THE SOVEREIGN FLOWER

THE
SOVEREIGN FLOWER

on Shakespeare as the Poet of Royalism
together with related essays and
indexes to earlier volumes

G. WILSON KNIGHT

*Professor of English Literature
in the University of Leeds*

Indexes composed by
PATRICIA M. BALL

*Assistant Lecturer in English at
Royal Holloway College, University of London*

> or so much as it needs
> To dew the sovereign flower and drown the weeds.
> MACBETH, v. ii. 29

Maybe in the next three or four thousand years
the word Kingdom will have disappeared—
Kingdom, Kingship, King—but I doubt it;
and if it does go something else equally fine will
take its place. It will be the same thing in a different dress. You can't invent anything finer than
Kingship, the idea of the King.
Edward Gordon Craig; *On the Art of the
Theatre*

METHUEN & CO LTD

36 ESSEX STREET · STRAND · LONDON WC2

CATALOGUE NO. 5990/U

PRINTED IN GREAT BRITAIN BY
BUTLER & TANNER LTD, FROME AND LONDON

Contents

Preface   *page* 7

I   This Sceptred Isle: a Study of Shakespeare's Kings
    (1940–1956)   11

II The Third Eye: an essay on *All's Well that Ends
    Well*   93

III What's in a Name?   161

IV The Shakespearian Integrity (1939)   203

V   Some Notable Fallacies   243

APPENDIXES

A   Literature and the Nation   263

B   The British Genius (1941)   266

C   A Royal Propaganda   273

D   The Second Part of *King Henry VI* and *Macbeth*
    (1927)   280

E   The Principles of Shakespeare Interpretation (1928)   287

INDEXES

A   Shakespearian Works   297

B   Shakespearian Themes   302

C   General   318

Preface

This is the last, and likely to remain the last, of my Shakespearian studies. The five main volumes form a set, with *The Mutual Flame* as a pendant. Indexes to this, and the other four volumes, are included, on a system explained below, (p. 295) by Dr Patricia Ball. My *Principles of Shakespearian Production* stands rather outside this sequence, being in a different vein. First published in 1936 by Messrs Faber & Faber, it was reissued in 1949 by Penguin Books, and is at present out of print: it will, I hope, eventually be reissued, perhaps with some additions.

The composition of this final volume caused some trouble. The first intention was to start with a narrative account of my work during the war on Shakespeare and the Nation, and to follow with the original text of *The Olive and the Sword*, as published in 1944 by the Oxford University Press. It was, however, considered by my advisers that so much war-time material would be out of place in a contemporary publication, and I have accordingly started with *The Olive and the Sword* under the title 'This Sceptred Isle', giving it new introductory and concluding sections, and removing references which might appear inapposite today. The new title had already been used for a 1940 booklet, and later for my various lecture-recitals culminating in the Westminster Theatre production of 1941; but its present use is reasonable, since from the start it has served as a generic title for this strand in my work. The 'narrative account' of my various war-time publications and recitals (of which some of the concluding passages are duplicated on pages 273–9 below) is now lodged, in typescript, under the title *A Royal Propaganda* in the British Museum and also in the Shakespeare Memorial Library of the Birmingham Reference Library. For the rest, I have remained content to supplement the statement of my first chapter by what is covered by Appendixes A, B and C. The general result is to shift the emphasis from Shakespeare as the poet of England to Shakespeare as the poet of royalism, in a wide sense; though it remains true that all the main points of royalistic thinking are to be found within the earlier statements.

The essay on *All's Well that Ends Well* is new, and so is the chapter on Shakespeare's Names, based on notes which I have had by me for many years, delivered as a lecture at the University of Liverpool in 1956, and now expanded for my present purpose. 'The Shakespearian Integrity,' first published in *The Burning Oracle* in 1939, constitutes my only comprehensive statement on Shakespeare. Elsewhere I concentrate on this or that aspect, with all the attendant risks of apparent over-emphasis. The essay is not faultless, and important considerations are lacking, but it serves to show the kind of thing I should have done, had I ever attempted a single discursive study of Shakespeare's total impact. The last chapter, 'Some Notable Fallacies', is new.

To Appendixes A, B and C, on work in the national and royalistic vein, I have already referred. Appendixes D and E are reprints of early essays, the second serving, if the matter be considered of any interest, to show that the main lines later taken by my Shakespearian investigations were in formulation two years before the publication of *The Wheel of Fire*.

Some notes as to other early pieces not included in my main volumes may here be in place. Contributions to *The Times Literary Supplement* from 1926 onwards can be traced through the indexes of that journal. My first published article was a note on Wordsworth's *Immortality Ode* in *The Adelphi* of September 1926. This was followed by an essay, which won a prize offered by John Middleton Murry as editor, called 'Brutus and Cassius', in *The Adelphi* of March 1927, and a note on tragedy in the following June.[1] The September 1928 article from *The Shakespeare Review* printed below as Appendix E was followed by another in October 1928 called 'The Poet and Immortality', outlining the thesis concerning Shakespeare's last plays which

---

[1] I have in my possession two bound volumes of *The Adelphi* from July 1926 to June 1927. These together constitute 'Volume IV' of the magazine and cover the contributions noted above. What is more important, they make a compact sample of the most vital 'little review' within living memory, at the height of its powers; and I intend eventually to lodge them in a library.

was published the following year in *Myth and Miracle*. The type-script of a full-length book on this same theme of the Final Plays, under the title *Thaisa*, had been searching for a publisher during 1928, and is now lodged in the Shakespeare Memorial Library at Birmingham. With it I have bound up the following papers: some letters concerning *Thaisa* from publishers, to-gether with one from the present Poet Laureate, Mr John Masefield; an inscribed copy of Mr T. S. Eliot's *Marina*, kindly presented to me on the publication of that exquisite poem in 1930; an accurate press report of a lecture on Shake-spearian tragedy, towards the end of 1927; a publisher's letter of 1925 on my first full-length, but quite unshaped, attempt at a work of Shakespearian interpretation; and the typescript of an immature essay written in 1924 on *The Tempest*.

The Shakespeare Memorial Library has also made, and now holds, a large scrap-book containing a full record of my dramatic activities since the twenties, including programmes, press-cuttings and a large number of photographs. This work is entitled, and indexed as, *Dramatic Papers: Material Relating to the Shakespearian and other Productions by G. Wilson Knight at Hart House Theatre, Toronto, and in England*. I may also leave, for a specific purpose (see p. 246 below), some records of my own speaking of Shakespeare. I would express my gratitude to the Librarian and Staff of the Birmingham Reference Library for their sympathetic and expert collaboration.

Among these *Dramatic Papers* I have included one non-dramatic item: an offprint of an article 'The Juxon Cups' by R. S. Forman[1] on certain family heirlooms, first published in *Notes and Queries* of 25 October and 22 November 1952 (Vol. 197, Nos. 22 and 24). This offprint, which may in due course be found in certain other libraries, contains a footnote, not printed in the *Notes and Queries* text, on the tracing of a direct line of descent, on the authority of J. H. Lawrence-Archer's *An Account of the Sirname Edgar: and particularly of*

---

[1] Mr Forman died shortly after completing the investigation, though he was able to see the article in print. With the kind permission of Mrs Forman the offprint bears my own name in addition to Mr Forman's. Though my own contribution was mainly secretarial and subsidiary, all the more professional part of the investigation having been done, with great brilliance, by Mr Forman at my request, it seemed advisable to include my name on the offprint to facilitate the tracing of it in libraries.

Wedderlie in Berwickshire (1873), from Malcolm II of Scotland, great-grandfather of Shakespeare's Duncan. It should be clear that my sympathetic handling of Macbeth in Shakespeare's play is free from prejudice.

Other unpublished works may eventually be lodged at Birmingham, including one entitled *Symbol of Man*, either in manuscript or typescript and supported by photographs, a study concerned, from the actor's view, with the more esoteric significances of the human form in repose and action.

Should any of my books be reset after my time, I should like to record that details of typography and usage of the more technical kinds should follow the texts of *The Wheel of Fire* and this volume rather than those texts which, through the exigencies of photography, have had to perpetuate earlier habits. I no longer refer to *Troilus and Cressida* as '*Troilus*', and *King Lear* is surely preferable to '*Lear*': once you start this you may, end up, as they sometimes do on the stage, by calling *As You Like It*, '*As You*'. All titles, for short or long works, are, with the exception of articles, now italicized; bird-imagery replaces 'bird' imagery; Ghost scene and Banquet scene are done with one capital but no hyphen; for 'the King' I use a capital; and play-titles in chapter-headings should be italicized.

Any improvements in technical convention and apparatus, in the dating of books referred to, and so on, would be in order. Were it ever possible, I could wish the title *The Shakespearian Tempest* altered to *Tempests and Music*.

I record my deep sense of gratitude to Dr Patricia Ball for the care, labour and *expertise* which she has so generously devoted to the making of my indexes. I would also express my thanks both to Professor Kenneth Muir and to the Publishers for advice in helping to decide on the construction of this final volume; to Miss Helen White for checking its references; and to my brother, W. F. Jackson Knight, for settling some of my queries on Greek derivation. My grateful acknowledgements are due to Mr Edward Gordon Craig and Messrs William Heinemann Ltd. for permission to use the passage quoted on my title-page. I follow the numerals of the Oxford Shakespeare, though sometimes departing from it in textual detail of punctuation.

G. W. K.

LEEDS *January* 1957

This Sceptred Isle

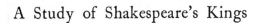

A Study of Shakespeare's Kings

This royal throne of kings, this sceptred isle,
This earth of majesty, this seat of Mars.
(Richard II, ii. i, 40)

This is a revised version of a monograph composed, except for the section 'Roses at War', in 1940 and published and reprinted in 1944 by the Oxford University Press under the title *The Olive and the Sword*. Originally designed for the war years, it is here presented as a study of Shakespeare's royalism. Fresh introductory and concluding sections have been written to replace the originals, and the footnotes are also new. The text of sections II, III, IV, and V follows, in the main, the 1944 reprint, except for some compression, a few expansions and additions, and the omission of contemporary references to which readers might respond less readily today than on the occasion of their first appearance: those who are interested in the original text must be referred to the libraries. The key to all my thinking on the British Crown during the last twenty years will be found at the conclusion of *Atlantic Crossing* (1936; pp. 327–35). For further information regarding my work on Shakespeare and the nation, see Appendix A.

I

The Shakespearian Royalty

If we were asked to state simply why the works of Shakespeare hold so inexhaustible an appeal, and why, moreover,
their popularity is steadily growing at this hour, surviving
the test of translation into strange tongues and spreading their
influence among foreign cultures, what should be our answer?
It could, certainly, be framed in general terms of human insight, wisdom, and poetic splendour; but should we try to
locate a more specific and concrete reason, we might perhaps
conclude by saying that it is because Shakespeare has throughout sounded, as has no other great poet or dramatist on record,
the note of royalty. His is a royal world.

Shakespeare's royalistic thinking is, for the most part,
patriotic, and his work from time to time spreads its wings in
national prophecy. Royalty and England tend to involve each
other, and these in turn involve strenuous themes of war and
peace, order and disorder, conflicts of personal ambition and
communal necessity, contrasts of tyranny and justice, the
whole stamped by the chivalric symbol of Saint George and
aspiring to Christian sanctions. This Shakespearian royalty,
conceived in the reign of Elizabeth I, is not dead; it has lived
since, within the story of Great Britain;[1] and it is alive today, in
the reign of Elizabeth II. Nor need it be limited to the fortunes, or destiny, of any one people: in it lies a yet greater conception, as a seed awaiting spring.

To understand all this we must allow the various dramas
to germinate within our minds. The Shakespearian play, designed in close relation to the queen-centred society of Tudor
England, owes much of the ease and the power of its accomplishment to the convergence of personal and communal issues

[1] For a development of this thought, see Appendix B, below.

in the figure of its king-protagonist. But some of the overtones can very easily be missed. Often in reading Shakespeare we do well to expand the obvious content, to put modern nations, or parties, for separate persons, and world-affairs for the turbulences of state.[1] Well-known works will at once start up into relief with new, because contemporary, meanings. The issues troubling our own world stand before us.

But we cannot capture the more universal meanings without first giving strict attention to the Shakespearian facts, as they exist within the dramatic poetry. In the following sections I shall trace, in a series of lightning sketches, this royal, and mainly English, or British, theme, untangling the golden thread which runs through Shakespeare's drama. The treatment will be brief and slight, but in no other way can we show, in one swift conspectus, how the whole series, except for the Comedies, which nevertheless have each its 'duke', can be felt to turn on a single axle, to exist within a single, national and royal, framework.

II

Roses at War

In Shakespeare's historical plays we have studies of internal disorder during the centuries leading to the England of Elizabeth I. We start with the three parts of *King Henry VI*.[2] Part I, the least important, is concerned with wars in France, Talbot playing the role of national hero and less than justice being done to Joan of Arc. Parts II and III are more important. These dramatize the Wars of the Roses, staging bitter animosities and bloody acts, as rival factions fight, like Lion and Unicorn, for the Crown. Shakespeare here resembles his wild contemporary Christopher Marlowe, but though the events are Marlovian, the treatment is not. From the start there is a basic sense of moral law:

---

[1] The process is well illustrated by Mr Peter Ustinov's recent play *Romanoff and Juliet*.

[2] For the dating of these plays, see my note on p. 280 below.

What stronger breastplate than a heart untainted!
Thrice is he arm'd that hath his quarrel just,
And he but naked, though lock'd up in steel,
Whose conscience with injustice is corrupted.

(*2 Henry VI*, III. ii. 232)

But more significant than any ethic is the prevailing tone
of piteous human feeling countering the ruthless savagery.
The pathetic and gentle-hearted Henry VI watches a battle
(*3 Henry VI*, II. v). First enters a 'son that hath killed his father,
with the dead body'; next 'a father that hath killed his son'.
Each in turn proceeds to plunder his prize only to be brought
up against the horror of his act. 'Pardon me, God, I knew not
what I did!' cries one; and the other, 'O pity, God, this
miserable age!' The King himself comments:

Woe above woe! grief more than common grief!
O that my death would stay these ruthful deeds!
O, pity, pity, gentle Heaven, pity!
The red rose and the white are on his face,
The fatal colours of our striving houses:
The one his purple blood right well resembles;
The other his pale cheeks, methinks, presenteth;
Wither one rose, and let the other flourish;
If you contend, a thousand lives must wither.

(II. v. 94)

'The red rose and the white are on his face': it is as though
blood were at war with flesh. Civil war is shown as paradoxical
and self-condemned, and no great imagination is today needed
to expand the condemnation. War makes beasts of men, and of
women too. Here is cruel Margaret, Henry's fierce queen,
depicted for us:

O tiger's heart wrapp'd in a woman's hide!
How could'st thou drain the life-blood of the child,
To bid the father wipe his eyes withal,
And yet be seen to bear a woman's face?
Women are soft, mild, pitiful, and flexible;
Thou stern, obdurate, flinty, rough, remorseless.

(*3 Henry VI*, I. iv. 137)

The savage actions of man are regularly characterized in bestial
terms.

The greatest things in these two plays arise from an over-powering sense of revulsion against insensate brutality:

> O, let the vile world end,
> And the premised flames of the last day
> Knit heaven and earth together!
> Now let the general trumpet blow his blast,
> Particularities and petty sounds
> To cease! Wast thou ordain'd, dear father,
> To lose thy youth in peace, and to achieve
> The silver livery of advised age,
> And, in thy reverence and thy chair-days, thus
> To die in ruffian battle? Even at this sight
> My heart is turn'd to stone: and while 'tis mine,
> It shall be stony.
>
> (*2 Henry VI*, v. ii. 40)

Shakespeare's poetry becomes more various and subtle, but, given a choice occasion, it already here achieves a maximum impact. Each person is a unit of passionate energy and the poetry blazes. Single lines start up in compacted force, as

> Mine eyes should sparkle like the beaten flint
>
> (*2 Henry VI*, iii. ii. 317)

and

> We set the axe to thy usurping root
>
> (*3 Henry VI*, ii. ii. 165)

and

> That stain'd their fetlocks in his smoking blood.
>
> (*3 Henry VI*, ii, iii. 21)

See how the impressions range over the human, animal, vegetable, and mineral creation, stung to life by each, making contact with the springs of existence. It is this which has caused critics to regard Shakespeare less as a literary artist than as a force of nature.

It has often been urged that a young man straight from Warwickshire could not have learnt so soon to speak with the accents of nobility; but we should also observe that the grand persons of *Henry VI* cannot open their mouths at a passionate moment without loading their speech with vivid analogies

from nature. Here, as later in *Coriolanus*, the many analogies
point us to a peculiarly clear contrast of beasts of prey and
gentle creatures; wolves, foxes, kites, against lambs, chickens,
and partridges; or even caterpillars and leaves (*2 Henry VI*,
III. i. 90). There is a quivering perception of animal suffering,
seeing a lion's prey 'that trembles under his devouring paws'
(*3 Henry VI*, I. iii. 13) and the 'trembling' wings of a bird
'limed in a bush' and now afraid to alight (*3 Henry VI*, v. vi. 14).
There are mild birds defending their young with ferocity, and
the 'fearful' hare flying from greyhounds whose eyes sparkle
with wrath (*3 Henry VI*, II. ii. 18; II. v. 130). All creation
seems at work preying, slaughtering, devouring:

> And as the butcher takes away the calf,
> And binds the wretch, and beats it when it strays,
> Bearing it to the bloody slaughter-house,
> Even so remorseless have they borne him hence;
> And as the dam runs lowing up and down,
> Looking the way her harmless young one went,
> And can do nought but wail her darling's loss,
> Even so myself bewails good Gloucester's case.
>
> (*2 Henry VI*, III. i. 210)

Man's brutality flowers only too naturally from a universe
apparently patterned of blood. And yet we are continually
pointed back to the unnaturalness of cruelty. The paradox is
left unresolved.

This vital feeling of beauty and agony within the very texture of physical existence naturally extends to a vivid awareness
of human physique too, the face especially, as in the lines

> He knits his brow and shows an angry eye
> (*2 Henry VI*, III. i. 15)

> Beaufort's red sparkling eyes blab his heart's malice
> (*2 Henry VI*, III. i. 154)

and

> Look pale as primrose with blood-drinking sighs
> (*2 Henry VI*, III. ii. 63)

or so fine a couplet as

> Upon thy eyeballs murderous tyranny
> Sits in grim majesty, to fright the world.
> (*2 Henry VI*, III. ii. 49)

B

The tragic events are presented with a vivid physical realism:

> See how the blood is settled in his face.
> Oft have I seen a timely-parted ghost,
> Of ashy semblance, meagre, pale, and bloodless,
> Being all descended to the labouring heart;
> Who, in the conflict that it holds with death,
> Attracts the same for aidance 'gainst the enemy;
> Which with the heart there cools and ne'er returneth
> To blush and beautify the cheek again.
> But see, his face is black and full of blood,
> His eye-balls further out than when he lived,
> Staring full ghastly like a strangled man;
> His hair uprear'd, his nostrils stretch'd with struggling;
> His hands abroad display'd, as one that grasp'd
> And tugg'd for life and was by strength subdued:
> Look, on the sheets his hair, you see, is sticking;
> His well-proportion'd beard made rough and rugged,
> Like to the summer's corn by tempest lodg'd.
>
> (*2 Henry VI*, III. ii. 160)

The impact may, as here, be gruesome; or it may come alive with a strong, maternal piteousness for a beautiful body broken and gashed, seeing a slaughtered youth as a 'tender spray' 'sweetly' sprung from his 'princely father' (*3 Henry VI*, II. vi. 47–51).[1] The blood of the slain is felt, by relative or supporter, as rich, sweet, potent, yet piteous. Neither side has any monopoly of these images: the terrible Margaret can be as pathetic as anyone.

In the three parts of *Henry VI* the horrors of war are carefully dramatized through a series of individual deaths: those of Salisbury, young Talbot, Talbot, Humphrey Duke of Gloucester, Cardinal Beaufort, Suffolk, Jack Cade, Clifford, the boy Rutland, York, young Clifford, Warwick, Prince Edward, and finally Henry VI himself. The succession of personal griefs gives a dramatic poignance no impressions of massed warfare could attain. The more generalized feeling that results is

---

[1] The passionate tenderness accorded slaughtered youth (discussed also in *The Mutual Flame*, pp. 109–10) directly recalls certain passages of Vergil's *Aeneid* (e.g., the deaths of Nisus, Euryalus, Lausus, and Pallas in Books IX–XI). The emphasis on young life, including the important prophecy (see p. 86 below, note) concerning 'this pretty lad', young Richmond (*3 Henry VI*, IV. vi. 70), is striking throughout.

phrased by King Henry in a fine speech of Shakespearian pastoralism:

> O God! methinks it were a happy life,
> To be no better than a homely swain;
> To sit upon a hill, as I do now,
> To carve out dials quaintly, point to point,
> Thereby to see the minutes how they run,
> How many make the hour full complete;
> How many hours bring about the day;
> How many days will finish up the year;
> How many years a mortal man may live.
> When this is known, then to divide the times:
> So many hours must I tend my flock;
> So many hours must I take my rest;
> So many hours must I contemplate;
> So many hours must I sport myself;
> So many days my ewes have been with young;
> So many weeks ere the poor fools will ean;
> So many years ere I shall shear the fleece:
> So minutes, hours, days, months, and years,
> Pass'd over to the end they were created,
> Would bring white hairs unto a quiet grave.
> Ah! what a life were this! how sweet! how lovely!
> Gives not the hawthorn-bush a sweeter shade
> To shepherds looking on their silly sheep,
> Than doth a rich embroider'd canopy
> To kings that fear their subjects' treachery?
> O, yes, it doth; a thousand-fold it doth.
> And to conclude, the shepherd's homely curds,
> His cold thin drink out of his leather bottle,
> His wonted sleep under a fresh tree's shade,
> All which secure and sweetly he enjoys,
> Is far beyond a prince's delicates,
> His viands sparkling in a golden cup,
> His body couched in a curious bed,
> When care, mistrust, and treason wait on him.
>
> (*3 Henry VI*, II. v. 21)

This is the central comment of the whole, just as the King himself, in his unworldly, generous weakness, is the central figure.

Much of Shakespeare's future drama is implicit in *Henry VI*, our thoughts being pointed ahead variously to other

Histories and greater plays like *Macbeth* and *Coriolanus*. The pity and the pastoralism are to run throughout, and so too is the keen sense of physical existence, in plant, animal, or man. Throughout the Crown is to burn, as it burns here in the ambitious craving of Richard, Duke of York and Richard, Duke of Gloucester (*2 Henry VI*, i. i. 241–60; *3 Henry VI*, iii. ii. 124–95), as an ultimate splendour, though there is to be a growing emphasis on its tragic weight. Indeed many important qualities of the Shakespearian humanism remain, in this early work, undeveloped. The people lack stature. In *Henry VI* we face a world of men and women violent, passionate, loyal, and pathetic. Frenzied actions make the victims' supporters stifle their natural instincts and commit more ruthless acts, which turn more hearts to stone: it is a vicious circle and, like the world today, they cannot get out of it. But, though violent, they are, in a deeper sense, all strangely passive: they are at the mercy of circumstances and their uncontrolled selves. So they are to end by handing the Crown to the wicked Duke of Gloucester, afterwards Richard III, who explicitly renounces all the 'soft laws' of 'nature' (*3 Henry VI*, iii. ii. 154) with a considered philosophy of egotism, saying 'I am myself alone' (*3 Henry VI*, v. vi. 83). He at least makes some sense of this chaos—for a while.

From now on, a new strength is to dominate Shakespeare's drama. More, his people themselves are henceforth greater. They may be either good or evil, but they exist in a new dimension. The people of *Henry VI* are marvellous creatures; but they are just that—creatures. They are neither good nor evil. Richard III, Faulconbridge in *King John*, Richard II, Henry IV, Hotspur and Falstaff, Henry V—all are variously, in a new sense, great; and so, we may add, are many of the people that surround them.

I shall not attempt to define this greatness here. It has much to do with Shakespeare's rooted naturalism and refusal to make any final distinction between man and the rest of God's creation, his ability 'to see how God in all his creatures works' (*2 Henry VI*, ii. i. 7). That gives him his insight into human energies and his trust in man as man. For the rest, its symptoms, irrespective of good or evil, are dignity and courage; the will to wrestle with a chaotic universe and make sense of it;

and spiritual depth. With this grows a new feeling for kingly office, and for England, as a nation. The greater persons to follow are all, good or bad, dedicated men; in a wider sense, the plays are dedicated plays—expressions of the poet's mind at grips with the problem of human discord and willing the mastery of its horrors.

III

Saint George for England

We have seen how Shakespeare's first historical study gave us the three parts of *Henry VI*, where the swaying internal discords of York and Lancaster, the Wars of the Roses, work to a conclusion; but that conclusion is a bitter one, throwing up, from this hell-cauldron of bloodshed and hate, a new danger in the satanic figure of Richard, Duke of Gloucester.

Richard III presents a reading of tyranny which we, in our time, should be in a peculiarly good position to appreciate. Richard suffers from a sense of inferiority caused by his deformed stature and chooses villainy, now that the fighting is over, as a compensation for lack of sexual appeal and the normal graces of peace. He is a master of hypocrisy, delighting to embarrass his enemies by playing on those Christian values which he nevertheless intends to repudiate. He swears continually by Saint Paul. Those surrounding the hero certainly seem nonentities in comparison. They belong still to the world of *Henry VI*, highly emotional, piteous, unprincipled, and finally enslaved. Richard is a greater than they: he is, for good or ill, master of his own fate.

His fate is, however, terrible enough. He suffers from 'timorous' dreams (iv. i. 84); his soliloquies in *Henry VI* show that he had from the first a clear conception of the gentler values; and at the play's close he sees ghosts. Under Richmond, whose role of saviour was foretold in *Henry VI*, a righteous force opposes his tyrannic rule, and on the eve of battle the souls of his victims enter his tent to pronounce doom

on their murderer and bless Richmond's sword. Dim figures
form round the sleeping Richard:

> Dream on, dream on, of bloody deeds and death:
> Fainting, despair; despairing, yield thy breath!
>
> (v. iii. 172)

Each ghost turns also to Richmond, assuring to his sword an
angelic strength. Richard starts from his sleep in terror. Here
is his soliloquy, playing on the enigma of conscience:

> Give me another horse, bind up my wounds!
> Have mercy, Jesu!—Soft! I did but dream.
> O coward conscience, how dost thou afflict me!
> The lights burn blue. It is now dead midnight.
> Cold fearful drops stand on my trembling flesh.
> What do I fear? myself? there's none else by:
> Richard loves Richard; that is, I am I.
> Is there a murderer here? No. Yes, I am:
> Then fly. What, from myself? Great reason why:
> Lest I revenge. What, myself upon myself?
> Alack, I love myself. Wherefore? for any good
> That I myself have done unto myself?
> O, no! alas, I rather hate myself
> For hateful deeds committed by myself!
> I am a villain; yet I lie, I am not.
> Fool, of thyself speak well: fool, do not flatter.
> My conscience hath a thousand several tongues,
> And every tongue brings in a several tale,
> And every tale condemns me for a villain.
> Perjury, perjury, in the high'st degree;
> Murder, stern murder, in the direst degree;
> All several sins, all used in each degree,
> Throng to the bar, crying all 'Guilty! guilty!'
> I shall despair. There is no creature loves me;
> And if I die, no soul will pity me.
> Nay, wherefore should they, since that I myself
> Find in myself no pity to myself?
> Methought the souls of all that I had murder'd
> Came to my tent, and every one did threat
> To-morrow's vengeance on the head of Richard.
>
> (v. iii. 178)

Something deep in Richard already sides with his accusers, but
his daylight will remains impregnable. When he recovers and

asserts 'Our strong arms be our conscience, swords our law'
(v. iii. 312) we recognize the philosophy. So in demonic pride
he goes to his bloody end:

> Let us to't pell-mell;
> If not to Heaven, then hand in hand to Hell!
>
> (v. iii. 313)

We cannot deny to Richard a certain semi-reluctant admiration. Though wicked, he remains great.

He is, in mind and body, deformed. His victims compare
him to beasts: ugly, reptilian, and dangerous. He is called a dog,
a 'bottled spider', a 'poisonous bunch-back'd toad', an 'elvish-
mark'd, abortive, rooting hog' (i. iii. 216–46), a 'hell-hound
that doth hunt us all to death' (iv. iv. 48), a 'cacodemon'
(i. iii. 144). Such inhuman evil is regularly opposed by Shakespeare's England. The central symbolism to which Shakespeare's
English warriors appeal before battle is Saint George, the
dragon-vanquisher. In the first part of *Henry VI* Talbot does
so, and in the civil warfare of the second and third parts both
sides cry on God and Saint George before battle. In *Richard III*
both Richard and Richmond do the same; both lay claim to
Saint George's protection. But can Richard properly do such a
thing? Once earlier, when he swore by his 'George', 'garter',
and 'crown', his interlocutor answered crisply, 'Profaned,
dishonour'd, and the third usurp'd' (iv. iv. 368). Whatever
courage he may show, Richard cannot with reason appeal to
Saint George. The whole play is against him. He is himself
nearer to the dragon, and is accordingly driven up against a
logical paradox:

> Our ancient word of courage, fair Saint George,
> Inspire us with the spleen of fiery dragons!
>
> (v. iii. 350)

It is the dragon of the emblem with which he recognizes
personal kinship, nor does he, like Richmond, couple the
Saint's name with 'God'. He is, in fact, himself the Dragon.

Here is Richmond's address to his soldiers:

> Yet remember this,
> God and our good cause fight upon our side;
> The prayers of holy saints and wronged souls,

Like high-rear'd bulwarks, stand before our faces;
Richard except, those whom we fight against
Had rather have us win than him they follow.
For what is he they follow? truly, gentlemen,
A bloody tyrant, and a homicide;
One rais'd in blood, and one in blood establish'd;
One that made means to come by what he hath,
And slaughter'd those that were the means to help him;
A base foul stone, made precious by the foil
Of England's chair, where he is falsely set;
One that hath ever been God's enemy.
Then, if you fight against God's enemy,
God will in justice ward you as his soldiers;
If you do sweat to put a tyrant down,
You sleep in peace, the tyrant being slain;
If you do fight against your country's foes,
Your country's fat shall pay your pains the hire;
If you do fight in safeguard of your wives,
Your wives shall welcome home the conquerors;
If you do free your children from the sword,
Your children's children quit it in your age.
Then, in the name of God and all these rights,
Advance your standards, draw your willing swords.

(v. iii. 240)

England is felt as ejecting from her own constitution, as a
foul disease, the tyrannous and bloody thing which she has so
often since opposed in other nations; and the play ends with
some great lines by Richmond on the peace won by his victorious arm. But that is not the whole story: for Richard's
address to his army wielded also a burly patriotism of its own;
an element of British virility is clearly part of him, and Shakespeare even underlines it by a reminder of Richmond's de-
pendence on a foreign army:

Let's whip these stragglers o'er the sea again,
Lash hence these overweening rags of France.

(v. iii. 328)

That, in Shakespeare's world, needs no comment.

Shakespeare in this early play saw deep into both the greatness and the short-lived success of such ambition as Richard's,
and was the better able, through the following series, King
John included, to hammer out his conception of how an

English king—that is, how England—should behave. After writing the three parts of *Henry VI* and *Richard III*, having brought the historic sequence almost to his own century, he goes farther back historically, though with an advancing conception. *King John, Richard II*, the two parts of *Henry IV* and *Henry V*, complete, for the time being, his structure.

In *King John* England is felt groping towards independence. The nation's relationship to the continent, and especially to the Church of Rome, is subtly presented, together with a feeling for England's true strength, dependent on two things, which are really the same, the coming home of her revolted barons, that is, unity; and truth to herself. Here is our final speech:

> This England never did, nor never shall,
> Lie at the proud foot of a conqueror,
> But when it first did help to wound itself.
> Now these her princes are come home again,
> Come the three corners of the world in arms,
> And we shall shock them. Nought shall make us rue,
> If England to itself do rest but true.
>
> (v. vii. 112)

This is spoken by the Bastard, Faulconbridge, the bluff, humorous, critical, warm-hearted and typically English son of Richard Coeur-de-Lion. Compare Hastings' words in *Henry VI*:

> *Hastings* Why, knows not Montague that of itself
> England is safe if true within itself?
>
> *   *   *   *
>
> Let us be back'd with God and with the seas
> Which he hath given for fence impregnable,
> And with their helps only defend ourselves;
> In them and in ourselves our safety lies.
>
> (*3 Henry VI*, IV. i. 39)

Faulconbridge's faith is not lightly held, for he speaks earlier what is as trenchant a criticism of international bargaining as you could wish, England being one of the parties criticized:

> Mad world! mad kings! mad composition!
> John, to stop Arthur's title in the whole,
> Hath willingly departed with a part:

> And France, whose armour conscience buckled on,
> Whom zeal and charity brought to the field
> As God's own soldier

—he, in short, has suddenly renounced his noble purpose for the sake of that 'sly devil', 'commodity', or self-interest:

> And this same bias, this Commodity,
> This bawd, this broker, this all-changing word,
> Clapp'd on the outward eye of fickle France,
> Hath drawn him from his own determined aid,
> From a resolved and honourable war,
> To a most base and vile-concluded peace.
>
> (II. i. 561)

Papal intrigue and national rivalry, hard-headed loyalty and semi-virtuous treachery, all jostle each other. Once, when Faulconbridge is shocked and baffled by young Arthur's death (IV. iii. 139–59), his words are poignant with a doubt and a foreboding of a kind to which modern scepticism will readily respond. But he finally rises above such uncertainties, urging John to be resolute in face of foreign invasion:

> Be great in act, as you have been in thought;
> Let not the world see fear and sad distrust
> Govern the motion of a kingly eye:
> Be stirring as the time; be fire with fire;
> Threaten the threatener, and outface the brow
> Of bragging horror: so shall inferior eyes,
> That borrow their behaviours from the great,
> Grow great by your example and put on
> The dauntless spirit of resolution.
> Away! and glister like the god of war
> When he intendeth to become the field:
> Show boldness and aspiring confidence.
> What! shall they seek the lion in his den
> And fright him there? and make him tremble there?
> O! let it not be said.
>
> (V. i. 45)

That infectious fervour is, nevertheless, countered by another, typically Shakespearian, reminder, spoken by Salisbury:

> O nation, that thou couldst remove!
> That Neptune's arms, who clippeth thee about,

Would bear thee from the knowledge of thyself,
And gripple thee unto a pagan shore;
Where these two Christian armies might combine
The blood of malice in a vein of league,
And not to spend it so unneighbourly!

(v. ii. 33)

Emphasis is thus laid on the un-Christian nature of war, and the confusion is at last ended by the Pope's legate, peace being forwarded by John's religious submission. But Cardinal Pandulph is an intriguer like the rest, and the voice of Faulconbridge has the final say, speaking only of England.

In *King John* we have a rather untidy story, which can only be understood as an artistic unit if we feel that the true hero is England, vaguely, and often unworthily, shadowed by John, King of England. That is why Faulconbridge, as the voice of England's destiny, assists a king who seems unworthy of so penetrating an intelligence. Cardinal Pandulph is at first an ambassador of powerful religious and political authority, inimical to John and his ways, but the play ends with John's submission and a consequent union which extends to friendship with France also. So much is simple. But there is also severe tragedy in the appalling sufferings caused by John to Constance and her boy, Arthur, presented with that tragic sympathy of which Shakespeare is the world's master. Should we not say, then, that Shakespeare's heart is in this, and the play's outward form of steady national accomplishment secondary? We can, if we like. Nationalism in Shakespeare is only so supremely important because, in the depths, he has a sense of the human essence, in joy or pain, which far outspaces all national and historic boundaries. But it is better to unify our impressions by saying that the process of England's rise to a national integrity is accompanied by terrible suffering. Every opposing argument to Shakespeare's national assertion is already potentially present, though sternly controlled, in this comparatively early work.[1]

England must be true to herself: that is the burden of Shakespeare's unsentimental patriotism. A characteristic blend of sharp criticism with patriotic fervour is compressed within

[1] This last paragraph has been removed to its present and logical position from its place in the original text.

a single speech of what was probably an earlier play, *Richard II.*
Old John of Gaunt, seeing himself as 'a prophet new inspired',
grieves in quavering, repetitive accents[1] at the spendthrift
king and the selfish prostitution of his country's soul to an
immediate, monetary, gain:

> This royal throne of kings, this scepter'd isle,
> This earth of majesty, this seat of Mars,
> This other Eden, demi-paradise;
> This fortress built by Nature for herself
> Against infection and the hand of war;
> This happy breed of men, this little world,
> This precious stone set in the silver sea,
> Which serves it in the office of a wall,
> Or as a moat defensive to a house,
> Against the envy of less happier lands;
> This blessed plot, this earth, this realm, this England,
> This nurse, this teeming womb of royal kings,
> Fear'd by their breed and famous by their birth,
> Renowned for their deeds as far from home,
> For Christian service and true chivalry,
> As is the sepulchre in stubborn Jewry
> Of the world's ransom, blessed Mary's Son;
> This land of such dear souls, this dear, dear land,
> Dear for her reputation through the world,
> Is now leased out, I die pronouncing it,
> Like to a tenement or pelting farm.
> England, bound in with the triumphant sea,
> Whose rocky shore beats back the envious siege
> Of watery Neptune, is now bound in with shame,
> With inky blots and rotten parchment bonds:
> That England, that was wont to conquer others,
> Hath made a shameful conquest of itself.
> Ah, would the scandal vanish with my life,
> How happy then were my ensuing death.
>
> (II. i. 40)

How illogical, to our way of thinking, seems this emphasis
on kings; but it is the royal soul of England which Shakespeare
is defining, just as the word 'prophet', used to introduce the

---

[1] The speech is written for an old man, and must be spoken in character; only so
will the repetitions seem natural and the gathering power, which should be felt breaking
through the impediment of age, receive definition. See p. 247 below.

passage, holds poetically a deeper content than the dramatic context would suggest. It is only too easy to miss some of the meaning. The speech does not so much emphasize the value of kings to the community as honour England for having produced a succession of noble kings. Royalty is the final value. But yet again, what exactly are these 'dear' (i.e. 'of great worth') 'souls'? The kings, or the community, the 'happy breed'? Is that 'breed' itself being regarded as, in part, royal? Whatever be the exact meaning, it is clear that the heart of the conception is royalty as a positive and self-sufficing value, with strong chivalric and Christian associations. The speech may be said to transcend its historic setting.

Such is the conception running as a golden thread through Shakespeare's drama. The Crown symbolizes the nation's soul-life, which is also the greater self of each subject. In Shakespeare's human kings we watch different persons daring to identify themselves with this supreme value; and we can view each personal king as a prototype of national action, as England herself, fulfilling or falsifying her destiny.

In *Richard II* we are shown the exact opposite of our other Richard. Here we have a weak, inefficient, luxury-loving king. Faced by dissension among his subjects, he tries to avoid trouble by the simple expedient of banishing those ready

> To wake our peace, which in our country's cradle
> Draws the sweet infant breath of gentle sleep,
>
> (I. iii. 132)

men who would involve his land in the 'dreadful bray' of trumpets and 'grating shock of wrathful iron arms' (I. iii. 136). But on the death of his father, the banished Bolingbroke lands in England to claim his inheritance.

On returning from his Irish expedition to meet the rebellion, Richard solicits our sympathy:

> I weep for joy
> To stand upon my kingdom once again.
> Dear earth, I do salute thee with my hand
> Though rebels wound thee with their horses' hoofs.
>
> (III. ii. 4)

He prays that the English countryside may offer only what is hateful and venomous to her sovereign's foe: how closely always in Shakespeare are England's natural sweets entwined with her human and political integrity. Richard's followers accuse him of enjoying too facile a 'security' while his enemies grow powerful. He answers by comparing himself to a rising sun putting criminals to shame, for

> Not all the water in the rough rude sea
> Can wash the balm from an anointed king;
> The breath of worldly men cannot depose
> The deputy elected by the Lord.
> For every man that Bolingbroke hath press'd
> To lift shrewd steel against our golden crown,
> God for his Richard hath in heavenly pay
> A glorious angel: then, if angels fight,
> Weak men must fall, for Heaven still guards the right.
>
> (III. ii. 54)

We can rely too confidently on Heaven's guardian might. Richard does so; and we should consider carefully the opposition Shakespeare draws of confidence and disillusion. In reading such a speech we must (i) respect the essence of divine authority as existent in its own right, although (ii) we are aware of the King's unsuitability for his high office.

Richard's assurance is swiftly reversed to a defeatist resignation:

> No matter where; of comfort no man speak:
> Let's talk of graves, of worms and epitaphs . . .
> Our lands, our lives, and all, are Bolingbroke's,
> And nothing can we call our own but death . . .
>
> (III. ii. 144)

He now recognizes that he is, after all, only a man: 'I live with bread like you, feel want, taste grief, need friends' (III. ii. 175). But, as the clouds gather, he grows in stature after the fashion characteristic of all Shakespeare's tragic heroes, and his utterance has a new depth and strength:

> We are amazed; and thus long have we stood
> To watch the fearful bending of thy knee,
> Because we thought ourself thy lawful king:
> And if we be, how dare thy joints forget

To pay their awful duty to our presence?
If we be not, show us the hand of God
That hath dismiss'd us from our stewardship;
For well we know, no hand of blood and bone
Can gripe the sacred handle of our sceptre,
Unless he do profane, steal, or usurp.
And though you think that all, as you have done,
Have torn their souls by turning them from us,
And we are barren and bereft of friends;
Yet know, my master, God omnipotent
Is mustering in his clouds on our behalf
Armies of pestilence; and they shall strike
Your children yet unborn and unbegot,
That lift your vassal hands against my head,
And threat the glory of my precious crown.
Tell Bolingbroke—for yond methinks he is—
That every stride he makes upon my land
Is dangerous treason: he is come to open
The purple testament of bleeding war;
But ere the crown he looks for live in peace,
Ten thousand bloody crowns of mother's sons
Shall ill become the flower of England's face,
Change the complexion of her maid-pale peace
To scarlet indignation, and bedew
Her pastures' grass with faithful English blood.

(III. iii. 72)

Whatever we think of Richard, some sacred essence, at once pastoral and royal, is being wronged: in no play is Shakespeare's royalism so poetically explicit. Moreover, this prophecy will be, after his death, fulfilled, and Richard's warning is not, if a long view be taken, misplaced. Next he slips into a luxuriant mysticism which has its own beauty, though further emphasizing his unsuitability for temporal office. But then again, when formally renouncing his crown, from height of a new tragic dignity, he denounces traitorous rebellion in scorching words, branding that 'heinous' deed, the 'cracking' of a sacred oath, with Heaven's curse, and comparing his tormentors to Judas and to Pilate, and himself to Christ; while even including himself in his denunciation:

> For I have given here my soul's consent
> To undeck the pompous body of a king;

> Made glory base and sovereignty a slave,
> Proud majesty a subject, state a peasant.
>
> (IV. i. 250)

Independent of any personal considerations, some essential, superpersonal, sovereignty takes on mysterious, compelling, glistening presence.

Richard meets his death with a towering courage:

> How now! What means death in this rude assault?
> Villain, thine own hand yields thy death's instrument.
> Go thou and fill another room in Hell.
> That hand shall burn in never-quenching fire
> That staggers thus my person. Exton, thy fierce hand
> Hath with the king's blood stain'd the king's own land.
>
> (V. v. 106)

He kills two of his assailants before himself falling; and this is Shakespeare's weak king. We are already a long way from Henry VI, and still farther from Marlowe's Edward II. Such innate royalty Marlowe never conceived.

Richard is compared both to Christ and to the sun. The king is Christ's deputy on earth, and should properly possess and exercise both divine and natural powers. Richard III certainly had too much of the beast in him, but Richard II, apart from his other failings, has too little; and when his queen and he part, she accuses of unmanly weakness one who should more properly be a 'lion' and 'king of beasts' (V. i. 34). His religious and tragic mysticism is poetically exquisite, but lacks practical relevance. Such is Shakespeare's judgement on a king who pursues reliance on divine sanctions, while lacking both the virtue and the virility without which temporal affairs cannot be ordered, nor the realms of justice and love be rendered secure.

Though Richard may be wrong, revolution—the thought is Shakespearian—cannot exactly be right. In *Richard II* a discrepancy exists between true sovereignty and its exponent, leading to disaster. Richard's successor, Bolingbroke, now Henry IV, though a strong man, is nevertheless worn down by civil disturbances, and hopes to cleanse his hands of Richard's blood by a crusade:

So shaken as we are, so wan with care,
Find we a time for frighted peace to pant,
And breathe short-winded accents of new broils
To be commenc'd in stronds afar remote.
No more the thirsty entrance of this soil
Shall daub her lips with her own children's blood;
No more shall trenching war channel her fields,
Nor bruise her flowerets with the armed hoofs
Of hostile paces . . . Therefore, friends,
As far as to the sepulchre of Christ—
Whose soldier now, under whose blessed cross
We are impressed and engag'd to fight—
Forthwith a power of English shall we levy,
Whose arms were moulded in their mother's womb
To chase these pagans in those holy fields
Over whose acres walk'd those blessed feet
Which fourteen hundred years ago were nail'd
For our advantage on the bitter cross.

(*1 Henry IV*, I. i. I)

But disorder at home continues and his purpose fails. The two parts of *Henry IV* show a nation condemned to a slow agony of self-conflict, in which both sides bear guilt. Here we have the Archbishop of York characterized as a rebel:

My Lord of York, it better show'd with you,
When that your flock, assembled by the bell,
Encircled you to hear with reverence
Your exposition on the holy text
Than now to see you here an iron man,
Cheering a rout of rebels with your drum,
Turning the word to sword and life to death.

(*2 Henry IV*, IV. ii. 4)

Shakespeare's Histories are rich with images of peace.

Henry is primarily a worried king, set half-way between Richard III and Richard II, with strength and weakness, determination and repentance, intermingling:

How many thousand of my poorest subjects
Are at this hour asleep! O sleep, O gentle sleep,
Nature's soft nurse, how have I frighted thee,
That thou no more wilt weigh my eyelids down,
And steep my senses in forgetfulness?

C

Why rather, sleep, liest thou in smoky cribs,
Upon uneasy pallets stretching thee,
And hush'd with buzzing night-flies to thy slumber,
Than in the perfumed chambers of the great,
Under the canopies of costly state,
And lull'd with sound of sweetest melody?
O thou dull god, why liest thou with the vile
In loathsome beds, and leav'st the kingly couch
A watch-case or a common 'larum-bell?
Wilt thou upon the high and giddy mast
Seal up the ship-boy's eyes, and rock his brains
In cradle of the rude imperious surge,
And in the visitation of the winds,
Who take the ruffian billows by the top,
Curling their monstrous heads, and hanging them
With deafening clamour in the slippery clouds,
That, with the hurly, death itself awakes?
Canst thou, O partial sleep, give thy repose
To the wet sea-boy in an hour so rude,
And in the calmest and most stillest night,
With all appliances and means to boot,
Deny it to a king? Then happy low, lie down!
Uneasy lies the head that wears a crown.

(*2 Henry IV*, III. i. 4)

How inward is the Shakespearian intuition of sovereignty, disclosing, beneath the show and trappings of world-power, its bitterness and unrest. Set beside this the barbaric Tamburlaine of Shakespeare's contemporary, Marlowe:

A god is not so glorious as a king.
To ask and have; command and be obeyed. . . .

(*1 Tamburlaine the Great*, II. v. 57)

The contrast shows the spiritual depth of the Shakespearian approach to power. King Henry's intention of voyaging to the Holy Land to wash the guilt of Richard's blood from his hands is never consummated; but in suggesting a humble reference of England's royal history to that higher court of justice and mercy overarching nations, it remains important. We can see this guilt-burdened king as a symbol of all secular authority, of any time or place.

Henry IV is also worried about his son, Hal, so dissolute

in comparison with the rebel Hotspur who is always thirsting
for military honour. Hal idles away his time with Falstaff, the
fat drunkard of philosophic humour and trenchant wit. Now
in Prince Hal Shakespeare is at work, throughout the two parts
of *Henry IV*, in constructing an ideal English type, with even
that streak of a politic worldly-wisdom not openly acknow-
ledged, a high seriousness unsuspected until the crucial
moment reveals it, which might be said to be a characteristic
of the national temperament. But first Shakespeare deliberately
apprentices him to Falstaff, who repudiates all heroisms. Here
he is, before the battle:

> *Falstaff* I would it were bed-time, Hal, and all well.
> *Prince* Why, thou owest God a death.
>
> [*Exit.*]
>
> *Falstaff* 'Tis not due yet; I would be loath to pay him before his
> day. What need I be so forward with him that calls not on me?
> Well, 'tis no matter; honour pricks me on. Yea, but how if honour
> prick me off when I come on? how then? Can honour set to a leg?
> no: or an arm? no: or take away the grief of a wound? no. Honour
> hath no skill in surgery, then? no. What is honour? a word. What is
> that word honour? air. A trim reckoning! Who hath it? he that died
> o' Wednesday. Doth he feel it? no. Doth he hear it? no. It is in-
> sensible, then? Yea, to the dead. But will it not live with the living?
> no. Why? detraction will not suffer it. Therefore I'll none of it.
> Honour is a mere scutcheon; and so ends my catechism.
>
> (*1 Henry IV*, v. i. 126)

Later, on the field of battle, seeing, and perhaps turning over
with his boot, Sir Walter Blunt's, probably ungraceful, dead
body, he says, 'There's honour for you' (v. iii. 33). He expands
that rough and burly common-sense in approaching kings and
all their ways which we noticed in Faulconbridge to a general
satire on martial heroism and all aristocratic valuation whatsoever, at one point even burlesquing the King himself in Hal's
presence.

The second part of *Henry IV*, a more bitter play than the
first, presents a dastardly example of treachery in Prince John
of Lancaster, a young man neatly criticized by Falstaff; and
here too Shakespeare ably satirizes the methods of the press-
gangs. Falstaff's comment on his ragamuffin army in Part I
had an undertone of bitterness:

> Tut, tut; good enough to toss; food for powder, food for powder;
> they'll fill a pit as well as better; tush, man, mortal men, mortal men.
>
> (iv. ii. 72)

It is a supreme stroke of Shakespeare to have apprenticed his
hero-to-be, Henry V, to such a tutor as Falstaff, because
within the very essence of the national temperament exists not
only a sense of humour but also a closely allied and deeply
satiric sense of the futility of military ambition, as an end in
itself: 'There's honour for you'. The more continental Hotspur, like Tybalt in *Romeo and Juliet*—we may remember the
very English Mercutio's caustic criticisms of Tybalt's explicitly continental swaggerings, honour-cult, and new-fangled
sword-play (*Romeo and Juliet*, ii. iv. 20–38)—seems trivial by
comparison; though of course Hal must be allowed to prove
himself the better soldier.

When Hal succeeds to the throne, his brothers and the
Chief Justice, who had once imprisoned him when Prince of
Wales, are at first fearful, but the new king disabuses them
in a phrase defining in Shakespearian terms the very soul of
true sovereignty:

> Brothers, you mix your sadness with some fear;
> This is the English, not the Turkish court;
> Not Amurath an Amurath succeeds
> But Harry Harry.
>
> (*2 Henry IV*, v. ii. 46)

A quotation for that most testing moment, the moment of
triumph, whether personal, official, or national. So, too, when
the Chief Justice, whom the new king addresses first with some
severity, offers a noble defence in terms of justice, he is
answered by a speech of youthful humility, unlike the words
of any previous king; for this king is to be different from
all predecessors, at once humble, religious, and assured in
action.

Richard III is terrifyingly powerful—but wicked. Richard
II is weak, but, under disaster, becomes almost a saint, religious
phraseology so appropriately accompanying practical failure
that a want in our religious tradition is suggested. The troubled
Henry IV is really neither one thing nor the other, neither
a first-class villain nor a beautiful failure. In the person of

Henry V Shakespeare attempts a blend of righteousness with power.

To fuse strong action with religious humility is, however, far from easy. In Marlowe's *Tamburlaine* we have an amazing tale of conquest, the hero starting as a peasant, conquering nation after nation in scene after scene, and ending as all but master of the world. His aspiring pride rises in rhetoric of ringing, resounding, clanging magnificence. City after city falls before him. The tone is pagan, barbaric, and often brutal. Tamburlaine makes cruel mockery of his enemies, subjugating them to his power-lust, his pagan splendour being, precisely, a denial of chivalry. Throughout he feels himself irresistible, backed by destiny, at once the overthrower of religions and himself 'the scourge' of God (*I*. III. iii. 44). Here we have a tyrannic progress shown with all its superficial glamour, but none of those inward depths of psychic conflict shadowed by Shakespeare even in *Richard III*. In *Henry V* Shakespeare, who parodies such bombast through the absurd braggadocio and Marlovian tags of Pistol, writes his *Tamburlaine*: and it is vastly different from Marlowe's.

Shakespeare's hero has already been contrasted with an Amurath, and is now to become a Christian warrior, leading, after long periods of civil war, a united nation to foreign conquest. Strands separated and frayed in *Henry IV* are close knotted in the person of Henry V, though Falstaff has been necessarily rejected, with a sharp repudiation of his all but irresistible wit—'Reply not to me with a fool-born jest' (*2 Henry IV*, v. v. 60)—marking a refusal to escape, or cloud responsibility by, humour. The stage is left free for a new epic and heroic drama, blending Christian virtue with martial prowess. The largeness of his theme, more epic than dramatic, embarrassed even Shakespeare, leading him to preface the separate acts of *Henry V* with a sequence of fine choruses. Here is part of the first:

> O for a Muse of fire, that would ascend
> The brightest heaven of invention,
> A kingdom for a stage, princes to act
> And monarchs to behold the swelling scene!
> Then should the warlike Harry, like himself,
> Assume the port of Mars; and at his heels,

> Leash'd in like hounds, should famine, sword, and fire
> Crouch for employment. But pardon, gentles all,
> The flat unraised spirits that hath dared
> On this unworthy scaffold to bring forth
> So great an object: can this cockpit hold
> The vasty fields of France? or may we cram
> Within this wooden O the very casques
> That did affright the air at Agincourt?

(I. Chorus)

Twice only throughout his work Shakespeare apologizes for the insufficiency of his art: here, and in the prologue to *Henry VIII*. 'Famine, sword, and fire': war is not sentimentalized. Though Shakespeare attempts to Christianize military conquest, he never lets us forget that it is military conquest, with its attendant terrors, that he is attempting to Christianize. Nor is the Falstaffian approach ever quite forgotten: though their massive progenitor be dead, Pistol, Bardolph, and Nym carry on, and are supported by that glorious comic triumvirate, the officers, Jamy the Scot, Macmorris the Irishman, and, best of all, Fluellen, the Welshman, chattering of military science, Monmouth, and the wars of Alexander.

King Henry is a deeply religious man, phrase after phrase showing his reliance on God. He will not fight until his claims on France are sanctioned in terms of 'law' and 'right' by the Archbishop of Canterbury, to whose legal scholarship he appeals (I. ii. 8–32), with a stern warning that no prevarication be allowed to twist the truth in a matter so likely to involve grievous sufferings: never does he forget those.

The King is to lead a united nation to war. Shakespeare's mood is accordingly ripe for some comments on national harmony:

> For government, though high and low and lower,
> Put into parts, doth keep in one consent,
> Congreeing in a full and natural close,
> Like music.

(I. ii. 180)

The precise ordering of the life of bees is adduced by the Archbishop as an analogy:

> They have a king and officers of sorts;
> Where some, like magistrates, correct at home;
> Others, like merchants, venture trade abroad;

Others, like soldiers, armed in their stings,
Make boot upon the summer's velvet buds,
Which pillage they with merry march bring home
To the tent-royal of their emperor.
Who, busied in his majesty surveys
The singing masons building roofs of gold,
The civil citizens kneading up the honey,
The poor mechanic porters crowding in
Their heavy burdens at his narrow gate,
The sad-eye'd justice, with his surly hum,
Delivering o'er to executors pale
The lazy yawning drone.

(i. ii. 190)

So King Henry, with a unified nation at his back, may safely set out for France.

The messenger from the Dauphin is called in, but is afraid to deliver his master's message. The King's comment is important:

We are no tyrant, but a Christian king;
Under whose grace our passion is as subject
As are our wretches fetter'd in our prisons.

(i. ii. 241)

You can see how carefully Shakespeare is labouring to create in Henry a blend of Christian faith and martial heroism. How neatly, too, the King is made to typify the English temperament when, discovering that the Dauphin's message is merely a gift of tennis-balls as a taunt against his own supposed decadence, he answers with a long speech of withering sarcasm prophesying the vengeance shortly to fall on France in response to this insult, and concluding:

But this lies all within the will of God,
To whom I do appeal; and in whose name
Tell you the Dauphin I am coming on,
To venge me as I may and to put forth
My rightful hand in a well-hallow'd cause.
So get you hence in peace; and tell the Dauphin
His jest will savour but of shallow wit,
When thousands weep more than did laugh at it.

(i. ii. 259)

It happened with Hotspur before; it has happened since.

Before embarking, the King discovers treachery in three
nobles, suborned by foreign money, and commits the culprits
to their doom, with a speech of scorching rhetoric on deception and ingratitude. In France he wins a swift victory at
Harfleur, preluded by the famous 'Once more unto the breach,
dear friends', urging his men to put by the 'modest stillness
and humility' so valued in peace, and instead now to 'disguise
fair nature with hard-favour'd rage' and 'imitate the action of
the tiger' (III. i. 1): a sharply realistic piece of advice facing the
inhumanity of war. Henry V is himself once, in the much
earlier play, *1 Henry VI* (I. i. 8–16), compared to an especially
dazzling, sun-brilliant, and therefore royal, dragon. Animal
strength holds various meanings drawn from both sides of the
Saint George symbolism, and the horses and greyhounds so
vivid in the first chorus of *Henry V* are fine beasts, corresponding to a strength which is virtue. Greyhounds occur again:

> On, on, you noblest English,
> Whose blood is fet from fathers of war-proof!
> Fathers that, like so many Alexanders,
> Have in these parts from morn till even fought,
> And sheathed their swords for lack of argument.
> Dishonour not your mothers; now attest
> That those whom you call'd fathers did beget you.
> Be copy now to men of grosser blood,
> And teach them how to war. And you, good yeomen,
> Whose limbs were made in England, show us here
> The mettle of your pasture; let us swear
> That you are worth your breeding; which I doubt not;
> For there is none of you so mean and base,
> That hath not noble lustre in your eyes.
> I see you stand like greyhounds in the slips,
> Straining upon the start. The game's afoot:
> Follow your spirit, and upon this charge
> Cry 'God for Harry, England and Saint George!'
>
> (III. i. 17)

The King had been sportive in his youth, and now war is conceived as a 'game', though without mitigation of its terror.
Later Henry implores the citizens of Harfleur to surrender,
warning them of the horrors which await them if once the
instincts of his soldiery are unleashed:

> Therefore, you men of Harfleur,
> Take pity of your town and of your people,
> Whiles yet my soldiers are in my command;
> Whiles yet the cool and temporate wind of grace
> O'erblows the filthy and contagious clouds
> Of heady murder, spoil, and villainy.
>
> (III. iii. 27)

It is a long speech. No more honest facing of war's brutality was ever penned.

As though to show us that such direct heroism is not, by itself, enough, we advance to the far more crucial battle of Agincourt. The English, as a fine chorus describes them, are now battle-worn and exhausted, and surrounded by a more powerful, and fresh, army. Only a miracle can save them. The King, disguising his anxiety, goes through his army cheering his men, like a 'sun', calling them 'brothers' (IV. Chorus); and later, putting on a disguise, hears the not unreasonable complaint of a common soldier, who knows nothing of the issues at stake, and, when told that the King's cause is just, answers, pithily, 'That's more than we know' (IV. i. 136). Left alone, the King meditates upon the all but intolerable burden laid on him:

> Upon the King! let us our lives, our souls,
> Our debts, our careful wives,
> Our children and our sins lay on the King!
> We must bear all. O hard condition,
> Twin-born with greatness, subject to the breath
> Of every fool, whose sense no more can feel
> But his own wringing! What infinite heart's-ease
> Must kings neglect, that private men enjoy!
>
> (IV. i. 250)

What joy does power give to compensate for this heavy, spiritual, weight? 'Ceremony', that is all, the tinsel trappings of material magnificence:

> And what art thou, thou idle ceremony?
>
> (IV. i. 260)

What a difference from *Tamburlaine*! Temporal power has its reverse side. All 'ceremony' is impugned, as an outward deceit:

Canst thou, when thou command'st the beggar's knee,
Command the health of it? No, thou proud dream,
That play'st so subtly with a king's repose;
I am a king that find thee, and I know
'Tis not the balm, the sceptre and the ball,
The sword, the mace, the crown imperial,
The intertissued robe of gold and pearl,
The farced title running 'fore the king,
The throne he sits on, nor the tide of pomp
That beats upon the high shore of this world,
No, not all these, thrice-gorgeous ceremony,
Not all these, laid in bed majestical,
Can sleep so soundly as the wretched slave,
Who with a body fill'd and vacant mind
Gets him to rest, cramm'd with distressful bread;
Never sees horrid night, the child of Hell,
But, like a lackey, from the rise to set
Sweats in the eye of Phoebus and all night
Sleeps in Elysium.

(IV. i. 276)

Yet, too, what deep burnishings of poetry Shakespeare accords those regal splendours. Indeed, it is precisely because he sees through them, knows their purely provisional value, that all Shakespeare's kingly impressions hold such lasting potency. They are always sinking into depths beyond our understanding, are fed from elsewhere; they are sacramental.

Next Henry throws himself and his army on God's mercy, confessing his father's crime against the sacred person of Richard; that is, confessing, as perhaps all temporal leaders must, the dubious nature of his own authority, bought and maintained in blood:

O God of battles! steel my soldiers' hearts;
Possess them not with fear; take from them now
The sense of reckoning, if the opposed numbers
Pluck their hearts from them. Not to-day, O Lord,
O, not to-day, think not upon the fault
My father made in compassing the crown!
I Richard's body have interr'd anew;
And on it have bestow'd more contrite tears
Than from it issued forced drops of blood:
Five hundred poor I have in yearly pay,

Who twice a day their wither'd hands hold up
Toward Heaven, to pardon blood; and I have built
Two chantries, where the sad and solemn priests
Sing still for Richard's soul. More will I do;
Though all that I can do is nothing worth,
Since that my penitence comes after all,
Imploring pardon.

(IV. i. 309)

The presence of Richard has, through repeated reminders, lingered as an accusing presence throughout *Henry IV*; but now that ghost is laid. From now on Henry is free, and when one of his nobles wishes for more men, accuses such fear with the finest heroic assurance in our literature.

We open with some twenty comparatively dull lines, and it is not till the word 'Crispin' appears that the speech catches poetic fire.[1] Observe the repeated use of the name 'Crispin' leading up to a double-barrelled use of it (for Crispinus and Crispianus), and watch for a subtle touch of humour:

This day is call'd the feast of Crispian:
He that outlives this day, and comes safe home,
Will stand a tip-toe when this day is named,
And rouse him at the name of Crispian.
He that shall live this day, and see old age,
Will yearly on the vigil feast his neighbours,
And say, 'To-morrow is Saint Crispian'.
Then will he strip his sleeve and show his scars,
And say 'These wounds I had on Crispin's day'.
Old men forget; yet all shall be forgot,
But he'll remember with advantages
What feats he did that day: then shall our names,
Familiar in his mouth as household words,
Harry the king, Bedford and Exeter,
Warwick and Talbot, Salisbury and Gloucester,
Be in their flowing cups freshly remember'd.
This story shall the good man teach his son;
And Crispin Crispian shall ne'er go by,
From this day to the ending of the world,
But we in it shall be remembered;
We few, we happy few, we band of brothers;

[1] The speech is a peculiarly good example of Shakespeare's rhetorical technique:
see p. 247 below.

> For he to-day that sheds his blood with me
> Shall be my brother; be he ne'er so vile,
> This day shall gentle his condition:
> And gentlemen in England now a-bed
> Shall think themselves accursed they were not here,
> And hold their manhoods cheap whiles any speaks
> That fought with us upon Saint Crispin's day.
>
> (IV. iii. 18)

Many other fights in which material weakness has prevailed against heavy odds have been more important to the world's history than Agincourt; many heroisms are more gripping to the imagination—Spartans at Thermopylae, Drake's seamen against the Armada; but none were ever so nobly honoured in verse, and indeed all find here their consummate expression. Earlier King Henry called on God and Saint George, and now we have Saint Crispin, a name whose very sound delicately suggests Christ; and yet how careful Shakespeare is to avoid directly associating Christ Himself with any martial assertion, however chivalrous. It has been observed that Shakespeare's Henry becomes here a comrade of his own men.[1] But there is no levelling down of the King to his subjects; rather his soldiers, through heroism, are lifted up to the stature of his own sovereignty. Notice, too, how this speech gains power from raising its hearers' own, deeper, selves: it appeals to their own judgements, asking them to be true to themselves, as in the earlier 'follow your spirit' (p. 40) or

> nought shall make us rue
> If England to itself do rest but true.
>
> (*King John*, v. vii. 117)

Such 'truth' is the key to much in Shakespeare.

When the battle of Agincourt is won, the King attributes the glory of it to God:

King Henry   O God, thy arm was here;
> And not to us, but to thy arm alone,
> Ascribe we all! When, without stratagem,
> But in plain shock and even play of battle,
> Was ever known so great and little loss
> On one part and on th'other? Take it, God,
> For it is none but thine!

---

[1] This was first, I think, emphasized by J. Middleton Murry in his book *Shakespeare*.

Exeter	'Tis wonderful!
King Henry	Come, go we in procession to the village:
	And be it death proclaimed through our host
	To boast of this or take the praise from God
	Which is his only.
Fluellen	Is't not lawful, an't please your majesty, to tell how many is killed?
King Henry	Yes, captain; but with this acknowledgement, that God fought for us.
Fluellen	Yes, my conscience, he did us great good.
King Henry	Do we all holy rites.
	Let there be sung 'Non nobis' and 'Te Deum';
	The dead with charity enclosed in clay:
	We'll then to Calais; and to England then;
	Where ne'er from France arrived more happy men.

(IV. viii. III)

In Henry Shakespeare characterizes a model of generalship. The King's humility is contrasted with his enemies' boasting; and during the battle of Agincourt criticism is levelled, by Fluellen, against the enemy's methods (IV. vii. I). A short passage sums up, in a more realistic manner, the kind of virtue intended:

> We would have all such offenders so cut off: and we give express charge that in our marches through the country there be nothing compelled from the villages, nothing taken but paid for, none of the French upbraided or abused in disdainful language; for when lenity and cruelty play for a kingdom, the gentler gamester is the soonest winner.

(III. vi. 116)

With that we may close our study of Henry's warring.

The play ends in concord. Peace is eulogized by the Duke of Burgundy and Henry woos Katharine of France. Here is Burgundy's speech, spoken before the two kings:

> Let it not disgrace me
> If I demand before this royal view,
> What rub or what impediment there is,
> Why that the naked, poor, and mangled Peace,
> Dear nurse of arts, plenties, and joyful births,
> Should not in this best garden of the world,
> Our fertile France, put up her lovely visage?

Alas! she hath from France too long been chas'd,
And all her husbandry doth lie on heaps,
Corrupting in its own fertility.
Her vine, the merry cheerer of the heart,
Unpruned dies; her hedges even-pleach'd,
Like prisoners wildly overgrown with hair,
Put forth disorder'd twigs; her fallow leas
The darnel, hemlock and rank fumitory
Doth root upon, while that the coulter rusts
That should deracinate such savagery;
The even mead, that erst brought sweetly forth
The freckled cowslip, burnet, and green clover,
Wanting the scythe, all uncorrected, rank,
Conceives by idleness, and nothing teems
But hateful docks, rough thistles, kecksies, burs,
Losing both beauty and utility;
And as our vineyards, fallows, meads, and hedges,
Defective in their natures, grow to wildness,
Even so our houses and ourselves and children
Have lost, or do not learn for want of time,
The sciences that should become our country,
But grow like savages—as soldiers will,
That nothing do but meditate on blood—
To swearing and stern looks, diffus'd attire,
And everything that seems unnatural.
Which to reduce into our former favour
You are assembled; and my speech entreats
That I may know the let why gentle Peace
Should not expel these inconveniences,
And bless us with her former qualities.

(v. ii. 31)

We may remember Henry VI's longing for nature's simple sweets. Burgundy's pastoral lines crown, as with a chaplet of flowers, Shakespeare's historic sequence.

This sequence, together with the comedies, whose resolving action, always in its way a definition of essential peace, is usually played out across a background of war and civil disturbance, makes up the first half of Shakespeare's work. The second half is a replica of the first, with a similar conclusion.

IV

Crack of Doom

In the plays so far noticed the conflict of human purpose and the will of God has not been resolved. *Henry V* is a magnificent attempt, but there are questions left over. Henry's warring is not all merciful: it could not be. Duke Theseus in *A Midsummer Night's Dream* comes near to personifying the desired union. He is gracious and kindly, though a great conqueror; but we do not actually *see* him at anything more bloodthirsty than hunting, and even then he seems mainly interested in the music of his hounds' baying, very much being subtly kept in the background. The Elizabethan age aspired to that synthesis of courtliness and prowess of which Sir Philip Sidney was a famed example; which breathes in Lyly's *Campaspe*; which Spenser's *Faerie Queene* labours to define and inculcate; and Shakespeare suggests in those lines attributing to Hamlet 'the courtier's, soldier's, scholar's, eye, tongue, sword' (*Hamlet*, III. i. 160).

The second half of Shakespeare's work does not repudiate the sequence leading to *Henry V*, but treats the old materials with a more deeply critical handling. The famous phrase 'Patriotism is not enough' might well be taken as a text for this new movement. It is as though Falstaff came back to life to inspire not comedy but tragedy. Falstaff becomes, as it were, violent; the mountain of a man turns out to be a volcano; there is earthquake and tempest, and seas grow tumultuous. This turbulence the ship of Shakespeare's national faith has to weather; and what a storm it is to be, upheaving waters and showing the slimy ocean bed, whirling you to the stars, dragging you out of your course. A veritable tornado is endured before that ship, in *Henry VIII*, comes to harbour.

Both *Julius Caesar* and *Hamlet* form a valuable contrast to *Henry V*, showing heroes deeply troubled by the necessity of stern action involving bloodshed. Brutus considers it to be his duty to assassinate his friend Caesar in the cause of political liberty, but, whereas Cassius on the one side and Antony on

the other are forceful and single-minded, he himself, though
acting for so pure an ideal as liberty, endures a severe conflict:

> Between the acting of a dreadful thing
> And the first motion, all the interim is
> Like a phantasma or a hideous dream.
> The genius and the mortal instruments
> Are then in council; and the state of man,
> Like to a little kingdom, suffers then
> The nature of an insurrection.
>
> (II. i. 63)

That is the new and deeper note.

In *Hamlet* we are shown a hero of sensitive temperament,
who learns from a ghost representing 'the majesty of buried
Denmark' (I. i. 48) that his royal father's untimely end has
been caused by the treacherous act of his own uncle, now king.
Hamlet's world is henceforth darkened, and society, to him,
diseased. Honour demands that he execute revenge, but his
will is paralysed. He typifies all those whose depth of insight
prevents them from obeying the calls of action in a disordered
world. He is, moreover, contrasted with Laertes and Fortinbras, strong young men serving ideals of conventional honour
without a questioning thought. 'Am I a coward?' Hamlet asks
himself (II. ii. 606), wondering if he is a greater or a lesser
than those around him. His two longest soliloquies, those
beginning 'O what a rogue and peasant slave am I!' (II. ii. 584)
and 'How all occasions do inform against me . . .' (IV. iv. 32),
are indicative: and both may serve to forecast the inevitable
self-conflicts which have since become apparent in any national
community whose depth of insight and maturity of experience
puts it at a disadvantage before the unprincipled energies of
seemingly more virile nations. Such a comparison has the
advantage of enabling all of us to live the experience of Shakespeare's play.

The action is given a war-like setting and these two soliloquies are occasioned directly by thoughts of war, its horrors
and heroisms, the one by the Player's speech on the sack of
Troy, the other by Fortinbras' expedition against the Poles:

> Now, whe'r it be
> Bestial oblivion, or some craven scruple

Of thinking too precisely on the event,
A thought, which, quarter'd, hath but one part wisdom,
And ever three parts coward, I do not know
Why yet I live to say 'This thing's to do';
Sith I have cause and will and strength and means
To do't. Examples gross as earth exhort me:
Witness this army of such mass and charge
Led by a delicate and tender prince,
Whose spirit with divine ambition puff'd
Makes mouths at the invisible event,
Exposing what is mortal and unsure
To all that fortune, death, and danger dare,
Even for an egg-shell. Rightly to be great
Is not to stir without great argument,
But greatly to find quarrel in a straw
When honour's at the stake. How stand I then,
That hath a father kill'd, a mother stain'd,
Excitements of my reason and my blood,
And let all sleep, while, to my shame, I see
The imminent death of twenty thousand men,
That, for a fantasy and trick of fame,
Go to their graves like beds, fight for a plot
Whereon the numbers cannot try the cause,
Which is not tomb enough and continent
To hide the slain? O! from this time forth,
My thoughts be bloody, or be nothing worth!

(IV. iv. 39)

'Bloody' here means 'virile' rather than 'murderous', as so often in Shakespeare.

Many of the more social and what might be called 'governmental' qualities lacking in Hamlet are to be found in the eminently courteous and efficient king, Claudius. Though a murderer, he is no Richard III, and indeed bears to Hamlet a relation not unlike the relation borne by King Henry to the tragic people in *Henry VIII*.[1] Both Claudius and Henry are regularly referred to as 'the King', the simple words, as in 'catch the conscience of the King' (II. ii. 642), sounding as a reminder of their function, for good or ill, as a reflection of society, the hub-like importance of kingship to the wheel of state being underlined by an important speech of Guildernstern (III. iii. 11–23), and its overtones of sanctity impressed

---

[1] See my footnote on p. 228 below.

D

on us by Claudius' 'There's such divinity doth hedge a king . . .' (IV. v. 123). And yet, at the end, 'the King, the King's to blame' (v. ii. 334). He is both an enlightened ruler and a criminal in direct contrast to the finely tuned but baffled Hamlet: the paradoxes go deep.

Hamlet's lack of virility is clearly one with his profundity, and Shakespeare's greater plays to follow preserve much of the Hamlet spirit: the poet is not content with military or political values alone, but remains deeply concerned with them, and henceforth submits each and all to a penetrating criticism, showing them in contrast, or collaboration, with greater, and mysterious presences. Shakespeare is himself now ghost-ridden and, like Hamlet, aims to penetrate below the surface of an unclean society, or 'king', by his own dramatic art: 'The play's the thing . . .' (II. ii. 641). So too, by the reverse process, we may ourselves search for solutions to our own problems in the mirror of our national drama.[1]

The order upheld by the King in *Hamlet* is efficient and humane, yet based on crime: that is the paradox which makes the play so baffling. The problem of government is certainly one of Shakespeare's most pressing concerns, and many variations are played on it. His thought is, as usual, characterized by a unique balancing of opposites, as when justice and Christian mercy are balanced in Portia's speech in *The Merchant of Venice*:

> The quality of mercy is not strain'd,
> It droppeth as the gentle rain from heaven
> Upon the place beneath: it is twice bless'd;
> It blesseth him that gives and him that takes;
> 'Tis mightiest in the mightiest; it becomes
> The throned monarch better than his crown.
> His sceptre shows the force of temporal power,
> The attribute to awe and majesty,
> Wherein doth sit the dread and fear of kings;
> But mercy is above this sceptred sway,
> It is enthroned in the hearts of kings,
> It is an attribute to God himself,
> And earthly power doth then show likest God's
> When mercy seasons justice. Therefore, Jew,

[1] These remarks on *Hamlet* should be supplemented by consideration of the essay 'Hamlet Reconsidered' in the enlarged edition of *The Wheel of Fire*.

Though justice be thy plea, consider this,
That in the course of justice none of us
Should see salvation: we do pray for mercy,
And that same prayer doth teach us all to render
The deeds of mercy.

(iv. i. 184)

The transcending of law is an attribute of royalty. A king is more than a governor: he is rather a mediator between the temporal and the eternal.

In *Measure for Measure* Shakespeare closely advances his analysis of a deeply disturbing problem. Is justice possible? The studious Duke of Vienna, whose psychological insight has convinced him so thoroughly of man's inability to pronounce judgement on his neighbour that his city becomes a riot of vice, hands over ducal authority to a man of stern rectitude and spotless reputation, and then returns, in the disguise of a friar, which may be allowed to adumbrate dramatically a synthesis of church and state, to watch the result.

Angelo, the substitute, is shown as failing under the test of authority and himself, at a key moment, guilty of the very fault he would punish. The whole play turns, as I have shown at length in *The Wheel of Fire*, on the serene but baffling teaching of Christ's gospel. Great things are spoken. Here is one:

Well, believe this,
No ceremony that to great ones 'longs,
Not the king's crown, nor the deputed sword,
The marshal's truncheon, nor the judge's robe,
Become them with one half so good a grace
As mercy does.

(ii. ii. 58)

And here another:

Why, all the souls that were were forfeit once;
And He that might the vantage best have took,
Found out the remedy. How would you be,
If He, which is the top of judgement, should
But judge you as you are? O! think on that,
And mercy then will breathe within your lips,
Like man new made.

(ii. ii. 73)

And this perhaps the best of all:

                                        O! it is excellent
    To have a giant's strength, but it is tyrannous
    To use it like a giant. . . . Could great men thunder
    As Jove himself does, Jove would ne'er be quiet,
    For every pelting, petty officer
    Would use his heaven for thunder; nothing but thunder.
    Merciful Heaven!
    Thou rather with thy sharp and sulphurous bolt
    Split'st the unwedgeable and gnarled oak
    Than the soft myrtle; but man, proud man,
    Drest in a little brief authority,
    Most ignorant of what he's most assur'd,
    His glassy essence, like an angry ape,
    Plays such fantastic tricks before high heaven
    As make the angels weep; who, with our spleens,
    Would all themselves laugh mortal.

                                        (II. ii. 107)

The lines register powerfully enough today; but we do well
to remember that they express an age-old and all but inevitable
aspect of government, against which Shakespeare pronounces
such judgements as these, following the gospel of Christ, who
himself uttered all but the last word on such oppositions:
'You could have no power over me were it not given you from
above (John, XIX, 11). And yet Shakespeare leaves us in no
doubt that Vienna needed a strong ruler.

    Temporal authority must, as things are, exist. In *Troilus
and Cressida* Agamemnon is too ready to fall back on semi-
mystic excuses of tragic philosophy—in which he bears some
resemblance to the Duke in *Measure for Measure*—for his,
and his army's, failure. He is answered by Ulysses with a
long speech on order,[1] pointing us to those parents of all
unity, reverence and respect. Factions, disorder, and disrespect
hold sway in sharp contrast to the cosmic scheme wherein the
Sun functions as king and all is harmony. Hierarchies are
necessary:

    Take but degree away, untune that string,
    And, hark! what discord follows; each thing meets

[1] Compare the opposition of Falstaff and the Chief Justice in *2 Henry IV* as analysed
by Dover Wilson in *The Fortunes of Falstaff*. Falstaff may be allowed to correspond to
the tragic spirit of later plays.

In mere oppugnancy: the bounded waters
Should lift their bosom higher than the shores,
And make a sop of all this solid globe:
Strength should be lord of imbecility,
And the rude son should strike his father dead:
Force should be right; or rather, right and wrong—
Between whose endless jar justice resides—
Should lose their names, and so should justice too.
Then every thing includes itself in power,
Power into will, will into appetite;
And appetite, a universal wolf,
So doubly seconded with will and power,
Must make perforce a universal prey,
And last eat up himself.

(i. iii. 109)

The slow working out of a stable system from chaos and conflict dramatized in the historical plays is here given its philosophy; and the philosophy is one which presses on us heavily
today with a summoning insistence, not merely as nations,
but as travaillers towards world-order. Notice how all Christian, and other civilized, values are by Shakespeare maintained;
values which any too masterful a will to a forced, inorganic,
order may be in danger of scattering to the four winds.

In *Troilus and Cressida* both government and war, as well
as love, the play's primary theme, are variously honoured and
satirized. On the Trojan side war is chivalrous and romantic,
with honour an infinite value, but among the Greeks it is
shown as brutal and all but absurd. The deformed and embit-
tered Thersites watches two lords fighting during a battle, and
cheers them on with bitter mockery (v. vii. 9–13). Elsewhere
he comments:

Lechery, lechery; still, wars and lechery: nothing else holds
fashion. A burning devil take them!

(v. ii. 192)

Remembering Falstaff we can feel Shakespeare wondering
whether all armed conflict is finally stupid and degrading, and
the history of modern Europe, as Swift saw it, poisoned at the
source of national action. Such bitterness is expanded further
in *Timon of Athens*.

Here Shakespeare sets his soul on paper as perhaps in no

other work, not even *Hamlet*. We are shown a generous and
lordly Athenian who exhausts his wealth and, all help from his
former friends being denied him, is struck to the quick by their
miserly ingratitude; next deserts humanity for a hermit's garb
and sea-shore cavern home, only to find more gold when digging
for roots; but, the iron having settled in his heart, refuses now
all compromise, pours out his new-found treasure to assist
Alcibiades to lead an army against Athens, and indeed gives
gold, with imprecations, to all who come; but himself will not
return, though the repentant city implores him to lend his
name and princely virtue to save it from destruction. We
must be ready to put London for Athens as we read Timon's
prophetic denunciations. Here, as in *Troilus and Cressida*,
Shakespeare uses a Greek setting for what appears to be a
mainly contemporary satire, whereas his Roman plays are very
differently modelled: in them ancient Rome, as Rome, dominates. So *Timon of Athens* shatters the smug surfaces of our
civilization with a piercing invective, exposing its sores and
shames and hideous communal wrongs:

> I know thee too; and more than that I know thee
> I not desire to know. Follow thy drum;
> With man's blood paint the ground, gules, gules;
> Religious canons, civil laws are cruel;
> Then what should war be?

(iv. iii. 57)

'Drum' is spoken with emphasized scorn of war's childish
ritual, while the charge against civil ordinances is levelled in
terms of cruelty. Hearing that Alcibiades is campaigning
against Athens, Timon gives him gold, and in part seriously
and partly in scathing irony—for detestation of war breathes
in every pitying yet condemning syllable—directs him to
violent excesses:

Timon   Warr'st thou 'gainst Athens?
Alcibiades Ay, Timon, and have cause.
Timon   The gods confound them all in thy conquest;
            And thee after, when thou hast conquer'd!
Alcibiades   Why me, Timon?
Timon   That, by killing of villains, thou wast born to conquer my
            country.
            Put up thy gold: go on—here's gold—go on;

Be as a planetary plague, when Jove
Will o'er some high-vic'd city hang his poison
In the sick air: let not thy sword skip one.
Pity not honour'd age for his white beard;
He is a usurer. Strike me the counterfeit matron;
It is her habit only that is honest,
Herself's a bawd. Let not the virgin's cheek
Make soft thy trenchant sword; for those milk-paps,
That through the window-bars bore at men's eyes,
Are not within the leaf of pity writ,
But set them down horrible traitors. Spare not the babe,
Whose dimpled smiles from fools exhaust their mercy;
Think it a bastard, whom the oracle
Hath doubtfully pronounc'd thy throat shall cut,
And mince it sans remorse. Swear against objects;
Put armour on thine ears and on thine eyes,
Whose proof nor yells of mothers, maids, nor babes,
Nor sight of priests in holy vestments bleeding,
Shall pierce a jot. There's gold to pay thy soldiers:
Make large confusion; and, thy fury spent,
Confounded be thyself! Speak not, be gone.

(IV. iii. 102)

What has become of the romantic Henry V? Yet even there
you will find, in Henry's own speeches, a closely similar
awareness of war's brutality.[1] Here words such as 'my country',
the various images of human appeal, the 'holy priests' and
'sacred vestments', all witness, are stamped with a recognition
of, those potential excellences which have been betrayed by a
decadent society. In another speech Timon's words labour
under an agonized sense of war's hideousness even when his
refusal to assist the Senate rings final:

Well, sir, I will; therefore, I will, sir; thus:—
If Alcibiades kill my countrymen,
Let Alcibiades know this of Timon,
That Timon cares not. But if he sack fair Athens,
And take our goodly aged men by the beards,

---

[1] *Timon of Athens* is forecast by much of Shakespeare's earlier work; by Romeo's
speech on gold to the Apothecary (*Romeo and Juliet*, V, 1, 80–3); by Falconbridge's
'Commodity' speech in *King John* (II, 1, 561–98); and by Jacques in *As You Like It*
(II. vii. 47–87). Shakespeare does not so much discover new thoughts in his later work
as make changes of emphasis and distribution.

> Giving our holy virgins to the stain
> Of contumelious, beastly, mad-brain'd war;
> Then let him know, and tell him Timon speaks it,
> In pity of our aged and our youth,
> I cannot choose but tell him, that I care not,
> And let him take't at worst.

(v. i. 173)

It may seem, indeed, that Shakespeare prefers Alcibiades, the man of soldierly honour, to the usurious and capitalistic senators. But Timon himself despises both, and all their ways and works:

> Be Alcibiades your plague, you his,
> And last so long enough.

(v. i. 194)

He exists on a height overlooking all military, or civil, ambitions.

The play does, however, forecast the greatest conflict of our time to the extent that it correctly diagnoses the forces at issue, the emerging opposition of (i) a peace-loving capitalism, rendered ugly in its 'dotage' by 'usury' (iii. v. 101) in high places, resting in 'great chairs of ease' (v. iv. 11) and relying, as do the Senators in their scene with Alcibiades, on smug concepts of law and justice; and (ii) stark, youthful, militarism in revolt.[1] Alcibiades certainly wins and establishes a new order. I read the play as a warning to Shakespeare's countrymen; as an extension of old John of Gaunt's denunciation of an England bound in by 'inky blots and rotten parchment bonds' (p. 28) in *Richard II*. If any doubts remain that Shakespeare's genius here senses the oncoming of vast, greed-engendered, conflicts, they should be dispelled by Timon's address (iv. iii. 25–44) to the gold-nugget he digs up, called by him a 'yellow slave' that can 'knit and break religions' and bend all mankind to its will, putting 'odds' (i.e. conflict) 'among the rout of nations':

---

[1] The analogy—it is no more—was obvious enough in 1940, and can be extended to include Apemantus as social revolutionary, or communist. Timon himself personifies *the one positive of which these others are all negative, and mutually destructive, shadows,* the denunciation, after the fashion of great poetry, covering *all* contemporary society, as we today know it.

O thou sweet king-killer, and dear divorce
'Twixt natural son and sire! thou bright defiler
Of Hymen's purest bed! thou valiant Mars!
Thou ever young, fresh, lov'd, and delicate wooer,
Whose blush doth thaw the consecrated snow
That lies on Dian's lap! thou visible god,
That solder'st close impossibilities,
And mak'st them kiss! that speak'st with every tongue,
To every purpose! O thou touch of hearts!
Think, thy slave man rebels, and by thy virtue
Set them into confounding odds, that beasts
May have the world in empire.

(IV. iii. 384)

'Beasts'. All Shakespeare's work aims variously at controlling, fighting, or, at the best, using, the 'beast' in man. His Saint George takes different forms, but the conflict of man's spiritual aristocracy and the various degrading shapes which so easily usurp power is recurrent. Greed is here the 'beast'. Disgusted, Timon imprecates all possible disorders on a civilization which has severed contact with the foundations of all true order: emotional sincerity, generosity, nobility. A certain sovereign essence has been wronged. *Measure for Measure* questions all temporal justice and authority; and *Troilus and Cressida* at one point asserts the absolute necessity of degree and order. But Timon personifies that indefinable essence of generosity and grace on which all such arguments pivot. The gold he gives to all who visit him may be allowed to symbolize the golden wisdom which burns alike in his early love and later hate. Here Shakespeare attacks a society, and that means to him England, for insincerity, for being false to itself, for selling its own nobility and generosity, its own best human and therefore royal excellence, its highest purpose on earth. If Shakespeare finally takes his stand, as he does, by his country's destiny, he has certainly shirked nothing. Timon is, indeed, far more than a critic of society. He is the soul of great poetry voyaging on a lonely quest, most truly at home with sun and moon and earth and all elements of nature, and listening from time to time to the sob and surge of the great seas into which his story fades. From the depths of eternity he pronounces judgement on the pettiness of man.

It may seem rash to search for any national message or meaning in such tragedies as *King Lear* and *Macbeth*. I here make no attempt to characterize the racked universe of the one or the demonic energies of the other. The two plays dig at the roots of evil, seeing political disruption as closely related respectively to (i) family disunion, and (ii) psychic disease and dark forces of the immaterial world. There is therefore a continuity, of a general kind, with our other political studies concentrating on order and disorder, and any explicit references to England fall accordingly into place.

Remember how important to Shakespeare is the unity, which is also the sincerity, of England; and how his history cycle shows the turmoils of civil war leading towards Tudor supremacy. Now Lear is King of Britain; and he is old. In old age he gives up his sovereignty in all but name, sentimentally wishing for ease, with his three daughters dividing the realm; and disaster follows. Reference to the future of Britain becomes explicit in an unfortunately obscure piece of doggerel spoken by the Fool, purporting half-mockingly to describe the conditions of the country's future disintegration, and ending:

> Then shall the realm of Albion
> Come to great confusion.

(III. ii. 91)

It is called a 'prophecy', and the lines perhaps represent a comic actor's distortion of an original which appeared, in Shakespeare's day, meaningless. Or maybe Shakespeare's instinct enjoys using the Fool's inconsequence to push the play's dim national feeling into the twilight of a semi-conscious, semi-purposeful, prophetic commentary. Anyone who has read Sackville's *Gorboduc*, an earlier play on a very similar theme, with its precise reference, through dumb-show, of the plot to a nation, and in particular Britain, in disunity, or realizes the fear of political disorder which existed in the Elizabethan mind, will recognize how much more nationally important to Shakespeare than to the modern reader, unless duly warned, was a story about a king of Britain who relinquishes authority and paves the way for chaos.

The play is written, broadly, from a sense of oncoming

disaster in Renaissance civilization related to lack of family piety:

> These late eclipses in the sun and moon portend no good to us: though the wisdom of nature can reason it thus and thus, yet nature finds itself scourged by the sequent effects. Love cools, friendship falls off, brothers divide: in cities, mutinies; in countries, discord; in palaces, treason; and the bond cracked between son and father. This villain of mine comes under the prediction; there's son against father: the king falls from bias of nature; there's father against child. We have seen the best of our time: machinations, hollowness, treachery, and all ruinous disorders, follow us disquietly to our graves.
>
> (I. ii. 115)

Like *Timon of Athens*, though less obviously, the play is a warning; and Lear's madness contains satire savage as Timon's, with a closely similar denunciation of civil justice (IV. vi. 163–73). Another passage rouses an easy response today:

> If that the heavens do not their visible spirits
> Send quickly down to tame these vile offences,
> It will come,
> Humanity must perforce prey on itself,
> Like monsters of the deep.
>
> (IV. ii. 46)

As in *Timon of Athens*, man's dangerous, lusting, brutality is compared, over and over again, to beasts; and in our last quotation they are water-beasts, like Tennyson's

> . . . dragons of the prime
> That tare each other in their slime

of *In Memoriam* (LVI), and the more apt, as in the emblem of Saint George, as symbols of unreclaimed instinct. These dread forces Lear's original foolishness has unloosed, and Goneril and Regan and Edmund have their way—for a time. They regard the good people as weaklings. Goneril scorns her gentle husband Albany, preferring Edmund, the conscienceless, panther-like, villain. The evil people degenerate swiftly, growing worse and worse. They become sadistically brutal. But saving powers return with the love of Lear's youngest daughter Cordelia, as in *Macbeth* through child-innocence and a holy king. Shakespeare sets against Machiavellian intrigue, crude force, and all lustful evils, such simple champions of grace.

The power-quest and tyrannic ambition explored in *Richard III* are in *Macbeth* presented at once more metaphysically and more imaginatively. In no other Shakespearian work are the symbols of royalty so weighty, so loaded with metaphysical significance. Though darkly shadowed, they seem to burn out with a richer solidity, a deeper cogency of meaning, for the murk that would engulf them, as in the accents of Lady Macbeth's 'all that impedes thee from the golden round' and 'give solely sovereign sway and masterdom' (i. v. 29, 71). 'Golden round': the crown is of gold, symbolizing a high value; and it is round, being an emblem of the eternal. It is to gain, and keep, this splendour for his own enjoyment that Macbeth plunges his country in chaos:

> . . . Alas! poor country;
> Almost afraid to know itself. It cannot
> Be call'd our mother, but our grave; where nothing,
> But who knows nothing, is once seen to smile;
> Where sighs and groans and shrieks that rent the air
> Are made, not mark'd; where violent sorrow seems
> A modern ecstasy; the dead man's knell
> Is there scarce ask'd for who; and good men's lives
> Expire before the flowers in their caps,
> Dying or ere they sicken.
>
> (iv. iii. 164)

Macbeth's mad and useless murders make Scotland a shambles. He has spies everywhere: 'There's not a one of them but in his house I keep a servant fee'd' (iii. iv. 131). Shakespeare's *Richard III*, *King Lear* and *Macbeth* isolate and intensify certain negative essences of the will to power, accompanied freely by deception and slaughter, which are not hard to recognize.

However irresistible the evil forces may seem, Shakespeare clearly defines the opposing powers of good. We have, first, the good King Duncan, whose murder is Macbeth's original crime:

> Besides, this Duncan
> Hath borne his faculties so meek, hath been
> So clear in his great office, that his virtues
> Will plead like angels trumpet-tongu'd against
> The deep damnation of his taking-off;

And pity, like a naked new-born babe,
Striding the blast, or Heaven's cherubin, hors'd
Upon the sightless couriers of the air,
Shall blow the horrid deed in every eye,
That tears shall drown the wind. I have no spur
To prick the sides of my intent, but only
Vaulting ambition . . .

(i. vii. 16)

Compare with this the vision shown Macbeth by the Weird
Sisters of a power combining child-purity, as in our 'naked new-
born babe', nature and true sovereignty, a combination which,
at long last, must win. The apparition is 'a Child Crowned,
with a Tree in his hand', and Macbeth addresses it:

What is this
That rises like the issue of a king,
And wears upon his baby-brow the round
And top of sovereignty?

(iv. i. 86)

In strong contrast is the other apparition, the 'Armed Head',
iron force severed from its body, the destructive and self-
destructive essence.[1]

The witches have prophesied that the descendants of
Banquo shall rule after Macbeth. Macbeth's kingship is lustful
and possessive, Banquo's un-selfseeking and creative; his
doomed to wither, Banquo's destined to immortality. The
thought of this torments Macbeth, who expresses his fears in
a soliloquy condensing vividly the essential insecurity and
uneasiness of a tyrannous rule:

To be thus is nothing;
But to be safely thus. Our fears in Banquo
Stick deep, and in his royalty of nature
Reigns that which would be fear'd: 'tis much he dares,
And, to that dauntless temper of his mind,
He hath a wisdom that doth guide his valour
To act in safety. There is none but he
Whose being I do fear; and under him
My genius is rebuk'd, as it is said
Mark Antony's was by Caesar. He chid the sisters

---

[1] The three Apparitions, Armed Head, Bloody Child and Child Crowned, are
exactly used. Their full significance is discussed in *The Shakespearian Tempest*, pp. 192–3.

When first they put the name of king upon me,
And bade them speak to him; then, prophet-like,
They hail'd him father to a line of kings.
Upon my head they plac'd a fruitless crown,
And put a barren sceptre in my gripe,
Thence to be wrench'd with an unlineal hand,
No son of mine succeeding. If't be so,
For Banquo's issue have I fil'd my mind;
For them the gracious Duncan have I murder'd;
Put rancours in the vessel of my peace
Only for them; and mine eternal jewel
Given to the common enemy of man,
To make them kings, the seed of Banquo kings!
Rather than so, come fate into the list,
And champion me to the utterance!

(III. i. 48)

He is further tormented by a vision of future Scottish kings
blending, after the union of realms under James I, during
whose reign this play was written, into a line of English kings
too; and the inevitable and expanding, organically growing,
power suggested, together with those deep burnishings of a
royal splendour so weighty throughout the poetry here, blend
naturally into Shakespeare's general feeling elsewhere for
England's, which is now also Scotland's, undying sovereignty:

Thou art too like the spirit of Banquo; down!
Thy crown does sear mine eyeballs; and thy hair,
Thou other gold-bound brow, is like the first:
A third is like the former. Filthy hags!
Why do you show me this? A fourth! Start, eyes!
What! will the line stretch out to the crack of doom?
Another yet? A seventh! I'll see no more:
And yet the eighth appears, who bears a glass
Which shows me many more; and some I see
That two-fold balls and treble sceptres carry.
Horrible sight! Now, I see 'tis true;
For the blood-bolter'd Banquo smiles upon me,
And points at them for his.

(IV. i. 112)

This line of kings is descended from Banquo, secure in an
integrity which, in the midst of suffocating evil, can yet say:

> In the great hand of God I stand, and thence
> Against the undivulg'd pretence I fight
> Of treasonous malice.
>
> (II. iii. 137)

In murdering Banquo, Macbeth tries to cut off Great Britain's future history at its root. But Fleance escapes.

In Macbeth and Banquo two ways of serving both time and eternity are contrasted, and they cannot readily mix. But notice that in this, Shakespeare's most profound dramatization of evil, Great Britain's destiny is at stake. This it is which wrestles with the power-lust and is shown, finally, as triumphant. *Macbeth* points directly to *Henry VIII*.

The saving powers are aligned with England. Thither the brave Macduff flies to join Malcolm, Scotland's true heir, and gather military assistance. A Scottish lord prays for angelic aid in his mission:

> Some holy angel
> Fly to the court of England and unfold
> His message ere he come, that a swift blessing
> May soon return to this our suffering country
> Under a hand accurs'd!
>
> (III. vi. 45)

And what of that English court? Here we have a scene of quiet, of peace, a backwater in the torrential action, together with a description of the holy English king, Edward the Confessor, and his miraculous powers against—how apt the name—a disease called 'the Evil':

> *Macduff* What's the disease he means?
> *Malcolm* 'Tis call'd the Evil
> A most miraculous work in this good king,
> Which often, since my here-remain in England,
> I have seen him do. How he solicits Heaven,
> Himself best knows; but strangely-visited people,
> All swoln and ulcerous, pitiful to the eye,
> The mere despair of surgery, he cures;
> Hanging a golden stamp about their necks,
> Put on with holy prayers; and 'tis spoken
> To the succeeding royalty he leaves
> The healing benediction. With this strange virtue,
> He hath a heavenly gift of prophecy,

And sundry blessings hang about his throne
That speak him full of grace.

(IV. iii. 146)

So Macduff and Malcolm, with an English army led by old Siward—'an older and a better soldier none that Christendom gives out' (IV. iii. 191)—set forth to conquer tyranny, with the aid of Birnam wood, all nature joining in the cause. Pushing through this play's structure rise, from the murk and the night-mare, solid shapes of a blessed power, with baby innocence and gentle nature as invincible allies, and an English king as mediator of grace.

There are many more implications in such plays as *King Lear* and *Macbeth* than I can here discuss. Notice how in all these greater plays the more spiritual conflict objectifies itself into armed opposition, with a final re-establishment of order, as in *Hamlet* and *Timon of Athens*, with Fortinbras and Alcibiades as arbiters. We can, however, notice also that in each some obvious outward shape of nobility, kingly rank or fine soldiership, is overthrown by an emotional force touching, except in *Timon of Athens*, some feminine relationship; for we must not forget the part played by Lady Macbeth. This pattern is clear in *Othello*. In the middle-action, as despair overwhelms him, Othello recalls his soldierly glory:

> I had been happy, if the general camp,
> Pioneers and all, had tasted her sweet body,
> So I had nothing known. O! now, for ever
> Farewell the tranquil mind; farewell content!
> Farewell the plumed troop and the big wars
> That make ambition virtue! O, farewell!
> Farewell the neighing steed, and the shrill trump,
> The spirit-stirring drum, the ear-piercing fife,
> The royal banner, and all quality,
> Pride, pomp, and circumstance of glorious war!
> And, O you mortal engines, whose rude throats
> The immortal Jove's dread clamours counterfeit,
> Farewell! Othello's occupation's gone![1]

(III. iii. 346)

[1] That Othello's soldiership is enlisted against the Turks tends, within the Shakespearian purview, to universalize him as a Christian warrior. This is the point of the reference in his final speech (V. ii. 351–5). Compare the passages quoted on pp. 36, 39.

This overthrowing of what might be termed a male value by a female force may be referred to those numerous women throughout the Histories in the background of martial action and political rivalry, variously watching, often suffering for and sometimes condemning, as from a deeper wisdom, man's turbulent and ambitious drama. The process is one with Shakespeare's spiritualized and tragic understanding of all temporal power; and it is precisely this that, in the long run, renders whatever military fervours or national gospel he may offer so peculiarly invulnerable. There are always cosmic powers waiting to shatter the brittle outside of over-confident and insubstantial appearance, and the rights Shakespeare ultimately believes in are only those which themselves derive sanction from this cosmic source, which becomes, at the limit, as with the English king in *Macbeth*, divine grace. With this tendency in mind let us glance shortly at *Antony and Cleopatra* and *Coriolanus*, in both of which soldierly pride is contrasted with a feminine allegiance.

Ancient Rome was to the Elizabethans a prototype and an exemplar. The issues raised in *Julius Caesar* of monarchy and freedom, of personal and symbolic sovereignty, Caesar the man and Caesar the spirit of imperial guidance, all have close, Tudor, implications. And so, when in *Antony and Cleopatra* one of Rome's joint imperial rulers throws away all soldierly honour and imperial sway for a woman's love, we have Shakespeare at work on a vital conflict. Without shirking the tragedy of Antony's fall, he expends his art lavishly on the cosmic powers of a great love, while his Cleopatra, into whom all his feminine understanding is condensed, is so amazing a creation that one is scarcely surprised at her victory. No Shakespearian hero, not even Othello, is so idealized in point of soldierly valour as Antony. He incorporates at its pagan best the primitive energies, and is therefore compared (iii. xi. 94–5) naturally to that golden and kingly beast, the lion, in contradistinction to the tyrant Macbeth, who is, at a similar moment, imaged as a 'bear' (*Macbeth*, v. vii. 2). Antony is a mighty oak of a man, a vast strength uprooted, and crashes in magnificent and rebounding echoes of poetry. The disrupting force is Cleopatra. He is masculinity personified, she expressly and universally feminine, with all peculiarly feminine traits of grace, merriment,

E

fascination, courage, weakness and, above and justifying, lending meaning to, all, love. She is, too, queen of Egypt: the play scintillates with splendours and, while an empire is split by civil war, love's presence itself assumes imperial stature. Beside Romeo's dream of re-union beyond death with its 'I revived and was an emperor' (*Romeo and Juliet*, v. i. 9) we may place Cleopatra's dream: 'I dream'd there was an Emperor Antony . . .' (v. ii. 76). We all but reach an equation of love and empire, just as Shakespeare's royalism may draw close to an erotic potency (e.g. *The Merchant of Venice*, III. ii. 178–84; *Troilus and Cressida*, III. ii. 35–9). In this golden play both soldierly honour and love blaze with noonday strength; and, though love wins and seems to lift the lovers beyond death to realms of eternal fruition, the two values are once, for a superb moment, as once also in *Othello* (IV. viii; II. i), felt as identical, and both are contrasted with the cool and calculating policy of Caesar. The general reference to Shakespeare's refusal of all simple solutions is obvious.

Coriolanus strikes home, as does no other play, to our most pressing contemporary horror: the horror of stark, unadulterated, militarism. Coriolanus is brought up by that stern Roman matron, Volumnia, his devoted mother, to honour, not Rome, but 'honour' itself, to be a veritable superman of a soldier. Both Coriolanus and Volumnia sin through pride and excessive concentration on an ambition which, if allowed to become an end in itself, proves suicidal. Warfare is shown as harsh, brutal, thunderous in impact, and Coriolanus stands as the honoured expert in its grim technique. His mother welcomes him home from the war, forgetting, as we are reminded (II. i. 197–8), the women of Corioli whom his success has left widowed or sonless.

But Volumnia has created a force which she cannot control and Coriolanus' pride becomes intolerable. We see now that he warred only for 'honour'; for himself, not for Rome. It is as though whoever puts an abstraction, a word, an ideology, before his God, his country, or his family, vital allegiances which may indeed themselves conflict but are all alike hostile to those insidious abstract virtues, whether they call themselves 'honour' or 'reason', and to whatever particular abstractions they may lead, will be, at the limit, found guilty of an egocentric idolatry. But against that little ego stands a greater self in us all; and that greater self, as with Enobarbus in *Antony and Cleopatra*, whose desertion swiftly faced him with self-condemnation, awaits its time. Coriolanus' pride refuses compromise; Rome finds him intolerable, his mother pathetically attempts to retrieve the error of his upbringing; he is banished.

Now the inherent paradox of the elevation of warrior-honour to a supreme value is driven home. Nursing his wounded pride, Coriolanus leads his one-time enemies against his own city. Encamped outside its walls, he has Rome at his mercy, and expects soon to taste the sweets of revenge. As a last hope, Rome sends his own mother, wife, and child to soften, if they may, his implacable will. It seems a forlorn hope. Here he is in his iron, dictatorial, dignity as described by the witty old aristocrat, Menenius:

> *Sicinius* Is't possible that so short a time can alter the condition of a man?
>
> *Menenius* There is differency between a grub and a butterfly; yet your butterfly was a grub. This Marcius is grown from man to dragon: he has wings; he's more than a creeping thing.
>
> *Sicinius* He loved his mother dearly.
>
> *Menenius* So did he me; and he no more remembers his mother now than an eight-year-old horse. The tartness of his face sours ripe grapes: when he walks, he moves like an engine, and the ground shrinks before his treading; he is able to pierce a corslet with his eye; talks like a knell, and his hum is a battery. He sits in his state, as a thing made for Alexander. What he bids be done is finished with his bidding. He wants nothing of a god but eternity and a heaven to throne in.
>
> *Sicinius* Yes, mercy, if you report him truly.
>
> *Menenius* I paint him in the character. Mark what mercy his mother shall bring from him: there is no more mercy in him than there is milk in a male tiger; that shall our poor city find.
>
> (v. iv. 10)

This is Shakespeare's mature commentary on self-centred devotees of military honour, men like Hotspur and Tybalt, types of which Homer's Achilles is an ancient literary example. Coriolanus has become inhuman: he is a 'dragon', or 'tiger'; or worse, a machine, a robot, almost un-alive. There is an implied criticism of pride and force corresponding to that in

the 'Armed Head' apparition of *Macbeth*, wherein violent
destructiveness is shown as both threatening and severed from
its organic body, and therefore rootless as well as sapless. In the
same way, Coriolanus' pride is now shown as self-contradictory
and suicidal.

His mother, wife, and son approach him. He stands firm,
and will not obey 'instinct' (v. iii. 35), already half-confessing
that his deepest self rejects his self-nursed ideal. When his
own mother kneels to him, that egocentric ideal seems like a
'pebble' on the beach insulting the stars, a 'cedar' striking
the sun (v. iii. 56–62); for his pride is a little, earthly thing,
and his love for his mother a great cosmic power. Yet he will
not give way. Volumnia speaks scathingly, scornfully, of his
treacherous intention, and, since his long story of pride derived
first from an inborn desire to deserve his mother's praise (i. i.
40), her scorn now, a voice drawing power from his deepest
childhood, disarms him. He 'holds her hand in silence', and
then:

> O, mother, mother!
> What have you done? Behold! the heavens do ope,
> The gods look down, and this unnatural scene
> They laugh at. O my mother! mother! O!
> You have won a happy victory to Rome;
> But, for your son, believe it, O! believe it,
> Most dangerously you have with him prevail'd,
> If not most mortal to him.
>
> (v. iii. 182)

She wins, unconditionally. At once this hard, metallic, play
brightens, and after four acts of city imagery, warring noise
and pride of unbending iron, suddenly the sun blazes and
music sounds (v. iv. 53–5). Coriolanus cannot live out to the
end the inhuman thing that he has worshipped, his own self
finally rejecting this lonely and barren quest of honour. Such
militaristic idolatry distorts human nature, which must sooner
or later reject those infertile values unsanctioned by the deeper
powers. The softer, more feminine, more filial and parental,
virtues may be, for a while, dormant, but await their turn; and
'mercy', as Sicinius suggests, remains basic to divine ordinance.

Towards the end of his life Shakespeare composed a series

of plays tinged with religious mysticism, as though the profundities of spiritual experience reached in the great tragedies
had forced his genius on to a realization of mystic wisdom and
resurrection beyond death. Such plays are *Pericles* and *The
Winter's Tale.* All along Shakespeare's historic and temporal
analysis has been closely aware of life's tragedy, though at the
same time recognizing the compulsion of noble effort in terms
of this human world. But in *Antony and Cleopatra* the tragic
defeat itself becomes a sublime victory, and at the end of
Shakespeare's writing career this spiritual insight grows
positive and assured, as in the bringing back to life of Thaisa,
Pericles' queen, by the saintly Cerimon, and the miraculous
resurrection of Hermione, supposed dead, at the close of *The
Winter's Tale.* There is, too, a strangely sweet concentration
on youth, with the recovery of long-lost, royal, children, as in
the wondrous return of Marina to her careworn father King
Pericles, and the amazing restoration of Perdita, reversing the
evil of Leontes' tyranny. How does this mood react on Shakespeare's more directly political and royal statement?

The best known of these plays is *The Tempest.* It is a symbolic work, whose fantasy-structure is used to sum up the
inward meanings of the long spiritual pilgrimage of the great
plays. Prospero, formerly Duke of Milan, and rather too
studious, like the Duke in *Measure for Measure,* for that office,
has been supplanted by a wicked brother and cast adrift on
the ocean to live a marooned existence, with his daughter
Miranda, on an island. Here he pursues his studies, grows
powerful in natural magic, and gets two semi-human creatures,
Caliban and Ariel, representative figures of animal and spiritual
energy, to serve his purposes. At last he charms his enemies to
the island, overpowers and forgives them, renounces his magic
and returns to re-engage his ducal responsibilities at Milan.
What are we to make of this queer story?

First, we can see an obvious re-working of *Measure for
Measure,* with mystic wisdom replacing psychological insight.
Both plays are concerned with the age-old problem of the
philosopher-king. Surely, one feels, the wisest type of man
should govern, and yet that type inevitably finds government
and temporal magnificence repellent, as does Cerimon, the
saintly recluse of *Pericles*:

> I hold it ever,
> Virtue and cunning were endowments greater
> Than nobleness and riches; careless heirs
> May the two latter darken and expend;
> But immortality attends the former
> Making a man a god.
>
> (III. ii. 26)

Our minds are thrown back on Shakespeare's religious Henry
VI and impractical but, as his story grows tragic, deeply
mystical, Richard II. Prospero is, with Ariel and Caliban, an
obvious repetition of much in Timon. Timon splits now into
three persons. Both Timon and Prospero are driven by human
ingratitude to a cave by the wild sea; Timon's spiritual aspiration and prophetic denunciations are in Ariel; and his return
to naked savagery has its parallel in Caliban. Here is Ariel's
accusation of Prospero's enemies, now helpless on the island,
which may be read as an accusation of all societies who have
wronged their truest good, their highest national possession,
as Athens wrongs Timon and Milan Prospero:

> You are three men of sin, whom Destiny—
> That hath to instrument this lower world
> And what is in't—the never-surfeited sea
> Hath caused to belch up you; and on this island
> Where man doth not inhabit; you 'mongst men
> Being most unfit to live. I have made you mad;
> And even with such-like valour men hang and drown
> Their proper selves. You fools! I and my fellows
> Are ministers of fate: the elements
> Of whom your swords are temper'd, may as well
> Wound the loud winds, or with bemock'd-at stabs
> Kill the still-closing waters, as diminish
> One dowle that's in my plume; my fellow-ministers
> Are like invulnerable. If you could hurt,
> Your swords are now too massy for your strengths,
> And will not be uplifted. But, remember—
> For that's my business to you—that you three
> From Milan did supplant good Prospero;
> Expos'd unto the sea, which hath requit it,
> Him and his innocent child: for which foul deed
> The powers, delaying, not forgetting, have
> Incens'd the seas and shores, yea, all the creatures,

Against your peace. Thee of thy son, Alonso,
They have bereft; and do pronounce, by me,
Lingering perdition—worse than any death
Can be at once—shall step by step attend
You and your ways; whose wraths to guard you from—
Which here in this most desolate isle, else falls
Upon your heads—is nothing but heart-sorrow
And a clear life ensuing.

(III. iii. 53)

Earlier tragic discords are clearly constituent to that inclusive harmony which *The Tempest* aims to define: the suffering Alonso searching for his child repeats the purgatory of Lear, while Sebastian and Antonio together act a miniature *Macbeth*. Prospero, like Lear, Pericles, and Leontes in *The Winter's Tale*, has a treasured daughter saved from the storms of chance. Miranda is threatened, but kept intact, and never lost, Prospero's wise guardianship differentiating him from the follies of former monarchs. Ariel's speech is spoken for all states at all times. Remember the poetic condemnation Shakespeare accorded those who too lightly thought to desecrate a Richard's kingly person. Something there is which we too, in our time, have scorned and cast out of our city, some Timon who might save us in the hour of peril, some Prospero of magical insight, some ruling power of wisdom and goodness; and a mighty sovereignty remains dethroned.

That sovereignty is not purely secular and rational, but rather mystic and poetic. It is both stern and loving. Prospero controls his Ariel and Caliban as man's judgement must control both ethereal fancy and physical instinct. Caliban is a half-fish, a monster both watery and earthy, a semi-devil, and must be referred to those numerous beasts throughout Shakespeare denoting an energy which, if allowed to distort human graciousness, gives us the 'cacodemon' Richard III, the 'dragon' Coriolanus, and the 'monsters of the deep' in *King Lear* (pp. 23, 67, 59): a close relationship, through his mother Sycorax, to black magic points also to *Macbeth*. But Prospero is the wise governor, the philosopher-king; and his stern, almost brutal, repression of Caliban, to whom the poet has nevertheless devoted a most exquisite creative sympathy, is in tone with Shakespeare's ethical self-control throughout his excursions among demonic, and often imaginatively attractive, energies. And what of Miranda, Prospero's daughter? She represents an innocence and a purity to be saved, guarded, and when the time is ripe restored, to redeem with her natural and unspoilt grace a sin-struck society.

Prospero lives half in eternity, and from that eminence sees beyond all temporal glories, as, indeed, did Richard II and Henry V, but presses yet further, beyond the different nihilisms of Macbeth and Timon, into the transience of the created universe itself:

> These our actors
> As I foretold you, were all spirits and
> Are melted into air, into thin air:
> And, like the baseless fabric of this vision,
> The cloud-capp'd towers, the gorgeous palaces,
> The solemn temples, the great globe itself,
> Yea, all which it inherit, shall dissolve,
> And, like this insubstantial pageant faded,
> Leave not a rack behind. We are such stuff
> As dreams are made on, and our little life
> Is rounded with a sleep.
>
> (IV. i. 148)

Yet, though living within the consciousness of such deep, though not bitter, wisdom, Prospero finally *returns to Milan*, to take up again his practical duties. He is conceived as a philosopher-prince, in descent from the Duke in *Measure for Measure* and the prophetic Timon; and when, after maturing his wisdom and magic in his island retreat, he finally overcomes his enemies and at a staggering climax—for so it should be presented—reveals himself suddenly *in his ducal robes*, he symbolizes magic, art, poetry returning to engage and control the temporal order. For true royalty is precisely, and only, poetry incarnate and in action: in Christian terms it corresponds to the return of Christ in power.

Prospero's renunciation of his more obviously magical powers, what he himself calls his 'rough' magic (v. i. 50), has often enough been considered the poet's autobiographical farewell to his literary career. So it may be. But *The Tempest* is not, as is popularly supposed, Shakespeare's last play; and, just as Prospero, the poet-seer, returns to his ducal office, so Shakespeare, after a long line of outwardly non-historical plays, plays not obviously concerned with England's destiny at all, yet each, as we have seen, closely concerned with the deepest and darkest issues raised by consideration of that destiny in his earlier work, after all this, Shakespeare writes, as his last play, *Henry VIII*. His bark has come to harbour. He returns to a national theme, set nearer his own day than any previous attempt, and deeply loads it with orthodox Christian feeling. Here the extravagances and profundities of the great sequence come, at the last, to rest.

V

Maiden Phoenix

Before, however, approaching *Henry VIII*, we must consider *Cymbeline*, written probably just before *The Tempest*. Here we find the not-too-obvious national interest of such works as *King Lear* and *Macbeth* maturing into a more explicit message, though the historic setting is, like theirs, ancient. Study of it should certainly make my remarks on those earlier plays appear less bold. Now, since a major purpose of *Cymbeline* is to celebrate the union of Rome and Britain, we must, for a moment, return our thoughts to Rome and all that it signified to Shakespeare.

Ancient Rome loomed vaster in the Elizabethan imagination than it does in ours. Alexander and Julius Caesar are recognized giants, prototypes of military conquest and imperial greatness: see how Hamlet introduces them into his graveyard meditations. In *Julius Caesar*, written probably about the time of *Hamlet*, Shakespeare feels into what was, to him, a key-moment in history. Roman history, with its early liberation from tyranny and subsequent commonwealth, the dictatorial powers of Caesar, and the imperial Rome that followed, raises all possible questions of government, and many of the political complexities of modern Europe are embryonic in Shakespeare's play. The cause of liberty solicits, through Brutus, our approval; but the assassination is felt as only provisionally successful, the 'spirit' of Caesar winning after Caesar's death. The old conflict

of *Richard II* is here given a far subtler presentation. Caesar is
not yet king and cannot claim divine office. Shall he be assass-
inated to prevent tyranny? Is kingship, as such, good or bad?
Caesar is, as it were, the symbol of kingship, though not yet
king; and yet again, weak, puny, as a man. As the plunging of
Brutus' dagger into his body approaches, it is as though history
itself quivers, totters, is gashed open, exposing ruinous self-
conflict above the streets of Rome:

> Fierce fiery warriors fought upon the clouds,
> In ranks and squadrons and right form of war,
> Which drizzled blood upon the Capitol;
> The noise of battle hurtled in the air . . .
>
> (II. ii. 19)

After the murder Antony prophecies war:

> Woe to the hand that shed this costly blood!
> Over thy wounds now do I prophesy,
> Which like dumb mouths do ope their ruby lips,
> To beg the voice and utterance of my tongue,
> A curse shall light upon the limbs of men;
> Domestic fury and fierce civil strife
> Shall cumber all the parts of Italy;
> Blood and destruction shall be so in use,
> And dreadful objects so familiar,
> That mothers shall but smile when they behold
> Their infants quarter'd with the hands of war;
> All pity chok'd with custom of fell deeds:
> And Caesar's spirit, ranging for revenge,
> With Ate by his side come hot from hell,
> Shall in these confines with a monarch's voice
> Cry 'Havoc!' and let slip the dogs of war;
> That this foul deed shall smell above the earth
> With carrion men, groaning for burial.
>
> (III. i. 258)

Nowhere is Shakespeare's trust in essential sovereignty more
vivid. In spite of nerve-racking cataclysm and murder, in spite
of his own triviality as a man, in spite of Brutus' noble re-
publicanism, the spirit of Caesar is yet all-potent:

> O Julius Caesar! thou art mighty yet!
> Thy spirit walks abroad, and turns our swords
> In our own proper entrails.
>
> (V. iii. 94)

In opposing the Caesarean essence—and it is that, the 'spirit', not merely the body, of Caesar at which they aim, as a speech of Brutus (ii. i. 167–70) asserts—the conspirators merely slay themselves, while that spirit moves on, indestructible. They aim, and it is the root-error of many a revolutionary, to slay not a man only but royalty itself; which must not, and indeed cannot, be done. Here all Shakespeare's thought and feeling on political discord, government, human history itself, is compacted, distilled, and rendered in a dynamic tension of opposites, above which some vague, undefined, imperial splendour stands like a Colossus.

Both *Antony and Cleopatra* and *Coriolanus* are relevant to our discussion, with a relevance not to be distinguished with any finality from their Roman settings; for it is the Roman Empire, with all that that means, which Antony barters for a supreme love, and Coriolanus' mother is a stern Roman matron who drives the Spartan pride of her kind beyond the limits of nobility. And this is my present, and all-important, point, without a clear understanding of which *Cymbeline* is a nearly meaningless play: Shakespeare, at the youth of Great Britain's imperial history, is necessarily fascinated by the accomplished imperialism of ancient Rome. He feels England now as inheriting the great destiny of Rome, with new strength incorporated from the centuries of Christendom. To point an imaginative similarity, let us turn to his early play, *Titus Adronicus*.[1] The story is set late in Rome's imperial history— and how neatly Shakespeare's four Roman plays cover the main periods of that history—and starts with noble phrases:

> I am his first-born son that was the last
> That wore the imperial diadem of Rome . . .
>
> (i. i. 5)

The political purity of 'royal Rome' must be maintained:

> And suffer not dishonour to approach
> The imperial seat, to virtue consecrate,
> To justice, continence, and nobility;
> But let desert in pure election shine,
> And, Romans, fight for freedom in your choice.
>
> (i. i. 13)

---

[1] A remarkable investigation into the deeper significances of this play is given by Mr C. Alan Sommers' 'Wilderness of Tigers', to appear in *Essays in Criticism*.

That is, precisely, what Shakespeare feels about England also. The action shows intrigue, faction, and hideous wrongs hatched by Tamora, queen of the Goths, and Aaron, the Moor. As usual, the evil is felt as bestial, and of Tamora, in the final speech, it is said, 'Her life was beast-like and devoid of pity' (v. iii. 199); for pity is constituent to Shakespeare's sense of greatness in man or nation. We must, however, observe that she originally suffers from the cruel slaughter of her own son, and herself implores mercy in true Shakespearian manner:

> But must my sons be slaughter'd in the streets
> For valiant doings in their country's cause?
> O! if to fight for king and commonweal
> Were piety in thine, it is in these.
> Andronicus, stain not thy tomb with blood:
> Wilt thou draw near the nature of the gods?
> Draw near them then in being merciful;
> Sweet mercy is nobility's true badge:
> Thrice-noble Titus, spare my first-born son.
>
> (i. i. 112)

The action dramatizes her revenge, leading to many horrors, but we return at the last to sanity, and a speech near the play's conclusion recalls both the final speech of *King John* and John of Gaunt's prophecy in *Richard II*:

> You sad-fac'd men, people and sons of Rome,
> By uproar sever'd, like a flight of fowl
> Scatter'd by winds and high tempestuous gusts,
> O! let me teach you how to knit again
> This scatter'd corn into one mutual sheaf,
> These broken limbs again into one body;
> Lest Rome herself be bane unto herself,
> And she whom mighty kingdoms curtsy to,
> Like a forlorn and desperate castaway,
> Do shameful execution on herself.
>
> (v. iii. 67)

Here is the very accent of Shakespeare's words on England. Now *Cymbeline* carefully dramatizes a union of Rome and Britain.

It is a complicated, semi-historical, work on the period of Britain's subjection to Rome, with many strands interweaving.

The two sons of King Cymbeline have been absconded in child-hood and brought up by a banished, but really faithful, lord, like Kent in *King Lear*, among the Welsh mountains. They live in a cave, ignorant, like Miranda, of their high birth, in close contact with nature, hunting and paying honour to the sun, adoring the heavens as 'a morning's holy office' (III. iii. 4). 'Hail, heaven!' they cry in turn (III. iii. 9). They have animal strength and pagan piety, but in them nature is itself half divine, and their deepest instincts are normally as gentle as that 'modest stillness and humility' King Henry counselled (*Henry V*, III. i. 3–6) as most worthy in times of peace, though, on occasion, they can show the 'tiger' strain he urged as best suited for war:

> O thou goddess!
> Thou divine Nature, how thyself thou blazon'st
> In these two princely boys. They are as gentle
> As zephyrs, blowing below the violet,
> Not wagging his sweet head; and yet as rough,
> Their royal blood enchaf'd, as the rud'st wind,
> That by the top doth take the mountain pine,
> And make him stoop to the vale. 'Tis wonder
> That an invisible instinct should frame them
> To royalty unlearn'd, honour untaught,
> Civility not seen from other, valour
> That wildly grows in them, but yields a crop
> As if it had been sow'd!
>
> (IV. ii. 169)

At the last, they are restored to Cymbeline. What are they? What must they mean to us? They represent strength with gentleness, possessing a semi-pagan virility with yet an innate sweetness. They are 'princely' boys; and that word 'princely' alone saves the conception from any dangerous paganism, dis-tinguishing them from ruthless acts and brutal self-assertion. These are the long-lost boys who are given back to Cymbeline, King of Britain, as the troubled action dissolves in national accord: 'Now these her princes are come home again . . .' (*King John*, v. vii. 115).

The fortunes of Posthumus Leonatus, the centre of dramatic interest, involve his separation from Imogen, his newly-married wife and daughter of the King; his deception

by Iachimo, a close cousin of Iago in *Othello*, who intrigues to
make him distrust his wife; and, finally, his recognition of
error and re-enjoyment of love. This loss of faith in matters
of love recurs throughout Shakespeare: in *Troilus and Cressida*,
Othello, *Timon of Athens*, and elsewhere. Sometimes the distrust is justified, sometimes erroneous, but, generally, we can
say that Shakespeare is trying to incorporate the full riches
of the erotic instinct in a final inviolable integrity. Therefore,
just as in *King Lear* lack of family piety is related to national
discord, so Posthumus' story blends with the recovery of
the two sons of Cymbeline, and all that that suggests, into
the play's more national structure. This is made clear by the
prophetic tablet left by Jupiter, king of the gods, after visiting
Posthumus in sleep:

> Whenas a lion's whelp shall, to himself unknown, without seeking
> find, and be embraced by a piece of tender air; and when from a
> stately cedar shall be lopped branches, which, being dead many years,
> shall after revive, be jointed to the old stock, and freshly grow: then
> shall Posthumus end his miseries, Britain be fortunate, and flourish
> in peace and plenty.
>
> (v. iv. 138)

The 'lion's whelp' is, according to the Soothsayer, Posthumus
Leonatus, and Imogen the 'piece of tender air'; the union
suggested, as the Soothsayer's words help to emphasize, being
that of strength with spiritual sincerity, manliness with
womanly gentleness (v. v. 444–53). The stately cedar, which
is a favourite Shakespearian symbol of steadfast power (as at
2 Henry VI, v. i. 205; *3 Henry VI*, v. ii. 11), and which we
shall meet again in *Henry VIII*, is Cymbeline, and the branches
his princely sons. So the story of Posthumus, who is conceived
as a typical, and indeed typifying, example of British manhood, dovetails with the wider national, and semi-allegorical,
prophecy, whose oracular manner recalls Lyly's *Endimion*.

The Romans are fighting the British for the tribute which
King Cymbeline has neglected to pay. Though Iachimo,
'slight thing of Italy' (v. iv. 64), is to be felt as a Renaissance
creature of contemporary, Machiavellian, intrigue, the Roman
army and 'imperial Caesar' (v. v. 475) are of the ancient
world. The use of anachronism appears deliberate, pointing

an important contrast. The Soothsayer who interprets the tablet has a vision of his own concerning the fighting:

> Last night the very gods show'd me a vision—
> I fast and pray'd for their intelligence—thus:
> I saw Jove's bird, the Roman eagle, wing'd
> From the spongy south to this part of the west,
> There vanish'd in the sunbeams; which portends,
> Unless my sins abuse my divination,
> Success to the Roman host.
>
> (IV. ii. 346)

His divination *is* wrong, however, for the British, with the help of Cymbeline's long-lost boys, win. And yet they act, paradoxically, as though they had lost, Cymbeline offering to continue as of old with the payments, and the play ending with a celebration of union. You can feel Shakespeare's sense of Rome's supremacy being set beside the new strength of Britain; but this strength must pay honour to that Roman greatness which is its prototype. The meaning is clearer if we return to the Soothsayer's vision: he saw the Roman eagle as dissolving into the sunbeams of Britain. When things turn out happily the Soothsayer re-interprets his vision, but, even so, never quite hits the more simple and obvious reading; while we, today, can feel Shakespeare's own comment over-arching the thoughts of his dramatic persons.

Here are the final speeches:

Cymbeline   Well;
    My peace we will begin. And, Caius Lucius,
    Although the victor, we submit to Caesar,
    And to the Roman empire; promising
    To pay our wonted tribute, from the which
    We were dissuaded by our wicked queen;
    Whom heavens—in justice both on her and hers—
    Have laid most heavy hand.
Soothsayer The fingers of the powers above do tune
    The harmony of this peace. The vision
    Which I made known to Lucius ere the stroke
    Of this yet scarce-cold battle, at this instant
    Is full accomplish'd; for the Roman eagle,
    From south to west on wing soaring aloft,
    Lessen'd herself, and in the beams o' the sun

> So vanish'd: which foreshow'd our princely eagle,
> The imperial Caesar, should again unite
> His favour with the radiant Cymbeline,
> Which shines here in the west.

Cymbeline　　　　　　　　　　　Laud we the gods;
> And let our crooked smokes climb to their nostrils
> From our bless'd altars. Publish we this peace
> To all our subjects. Set we forward: let
> A Roman and a British ensign wave
> Friendly together; so through Lud's town march:
> And in the temple of great Jupiter
> Our peace we'll ratify; seal it with feasts.
> Set on there. Never was a war did cease,
> Ere bloody hands were wash'd, with such a peace.
>
> 　　　　　　　　　　　　　　　(v. v. 459)

A noble conclusion to this most majestic play. The end is peace through union, bitter reading, perhaps, in such an age as ours. But there is also a pagan grandeur, a burning virility, hinted throughout, which we do well to examine. The two wild yet princely boys and their sun-worship, their song about 'golden lads and girls' (iv. ii. 262), and the gold blaze of 'radiant Cymbeline', all balance the subtler story of Posthumus' and Imogen's attainment of marriage integrity, to build a comprehensive statement of Britain's potential beauty and power. Even more clearly than in *Macbeth* and *King Lear*, those historical plays which nevertheless do not appear, on the surface, to hold precise contemporary meanings, you can feel in *Cymbeline*, through the often fanciful plot, a sense of national destiny pushing through.

In *Henry VIII* Shakespeare ends his life-work with a massive and closely realistic working out of events within living memory. If *Cymbeline* surveys Britain's past and *The Tempest*, with its overtones of colonization, touches the future, *Henry VIII* is conceived as a study of the present. This great play is Shakespeare's crowning achievement, though the understanding of it has been hampered by a suspicion, to which I have elsewhere given my answer, that some scenes are un-Shakespearian.[1] *Henry VIII* is no mere historical pageant: it is far nearer a prophetic document, possessing a similarly cul-

---

[1] See my complete study of *Henry VIII* in *The Crown of Life*.

minating importance in the last half of Shakespeare's life-work to that of *Henry V* in the first; and indeed these two plays alone deliberately solicit the audience's sympathetic co-operation, as though the task seemed too heavy. The one prologue echoes the other. Compare

> . . . think ye see
> The very persons of our noble story
> As they were living . . .
>
> (Prologue, 25)

with

> Think, when we talk of horses, that you see them
> Printing their proud hoofs i' the receiving earth.
>
> (*Henry V*, I. Chorus, 26)

Both plays have contemporary impact: Henry V was compared directly to the Earl of Essex (*Henry V*, v. Chorus, 29–35). At first sight the plan of *Henry VIII* seems unco-ordinated and loose, but it obeys the same law as Shakespeare's earlier national play, *King John*. In both the tragedies of individual persons are constituent to a pattern in which the preservation of the King, or England, is to be regarded as our ruling, and over-ruling, theme.

All worldly power is, indeed, sin-struck at the core; and one cannot finally call any country a merciful power whilst year after year men and women, who are, in the depths, no more guilty than their neighbours, are sent to prison and, at the worst, death, for deeds which they have, certainly, committed, but concerning which the courts of divine understanding will make a different ruling from the courts of man. We may remember Portia's speech in *The Merchant of Venice*, the whole of *Measure for Measure*, Lear's words in madness on the futility of all justice, and Timon's curses. All this Shakespeare's genius takes into account; and, just as in the early *King John* he works through appalling sufferings of woman and child— and how often in Shakespeare a woman suffers for or redeems man's turbulent course—to a final trust in England's destiny, so the whole sequence of great plays from *Hamlet* to *The Tempest* returns, just as the earlier sequence of tragic and burdened kingship and Falstaffian criticism culminated in *Henry V*,

F

to a play explicitly asserting the importance of Great Britain's historic mission.[1]

Alone among the Histories *Henry VIII* is a play of peace throughout, the required note being struck in the first scene by the magnificent description of the Field of the Cloth of Gold. In the world of Shakespeare's Histories war means either (i) civil war or (ii) war between England and France. In *Henry V* the one, and in *Henry VIII* the other, is transcended. For the rest, the plan of *Henry VIII* resembles that of *King John*, but is more consciously and symmetrically designed. There are three individual tragedies, all very similar; but the King rises. We watch, in succession, the falls of Buckingham, Wolsey, and Queen Katharine. They are all haughty people but, at their fall, characterized by acceptance and a sense of being, as Buckingham says of himself, 'half in Heaven' (II. i. 88). There is nothing nobler in all Shakespeare than Buckingham's farewell speech on his way to execution. Many variations can and should be developed in the acting. This is my reading. Feeling deeply wronged, he shows at first a balance of controlled bitterness and noble resignation; is momentarily disturbed by what may be considered a peculiarly testing request from Lovell, but, mastering himself, rises to a sublime Christian forgiveness; is next stung by another, and this time maddening, interruption, which lances him on the very spot where the accumulated poison of pride and bitterness yet lingers, so that he gives way to scathing denunciation; and, last, at the second 'all good people', realizes how far he has fallen below that Christlike serenity he had thought to preserve:

> All good people,
> Pray for me! I must now forsake ye: the last hour
> Of my long weary life is come upon me.
> Farewell:
> And when you would say something that is sad,
> Speak how I fell. I have done; and God forgive me!
>
> (II. i. 131)

Never were the unscalable heights of Christian humility more

---

[1] Observe that Shakespeare's life-work develops, as do so many of his rhetorical speeches, in *two waves*, the second rising above the first. See my remarks on Shakespeare's rhetoric on p. 246 below.

subtly defined. Though he fails of that, see how he regards, like Henry V, his own faithful retainers as his 'fellows' (II. i. 73). There is nothing ungenerous or socially exclusive in the Shakespearian nobility. What essential grace, what innate aristocracy, these people express, almost irrespective of their faults and virtues: they tread the stage like beings of a higher world than ours.

It is the same with Wolsey. It was Wolsey who brought about the disgrace and death of Buckingham, and now he falls in his turn, and speaks in much the same idiom of religious assurance. He realizes that ambition has taken him far beyond his 'depth' (III. ii. 362). He is an exemplar of all power-seeking whatsoever, of man, or party, that does not realize that final power must reside in that which is beyond man, the Crown, or some other such semi-divine medium; in the highest courts of appeal, that greater mediator, Christ. He speaks to his secretary, Thomas Cromwell:

> Say, Wolsey, that once trod the ways of glory,
> And sounded all the depths and shoals of honour,
> Found thee a way, out of his wrack, to rise in;
> A sure and safe one, though thy master miss'd it.
> Mark but my fall, and that that ruin'd me.
> Cromwell, I charge thee, fling away ambition:
> By that sin fell the angels; how can man then,
> The image of his Maker, hope to win by't?
> Love thyself last: cherish those hearts that hate thee;
> Corruption wins not more than honesty.
> Still in thy right hand carry gentle peace,
> To silence envious tongues: be just, and fear not.
> Let all the ends thou aim'st at be thy country's,
> Thy God's, and truth's; then if thou fall'st, O Cromwell!
> Thou fall'st a blessed martyr. Serve the King;
> And—prithee, lead me in:
> There take an inventory of all I have,
> To the last penny; 'tis the King's: my robe,
> And my integrity to Heaven is all
> I dare now call mine own. O Cromwell, Cromwell!
> Had I but serv'd my God with half the zeal
> I serv'd my king, he would not in mine age
> Have left me naked to mine enemies.
>
> (III. ii. 436)

Without service to God, true service to the King is itself impossible, and so Wolsey must fall. His faith to both, at the last, remains: of the King he says 'That sun, I pray, may never set' (iii. ii. 416). Buckingham, too, asserted to the last his allegiance to 'the King' (ii. i. 88); the whole play's theme is, indeed, 'God save the King'.

Similarly Queen Katharine, cast off, unjustly divorced, and dying in loneliness, yet blesses the King 'in death' (iv. ii. 164). She, too, was proud, and bitter against Wolsey, her wronger. But a sublime charity breathes throughout this cathedral of a play. Griffith, an ordinary gentleman, in soft tones speaks of Wolsey's better qualities (iv. ii. 48–68), and the Queen, listening, accepts the charitable judgement. She is the last and greatest of Shakespeare's wronged women, and she, in her dying, enjoys through that new and purposive mysticism so urgent in Shakespeare's latest work, a direct vision of Paradise, angels appearing to her in sleep and wafting her to the joy her earthly pilgrimage has not known.

Now slowly rises the last movement. The cardinals, Wolsey and Campeius, recalling Cardinal Pardulph in *King John*, have been important to the action. But the King begins to chafe under their control, becoming irritated with 'Rome' (ii. iv. 235) and crushing the too ambitious Wolsey, whose place is taken by Cranmer, destined to be a martyr to the cause of the Reformed Church in England and therefore a type of English, as opposed to continental, religious autonomy.[1] Whereas our three tragic heroes were excessively proud and fell, each by the King's rejection, so Cranmer is excessively humble and rises, by the King's grace. Though the play seems at first merely to record certain known events, a most subtle treatment is all the time suggesting deeper and more perennially important significances. The persons are all more than themselves: they are instruments, as it were, in the creation of that England from which Shakespeare's work flowers. So, though the King's divorce of the childless Katharine is hard to justify, especially since there is no doubt about the part played by Anne Bullen's attractions, we may yet feel a deeper compulsion working

---

[1] This particular theme is developed in Tennyson's three plays, *Harold*, *Becket*, and *Queen Mary*, all of which turn on a balanced opposition of England and Catholicism.

through King Henry's virtues and vices alike, his considered plans and wayward desires. Moreover, the synthesis of religious mysticism with national purpose is not accomplished in the King himself, but rather in the royal child, Elizabeth. In thus laying the full weight of prophetic emphasis on a child Shakespeare obeys a fundamental law of the human imagination with analogies in Isaiah, Vergil, and Christianity; for in a child eternity and time necessarily embrace, and futurity lies curled. Therefore we are directed (III. ii. 48–52; IV. i. 42–7) to rejoice in the King's marriage; we applaud his gracious support of the good Cranmer, and the massive play ends with the christening ceremony of the baby Elizabeth, over whom Cranmer speaks the final prophecy, Shakespeare's last word to his countrymen:

> Let me speak, sir,
> For Heaven now bids me; and the words I utter
> Let none think flattery, for they'll find 'em truth.
> This royal infant—heaven still move about her!—
> Though in her cradle, yet now promises
> Upon this land a thousand thousand blessings,
> Which time shall bring to ripeness: she shall be—
> But few now living can behold that goodness—
> A pattern to all princes living with her,
> And all that shall succeed: Saba was never
> More covetous of wisdom and fair virtue
> Than this pure soul shall be: all princely graces,
> That mould up such a mighty piece as this is,
> With all the virtues that attend the good,
> Shall still be doubled on her; truth shall nurse her;
> Holy and heavenly thoughts still counsel her;
> She shall be lov'd and fear'd; her own shall bless her;
> Her foes shake like a field of beaten corn,
> And hang their heads with sorrow; good grows with her.
> In her days every man shall eat in safety
> Under his own vine what he plants; and sing
> The merry songs of peace to all his neighbours.
> God shall be truly known; and those about her
> From her shall read the perfect ways of honour,
> And by those claim their greatness, not by blood.
> Nor shall this peace sleep with her; but as when
> The bird of wonder dies, the maiden phoenix,
> Her ashes new-create another heir

As great in admiration as herself,
So shall she leave her blessedness to one—
When Heaven shall call her from this cloud of darkness—
Who, from the sacred ashes of her honour,
Shall star-like rise, as great in fame as she was,
And so stand fix'd. Peace, plenty, love, truth, terror,
That were the servants to this chosen infant,
Shall then be his, and like a vine grow to him:
Wherever the bright sun of heaven shall shine,
His honour and the greatness of his name
Shall be, and make new nations; he shall flourish,
And, like a mountain cedar, reach his branches
To all the plains about him; our children's children
Shall see this, and bless heaven.

(v. v. 15)[1]

As in the early *King John*, we end with a speech of national prophecy, though this has a depth and assurance born of the great soul-adventures which followed. Every phrase must be weighed, including the reminders of 'fear' and 'terror'. The 'stately cedar' of *Cymbeline* is transferred to a contemporary monarch, James I, under whom England's destiny is to expand. Every tragic insight, every penetrating sting of satire, every deepest religious intuition, of the greater plays, every lyric love of England's natural sweetness, is subdued within this last, ritualistic, offering by Shakespeare of himself and his deepest poetic wisdom to Elizabeth and James, the two sovereigns under whom he lived, wrote his plays, and died. Throughout my essay I have tried to listen to the subtler voice of Shakespeare's poetry, to show how his speeches and persons are more than they seem to the unresponsive ear; and surely here, if never elsewhere, we can feel that this prophecy is offered not to two temporal rulers alone, but to the essential sovereignty, the golden thread in England's story, that line of kings in *Macbeth* stretching out 'to the crack of doom' (iv. i. 117), handed down from his day to ours. *Macbeth* was recalled, and Cranmer's line forecast, by the 'emblems' used

---

[1] In this speech the wheel of Shakespeare's work comes full circle, harking back to Henry VI's prophecy, suggested by 'secret powers' to his 'divining thoughts', over the young Henry, Earl of Richmond, later Henry VII, the first of our Tudor sovereigns and grandfather of Elizabeth I, whose looks are said to be 'full of peaceful majesty' (*3 Henry VI*, iv, vi, 68–76).

at Anne Bullen's coronation: holy oil, Edward the Confessor's crown, the rod and the 'bird of peace' (IV. i. 88–9). The conclusion to *Henry VIII* is no mere record of an historic past, but rather as fine a statement as we shall find in any literature of that peace which the world craves and for which Great Britain labours.

VI

The Golden Thread

We should not be surprised to find Shakespeare concluding his great sequence of visionary dramas with so realistic, and near-distance, a piece as *Henry VIII*. Our greater poets do not remain content with generalities: Isaiah, Aeschylus, Vergil, Dante—all speak prophetically, for and from their own place and time. The national thinking of such poet-prophets *is* national, remaining, as Wordsworth in his poem *To a Skylark* has it, 'true to the kindred points of Heaven and home'. But theirs is also a spiritualized patriotism outlasting contemporary significance: while speaking of their own time, they simultaneously render it symbolic and eternal. So, too, should it be with us all. In these matters we must observe strict regard to the immediate and the actual, refusing to dissolve our problems into generalities, abstractions and ideologies. Royalty, which means the attunement of man's troubled affairs to divine grace, is always for us, here and now; and it is the here and now of our labouring world that cries for royalty.

It may seem that kingship as we know it has little in common with the Shakespearian conception; but that is not so. The same essence, or elixir, exists in the one as in the other, and indeed it is precisely, and only, the essence which has been preserved. In Shakespeare we find a divergence between man and office; there is no *perfect* king among his protagonists. Even the study of Henry V cannot, in view of the works which followed, be regarded as more than a provisional and strictly limited attempt, with many doubts adumbrated and questions left unanswered. The true royalty always exists in the poetry, not in the man, except in so far as the man himself is, as are both the prophetic Timon and the magician Prospero, a more purely poetic and symbolic conception.[1] We could say that it is the *contrast* of man and office in *Richard II* which corresponds to what we, today, call a 'constitutional monarchy', and that all Shakespeare's royalistic dramas are, in terms of a succession of partial failures, working to define that for which our constitutional monarchy also stands. Religious categories are necessarily involved, and we can indeed detect within Shakespeare a steady drive towards what might be called a peculiarly 'spiritualized royalty', found in the religious speeches of *Richard II*, in Lear's crown of flowers, in the philosopher princes of *Measure for Measure* and *The Tempest*, a vein perhaps most exquisitely expressed by the saintly Henry VI:

> My crown is in my heart, not on my head;
> Not deck'd with diamonds and Indian stones,
> Nor to be seen. My crown is call'd content:
> A crown it is that seldom kings enjoy.
>
> (*3 Henry VI*, iii. i. 62)

But that is not by itself enough, and we always have to return, as Prospero returns, to the greater complexities, which it is, of course, far easier to resolve by direct poetic statement than by dramatic action, as in the prophetically impregnated and perhaps consciously exaggerated limning of Elizabeth I in Cranmer's prophecy. The main thing to remember is that the royalty exists in the poetry, and that it is all far from simple.

In our system the Crown functions symbolically, or poetically: its purpose is to maintain this highest value and power, to which the sovereign no less than the subject exists in strictest vassalage, before our eyes and in our thoughts. There is properly no contradiction between royalty and democracy; rather they supplement and complete each other. We can say that royalty at its best has always functioned in unison with a willing allegiance, and has been to that extent dependent on freedom; and that any wise authority will always aspire to become, as Byron in his noble *Sonnet to George IV on the Repeal*

---

[1] For the more symbolic qualities of Timon's personality, see *Christ and Nietzsche*, pp. 223–9.

of Lord Edward FitzGerald's Forfeiture puts it, 'omnipotent by mercy's means', thus ruling less by force than through 'the heart'.[1] Nor can there be any perfected democracy until, to repeat a well-known thought, every man is, in his own proper self, a king; and here we are brought up against the tragic inadequacies of mankind.

These are, in the phrase of the old Shepherd in *The Winter's Tale*, 'heavy matters'. We are all, both as individuals and as communities, very far from perfection; and that is, precisely, why today we, as a royalistic community, *act* what we cannot, as individuals or community, *be*, or even fully understand. Like the audience at a stage performance, we have, freely, to play our part: we have to collaborate; even, if you like, pretend. Royalty in this sense is less a constricting of our freedom than an expansion of it; we are compelled to be free, to collaborate, to attune our imagination to a dramatic conception which states more than our minds can fathom. What is it we see in the king-protagonists of drama, Greek or Shakespearian? Surely it is our own highest, eternal selves; and it is precisely these that are symbolized within our constitution by royalty. In it we find, not merely a fiction, but a drama; and a drama which is the drama of our own, greater, more communal and eternal, yet still intensely personal, being; and only through such a realization can true freedom be known.

The association of stage and royalty throughout the ages is no chance. Theatres today, as well in their gilt enscrollings as in their names, sound still a royal note. In the past, actors have often been simple souls; vagabonds, strolling players, wandering minstrels; and if that element in acting ever completely goes, if the profession becomes too respectable, a vital element may be lost. Theatrical history indeed appears, from time to time, to introduce us to two extremes: these are (i) the vagabond, or otherwise non-respectable, players who (ii) enjoy the support of royalty; whereas the middle classes are usually the butts of comedy. We find it all very neatly set out for us in our Poet Laureate's *King Cole*, where the bedraggled and unhappy circus takes on, to the magic music of the wandering and wraithly king, a golden splendour, which is said to be the

[1] The importance of this sonnet is discussed in my *Lord Byron: Christian Virtues*, pp. 287–8.

splendour of each struggling artist's dreams, and therefore of his true self; and their performance is next graced by the presence of the reigning sovereign. We can thus visualize a recurring balance, or association: of king and vagabond, of nobility and simplicity, of seer and child. In the Christian story the Son of God was laid in a manger.

Kingship is golden; and gold still exerts imaginative power. It is, after all, solid sunlight, and the sun remains visible king, and nothing, as Keats found when writing his *Hyperion*, can quite dethrone him. In poetry king and sun are all but equivalents, and have been since time immemorial in the thought of ancient peoples. These atavistic powers are still alive, speaking to what Shelley in his *Defence of Poetry* called 'that imperial faculty whose throne is curtained within the invisible nature of man'. Though we live in an age of rationalism and attempts to raise man as man, with little conscious admission of man as a crowned or crowning being, we go sadly astray if we forget them. In all matters engaging the most immediate and fearful problems of our existence we know that drama, the opposition of parties in Parliament and Court of Justice, is our first guide; but there is always also, as in a work of art, some symbol, some higher fusing power, or its emblem, to unify our opposites, or at least to suggest their unification. If we cannot resolve our conflicts, we must at least imagine a dimension in which they are, or might be, resolved; which perhaps means, in Christian terms, looking forward, or up, to the advent of Christ in glory. Such, then, is the symbolic function of the Crown, not only itself dramatic, but also signifying the resolution and the purpose of the drama within and beyond which it exists. Drama is more than entertainment; it exists as our finest medium for truth, whether in the theatre or in the life of our community. This truth is only conjured into existence by what Coleridge called our 'willing suspension of disbelief', by an act of imaginative faith; and its one condition is, from the nursery onwards, 'Let's pretend'.[1]

This is, fundamentally, why Shakespeare's work is so royally alive in our time; why it is acted, not only in Britain and America, but in Europe, in India and Japan; and in

[1] For some additional thoughts on the Crown's function today and its relation to world-order, see Appendix C.

Russia. Shakespeare's drama, with its fanfares and ceremonial, abounds in kingly ritual; and his people speak, move, act royally. Villains or heroes, it is no matter; it all lies deeper than ethic. We have for long talked of the Crown as the link binding an empire of free communities: that is true, and it is a great conception, herald and pattern, it may be, of a yet greater. But meanwhile we can speak of another, and related, link, which may indeed prove to have some bearing on that greater conception as yet unshaped; a link, or rather a golden thread, putting, as Puck has it in *A Midsummer Night's Dream* (II. i. 175), 'a girdle round about the earth'; the golden thread of Shakespeare's poetic royalism which, despite all barriers, yet binds, as does nothing else, the world.

The Third Eye

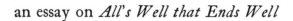

an essay on *All's Well that Ends Well*

> On's bed of death
> Many receipts he gave me; chiefly one
> Which, as the dearest issue of his practice,
> And of his old experience the only darling,
> He bade me store up as a triple eye,
> Safer than mine own two, more dear.
>
> (II. i. 107)

This play presents many difficulties. There is nothing quite like it in Shakespeare. It has not the humorous buoyancy of the Comedies, the narrative appeal of *Romeo and Juliet*, or the intellectual texture of *Troilus and Cressida* and *Measure for Measure*; it resembles none of the Tragedies, nor, in story-structure at least, the Final Plays, though much of it is on their wavelength;[1] and much of what is not on that wavelength recalls the Sonnets more nearly than any play. We naturally look for a unity of meaning such as that which interpretation has been able to reveal in other works, but the coherence of *All's Well that Ends Well* is far less easy to demonstrate. We seem at first to find Shakespeare taking from *The Decameron*, probably through the medium of Paynter's *Palace of Pleasure*, a plot of no particular interest and some silliness into which he has been able to inject comparatively little vitality. Conventional trickery is found in other plays, but does not matter. Here it tends to stick out; we complain that a field of meaning strong enough to assist our 'willing suspension of disbelief' has not been generated; and we are accordingly repelled.

Some of our own values are, moreover, positively contradicted. We seem to be invited to watch an over-praised heroine remorselessly tracking down an unwilling young man and finally forcing him to accept her against his will; and things are not made much the better by the young man himself being drawn as a dissolute cad. This is how we are tempted to see the play, but we may be wrong. It was a particular favourite of Bernard Shaw; and Coleridge called Helena Shakespeare's 'loveliest character'. It is scarcely likely that they were being deceived by a sham.

Shakespeare may have been working over an old play.

[1] For my earlier remarks on its relation to the Final Plays see *Christ and Nietzsche*, p. 122, note; *The Crown of Life*, pp. 70, 127–8, note; and *The Mutual Flame*, p. 54.

Our text comes from the Folio, and there is no certain evidence of anything earlier, in either print or production. It is sometimes supposed that the play contains different strata, but if so they are not of the sort that may be suspected in *Pericles*, which has obvious patches of what at least looks like early work. Here, there are no such patches; where we find a sonnet, or chant, or use of rhyme, there is good reason for it. This at least we can say: whatever earlier pieces may have been incorporated into the final text, the more mature pieces, and these constitute the greater part of the play, cannot well be early. They are late; some may even be very late.

Gnomic rhymes, such as those of Helena's soliloquy at I. i. 235–48 and the King's speech at II. iii. 124–51, are not by themselves evidence of early composition: the Duke of Venice uses them, with a slightly different accent, in *Othello* (I. iii. 202–9). Those in *All's Well that Ends Well* show much the same tone and timbre as certain passages in *Pericles* which we have no good reason to suppose to be early. The more formal rhymed movements in both may be roughly aligned with the language regularly used for theophanies, which show a formality less pleasing to our ears than either Shakespeare's normal manner or his earlier rhymes. But there is more than formality in the rhymes of *All's Well that Ends Well*, the interplay of prose and rhyme in the scene between Helena and the King (II. i) being extraordinarily subtle.

We find many parallels in phrase and thought to the latter half of Shakespeare's work. Lafeu's 'Moderate lamentation is the right of the dead; excessive grief the enemy to the living' (I. i. 65) inevitably recalls Claudius' advice in *Hamlet*, and this is followed directly by some lines which cannot well have been written before the composition of Polonius' farewell to Laertes:

> Be thou blest, Bertram, and succeed thy father
> In manners, as in shape! Thy blood and virtue
> Contend for empire in thee, and thy goodness
> Share with thy birthright! Love all, trust a few,
> Do wrong to none: be able for thine enemy
> Rather in power than use; and keep thy friend
> Under thy own life's key. Be check'd for silence,
> But never tax'd for speech. What Heaven more will

That thee may furnish, and my prayers pluck down,
Fall on thy head!

(I. i. 71)

Such a condensed version with its easy, almost perfunctory, covering of the ground, is unlikely to have been written before, and indeed seems, from its style, to have been written considerably later than, *Hamlet*.

Parallels to work later than *Hamlet* are fairly numerous. 'There's honour in that theft' (II. i. 34) recalls Malcolm's 'there's warrant in that theft' in *Macbeth* (II. iii. 152), the contexts being similar, with the thought of slipping away in secret. Here the 'constancies' of the younger generation 'expire before their fashions' (I. ii. 63), reminding us of those 'good men's lives' which 'expire before the flowers in their caps' in *Macbeth* (IV. iii. 172). The Clown's 'flowery way that leads to the broad gate and the great fire' (IV. v. 58) balances the Porter's 'primrose way to the everlasting bonfire' in *Macbeth* (II. iii. 22). When the King says:

> I am not a day of season,
> For thou may'st see a sunshine and a hail
> In me at once,

(v. iii. 32)

we think of Cordelia described in terms of 'sunshine and rain at once' in *King Lear* (IV. iii. 20). The King also reminds us of Antony's 'She's good, being gone' (*Antony and Cleopatra*, I. ii. 135) when he tells us that

> love that comes too late,
> Like a remorseful pardon slowly carried,
> To the great sender turns a sour offence,
> Crying, 'That's good that's gone'.

(v. iii. 57)

So, too, when the Clown talks of 'one good woman in ten' he is pursuing a train of thought parallel to that of the other, rustic, clown, the fig-seller, in *Antony and Cleopatra*, who tells us that the devils mar 'five' women for every 'ten' made by the gods (I. iii. 87; *Antony and Cleopatra*, v. ii. 278). Nature is here conceived in a manner corresponding to the phrase 'nature's

G

infinite book of secrecy' of *Antony and Cleopatra* (i. ii. 11), as a mystery, an infinitude:

> Plutus himself
> That knows the tinct and multiplying medicine
> Hath not in nature's mystery more science
> Than I have in this ring.
>
> (v. iii. 101)

The lines make us think of Cerimon's art in *Pericles* and of the general view of nature in *The Winter's Tale*.

The *Winter's Tale* is insistently recalled. The Countess addresses her adopted daughter, Helena:

> I say, I am your mother;
> And put you in the catalogue of those
> That were enwombed mine. 'Tis often seen
> Adoption strives with nature, and choice breeds
> A native slip to us from foreign seeds.
>
> (i. iii. 150)

Both the word 'slip' and the contrast of nature with human purposes recalls Perdita's flower-dialogue, and the social valuation, since Helena is of low birth, condenses the social valuations of the sheep-shearing scene (*The Winter's Tale*, iv. iii. 92–100; 454–9). In both plays human birth is given fine physical expression as part of nature's miracles. When Bertram's likeness to his father recalls to the King his own youth, we are reminded of Florizel's arrival at the court of Leontes. Here the King says:

> Youth, thou bear'st thy father's face.
> Frank nature, rather curious than in haste,
> Hath well composed thee. Thy father's moral parts
> May'st thou inherit too!
>
> (i. ii. 19)

The thought resembles that more elaborately expressed in Leontes'

> Your mother was most true to wedlock, prince;
> For she did print your royal father off,
> Conceiving you. Were I but twenty-one,
> Your father's image is so hit in you,
> His very air, that I should call you brother,

> As I did him, and speak of something wildly
> By us perform'd before.
>
>   (*The Winter's Tale*, v. i. 124)

So, too, our King here remembers his youth:

> I would I had that corporal soundness now
> As when thy father and myself in friendship
> First tried our soldiership!
>
>   (I. ii. 24)

It might be Leontes speaking when he murmurs: 'It much repairs me to talk of your good father' (I. ii. 30), the quiet yet weighty accent being exactly that of Leontes. Time is poignantly felt in both plays:

> But on us both did haggish age steal on,
> And wore us out of act.
>
>   (I. ii. 29)

We think of Pericles' vision of Patience

> gazing on kings' graves and smiling
> Extremity out of act.
>
>   (*Pericles*, v. i. 140)

The reminders cluster.

The stylistic movement, the rhythmic accent, of such passages seems to be late. Here is another, pointing to *The Winter's Tale*:

> But with the word the time will bring on summer,
> When briers shall have leaves as well as thorns,
> And be as sweet as sharp.
>
>   (IV. iv. 31)

The correspondence is not, perhaps, exact, and it is seldom safe to deduce too much from Shakespeare's poetic manner, since his methods are liable to many variations within a single play. But in the use of prose we have a far more telling correspondence.

In my extended study of *The Winter's Tale*, I drew attention to the dialogue of the three Gentlemen who describe the reunion of Leontes and Perdita. Though it is a courtier's talk, the subject matter is weighty enough and might seem to be receiving an inappropriate style were it not justified by the effect obtained. We have a light, almost mocking, bandying about of the vast issues raised by both this seemingly miraculous reunion and the extraordinary statue which we are shortly to see. Now *All's Well that Ends Well* has many passages in precisely this style put to a not dissimilar purpose. Metaphysical thought is contained, but it is lightly handled, played with by antithesis and paradox. Lafeu speaks of the sick King:

> He hath abandoned his physicians, madam; under whose practices he hath persecuted time with hope, and finds no other advantage in the process but only the losing of hope with time.
>
> (I. i. 15)

Speaking in the same manner of the old physician, Helena's father, the Countess remarks that, had his skill equalled his honesty, it 'would have made nature immortal, and death should have play for lack of work' (I. i. 23). Lafeu replies:

> He was skilful enough to have lived still, if knowledge could be set up against mortality.
>
> (I. i. 35)

Compare the Third Gentleman's words on Julio Romano

> who, had he himself eternity and could put breath into his work, would beguile Nature of her custom, so perfectly he is her ape.
>
> (*The Winter's Tale*, v. ii. 109)

In both speeches the thought of a more than natural skill is suggested in the very act of its denial: the same mental process is at work. *All's Well that Ends Well* shows striking examples of this style. The First Lord in the fourth act uses it to fine narrative effect, as it is used in *The Winter's Tale*, but with a slightly weightier accent:

> Sir, his wife some two months since fled from his house: her pretence is a pilgrimage to Saint Jaques le Grand; which holy undertaking with most austere sanctimony she accomplished; and, there residing, the tenderness of her nature became as a prey to her grief; in fine, made a groan of her last breath, and now she sings in Heaven.
>
> (IV. iii. 56)

There are other examples.

It is, indeed, an exquisite style, the style perhaps of a writer who, having mastered all passionate intensities, can the more easily handle them with the deft touches of a courtier's prose. It is not wholly new: its origin may be traced to Lyly, and a forecast of it appears in the Messenger's speeches in the first scene of *Much Ado about Nothing*. But it is not used for religious and miraculous categories until *All's Well that Ends Well* and *The Winter's Tale*. In both plays prose can be used to report heavy matters with a touch of humour, as again when Lafeu and Parolles comment on the King's recovery, in a delightful dialogue (II. iii) blended of Lafeu's courtly, and grave, talk and Parolles' comic attempt to compass a similar stylistic assurance. Throughout prose is varied and vivid. The examples we have quoted strike only one note of many. Some of it is weighty; and in both modes, light and weighty, it can be used as the language of miracle.

For *All's Well that Ends Well* is a play, like *Pericles* and *The Winter's Tale*, about the miraculous. Helena is introduced to the sick king and cures him, just as Marina is brought with her 'sacred physic' and 'skill' to cure Pericles (*Pericles*, v. i. 74, 76). They are introduced with the same kind of praise:

> I have spoke
> With one that, in her sex, her years, profession,
> Wisdom and constancy, hath amazed me more
> Than I dare blame my weakness.
>
> (II. i. 85)

So was it in *Pericles* (v. i. 44–9). The result in both is an event impregnated with miraculous feeling. Nor are we far from the final miracle of *The Winter's Tale*. One of Lafeu's speeches points directly to it:

> I have seen a medicine
> That's able to breathe life into a stone,
> Quicken a rock, and make you dance canary
> With spritely fire and motion; whose simple touch
> Is powerful to araise King Pepin, nay,
> To give great Charlemain a pen in's hand,
> And write to her a love-line.
>
> (II. i. 75)

Again, this time in verse, we find the miraculous lightly handled. From thought of a stone coming to life we pass to thought of raising the dead.

In *All's Well that Ends Well* the gods, especially Diana and Mars, are used as near personalities, and, though they do not actually appear, are felt vividly, as in the Final Plays. Bertram's cryptic and oracular letter to Helena recalls Apollo's oracle in *The Winter's Tale* (III. ii. 133) and Jupiter's tablet in *Cymbeline* (v. iv. 138):

> When thou canst get the ring upon my finger, which never shall come off, and show me a child begotten of thy body that I am father to, then call me husband: but in such a 'then' I write a 'never'.
>
> (III. ii. 59)

The words 'One that's dead is quick' (v. iii. 308) balance 'The same dead thing alive' in *Cymbeline* (v. v. 124).

It would accordingly seem reasonable to date the play in its final form not, as has hitherto been usual, about 1600–1602, but rather among the last group, perhaps after *Pericles* and *The Winter's Tale*. But even such correspondences as those which we have noted cannot be regarded as final evidence, which is always hard to come by failing external corroboration; and in one respect, the treatment of old and new generations, there is a definite divergence drawing us rather to the thought of the Sonnets. There are, indeed, as we shall see, strong Sonnet affinities, but this is less an argument for any particular date of composition than for the presence of some peculiarly personal element in the composition (p. 157 below). Dating is seldom easy, nor perhaps so important as we tend to think it. But these points of contact with the Final Plays certainly serve to direct our understanding: the play is more than a problem play like *Troilus and Cressida* and *Measure for Measure*. So much for our preliminary survey, which may at least serve as a helpful prelude to interpretation.

II

Since we shall be steering our course without too close an attention to narrative sequence it may be as well to remind the reader of our story. The widowed Countess of Rousillon has a son Bertram and an adopted daughter, Helena, whose father, recently deceased, had been a remarkable physician. Helena loves Bertram, and in pursuance of her love uses one of her father's remedies to cure the King of France from a deadly disease, and in return asks to be allowed to choose what husband she pleases. She chooses Bertram. He is furious at being told to marry beneath him, and, though forced to do so, leaves directly after the ceremony for the wars in Italy with Parolles, a licentious braggart whom he admires, and who, after Bertram has distinguished himself as a soldier, seduces him into vicious behaviour. Bertram engages in a liaison with an Italian girl, Diana. Diana pretends to give way, but Helena, who has undertaken a pilgrimage which brings her to the scene of Bertram's love-making, takes her place, and the marriage is consummated without his knowledge. After that, Parolles is proved to be a coward in the presence of Bertram, who is thus made to realize his own paucity of judgement. They all return to France. The threads are untangled in the last act, Bertram admits his fault in rejecting Helena, and all ends happily.

My remarks have already hinted that our play contains profundities, and we must next ask whether our usual method of interpretation can serve here, as elsewhere, to resolve our difficulties? Is there any dominating atmosphere, or idea? 'Atmosphere' is not, perhaps, the word for what we find, but there is what may be called a 'climate of thought' concerned with certain definable values. Our response depends largely on our ability to regard Helena as throughout sympathetic and Bertram as, in the main, faulty; above all we must try to realize why his rejection of Helena is considered so grave a lapse. To do this we must try to understand the play's scale of values.

This is far from easy, since they are not strictly ethical; where, as in the Clown's talk (i. iii. 30–9), they are so, we are invited to regard human instinct as, pretty nearly, poisoned at the source. He and Parolles, who has no morals, exist at extremes; but, since neither offer us a code to live by, some compromise must be reached. The more important thinking here avoids questions of right and wrong as sharply opposed absolutes—the Clown is there to point the difference—and concentrates rather on a territory where exactitudes are impossible because ethical ideals and human stuff, personal or communal, are in such conflict that some compromise, some unwritten code for living and action, must be devised; and the more insecure such a code may seem, the greater will be the responsibility on the individual to preserve it, or at the least, for society's sake, to maintain the reputation of its preservation. The well-worn term for such provisional values is 'honour'; and since the most pressing human problems of *action* are involved, and since, in our present state of uncertainty, there may be no easy and clear-cut solutions, the highest and noblest qualities of initiative, self-control and self-sacrifice may be called into play. 'Honour' reflects man's wholeness, both good and evil; it is the inmost secret and gem of the total personality. Ethical absolutes are, in comparison, crude; and that is why their main spokesman here is the comparatively simple-minded Clown named 'Lavache'.[1] Our chief persons engage the complexities of one or another variety of 'honour'. Nor is this easy. The nature of the responsibility marks the quality of soul demanded.

The two most urgent matters where such qualities are called into play are: (i) the exercise of power among men and nations, involving duels, war, statecraft, and (ii) sexual relationships. That ethical absolutes are not alone enough can be seen from the way duelling was for so long simultaneously punishable by law and yet demanded by the code; and in matters of international relationship and war we are today in a precisely similar position with respect to Christian teaching. Where sexual relationships and actions are concerned, it would be idle to suppose that we have as yet reached a wholly satisfying ethical solution; the pressure is still on the individual, and here, as so often in matters of 'honour', there may be the compulsion to preserve the reputation, the 'name', even at the cost of a certain falsification. 'Honour' is, partly at least, a communal reality, but the most intimate centres of the individual's dignity, soul-worth, and pride are also at stake: his pride particularly as a member of society. In sexual matters the comparative freedom of western society throws a weight of personal responsibility on the woman, and it is on her that the calls of this sort of honour most insistently converge; and that it is not all easy may be seen from Shakespeare's handling of the plight of Isabella in *Measure for Measure*. We observe that our two main

[1] The Folio spelling (v, ii. 1) is 'Lauatch', but the reading 'Lavache' has been generally accepted.

types of honour may be said to concern respectively the two sexes, male and female. Our play is deeply concerned with this sexual opposition.

It is true that 'honour' itself tends to solidify into a system, what we have called the 'code'; but it is not properly to be so limited. Even where a woman's chastity is concerned, there is room at least for discussion, as both *Measure for Measure* and our present play make clear; and so female lapses have often enough been allowed in practice, as they are today, provided that appearances are preserved. 'Honour' is a way of life, not easy to define or explain, and that is why birth and breeding so often appear to condition it: it is our Clown, who has neither, who relies entirely on ethical absolutes.

High birth is here emphatic. Bertram is thus 'of honoured name' (i. iii. 164). Honour may be almost a visible splendour, as when Helena addresses a lord:

> The honour, sir, that flames in your fair eyes,
> Before I speak, too threateningly replies.
>
> (ii. iii. 86)

If all goes well, breeding and virtue—which is not quite 'honour'—should go hand in hand, and so the Countess expects as much of her son Bertram:

> Thy blood and virtue
> Contend for empire in thee, and thy goodness
> Share with thy birthright!
>
> (i. i. 72)

It is, of course, inevitable that people should always be trying to equate true honour with virtue. Lafeu tells Parolles that he is more 'saucy' with lords than 'the heraldry of your birth and virtue'—though here 'virtue' may hold suggestion of courage too—gives him 'commission' (ii. iii. 277–80). Indeed, if enough virtue be present, we can do without breeding: 'all her deserving is a reserved honesty' (iii. v. 61). Sometimes true 'honour' is all but equated with goodness, as when the King hopes that Bertram's deeds may prove his 'honour' to be 'fairer' than he is inclined to think it (v. iii. 185). Certainly the outward show of honour may be deceptive. Parolles apes it, and we have some telling court satire from the Clown

(II. ii). It is driven home on us, by the King pre-eminently, that goodness is independent of such inessentials as noble birth: 'Good alone', he says, 'is good without a name' (II. iii. 135). We remember Perdita's similar claims, and indeed the whole tenour in social implication of the sheep-shearing festival, in *The Winter's Tale* (IV. iii. 454–9).

This then, is the mental context for our story, which shows us Helena, a girl of low birth, aspiring to the hand of Bertram, a young nobleman. We have to place these two persons in relation to the concept 'honour', having regard to what may be superficial in the conventions of an aristocratic society. But many complexities are involved, and honour takes other forms too, and these may differ according to sex.

'Honour' for a man of birth is, as we have seen, generally taken to be a matter of correct behaviour among men, especially in matters of life and death, such as duelling and war. That is, so far as it goes, simple enough; but our play is to show that there is a serious lack in such a conception. Man's sexual instincts cannot be ignored, and they also involve honourable or dishonourable behaviour. Much of man's main activities are necessarily deployed in the world of action, and on those his reputation depends. Meanwhile the sexual problem is allowed to converge rather unfairly on the woman, and here matters are very far from simple, if only because male instincts are irrepressible and often promiscuous. This is, indeed, one of our main problems. So, without at present saying anything more regarding Bertram's military prowess, which is considerable but easily placed, we shall turn next to the reiterated emphasis, from the woman's viewpoint, on chastity.

'Honour' for a woman usually means chastity, and much of our thinking revolves about the question of honourable and dishonourable sexual behaviour. Virginity is a key-thought, directly related to 'honour'. 'The honour of a maid', says the Widow, 'is her name; and no legacy is so rich as honesty' (III. v. 12). Again, one of the Lords, speaking of Bertram, tells us: 'He hath perverted a young gentlewoman here in Florence, of a most chaste renown; and this night he fleshes his will in the spoil of her honour' (IV. iii. 17). The association is insistent: 'My honour's paid to him', runs Diana's letter

(v. iii. 143). It can be used by a man when Bertram says that, being married, he could not—though the phrase on his lips does not ring true—'answer in that course of honour' corresponding to a lady's advances (v. iii. 98).

'Virginity' is a recurring theme. There is the early dialogue between Helena and Parolles on the subject, commencing with Parolles 'Are you meditating on virginity?' (i. i. 122). Parolles takes his stand, like Lucio in *Measure for Measure*, on the social necessity of sexual activity:

> It is not politic in the commonwealth of nature to preserve virginity. Loss of virginity is rational increase, and there was never virgin got till virginity was first lost. That you were made of is metal to make virgins. Virginity by being once lost may be ten times found; by being ever kept, it is ever lost: 'tis too cold a companion; away with 't.
>
> (i. i. 139)

He continues with other, and some of them strong, arguments, accusing virginity of 'self-love, which is the most inhibited sin in the canon' (i. i. 159). We are not to regard Parolles' attitude, which recalls Lucio's in *Measure for Measure* (i. iv. 39–44) and forecasts Comus' defence of his position in Milton's *Comus*, as wholly fallacious. It, like the Clown's, of which it is the exact obverse, is an over-developed truth. Were it wholly false, we should not need to use the provisional yet compelling word 'honour' so much: it would be a straight question of right or wrong. Nor must we ever regard Parolles as a fool: he may be a braggart and a coward, but he is an astute thinker. Indeed, he possesses a warm humanity causing Helena to prefer him with all his falsities, which may be called the extreme limit of honour-worship at its lowest, to 'virtue's steely bones' looking 'bleak in the cold wind' (i. i. 115); for the honour-values, even those of a Parolles, may well contain human ingredients which absolute virtue would seem to exclude. Whatever the truth of it, we must recognize that we are being forced to question these problems very deeply.

Virginity is here seriously questioned. But Helena's dialogue with Parolles is finally crowned by her exquisite if enigmatic lines, to which we shall return: 'Not my virginity yet . . .' (i. i. 181).

In the Steward's report to the Countess of Helena's

soliloquy—'the most bitter touch of sorrow that e'er I heard
virgin exclaim in'—it is said that she complained of the callous-
ness of three goddesses, 'Fortune', 'Love' and the 'Queen of
Virgins', or Diana (i. iii. 117–21). And indeed, Diana is here a
presiding deity, used rather as she is in *Pericles*, though she
does not actually appear. But marriage is, as our story shows,
also a high ideal, and we seem at first to be in some confusion,
since Helena, whose virginity is so emphatic, aspires with
considerable fervour to a husband. The problem is as good as
admitted when Helena says to the Countess

> but if yourself
> Whose aged honour cites a virtuous youth,
> Did ever in so true a flame of liking
> Wish chastely and love dearly, that your Dian
> Was both herself and love . . .
>
> (i. iii. 217)

The essence of virginity is somehow felt to be carried over into
sexual love. Later, in choosing Bertram, Helena deliberately
takes this step:

> Now, Dian, from thy altar do I fly,
> And to imperial Love, that god most high,
> Do my sighs stream.
>
> (ii. iii. 80)

We are probably to assume that Helena, whose purity is
idealized to excess, is laying claim to a love beyond the normal,
a love which the Clown, so firm, as we shall see, in his conviction of sexual evil, would scarcely believe in were it not for
Helena, whom he may be supposed to regard as an exception
(p. 145). Marriage at its most perfect may, it seems, be as
noble a state as virginity. Parolles well phrases its majesty:

> The great prerogative and rite of love
> Which, as your due, time claims, he does acknowledge.
>
> (ii. iv. 43)

We have watched a movement from virginity to marriage.

And yet virginity persists as a dominating theme. When
Helena leaves the goddess Diana for a husband, its place as a
dominating value is carried on into *the girl called Diana*: she

replaces the goddess. Mariana warns her against the deceits of
Bertram and Parolles:

> Beware of them, Diana; their promises, enticements, oaths, tokens,
> and all these engines of lust, are not the things they go under. Many
> a maid hath been seduced by them . . .
>
> (III. v. 18)

Her prophecy is correct, and Bertram pursues his seduction
in fine poetic style, following closely the thought already expressed by Parolles:

> *Bertram* They told me that your name was Fontibell.
> *Diana*   No, my good lord, Diana.
> *Bertram*   Titled goddess!
>   And worth it, with addition! But, fair soul,
>   In your fine frame hath love no quality?
>   If the quick fire of youth light not your mind,
>   You are no maiden, but a monument:
>   When you are dead, you should be such a one
>   As you are now, for you are cold and stern;
>   And now you should be as your mother was
>   When your sweet self was got.
> *Diana*   She then was honest.
>
> (IV. ii. 1)

Bertram's argument recalls those early Sonnets of Shakespeare
where the poet urges the loved youth to marry. Again, we are
not to regard the seducer's case as wholly fallacious: there *is*
an element of truth in it, as Browning shows in *The Statue and
the Bust*. Bertram says that 'love is holy' and insists, like
Troilus, on his 'integrity' (IV. ii. 32–3). Diana asks for his
ancestral ring which he at first refuses, since he is in honour
bound not to part with it, and she answers that her maiden
honour is itself just such a ring. So we have an argument
playing on the dual, male and female, principles of 'honour',
with Bertram's ring as ancestral heirloom on the one hand and
Diana's 'chastity' as a 'jewel' 'bequeathed' to her from her
'ancestors' on the other, and the neat conclusion:

> Thus your own proper wisdom
>   Brings in the champion Honour on my part
>   Against your vain assault.
>
> (IV. ii. 42–51)

This is interesting: the two honours, male and female, are fighting out their difference. The problem is, and is meant to appear, rather different as viewed from different sexual standpoints, and we cannot assume that Bertram is here being wholly repudiated: the quality of the poetry alone forbids that. In the last act, in a context of clustering references to 'honour' —'my honour's paid to him' (v. iii. 143)—Diana again sounds the note of virginity:

> Good my lord,
> Ask him, upon his oath, if he does think
> He had not my virginity.
>
> (v. iii. 186)

From first to last the word rings through the play.

That we are indeed faced by a peculiar antagonism and interweaving of male and female values is further indicated by the many passages where the woman's defence of her honour is expressed in war-like terms. Woman has, herself, a battle to fight. Helena's dialogue with Parolles on virginity plays curiously with metaphors from war. The association is found elsewhere, but here its development is emphatic. How is woman to 'barricade' her honour against the 'enemy', man? Some 'warlike resistance' is needed. Is there no 'military policy' for the women, on their side, to use in attack? But man, says Parolles, will nevertheless 'undermine you and blow you up', whatever schemes you employ; and so on (i. i. 124–39). There are other such phrases: the goddess Diana, 'queen of virgins' is blamed for leaving Helena 'her poor knight'— observe that she is given the *male* term—'without rescue in the first assault' of love, and with no hope of ransom (i. iii. 121–3); a young man is 'shot at with fair eyes' (iii. ii. 110); a maid is 'arm'd' against a seducer and 'keeps her guard in honestest defence' (iii. v. 73); Bertram 'lays down a wanton siege' before Diana's 'beauty' (iii. vii. 18); Diana talks of Bertram's 'vain assault' (iv. ii. 51) and, after pretending to give way, looks to the time 'when you have conquered my yet maiden bed' (iv. ii. 57). And it can happen the other way round. The King urges on the young men going to the wars with a metaphor from marriage:

See that you come
Not to woo honour, but to wed it; when
The bravest questant shrinks, find what you seek,
That fame may cry you loud.

(II. i. 14)

Conversely he warns them to beware of themselves becoming
'captives' to 'those girls of Italy' (II. i. 19–21). A similar
thought is expressed by Parolles in his licentious way:

To the wars, my boy, to the wars!
He wears his honour in a box unseen,
That hugs his kicky-wicky here at home,
Spending his manly marrow in her arms
Which should sustain the bound and high curvet
Of Mars' fiery steed!

(II. iii. 295)

'Mars' is here another important deity, balancing 'Diana' and
'imperial Love'. Parolles speaks finely of war, as he did of
marriage (p. 108).

The warrior-values are comparatively simple, but with
sexual relationships the problem is harder; nor are we, today,
in a position to regard it as settled. Seduction may look bad,
but the fault is less in man's moral will than in his psychic
and physical construction. This is emphasized for us through
a skilful use of the Clown, who, like Pompey in *Measure for
Measure* (II. i. 248–63), is made the voice for questionings
which are at once comic, obvious, and disturbing:

Countess Tell me thy reason why thou wilt marry.
Clown My poor body, madam, requires it. I am driven on by
the flesh, and he must needs go that the devil drives.

(I. iii. 29)

We remember Touchstone (*As You Like It*, III. iii. 85–8).
The Clown has 'other holy reasons':

I have been, madam, a wicked creature, as you and all flesh and blood
are; and, indeed, I do marry that I may repent.

(I. iii. 38)

Despite her rank, the noble and good Countess is considered,
from this inclusive view of human frailty, to be as bad as anyone else; only a Clown dare say that, but we recognize an

obvious, if not very helpful, truth. There are other expressions of this truth, which we shall in due course review.

So we are not to regard the sexual laxity of people in our play as a simple sin, but rather as an aspect of a fundamental and disturbing problem. And yet it is in this world of lustful desires and indecisive morals that Helena's virgin honour not only itself burns as a pure flame, but wills, as an active power, to engage the desires of the flesh in marriage, without losing one whit of its virgin purity. The thought recalls that strange line in *The Phoenix and the Turtle*: 'It was married chastity'. The meaning of that is not simple, nor is anything in our play simple. But some at least of our obscurities will be clarified if we recall the metaphors from war used by Helena and Parolles in the discussion of virginity, and observe next how the woman, as Diana's 'knight' (I. iii. 121), *here assumes, for once, the male prerogative of action*. Helena goes out as a Saint Joan to fight for the female values, for the female honour, for 'virginity' as a conquering power. That is her role; and it includes a miracle.

III

Such is the philosophic atmosphere within which the story of Helena and Bertram is played out. Our sympathies are throughout directed towards Helena, and, if we are to make sense of the play we must see where and why Bertram is at fault in rejecting her. We shall now consider his behaviour.

He is conceived as a normal young man of good birth, but showing lack of judgement and an inadequate scale of values. He has the failings of pride and of licentiousness. But he exists in a society where a man does not lose his honour by sexual laxity, as does a woman. He does lose it if, like Parolles, he is proved a coward, but Bertram is no coward: far from it. Like the not dissimilar Claudio in *Much Ado about Nothing*, he is a fine soldier, and soldiership is a high male value. Certainly it seems hard not to sympathize with him just when the play itself appears to regard him as most grievously at fault: that is, when he rejects the advances of Helena, who has been given the right to choose whom she will as a husband in return for restoring the King's health. Surely, we must insist, this is unfair; and if it be so, we cannot respond as we are meant to as we watch Helena tracking him down and finally victorious.

We shall do our best to counter these admittedly serious objections. First, we must realize that in return for having cured the King Helena has asked for the right to choose a husband only from among those whose marriage is at the royal disposal (ii. i. 197). The young lords paraded before her are at the King's 'bestowing'; he has over them 'both sovereign power and father's voice' (ii. iii. 59–60). We are in a society where the son would probably be in duty bound to obey a parent's choice, and the King's command holds yet greater cogency, the more so since his obligation to Helena, and therefore his own honour, is involved. Bertram is accordingly countering the behaviour expected of him.

We must realize, too, that the play's thought depicts a world where the sexual instincts of the male are almost automatic, and the female regularly on the defensive. Bertram should have had no difficulty in accepting any normally good-looking woman, provided that the marriage was honourable to him, and this marriage will be made so, as the King clearly asserts. Love in our sense would scarcely be an essential. Such a husband would have no inhibitions as to satisfying his romantic impulses elsewhere, and society would accept the solution, after the manner of Macduff's 'We have willing dames enough' (*Macbeth*, iv. iii. 73). The only sensible argument on Bertram's side is offered much later, when he claims, in a passage to which we shall return, that his admiration for Lafeu's daughter played its part; but he says nothing of this at the time, and it is clear that, unless there were some other all-powerful reason, he would automatically have accepted the girl on the King's command. In such a society, that was no less than a plain duty.

Why, then, does he reject Helena? Almost entirely, we are led to suppose, on grounds of birth. The issue is already clearly before us. Helena has known it all along:

> It were all one
> That I should love a bright particular star,
> And think to wed it, he is so above me:
> In his bright radiance and collateral light
> Must I be comforted, not in his sphere.
> The ambition in my love thus plagues itself:

> The hind that would be mated by the lion
> Must die for love.
>
> (I. i. 97)

Her 'baser stars' shut her up in a world of 'wishes' (I. i. 199); she is 'from humble, he from honour'd name'; he is her 'master' and 'dear lord' (I. iii. 164–6). But Fortune is no just goddess to 'put such difference' between their 'two estates' when they are level in 'qualities' (I. iii. 118). It is felt as unfair, and we must assume that her chances would otherwise have been good. Even after Bertram is forced to marry her she knows that her 'homely stars' do not really balance her 'great fortune' (II. v. 81). And yet we are not to suppose that such a view is just. The Countess recognizes in Helena a supreme worth, and is furious at her son's behaviour:

> There's nothing here that is too good for him
> But only she; and she deserves a lord
> That twenty such rude boys might tend upon
> And call her hourly mistress.
>
> (III. ii. 82)

That is what we are directed to believe.

Let us glance at the rejection. Helena, as the King's saviour, has proved herself unique, and chooses Bertram as her reward. The dialogue goes:

King   Why, then, young Bertram, take her; she's thy wife.
Bertram My wife, my liege! I shall beseech your Highness
           In such a matter give me leave to use
           The help of mine own eyes.
King   Know'st thou not, Bertram,
           What she has done for me?
Bertram   Yes, my good lord;
           But never hope to know why I should marry her.
King   Thou know'st she has raised me from my sickly bed.
Bertram But follows it, my lord, to bring me down
           Must answer for your raising? I know her well:
           She had her breeding at my father's charge.
           A poor physician's daughter my wife! Disdain
           Rather corrupt me ever!
King   'Tis only title thou disdain'st in her, the which
           I can build up.

(II. iii. 112)

Bertram's dislike of such a marriage is, in its social context, understandable, but his manner of address is ugly. It is unworthy of his father, whom the King has earlier praised for his utter lack of 'contempt' or 'bitterness', and for treating those 'who were below him' as creatures 'of another place'; that is, as his equals (I. ii. 36, 41). So now the King, pursuing his earlier thought, delivers a sermon of considerable importance:

> 'Tis only title thou disdain'st in her, the which
> I can build up. Strange is it, that our bloods,
> Of colour, weight, and heat, pour'd all together,
> Would quite confound distinction, yet stand off
> In differences so mighty. If she be
> All that is virtuous, save what thou dislikest,
> A poor physician's daughter, thou dislikest
> Of virtue for the name: but do not so:
> From lowest place when virtuous things proceed,
> The place is dignified by the doer's deed:
> When great additions swell's, and virtue none,
> It is a dropsied honour. Good alone
> Is good without a name. Vileness is so:
> The property by what it is should go,
> Not by the title. She is young, wise, fair;
> In these to nature she's immediate heir,
> And these breed honour. That is honour's scorn,
> Which challenges itself as honour's born,
> And is not like the sire: honours thrive
> When rather from our acts we them derive
> Than our foregoers. The mere word's a slave
> Debosh'd on every tomb, on every grave
> A lying trophy; and as oft is dumb
> Where dust and damn'd oblivion is the tomb
> Of honour'd bones indeed. What should be said?
> If thou cans't like this creature as a maid,
> I can create the rest: virtue and she
> Is her own dower; honour and wealth from me.
>   (II. iii. 124)

Bertram still refuses. The King insists, calling him a 'proud, scornful boy', guilty of 'vile misprision'; that is, misvaluation. He is told to check his 'contempt' and 'disdain'; it is for his own 'good' (II. iii. 158–66). It is emphasized that his sin is an error in valuation, and also *a sin against himself*. Bowing to the King's power, Bertram gives way, but directly after the marriage leaves for the wars.

Bertram's own mother, the Countess, takes, as we have seen, precisely the same view of his behaviour as does the King, saying, when she hears of it: 'This is not well, rash and unbridled boy'; such as he are no better than 'rude'—i.e. untaught, undisciplined—'boys' (iii. ii. 30, 84).

That on the one side. On the other we have Bertram's hurried escape from 'the dark house and the detested wife' (ii. iii. 309), and his telling words, on seeing Helena's approach, 'Here comes my clog' (ii. v. 59). When he tells Diana 'I was compelled to her' (iv. ii. 15), he speaks the truth. We cannot altogether stifle our sympathies, and must even be prepared to recognize a possible undercurrent of satire against such conventional and arbitrary marriages. It is, in part, such marriages which encourage sexual licence, and we are shortly to watch Bertram so engaging himself.

What we can say is that, though no one could blame him for not loving Helena, and though we cannot wholly blame him for acting as he does if he really cannot even like her, we can, and are meant to, realize that he can indeed be blamed for positively disliking her: his values, mainly based on matters of rank, are all wrong. Meanwhile, we are invited to feel that not only has his too superficial understanding of honour plunged him into a great sin, but that only Helena can save him. The Countess speaks:

> What angel shall
> Bless this unworthy husband? He cannot thrive
> Unless her prayers, whom Heaven delights to hear
> And loves to grant, reprieve him from the wrath
> Of greatest justice.
>
> (iii. iv. 25)

In scorning Helena he has all but scorned divinity; but she, in her turn, may be his saviour.

In leaving for the wars, Bertram aspires to a high male value, and can be to that extent applauded. The King has already recalled the time when he and Bertram's father 'first tried our soldiership' (i. ii. 26), continuing:

> He did look far
> Into the service of the time, and was
> Discipled of the bravest.
>
> (i. ii. 26)

It is to be expected that Bertram will prove true to his father's memory, and as a soldier he does so, however far beneath him he falls in social understanding. Before Helena's choice of him, he had wanted to leave female charms and all the dalliance of court life for the battle-field:

> *Bertram*   I shall stay here the forehorse to a smock,
> Creaking my shoes on the plain masonry,
> Till honour be bought up, and no sword worn
> But one to dance with! By heaven, I'll steal away.
> *First Lord* There's honour in the theft.
>
> (ii. i. 30)

After Helena's choice, he is determined:

> Go thou toward home; where I will never come,
> Whilst I can shake my sword, or hear the drum.
> Away, and for our flight!
>
> (ii. v. 96)

The lines are spoken in the mood of Hotspur's 'Come, let me taste my horse . . .' (*1 Henry IV*, iv. i. 119). The poetry re-sounds with nobility and courage. His purpose is recognized as 'noble' (iii, ii. 73).

From now on war charges the atmosphere. There are war-sounds and war-sights. Soldiers pass in fine show across the stage (iii. v.). The drum captured by the enemy is impor-tant to the action (iii. vi; iv. i). Sound-effects of drum and trumpet (as at iii, iii) are important and should be amplified. We are in a world where 'a scar nobly got, or a noble scar, is a good livery of honour' (iv. v. 106).

In such a world Bertram is thoroughly at home, and his values in good trim. As a soldier he knows himself, and is accordingly, as are most of us regarding our real abilities, capable of humility. The Duke of Florence gives him a high command:

> *Duke*   The general of our horse thou art; and we,
> Great in our hope, lay our best love and credence
> Upon thy promising fortune.

>Bertram   Sir, it is
>A charge too heavy for my strength; but yet
>We'll strive to bear it for your worthy sake
>To the extreme edge of hazard.
>
>Duke   Then go thou forth;
>And fortune play upon thy prosperous helm,
>As thy auspicious mistress!
>
>Bertram   This very day,
>Great Mars, I put myself into thy file:
>Make me but like my thoughts, and I shall prove
>A lover of thy drum, hater of love.
>
>   (III. iii. 1)

The words 'mistress' and 'lover' again remind us of the intermingling of male and female valuations. Bertram is seen
deliberately rejecting, not merely Helena, but all the so-called
softness of feminine love. And he justifies the Duke's confidence: his deeds of prowess are outstanding, his service called
'honourable' and 'worthy', people speak 'nobly' of him, and the
King receives letters setting him 'high in fame' (III. v. 3–7,
48, 50; v. iii. 31).

Were there no more to be said, were Bertram simply one
who rejects love for military honour, there might be little
complaint. But there is very much more to say. In rejecting
love, he has not rejected sex, and in sexual matters is quite
undisciplined; indeed, his sexual being is in chaos.

Bertram and Parolles together exist as a centre to many
easily recognized Shakespearian faults, including showiness
and superficiality; and, though in matters of prowess Bertram
himself is genuine, he remains in danger, once off the battle-
field, of succumbing to a number of faulty valuations. His lack
of discrimination is emphasized by his relationship to Parolles
in whose courage and supposed experience he has complete
faith.

Parolles belongs to a well-known contemporary type of
which Falstaff and Ben Jonson's Bobadil are variants. He is less
sympathetic than Falstaff, and more warmly conceived than
Bobadil. We have seen that his attack on virginity holds wit
and sense. He brilliantly creates for himself an aura of heroism:

>Noble heroes, my sword and yours are kin. Good sparks and lustrous,
>a word, good metals: you shall find in the regiment of the Spinii

one Captain Spurio, with his cicatrice, an emblem of war, here on his
sinister cheek; it was this very sword entrenched it. Say to him, I
live; and observe his reports for me.

(II. i. 40)

His god is 'Mars' (II. i. 48). Besides being a braggart, he
aspires to be a courtier. We have court satire from the Clown
(in II. ii): it is one strand in the play's labouring towards a
distinction between true and false values, show and integrity.
Parolles is wholly dedicated to the show, the outward appearance: he is off to the Court and means to 'return perfect courtier'
(I. i. 225). After the healing of the King he vies with Lafeu in
attempt to find choice phrases to describe the miracle (II. iii.
1–45). He poses as a traveller, and exhibits those fantastical
styles of dress which are so often the subject of Shakespearian
satire. Lafeu, the experienced old courtier, easily penetrates his
mask:

> I did think thee, for two ordinaries, to be a pretty wise fellow; thou
> didst make tolerable vent of thy travel; it might pass. Yet the scarfs
> and the bannerets about thee did manifoldly dissuade me from believ-
> ing thee a vessel of too great a burden.

(II. iii. 210)

Lafeu 'looks through' him (II. iii. 225) easily, regarding him
as 'a general offence', a 'vagabond', and 'no true traveller'
(II. iii. 270, 277). He 'garters up his arms' (II. iii. 265), 'the
soul of this man is in his clothes' (II. v. 49). To others he is a
'vile rascal' and 'that jackanapes with scarfs' (III. v. 84–5).
Finally he is

> Monsieur Parolles, the gallant militarist—that was his own phrase
> —that had the whole theoric of war in the knot of his scarf, and the
> practice in the chape[1] of his dagger.

(IV. iii. 162)

His soldiership is false through and through.

During the war Bertram's brother-officers devise the
practical joke to reveal his cowardice. They recognize that his
proposed expedition to recapture the lost Drum is a pretence,
expecting him to 'return with an invention, and clap upon you
two or three probable lies' (III. vi. 104). This is true: he deliberately, like Falstaff, plans to give himself 'some hurts' and say

---

[1] The metallic part at the end of the scabbard.

he got them 'in exploit'; and yet he would much prefer merely to cut his 'garments' and break his 'Spanish sword' (IV. i. 40–52). But the trap is set, he is captured and blindfolded by his comrades, whom he thinks the enemy; shows himself for what he is; and finally faces his compatriots a confessed coward and traitor.

And here we come up against his remarkable bearing; for he comes out of it well. What we admire in him is his utter lack of self-deception, which is more than we can say for many of Shakespeare's greater persons: he is, with himself, sincere. From the start Helena, though well aware of his faults, could yet recognize, with a truly Shakespearian insight, a peculiar self-consistency, and therefore harmony, in the friend of her beloved Bertram:

> Who comes here?
> One that goes with him: I love him for his sake;
> And yet I know him a notorious liar,
> Think him a great way fool, solely a coward;
> Yet these fix'd evils sit so fit in him,
> That they take place, when virtue's steely bones
> Look bleak i' the cold wind: withal, full oft we see
> Cold wisdom waiting on superfluous folly.
>
> (I. i. 110)

This might seem at first to say merely that his play-acting is so convincing that it gives him precedence ('place') over the virtuous. But it is not his show of good, but the 'evils', which are said to seem 'fit'; and, despite the conclusion, which comes in as a concession to morality, the other thought, supported by the imagery, lingers. If my reading is correct, this must be the only instance we have of a Shakespearian person expressing for us that sense of a beyond-good-and-evil harmony which we ourselves so often experience in face of the Shakespearian creation (see p. 140 below; also *The Mutual Flame*, pp. 49–52, 119–21). Later Helena tells Parolles that the 'composition' of his 'valour and fear', makes a 'virtue' which pleases her (I. i. 221–3).

When one of the lords overhears his deliberate plans to cover his own admitted cowardice one comments: 'Is it possible he should know what he is and be that he is?' (IV. i. 48). It is possible: and it is possible because, with an unusual honesty, he knows, precisely, *what he is*; what he can, and cannot, do. He does not offend against the law 'To thine own self be true' (*Hamlet*, I. iii. 78). So, after his final unmasking, he first finds the perfect reply: 'Who cannot be crushed with a plot?' (IV. iii. 364); and then, left alone, speaks with staggering simplicity:

> Yet am I thankful: if my heart were great,
> 'Twould burst at this. Captain I'll be no more;
> But I will eat and drink, and sleep as soft
> As captain shall: simply the thing I am
> Shall make me live.
>
> (IV. iii. 370)

Like Cardinal Wolsey at a similar crisis he perhaps feels his 'heart' 'new-open'd', and can say, with greater right since it is really no new discovery, 'I know myself now' (*Henry VIII*, III. ii. 367, 379). He is now 'safest in shame', for 'there's place and means for every man alive' (IV. iii. 378–9). There is a sense of relief in giving up the foolish struggle to create appearances. The comment on all show, all appearances of honour, is keen.

That is his personal tragedy, and, like the greater tragedies in Shakespeare, it is, in its way, a victory. Parolles has honesty unfettered by principle. He sees the nobler values, and can speak finely of both marriage and war (pp. 108, 111); where war is concerned he not only apes, but genuinely likes, them, though well aware that he cannot live them. He never deceives himself, and perhaps he and Helena alone of our people have this integrity; and that may be why she from the start recognized in him a certain harmony (p. 120). His very being, like Falstaff's, constitutes a subtle attack on military honour, and after his fall he realizes that one can live without it.

He has, of course, to endure his shame. In the last act he enters with his fine clothes all bedraggled and smelling rank (v. ii. 1–27) from, presumably, a ducking, the indignity suffered by Falstaff in *The Merry Wives of Windsor* and Caliban, Stephano, and Trinculo in *The Tempest*. The pond, like those in *The Tempest* (IV. i. 182) and the story of 'Poor Tom' in *King Lear* (III. iv. 137), appears to have been stagnant and evil-smelling. Such ponds are in Shakespeare natural associations to vice and degradation. But his wit remains, and he bears himself well.

So much for his personal drama: his relation to Bertram raises other issues. He is, of course, on the surface, a dangerous influence, as is Falstaff in respect to Prince Hal. This we have to recognize in distinction from our own sympathies. He is a perverter of youth, as summed up by Lafeu:

> No, no, no, your son was misled with a snipt-taffeta fellow there, whose villainous saffron would have made all the unbaked and doughy youth of a nation in his colour.
>
> (IV. V. I)

Bertram had been, indeed, easily gulled, saying to Lafeu: 'I do assure you, my lord, he is very great in knowledge, and accordingly valiant' (II. v. 8). Here we have an example of Bertram's chief failing: a failure in judgement, or recognition. Helena and Lafeu saw through him easily. So does the Countess:

> A very tainted fellow, and full of wickedness.
> My son corrupts a well-derived nature
> With his inducement.
>
> (III. ii. 89)

It is Parolles who stimulates Bertram to licentiousness: 'I know that knave', says Mariana; 'Hang him! One Parolles: a filthy officer he is in those suggestions for the young earl' (III. v. I 7). Again, from Diana:

> Yond's that same knave
> That leads him to these places: were I his lady,
> I would poison that vile rascal.
>
> (III. v. 82)

Bertram's friends expose Parolles in order to reveal to him his own lack of judgement:

> I would gladly have him see his company anatomized that he might take a measure of his own judgements, wherein so curiously he had set this counterfeit.
>
> (IV. iii. 36)

Parolles, of course, does not believe in virginity, and has his own defence (p. 107). But he is sexually quite a-moral. So, in his youthful fashion, though without knowing it, or indeed troubling to think seriously about it at all, is Bertram. This his friends recognize, and their easiest way of revealing to Bertram his own lack of balance is to reveal Parolles' patent cowardice, since this at least he will understand.

Bertram's love-making in Italy is carefully shown to us. His dissolute life is strongly contrasted with his noble bearing:

Helena   Which is the Frenchman?
Diana   He.
 That with the plume; 'tis a most gallant fellow.
 I would he loved his wife: if he were honester
 He were much goodlier: is't not a handsome gentleman?
           (III. v. 77)

The contrast is pathetic, and there is even pathos in Bertram's attempt to win Diana to his desires. One of his poetic speeches we have already (p. 109) quoted. Here is another, phrased again with a poetic conviction[1] worthy of Troilus:

 Be not so holy-cruel: love is holy;
 And my integrity ne'er knew the crafts
 That you do charge me with. Stand no more off,
 But give thyself unto my sick desires
 Who then recover: say thou art mine, and ever
 My love as it begins shall so persever.
           (IV. ii. 32)

This is spoken from a genuine infatuation, and it is hard to see why such love, whilst it lasts, is not 'holy'. The trouble is, and his words admit it despite his protestations, that the 'sick desires' will indeed 'recover', and leave him heart-whole and independent; and his following denial merely emphasizes his lack of self-knowledge. We have a normal example of a young

[1] Poetic sincerity may often in Shakespeare express weaknesses which are satirized in another's prose, as happens with Orsino and Feste, Claudio and Beatrice, Jacques and Touchstone, Hotspur and Falstaff, Glendower and Hotspur, Othello and Iago, Lear and the Fool, Antony and Enobarbus. But the poetry nevertheless holds an emotional content which prose normally does not, and to undervalue the dignity of its speaker would be a folly reducing a complex antagonism to simple satire. Prose scores more heavily in the Comedies, poetry in the Tragedies. Our brief statement is necessarily crude: Shakespearian prose can be highly imaginative, and is so particularly in *All's Well that Ends Well*. But, with this reservation, we might almost say that Shakespeare's life-work, like Byron's, could be defined as a wrestling of prose and poetry, with a victory, in the last plays, for the poetry.

man who does not understand himself, and indeed finds it convenient not to do so. It is regarded as quite normal:

> My mother told me just how he would woo
> As if she sat in's heart; she says all men
> Have the like oaths.

(iv. ii. 69)

The scene is composed from the viewpoint of the worldly-wise Polonius, who regards it as perfectly natural that Hamlet should try to seduce Ophelia if he gets the chance: it is, indeed, only by ourselves allowing for such a view that we can make any sense of Polonius' opposition to Hamlet's suit. Nor does he think that sexual licence will dishonour Laertes in France. Shakespeare himself appears to regard Cassio's affair with Bianca as the normal behaviour of a young man on active service.[1] That he continually drives home the ethical corollaries with a fine penetration should not prevent us from realizing that Shakespeare understood the society of his day and recognized the strength of human instinct.

Bertram has complete integrity in matters of war, but is both ignorant of himself and without principle in matters of sex. It is accordingly a just and truly exquisite stroke that, when Bertram joins in the tricking of Parolles and is enjoying his scorn of the man's cowardice, the blindfolded Parolles, who thinks that he is among enemies, should describe Bertram to his face and before his fellow-officers as 'a foolish idle boy, but for all that very ruttish'; as 'a dangerous and lascivious boy, who is a whale to virginity and devours up all the fry it finds'; and as 'that lascivious young boy, the Count' (iv. iii. 242, 249, 337). Parolles has himself encouraged him in such vices, but it remains to his credit that no one in the play could so well have phrased Bertram's faults in an idiom that would strike home both to him and to us. With an exquisite irony Bertram is fooled by the plot quite as much as is Parolles himself, to the inner satisfaction, no doubt, of his friends, who have indeed engineered it in order to bring him to his senses.

---

[1] Mr Paul N. Siegel has recently gone some way towards placing Cassio's loose behaviour by observing its function within the web of Iago's plot (*Shakespearean Tragedy and the Elizabethan Compromise*, New York, 1957). The point is worth making and can be accepted without subscribing to Mr Siegel's argument concerning damnation (see p. 250 below).

They have already been heard discussing his 'unchaste' liaison, and deploring such 'rebellion' (i.e. upsurge of sexual instinct) as a universal split in man:

> *First Lord* Now God delay our rebellion! as we are ourselves, what things we are!
> *Second Lord* Merely our own traitors. And as in the common course of all treasons, we still see them reveal themselves, till they attain to their abhorred ends, so he that in this action contrives against his own nobility, in his proper stream o'erflows himself.
>
> (IV. iii. 23)

Helena also in effect makes the same point, dwelling on the ease with which Bertram could enjoy union with her in mistake for Diana:

> But, O strange men!
> That can such sweet use make of what they hate,
> When saucy trusting of the cozen'd thoughts
> Defiles the pitchy night: so lust doth play
> With what it loathes for that which is away.
>
> (IV. iv. 21)

The particular deception is used for a general indictment of lust as self-deceit, recalling the famous sonnet (129) on lust. Clearly, as the Clown has already (p. 111) explained to us, we are to recognize a universal split in man whereby his sexual instincts fight against his better self.

And yet society is also at fault in too readily condoning such male licence, especially in men of birth. Parolles later neatly expresses for us this strangely lax code. When questioned by the King as to Bertram's affair with Diana, he says that his master is indeed 'an honourable gentleman', but with 'tricks' in him 'which gentlemen have'. The King is unsatisfied, and asks if he loved her:

> *Parolles* Faith, sir, he did love her; but how?
> *King* How, I pray you?
> *Parolles* He did love her, sir, as a gentleman loves a woman.
> *King* How is that?
> *Parolles* He loved her, sir, and loved her not.
>
> (V. iii. 245)

That is as good an account as we shall get, though Parolles continues to insist that Bertram *did* in his lustful way love her, and was indeed 'mad for her', talking 'of Satan, and of Limbo and of Furies' (v. iii. 264). The whole question of sex-relationships, and particularly of aristocratic behaviour, is posed. We may remember that 'gentle sport' in Sonnet 96 means 'wanton behaviour becoming to a gentleman' (blending T. G. Tucker's notes to Sonnets 95 and 96; *The Mutual Flame*, p. 22).

In Bertram and Parolles we have a goodly range of satirized qualities which make one complex. They are, briefly, the conventional values of the young aristocrat, clustering about the concept 'honour'. Bravery, indeed, is there, but it exists on a precipice, always ready to descend to the falsities of court-fashion and, at the limit, the lying braggadocio of such frauds as Parolles. Sexually, it has no values, or those that exist are quite unreliable. Man is divided into honourable soldiership and dishonourable sex, and the way is opened for a number of other falsities, his sexual failings eventually, in the play's final scene, forcing Bertram into barefaced lying. To put it briefly, such 'honour' as his, grand on the battlefield, is not enough: no finer values are present, and he is left at the mercy of a Parolles. In some respects he is Parolles' inferior, since he lacks those primary virtues which Parolles, in the depths, possesses: self-knowledge and humility.

All this was probably felt by Shakespeare as a *contemporary* danger. Braggart travellers in fantastic dress like Parolles and Italian vice such as Bertram's, for it was—as the King warned his young officers (ii. i. 19–22)—in an Italian atmosphere that such things were likely to occur, were both well-worn themes to Shakespeare and his contemporaries. The charge against Bertram resembles that levelled against Claudio, who is also a fine soldier, in *Much Ado about Nothing* (i. i. 12–17; v. i. 92–8). Modern superficiality and vice are to be contrasted with the established values of an older world. Parolles significantly compares virginity to 'an old courtier', dressed 'out of fashion', all 'richly suited, but unsuitable' (i. i. 171): virtue is now out of fashion. At the limit, it is a contrast of Renaissance humanism and medieval society. The one is fine in masculine ambition and war, but has many gross failings; the other has a more feminine, more spiritualized, way of life to offer, maintaining respect to the feminine values. We may note that war in this play is, more vividly than anywhere else in Shakespeare, except perhaps in *Othello*, conceived as contemporary war, with bullets (p. 142).

New and old are emphatically contrasted. There are two primary personifications of the old order, the King and the Countess. The King, after recalling his friendship with Bertram's father, deplores the superficialities of the new generation:

> In his youth
> He had the wit, which I can well observe
> Today in our young lords; but they may jest
> Till their own scorn return to them unnoted
> Ere they can hide their levity in honour . . .
>
> (I. ii. 31)

Remembrance of his friend makes the King dubious of progress:

> Such a man
> Might be a copy to these younger times;
> Which, follow'd well, would demonstrate them now
> But goers backward.
>
> (I. ii. 45)

Bertram's father was a man of wisdom, who feared the on-coming generation:

> ' Let me not live', quoth he,
> 'After my flame lacks oil, to be the snuff
> Of younger spirits, whose apprehensive senses
> All but new things disdain; whose judgements are
> Mere fathers of their garments; whose constancies
> Expire before their fashions'.
>
> (I. ii. 58)

All this is spoken, with sharp dramatic irony, to Bertram, whom we are soon to watch in high 'disdain' and failing grievously in 'judgement'.

The Countess had hoped that he would succeed his father in 'manners', and that his 'birthright' and 'goodness' would go hand-in-hand (I. i. 70). But we find him horribly falsifying his birthright, and the symbol of that falsification is the ancestral ring which he gives to Diana during his wooing of her, in exchange for a transient pleasure. It was Helena's idea that she should ask for it:

> Now his important blood will nought deny
> That she'll demand: a ring the county wears
> That downward hath succeeded in his house
> From son to son, some four or five descents
> Since the first father wore it. This ring he holds
> In most rich choice; yet in his idle fire
> To buy his will, it would not seem too dear,
> Howe'er repented after.
>
> (III. vii. 21)

Diana follows Helena's suggestion. At first Bertram is reluctant:

> It is an honour 'longing to our house,
> Bequeathed down from many ancestors;
> Which were the greatest obloquy i' the world
> In me to lose.
>
> (IV. ii. 42)

This is the ring which Diana compares with her own sexual 'honour' as just such a 'ring' likewise 'bequeathed down from many ancestors' (IV. ii. 45). In parting with the ring Bertram falsifies those two values which the Countess grouped together: 'blood' and 'virtue', 'birthright' and 'goodness' (I. i. 72, 70). He offends against both. His fault is underlined for us by one of his friends:

> He hath given her his monumental ring, and thinks himself made in the unchaste composition.
>
> (IV. iii. 20)

It is a sacrifice of a great permanency to a temporary and immoral enjoyment. The ring is again highly charged with radiations in the last act, the Countess being deeply shocked at her son's irresponsibility:

> He blushes, and 'tis it.
> Of six preceding ancestors that gem
> Conferr'd by testament to the sequent issue,
> Hath it been owed and worn.
>
> (V. iii. 197)

The ring performs a function similar to that 'antique token', the handkerchief, in *Othello* (v. ii. 214), the loss of both being regarded as a betrayal of sanctities. 'Antique' reminds us of the Sonnets, where it is a key-word in the contrast of modern falsities and old-world piety and integrity.[1] In *All's Well that Ends Well* it occurs once only, when Parolles accords Lafeu 'the privilege of antiquity' (ii. iii. 219), but the general contrast here is the same as that of the Sonnets, and to be distinguished from the deployment of old and new generations in the Final Plays.

We are directed to think that his acceptance of Helena can alone settle Bertram's problems for him. In the last act the King, the Countess, and Lafeu discuss his original fault as a failure in 'estimation', or valuation, to be perhaps excused on grounds of hot-headed youth, but nevertheless 'an offence of mighty note' done to the King and to his mother, and 'to himself the greatest wrong of all' (v. iii. 1–15). For such self-delusion is a self-wronging; a wronging of his nobler, and therefore true, self.

The news of Helena's death may be considered to act on him as does that of Fulvia on Antony. The letter which, presumably, tells him of it affects him deeply: 'There is something in't that stings his nature, for on the reading it he changed almost into another man' (iv. iii. 8). True, he speaks lightly of her death soon after (iv. iii. 101), but we later find him admitting his fault, and claiming now to love her. It is here that he mentions Lafeu's daughter, of whom we had not previously heard, as, in part, his excuse. Asked by the King if he recalls that lady, he answers:

> Admiringly, my liege, at first
> I stuck my choice upon her, e'er my heart
> Durst make too bold a herald of my tongue:
> Where the impression of mine eye infixing,
> Contempt his scornful perspective did lend me,
> Which warp'd the line of every other favour;
> Scorn'd a fair colour, or express'd it stolen;
> Extended or contracted all proportions
> To a most hideous object: thence it came

[1] In my discussion of the word 'antique' in the Sonnets (*The Mutual Flame*, pp. 82–5) I omitted to mention both the 'antique token' of *Othello* (v. ii. 214) and the 'old and antique song' in *Twelfth Night* (ii, iv, 3).

> That she whom all men praised and whom myself,
> Since I have lost, have loved, was in mine eye
> The dust that did offend it.
>
> (v. iii. 44)

This is the exact obverse of the state of harmony in vision claimed by Shakespeare himself in Sonnets 113 and 114 (discussed in *The Mutual Flame*, pp. 119–22). It is a state of distorted vision and consequent scorn: that is what we are to suppose was wrong with him.

That he is still far from a state of grace may be assumed from his behaviour when cornered. First, he lies mightily about the ring given him by Helena (v. iii, 92–101). Then, when faced by Diana, whom he had wooed so fervently, his words are disgraceful and unchivalrous. Asked if he intends to marry her, he replies:

> Let your highness
> Lay a more noble thought upon mine honour
> Than for to think that I would sink it here.
>
> (v. iii. 181)

The very use of 'honour' in such a context is now, from his lips, a blasphemy. We must, I suppose, realize that when he describes how he 'boarded her i' the wanton way of youth' after she 'did angle' for him, showing both 'infinite cunning' and 'modern grace' (v. iii. 212), this is presumably how he saw her behaviour, in male fashion, after he thought that he had seduced her. But it is bad enough: every phrase rings with the callous attitude of the conventional code.

Such is our study of Bertram. As one of the Lords says:

> The web of our life is of a mingled yarn, good and ill together: our virtues would be proud if our faults whipped them not; and our crimes would despair if they were not cherished by our virtues.
>
> (IV. iii. 83)

That may serve as a just comment. We have now to consider Helena.

IV

Helena possesses those old-world qualities of simplicity, sincerity, and integrity which Bertram lacks. She is loving, humble, and good, and in her there is no lack of piety to her forbears: indeed, her father's art descends to, and is used by, her.

Her first words sound a note of wistful suffering. The Countess thinks that she is grieving for the loss of her father:

> *Countess* No more of this, Helena, go to, no more; lest it be rather thought you affect a sorrow than have it.
> *Helena* I do affect a sorrow, indeed, but I have it too.
>
> (I. i. 60)

The note is that of Julia's 'The musician likes'—i.e. 'pleases'— 'me not' in *The Two Gentlemen of Verona* (IV. ii. 58); and of Imogen in *Cymbeline*. Helena, like those, might seem to be going to play the part of a wronged woman, suffering for love. But there is a difference: her feminine humility becomes an active and challenging, almost a *male*, force.

She is generally praised. From her father she inherits fine qualities, and shows honesty and goodness (I. i. 45–53); the Countess regards her as, in effect, her daughter (I. iii. 150–61; IV. v. 11–13); she possesses 'wisdom and constancy' amazing in one of her age (II. i. 86–8). But she is always 'humble' (II. iii. 89), and will only have Bertram on terms just to him: 'Nor would I have him till I do deserve him' (I. iii. 207). Even when her healing of the King has proved her desert, her way of choosing Bertram is to offer her 'service' to his 'guiding power' in uttermost feminine humility (II. iii. 109): that is her conception of marriage, recalling Portia's in *The Merchant of Venice* (III. ii. 149–75). The Countess clearly asserts that she 'deserves a lord that twenty such rude boys' as her own son should 'tend upon' whilst calling her 'mistress', and regards her supposed death as 'the death of the most virtuous gentlewoman that ever nature had praise for creating' (III. ii. 83; IV. v. 9). Our social valuations are reversed: nature's aristocracy, as in the poetry of *The Winter's Tale* (p. 106), replaces

man's. 'We lost a jewel of'—i.e. 'in'—'her', says the King
(v. iii. 1), the image recalling Thaisa in *Pericles*. Again

> He lost a wife
> Whose beauty did astonish the survey
> Of richest eyes, whose words all ears took captive,
> Whose dear perfection hearts that scorn'd to serve
> Humbly called mistress.
>
> (v. iii. 15)

She is almost beyond the human, with the kind of idealization
accorded Thaisa, Marina, and Hermione. She is one whose
'prayers' Heaven itself 'delights to hear and loves to grant'
(iii. iv. 27). But she is not showy: 'all her deserving is a reserved honesty' (iii. v. 61). Nor is there anything priggish in
her. She can, as we have seen (p. 110), engage in broad sex-talk
with Parolles. She alone of our people has the sympathy to
recognize in this strange creature, whom she loves for Bertram's 'sake', both the vicious falsity of his play-acting and yet
a certain fitness in his scandalous behaviour which somehow
wins our approbation whilst 'virtue's steely bones' are left
'bleak i' the cold wind'. To this point the contrast is in Parolles'
favour: the imagery of cold contrasted with the rich humour
of his shameless absurdity constitutes a kind of approbation,
aesthetic rather than moral; and though in her next lines,
calling it an example of the way 'cold wisdom' often has to take
second place to 'superfluous folly' ('luxurious folly'), she
registers a disapproval, the point has, poetically, been made
(i. i. 111–17; see p. 120). However that may be, Helena herself
certainly stands for more than an ethical ideal; she is feminine
'honour' incarnate, her excellence a way of life, to be interpreted in the realm of being rather than of precept.

Helena can best be discussed under two main headings,
and we shall next consider her as (i) the supreme development
of Shakespeare's conception of feminine love, and (ii) as
miracle worker.

In 'The Shakespearian Integrity' (pp. 218–22) and in my
recent study of the Sonnets I have suggested that Shakespeare's
women lovers may be said to have been created from the
female element in his own soul. But that does not mean that
they are unsatisfactory as studies of women: on the contrary,
they are created from an exact, because personal, experience.

There is no need to emphasize the depth and subtlety of the love of Viola and Rosalind, or the dramatic force of Juliet and Cleopatra. Love is woman's peculiar domain, whereas the men are pre-eminent in war and tragedy. The sexes play differing parts, and the woman is at her finest in submission, as in Katharina's final speech in *The Taming of the Shrew* (v. ii. 137–80) and Portia's surrender to Bassanio in *The Merchant of Venice* (iii. ii. 149–75); in the other Portia's admission of feminine weakness in *Julius Caesar* (ii. iv. 39); and in Cleopatra's resignation of her claims on Antony, respect for his 'honour', and invocation of 'laurelled victory' on his arms (*Antony and Cleopatra*, i. iii. 93–101). Examples of this particular contrast of male and female abound; and just such is the contrast of Helena and Bertram.

But there is a difference. Here the contrast of woman and man is pretty nearly our whole theme; it is our motivating principle throughout; once recognized, you find it in speech after speech. All our thoughts on 'honour', 'virginity', and the intermixing of sex and war in metaphor, come to mind. More: not only is Helena, even more than Imogen, the distilled essence of Shakespeare's view of feminine love, but the woman's humility, her anxiety to serve, *becomes for once itself dynamic and assertive*. She fights for her love against all odds, and wins: the feminine principle of love asserts itself against the masculine principle of warrior-courage, 'virginity' here naturally assuming, as we have seen, terms drawn from warfare (p. 110). Shakespeare's heroines are, of course, active and adventurous elsewhere, and sometimes, as do Portia in *The Merchant of Venice* and Beatrice in *Much Ado about Nothing*, act deliberately to untangle male error and confusion. They often dress as boys, thereby, perhaps, reflecting both the bisexuality of their creator and that of his 'master-mistress' ideal (Sonnet 20; and compare the 'maiden-tongued' youth of *A Lover's Complaint*, 100). But Helena's bisexuality is at once more realistic and more impressive, relying not at all on the pictorial fiction of disguise, but springing direct from her womanly self. There is never any abrogation of femininity in Shakespeare's women, whatever the male disguises and bisexual inclusions; and so here we have femininity paradoxically invading the male prerogative of initiative and action.

Normally Shakespeare's women are not brave in face of physical danger: Viola is afraid of the duel, Rosalind faints at the sight of a blood-stained handkerchief, Desdemona goes to her death in terror, Portia in *Julius Caesar* collapses under the strain of the conspiracy, Lady Macbeth faints, Cleopatra flies from the battle of Actium; and though Juliet's terror in the Potion-scene is less physical than imaginative, resembling that of Faustus at the end of Marlowe's play, it marks an extremity which no Shakespearian *hero* would be allowed to reach. But, as we shall see (p. 152), Helena, Diana's 'knight' (I. iii. 122), *risks torture and death in order to save the King and win a husband.* The female values for once become on every level the equal, or superior, of the male. Nowhere else does this happen.

The feminine challenge here so directly dramatized can nevertheless be said to be implicit throughout Shakespeare. In all the greater plays we are aware of the female principle challenging the male principle in direct descent from the part played by women in the Comedies. The protagonist, king or soldier, is regularly overthrown by, or subdued to, that in himself which is involved in his relationship to a woman; as in *Othello, Macbeth, King Lear, Coriolanus, Antony and Cleopatra*; and both sexual elements can be felt active within the spiritualized strength forming in the protagonist towards the end, and in the final tragic harmony. The dominating importance of women in the Final Plays, except for *The Tempest*, is clear enough. Now this intuition, ranging from the earliest to the latest plays, is given personal projection in the plot of *All's Well that Ends Well*, with Helena as agent. She makes the plot, as do the Duke in *Measure for Measure* and Prospero in *The Tempest*.

We shall next demonstrate more exactly Helena's function as Shakespeare's supreme expression of a woman's love. It will be, mainly, a matter of poetry.

She is utterly humble. Her love is characterized less by desire and possessiveness than by service and adoration, reminiscent of the Sonnets. Her father is forgotten:

> What was he like?
> I have forgot him: my imagination
> Carries no favour in't but Bertram's.
> I am undone: there is no living, none,

If Bertram be away. 'Twere all one
That I should love a bright particular star
And think to wed it, he is so above me:
In his bright radiance and collateral light
Must I be comforted, not in his sphere.
The ambition in my love thus plagues itself:
The hind that would be mated with the lion
Must die for love. 'Twas pretty, though a plague,
To see him every hour; to sit and draw
His arched brows, his hawking eye, his curls,
In our heart's table; heart too capable
Of every line and trick of his sweet favour:
But now he's gone, and my idolatrous fancy
Must sanctify his reliques.

(1. i. 93)

Here is a Bertram very different from the man we have been discussing; it is Bertram known by love; the potential, perhaps the real, man. Observe that Helena herself subscribes whole-heartedly to those social and aristocratic valuations which her own personality, as a dramatic force, serves to attack. Notice, too, the peculiar tone of it, like Paulina's words over Leontes' child (*The Winter's Tale*, II. iii. 97–102), exquisitely handling physical detail with a consummate purity of perception. 'Our heart's table' recalls the difficult Sonnet 24 on perfect love-sight (*The Mutual Flame*, pp. 40–1).

Here is another revealing passage, spoken to the Countess:

Then I confess,
Here on my knee, before high Heaven and you,
That before you, and next unto high Heaven,
I love your son.
My friends were poor, but honest; so's my love.
Be not offended; for it hurts him not
That he is loved of me. I follow him not
By any token of presumptuous suit;
Nor would I have him till I do deserve him;
Yet never know how that desert should be.
I know I love in vain, strive against hope;
Yet in that captious and intenible sieve,
I still pour in the waters of my love,
And lack not to lose still: thus, Indian-like,
Religious in mine error, I adore
The sun, that looks upon his worshipper,

But knows of him no more. My dearest madam,
Let not your hate encounter with my love
For loving where you do: but if yourself
Whose aged honour cites a virtuous youth,
Did ever in so true a flame of liking
Wish chastely and love dearly, that your Dian
Was both herself and love; O, then give pity
To her, whose state is such, that cannot choose
But lend and give where she is sure to lose;
That seeks not to find that her search implies,
But riddle-like lives sweetly where she dies.

(i. iii. 199)

Here I point less to any especial accents in the poetry than to
the statement. 'Next high Heaven' recalls 'next my Heaven
the best' in Sonnet 110. Especially important is the reference
to Dian, our central deity. Helena's love exists at the meeting-
place of Dian and desire: 'was both herself and love'. We are
continually forced towards a paradoxical identification of *virginity* and *sexual love*, pointing to the 'married chastity' of *The
Phoenix and the Turtle*. That, if it means 'married virginity',
cannot be, and is not, dramatically maintained; but the
equivalent of purity may have been maintained in Shakespeare's
personal love for the Fair Youth adored in the Sonnets; and
he may be working from that.

The powers of virgin love are exquisitely described in one
of Helena's early speeches. Parolles has been arguing against
virginity, and she breaks in with:

Not my virginity yet:[1]
There shall your master have a thousand loves,
A mother and a mistress and a friend,
A phoenix, captain and an enemy,
A guide, a goddess, and a sovereign,
A counsellor, a traitress, and a dear;
His humble ambition, proud humility,
His jarring concord, and his discord dulcet,
His faith, his sweet disaster; with a world
Of pretty, fond, adoptious christendoms
That blinking Cupid gossips. Now shall he—
I know not what he shall. God send him well!
The court's a learning place, and he is one—

(i. i. 181)

[1] I follow the Folio pointing in printing a colon here.

The lines, with their broken conclusion, insistently remind us of Viola's semi-confession of her love to Orsino in *Twelfth Night*, breaking off on 'Sir, shall I to this lady?' (II. iv. 105-24); and of Cleopatra's

> Sir, you and I must part, but that's not it;
> Sir, you and I have loved, but there's not it;
> That you know well. Something it is I would—
> O, my oblivion is a very Antony,
> And I am all forgotten.
>
> (*Antony and Cleopatra*, I. iii. 87)

The thoughts are different, but the hesitant phrasing, the sense of unutterable worlds behind, is the same in each. The only other comparison I recall which seems at all adequate is Tolstoy's description of the birth of Prince Andrew's love for Natasha in the Nineteenth Chapter of the Sixth Book of *War and Peace*:

> In the midst of a phrase he ceased speaking and suddenly felt tears choking him, a thing he had thought impossible for him. He looked at Natasha as she sang, and something new and joyful stirred in his soul. He felt happy, and at the same time sad. He had absolutely nothing to weep about yet he was ready to weep. What about? His former love? The little princess? His disillusionments? . . . His hopes for the future? . . . Yes and no. The chief reason was a sudden, vivid sense of the terrible contrast between something infinitely great and illimitable within him, and that limited and material something that he, and even she, was. This contrast weighed on and yet cheered him while she sang.
>
> (*World's Classics*, Vol. II, pp. 67-8)

It is perhaps not surprising that on this particular ground these two most unchallengeable human delineators of the modern era stand so close together.

Helena's speech is difficult, but there is no reason to suppose a missing line. 'There' cannot surely, as has sometimes been argued, mean 'at the Court'. Helena's words show an enjoyed *fondling* of love-thoughts, and must accordingly refer to her own love of Bertram rather than that of any rival, or rivals. The opening I take, in direct succession to her preceding remarks to Parolles, to mean: 'I shall not part with my virginity to anyone yet, because therein your master has an infinite love'. I do not think that, at this early stage in her

story, it can mean 'In giving your master my virginity I shall
give him a thousand loves', since she has no good reason at
this stage to expect such an event. Not that the total meaning
would be so very different, either way, since virginity, given
or withheld, remains the key-thought. As in the Christian
scheme virginity is here less the denial of love than an expression of it: it is conceived as a positive power. In *The Christian
Renaissance* (p. 39) I have, in emphasizing the importance of
virginity in Christian dogma, suggested that 'to hold up virginity as an ideal is merely to raise sex to an infinite value'.
That is what happens here: the love is infinite, 'a thousand
loves'; it is the window to a great insight. It may be related to
the state of perfect integration from which poetry is born, a
state which is, as Shelley in his *Defence of Poetry* tells us, 'at
war with every base desire'. Such a state is a state of inclusion,
wisdom, and forgiveness: this Helena claims, and her ability
later on to work the miracle is evidence of her right.[1]

This love, like Shakespeare's own ranging poetic vision,
is universal and so a number of human categories are contained. It is not sexually limited: it is simultaneously maternal,
sexual, and a friendship in the Elizabethan sense, whereby
'friend' was as strong a term as 'lover', partly perhaps because
of the many ardent man-to-man friendships and idealizations,
such as Shakespeare's in the Sonnets. The 'Phoenix' must be
understood in terms of its use throughout *Love's Martyr*, the
collection in which Shakespeare's *The Phoenix and the Turtle*
appeared. The symbol appears at key-moments in Shakespeare's esoteric thought from *Timon of Athens* onwards, and
is fully discussed in *The Mutual Flame*. The Phoenix is bisexual, an idealized creature, and chaste. In precise terms of
'Phoenix' and 'Turtle' Bertram, from Helena's view, would
more exactly be 'Phoenix', with her adoring self as 'Turtle';
but she is imagining herself as she might be from his view,

---

[1] Helena's *virginity* must be related to both (i) her love-insight and (ii) her subsequent function as miracle-worker. For (i) the revelationary properties of virginity,
compare Mr John Cowper Powys' words in *The Brazen Head* (1956): 'that unique
power of revelation, of illumination, of ultimate vision, that virgins alone possess'
(p. 207). For (ii) its specifically *magical* properties in action, see *The Brazen Head*,
pp. 81–3; also pp. 267, 270–1, 337, 341; and for a reference to Christian myth
and dogma, p. 290. See also *Maiden Castle* (1937), pp. 236, 240, 482–3; *Jobber Skald*,
pp. 266, 276–7, 310; *Dostoievsky*, p. 48.

and her own bisexuality, her blend of female love and male
vigour, her virgin chastity combined with beauty and wisdom,
all entitle her to the term as that to which he might, and
should, aspire. War categories are also involved: she will be
both his 'captain' and his 'enemy'. All Bertram's interests and
ambitions as warrior are somehow contained, and the male
values safeguarded, Helena boldly entering this domain as his
'captain', so asserting the priority of her love, and even as his
'enemy'. Why? The next lines clarify the word. This love is as
a 'guide'; being in touch with his greater self and speaking
thence, it naturally becomes a 'goddess' and, in human terms,
his 'sovereign'. Every value, sacred or secular, is included,
and from this height Bertram is to be counselled, advised,
warned, even opposed, for his failings are admitted; and so her
love is, in its way, a 'traitress', aligning itself with opposing
forces, and yet simultaneously, and accordingly, a 'dear', or
thing of highest worth.

Paradox is involved, and becomes now explicit. Love such
as Helena's is, at its best, a great aspiration, and yet one born
of humility; in her pride and humility are unified; and this is
one with *his* reasons for both pride and humility. She has
become almost a divine or poetic principle, overruling, watching, containing him; or rather it is not she, but the Love over-
arching, overruling, both, as we find it in the Sonnets (*The
Mutual Flame*, pp. 41, 61, 94). 'His jarring concord and his
discord dulcet' suggests the whole Shakespearian universe in
its blend of tempests and music; but here in particular it
denotes both Helena's effect on him and also his own lack of
integration as surveyed by the now almost impersonal Love
for which it exists as harmony; as when Helena accepts
Parolles' faults since 'they sit so fit in him' that 'virtue' appears
'bleak', 'cold', and metallic in comparison (i. i. 113; p. 120).
This is the poetic, Shakespearian, view of man. Helena's love
sees Bertram as he potentially is, that core and inmost music
of his personality which no faults can disturb—Parolles'
'simply the thing I am' (p. 121)—and this outspaces the moral
judgement, which, though present, is surpassed, as when
Mariana says of Angelo that she craves 'no other nor no better
man,' since 'best men are moulded out of faults' (*Measure for
Measure*, v. i. 440). So here Helena is 'his faith', that which

believes in, recognizes, and works for, his own highest good and potential excellence; but, since that may, as in the greater scheme of God's dealings with man—and these are never far from Helena's thinking—bring suffering, she, or the great Love, is, too, his 'sweet disaster', recalling Saint Paul's sense of happy bondage in servitude to Christ. But the thought is getting too weighty, and returns to all the little ways and sentimentalities of love, though even here remembering religion in the word 'christendoms', Christian names or nicknames, sponsored by ('gossips') blind ('blinking') Cupid.

The speech offers a definition of perfect love, which labours for its object's good; which, seeing the 'heart' (*A Midsummer Night's Dream*, II. ii. 155), the Hindu *atman*, or divine spark, knows, includes, and forgives all; and which, in Shakespeare's own experience, made him see all humanity, including all that was evil and ugly, as aspects, like Helena's understanding of Parolles, of the wondrous being whom he loved (Sonnets 113 and 114): this is the exact opposite of Bertram's distorted, scornful vision of man already (p. 130) discussed. What Helena is describing is an authentic part of the great poetic panorama, of the same stuff and significance as the lucid patterns of Pope's *Essay on Man* and Shelley's *Defence of Poetry*.[1]

This careful definition serves as a prologue to Helena's story. Directly after it we find her love beginning to *act* in her as a source of magical power:

> Our remedies oft in ourselves do lie
> Which we ascribe to Heaven: the fated sky
> Gives us free scope; only doth backward pull
> Our slow designs when we ourselves are dull.
> What power is it which mounts my love so high,
> That makes me see, and cannot feed mine eye?
> The mightiest space in fortune nature brings
> To join like likes, and kiss like native things.
> Impossible be strange attempts to those
> That weigh their pains in sense, and do suppose
> What hath been cannot be: who ever strove
> To show her merit that did miss her love?

---

[1] These are discussed in *Christ and Nietzsche*, p. 20. For Sonnets 113 and 114, see *The Mutual Flame*, pp. 119–21.

The King's disease—my project may deceive me,
But my intents are fixed, and will not leave me.

(i. i. 235)

This is the moment of conception. Emphasis is laid on man's,
or woman's, 'free' abilities, given by the 'sky', to use what is
'in' himself, the more cosmic suggestion of 'sky' marking a
distinction from reliance on a transcendental, or theological,
'Heaven'. The psychic potentialities in question are hampered
by the 'dull' elements of material inertia (as at Sonnet 44).
The 'power' is either directly born of Helena's love, or at least
intimately associated with it, infusing it with confidence, even
pride ('mounts . . . high'): we may recall the powers of love
described by Biron in *Love's Labour's Lost* (iv. iii. 289–365).
It is recognized as a reality beyond sense-perception ('That
. . . eye'), which can break through even the strongest ('mighti-
est space') social barriers in the cause of *natural* affinity
('nature . . . things'). We must not stifle enterprise by assess-
ing difficulties in terms of common sense ('weigh . . . sense'),
nor forget that such things have happened before.

The emphasis falls on natural, yet spiritual, power, though
the contrast of 'Heaven' and 'sky' is not elsewhere maintained,
the more orthodox concepts being generally used. The distinction, though often valuable and sometimes inevitable, cannot be more than provisional. So Helena goes ahead with her
plan to heal the King, and succeeds. The actual healing we
shall discuss later.

Helena claims always to serve Bertram; he remains her
master. When, after the healing, she chooses him for her
husband, she first takes the great step from Dian to Love,
from virginity to marriage:

Now Dian, from thy altar do I fly;
And to imperial Love, that god most high,
Do my sighs stream.

(ii. iii. 80)

Then, coming to Bertram, she proposes as follows:

I dare not say I take you; but I give
Me and my service ever whilst I live,
Into your guiding power.

(ii. iii. 109)

She speaks like other Shakespearian heroines, recognizing the man as her lord and master; and yet here that very recognition has taken the initiative, assuming the male prerogative.

After Bertram has gone to the war, she recognizes that she has driven him away, and speaks poignantly of his danger. It is, as a Shakespearian woman, her part both to fear and to respect, like Katharina (*The Taming of the Shrew*, v. ii. 148-52), the hardships and dangers which fall to man. She, whose art is healing, fears the very thought of the dangers which Bertram must incur.

He has written: 'Till I have no wife, I have nothing in France' (III. ii. 77). So in remorse she will leave France. Here is her soliloquy, remarkable for its maternal, protective, tone, for its fine depicting, unusual in Shakespeare, of contemporary warfare, and above all for the sudden dignity, witnessing to the ability of Shakespeare's poetry to live its own lines of thought, with which she, who has long recognized his nobler self, now, as it were, crowns the scornful young man before our eyes by the simple use of his title. The name 'Rousillon' (spelt in the Folio 'Rossillion') sounds twice, like an awakening, and perhaps nowhere else in Shakespeare is a name used with so resounding an effect:

> Nothing in France until he has no wife!
> Thou shalt have none, Rousillon, none in France;
> Then hast thou all again. Poor lord! is't I
> That chase thee from thy country and expose
> Those tender limbs of thine to the event
> Of the non-sparing war? And is it I
> That drive thee from the sportive court, where thou
> Wast shot at with fair eyes, to be the mark
> Of smoky muskets? O you leaden messengers,
> That ride upon the violent speed of fire,
> Fly with false aim; move the still-piecing air
> That sings with piercing; do not touch my lord.
> Whoever shoots at him, I set him there;
> Whoever charges on his forward breast,
> I am the caitiff that do hold him to't;
> And, though I kill him not, I am the cause
> His death was so effected; better 'twere
> I met the ravin lion when he roar'd
> With sharp constraint of hunger; better 'twere

That all the miseries which nature owes
Were mine at once. No, come thou home, Rousillon,
Whence honour but of danger wins a scar,
As oft it loses all: I will be gone;
My being here it is that holds thee hence.
Shall I stay here to do 't? No, no, although
The air of paradise did fan the house
And angels officed all. I will be gone,
That pitiful rumour may report my flight,
To consolate thine ear.

(III. ii. 103)

Here there is full recognition both of her own fault, if for once
we may so call it, and also of the true greatness of her husband;
for a warrior's is a great calling. From a woman's, maternal,
view, she surveys its terror, the danger it is to be a man. So
Bertram is twice given his title, 'Rousillon'. In direct contrast
to her earlier soliloquy she here resigns her rights to the inti-
macy of a Christian name, while freely allowing him *his* rights
to all that aristocratic honour which made him reject her, but
which she herself never repudiates; and on her lips the splendid
name makes him indeed noble, creating for us his true self,
known by love, the word's music sounding as the music of his
young warrior soul.

So she composes a letter in sonnet-form for the Countess,
admitting the fault of her 'ambitious love' and saying how she
will do penance as a pilgrim, and labour to 'sanctify' her husband's 'name' with a 'zealous fervour' (III. iv. 4–17). It is a
religious and penitential act; she is still labouring to serve his
interests.

Whether we can respond as we are meant to to her later
actions is less certain. Though she certainly knew that Bertram
had gone to serve the Duke (III. i. 54), we must not suppose
that her finding him in Florence was part of a deliberate plan,
since her letter to the Countess had already urged his immediate return to France (III. iv. 8); and as for her substituting
of herself for Diana as the object of Bertram's passion, we can
at least note that in doing this she is in effect saving him from
a sin which, as we have seen (p. 125), she regards as serious:
again she is, in fact, serving his best interests. As for the
symbolic ring which she wins from him, we can endow this

with whatever ancestral powers we like: possessing that, she may be supposed to know that, according to the terms of his own semi-oracular letter (III. ii. 60), she will eventually possess his love. All this we must accept as best we may: we have to forgive as much, as Tolstoy saw, in most of Shakespeare's plays. No doubt such dramatists could do better were we willing to sit in the theatre for treble the time they normally demand, but we are not. What we can say is this, that her later actions all tend, finally, to serve and rebuild Bertram's better self; and whatever we think of these scenes, they do certainly serve to show that, except when on the field of battle, Bertram needs guiding, since his judgement is immature and his values in chaos. It may seem presumptuous in Helena to cast herself for such a role, but she is no ordinary woman; or rather she has the best qualities of an ordinary woman developed to so high a pitch that she becomes almost a saint.

Religious categories are involved: they cluster round her as the values of war surround Bertram; and she actually performs a miracle. We pass now to consider Helena as miracle-worker.

The miracle grows from a world well saturated with religious thought and language. Religious phrases are continual, such as: 'Heaven aiding', 'Doubt not but Heaven', 'O dear Heaven, bless' (IV. iv. 12, 18; v. iii. 71); and so on. A 'quarrel' may be called 'holy'; so may love, even by a seducer (III. i. 4; IV. ii. 32). Theological terms occur: 'With the divine forfeit of his soul', 'He will sell the fee-simple of his salvation'; 'Dost thou put upon me at once the office of God and the Devil?' (III. vi. 33; IV. iii. 314; v. ii. 52). The Countess' prayers hope to 'pluck down' blessings on her son's head (I. i. 79); Helena has influence with a religious dignitary said to be 'one of the greatest in the Christian world' (IV. iv. 2). Parolles tells how Bertram in love 'talked of Satan, and of Limbo, and of Furies' (v. iii. 264). People moralize naturally on human life as 'a mingled yarn' of 'good and ill', of virtues and vices (IV. iii. 83; p. 130). The Clown, as we have seen, knows himself a 'wicked creature', and marries in order to 'repent' (I. iii. 38), going on to talk of 'young Charbon the puritan and old Poysam the papist' (I. iii. 58). The Countess, he says, is well but for two things:

One, that she's not in Heaven, whither God send her quickly! the
other, that she's in earth, from whence God send her quickly!

(II. iv. 12)

He takes, indeed, a bitter view, talking of 'the black prince',
'the prince of darkness', 'the devil', and continuing:

> I am a woodland fellow, sir, that always loved a great fire; and the
> master I speak of ever keeps a good fire. But, sure, he is the prince
> of the world; let his nobility remain in's court. I am for the house
> with the narrow gate, which I take to be too little for pomp to enter.
> Some that humble themselves may; but the many will be too chill
> and tender, and they'll be for the flowery way that leads to the broad
> gate and the great fire.

(IV. v. 50)

'Pomp' is satirized, and humility, the humility of a Helena,
honoured. The speech marks a complete surrender to the
religious, ascetic, point of view. Naturally it displeases Lafeu,
the Lord. It is not so much that the Clown is wrong as that
this recognition of human evil is just where the real problem
of living, as Lafeu would see it, begins. Parolles has no morals;
the Clown has little else. Neither face the complexities of life.

Helena functions as a *bridge* between religion and the
court, between humility and honour. In a world of divided,
sin-struck humanity she is a redeeming power, a perfect unit:
that is her function. Even the Clown admits 'that she was the
sweet marjoram of the salad, or rather the herb of grace'
(IV. v. 17). She it is who can speak words which Imogen might
have spoken, like:

> No, no, although
> The air of paradise did fan the house
> And angels officed all.

(III. ii. 127)

Her very prayers, according to the Countess, are peculiarly
valid:

> What angel shall
> Bless this unworthy husband? He cannot thrive
> Unless her prayers, whom Heaven delights to hear
> And loves to grant, reprieve him from the wrath
> Of greatest justice.

(III. iv. 25)

K

She functions, within the play, almost as Christ within the Christian Scheme. The play is a microcosm of that scheme. Naturally, her love is 'religious':

> Thus, Indian-like,
> Religious in mine error, I adore
> The sun, that looks upon his worshippers
> But knows of him no more.
>
> (I. iii. 212)

That is spoken from her humility: we are not to regard her love as idolatry. Her love possesses, as we have seen, both poetic integrity and religious purity, and it is right that in its pursuit she should become a pilgrim in holy dress, going to the sanctuary of Saint Jaques le Grand and lodging 'at the Saint Francis' (III. v. 34–7), the whole venture being called 'a holy undertaking' accomplished 'with most austere sanctimony' (IV. iii. 59). Like the Duke's disguise as a Friar in *Measure for Measure*, all this has a more than plot-meaning: associatively and visually it marks an addition to the protagonist's stature. And yet there is nothing prudish or ascetic about her. Nor does she in any sense oppose the courtly, aristocratic, valuations. She both accepts and admires them: they are part of her.

The idealization is so uncompromising, and yet so inclusive and so firmly based, since, as we have seen, her consciousness functions on the plane of Shakespearian poetry itself, that we are all but forced to believe that her very being is beyond criticism, and see Bertram's behaviour accordingly. This is, pretty nearly, equivalent to calling the play a religious morality, with Helena as a semi-divine person, or some new type of saint. And it is true that our central scenes are formal and ritualistic, rather like the formality of the tournament in *Pericles* (II. ii). Her choosing of a husband is formal: she passes from lord to lord as in a sort of trance, her rhymed speeches driving home the ritual meaning.

The earlier and crucial scene of the healing is also ritualistically felt, with formal rhymes and chant. And here indeed we approach the play's heart. For, whatever the poetry says it is hard to believe it alone: we want dramatic action. Here we have it. Helena from the start insisted that she did not want

Bertram until she deserved him (p. 135). She wins her right by the miracle, and by that alone; and yet the miracle is itself, as we shall see, a derivative from her love.

We shall now inspect this crucial event. It is, as happens in other late plays, a development on a more metaphysical level of dramatic patterns in the Comedies: here we can point to Rosalind functioning as miracle-worker in *As You Like It*. Our nearest analogy from the latest plays is the art of Cerimon, together with the 'sacred physic' and 'skill' of Marina, in *Pericles* (iii. ii; v. i. 74, 76). But our present miracle is not quite like anything else in Shakespeare: it is closer to us, more realistically conceived in point of detail, it speaks less to a 'mystical' than to what might be called a psychical or 'spiritualistic' understanding. Since Helena's function is so clearly stated to be that of a medium only for the greater powers, we have the less excuse for questioning it on grounds of probability.

Helena comes to the King with a power which descends from her father. She is thus credited with preserving and using her parental heritage in contrast to Bertram whose qualities are precisely those which did not characterize his father (p. 115), and who parts with his ancestral ring.

Her father, Gerard de Narbon, was more than an ordinary physician, and nearer to Cerimon in *Pericles*, who says:

> I hold it ever
> Virtue and cunning were endowments greater
> Than nobleness and riches. Careless heirs
> May the two latter darken and expend,
> But immortality attends the former,
> Making a man a god.
>
> (*Pericles*, iii. ii. 26)

So, too, de Narbon's skill is closely associated with 'honesty', or integrity. He was one, according to the Countess,

> whose skill was almost as great as his honesty; had it stretched so far, would have made nature immortal, and death should have play for lack of work.
>
> (i. i. 22)

Indeed, adds Lafeu, 'he was skilful enough to have lived still, if knowledge could be set up against mortality' (i. i. 35). The skill concerned appears to exist in close relation to its owner's

personal virtues ('honesty'), and to be nearer to some variety
of occult wisdom, or spirit-power, than to anything which we
can call medical science. As in *The Winter's Tale*, only with
more of a close-pinned realism, such esoteric secrets are, so
far as may be, hinted, and indeed emphasized, without breaking the bounds of dramatic propriety, as normally understood.
Helena possessed her father's notes:

> You know my father left me some prescriptions
> Of rare and proved effects, such as his reading
> And manifest experience had collected
> For general sovereignty; and that he will'd me
> In heedfull'st reservation to bestow them
> As notes, whose faculties inclusive were,
> More than they were in note; amongst the rest,
> There is a remedy, approved, set down,
> To cure the desperate languishings whereof
> The king is render'd lost.
>
> (I. iii. 229)

This is the basis of our miracle. It sounds at first ordinary
enough; but we may observe that the notes are considered of
more general ('inclusive') application than a superficial reading would suggest.

The Countess fears that the King and his physicians would
scorn a 'poor unlearned virgin' after the 'doctrine' of their
'schools' has already pronounced its verdict (I. iii. 243–50).
This may appear strange in view of her earlier remark that,
had de Narbon been alive, the King might have been cured
(I. i. 25), but the discrepancy is, as we shall see, part of the
dramatic plan. Helena replies:

> There's something in't,
> More than my father's skill, which was the great'st
> Of his profession, that his good receipt
> Shall for my legacy be sanctified
> By the luckiest stars in Heaven.
>
> (I. iii. 250)

The lines are obscure: I take 'receipt' to refer to the pre-
scription (as at II. i. 108), rather than to the King's 'acceptance'.
If so, it means: 'There is more to it than my father's skill, for
I feel that his valuable prescription will in my hands ("for my

legacy") somehow be blessed by God.' She herself, whose prayers, as we are elsewhere (p. 145) told, are peculiarly valid, is claiming to have divine assistance and support. And here we may recall that her plan's *original conception* (i) grew directly from out of her own love of Bertram and (ii) entered her consciousness as a power independent of sense-perception:

> What power is it which mounts my love so high,
> That makes me see, and cannot feed mine eye?
>
> (I. i. 239)

Her determination to visit the King flowered directly from a state of strong spiritual impregnation, born of love. So now, asked if she really believes in divine support, she answers briefly: 'Ay, madam, knowingly' (I. iii. 258). We are beyond science: transcendental, or occult, categories have entered our field. She goes to Paris.

We are, as happens in *The Winter's Tale*, gradually attuned to the possibility of miracle by Lafeu's introductory speech to the King, wherein he reports, in a light semi-humorous style, that he has seen a medicine 'able to breathe life into a stone', and raise the dead. Next, claiming to have left his 'light deliverance' for serious talk, he tells how he has spoken

> With one that, in her sex, her years, profession,
> Wisdom and constancy, hath amazed me more
> Than I dare blame my weakness.
>
> (II. i. 86)

Will the King see her, and after that 'laugh' (II. i. 90) at him, if he wishes to? Again, we see that it is not all 'science'; Helena's own qualities are involved. Lafeu is amazed at her blend of female with male 'wisdom' and 'constancy'. It is all very strange. Observe that there is some risk of *mockery*.

Helena is brought before the King, and tells him of her father's art:

> On's bed of death
> Many receipts he gave me; chiefly one
> Which as the dearest issue of his practice,
> And of his old experience the only darling,
> He bade me store up as a triple eye,
> Safer than mine own two, more dear. I have so;
> And, hearing your high majesty is touch'd

> With that malignant cause, wherein the honour
> Of my dear father's gift stands chief in power,
> I come to tender it and my appliance,
> With all bound humbleness.
>
> (II. i. 107)

The legacy appears now to be rather more than a written prescription. It is a choice secret, to be 'stored up', and actually compared to a 'triple eye'. This is the 'third eye' of occult doctrine and practice, located on the forehead and used in spirit-healing as a source of powerful rays.[1] It is here regarded as a sense more valuable ('dear') than the physical senses, and we shall naturally relate it to that experience of a love-born power offering a *sight* other than *sense-perception* (p. 141) which was the motivating impulse of Helena's whole scheme. Helena accordingly offers not merely a 'prescription', but rather this secret together with her own 'appliance'. Her own mediumistic gifts, developing from love, will be engaged; but it is all offered with humility.

The King is at first incredulous. But why? We know that he has been speaking 'mourningly' of de Narbon (i. i. 35), and we have heard him remark to Bertram, 'If he were living, I would try him yet', since the other doctors have only worn him out 'with several applications' (i. ii. 73). Now he gets a wonderful posthumous opportunity, and refuses:

> We thank you, maiden;
> But may not be so credulous of cure
> When our most learned doctors leave us, and
> The congregated college have concluded
> That labouring art can never ransom nature
> From her inaidable estate. I say we must not

---

[1] The 'third eye' is said to be situated between and above the two physical eyes. In 'absent healing' an image of the patient is focussed as the apex of a pyramid of which the three eyes are the base (*Reality*, Simcot Press, Blackpool; 3 July 1953): the triangular mechanism here indicated helps to explain Shakespeare's use of the word 'triple', as at *Antony and Cleopatra*, I. i. 12.

For the more general significances, see *The Tibetan Book of the Dead*, by W. Y. Evans-Wentz (2nd edn., 1949, p. 216); also *The Finding of the Third Eye* by Vera Stanley Alder (1938; last reprint, 1955), a neat introduction to many aspects of occult wisdom, containing some valuable remarks on bisexuality and the spiritualistic powers of sexual instinct (Ch. VI, 'Male and Female'); *Man: The Grand Symbol of the Mysteries*, Manly Hall, 1932; Ch. XVI; and *The Third Eye*, T. Lobsang Rampa, 1956.

So stain our judgement, or corrupt our hope,
To prostitute our past-cure malady
To empirics, or to dissever so
Our great self and our credit, to esteem
A senseless help, when help past sense we deem.

(II. i. 117)

This constitutes a contradiction, both of the King's own
former speech—though perhaps even there 'try him' underlined a doubt—and of the general recognition, by the Countess
and Lafeu, of de Narbon's superlative abilities. And yet it is
easy to see what is happening. The Countess has already
warned us that the King will refuse, and we can say that
Shakespeare has been very subtly at work attuning us by
degrees to regard Helena's cure as within the realm of spirit-
healing in strong contrast to the official services of the medical
profession.[1] We could only make complete sense of the King's
attitude by supposing that the term 'triple eye' has made him
realize that more was involved in de Narbon's art than he had
supposed. Either way, the main issue is clear, and from now
on there is no doubt. The King, to put it bluntly, is afraid
of making a fool of himself.

Helena's argument in reply is important. She does not
waste time urging her father's famous skill, but rather insists
that divine powers can work through so humble an instrument
as herself. Hitherto, except for two concluding and *abrupt*
couplets from the King, both have spoken in blank verse, but
now Helena speaks wholly in rhyme:

What I can do can do no hurt to try,
Since you set up your rest 'gainst remedy.
He that of greatest works is finisher
Oft does them by the weakest minister:
So holy writ in babes hath judgement shown,
When judges have been babes; great floods have flown
From simple sources; and great seas have dried
When miracles have by the greatest been denied.
Oft expectation fails, and most oft there
Where most it promises; and oft it hits
Where hope is coldest, and despair most fits.

(II. i. 137)

[1] Precisely the same issue is today being fought out by that famous healer of the
spiritualist movement, Mr Harry Edwards, and the British Medical Association.

Observe the gnomic, formal, incantatory quality of the rhymes, functioning, as in Helena's first recognition of her own magical powers (p. 140), as the language of inspiration: she seems to be mesmerizing the King. He is, however, still reluctant, though from now on the two speakers interweave with each other in rhyme. Helena continues, in directly religious, and here orthodox, terms:

> Inspired merit so by breath is barr'd:
> It is not so with Him that all things knows,
> As 'tis with us that square our guess by shows;
> But most it is presumption in us when
> The help of Heaven we count the act of men.
> Dear sir, to my endeavours give consent;
> Of Heaven, not me, make an experiment.
>
> (II. i. 151)

The King asks how long the cure will take? She answers in powerful incantatory style:

> The great'st grace lending grace,
> Ere twice the horses of the sun shall bring
> Their fiery torcher his diurnal ring;
> Ere twice in murk and occidental damp
> Moist Hesperus hath quench'd his sleepy lamp;
> Or four and twenty times the pilot's glass
> Hath told the thievish minutes how they pass;
> What is infirm from your sound parts shall fly
> Health shall live free, and sickness freely die.
>
> (II. i. 163)

Uttermost humility is maintained: Helena claims no power of her own. Even on the plane of nature, it is clear that no health is given; it is there already; only the obstruction is removed, so that nature, the full cosmic powers, may function unimpeded.

The King asks Helena what she is prepared to stake on her own belief. She has already told the Countess that she is prepared to risk her life (I. iii. 255–7) and now proposes the alternative of death with torture. It is precisely this willingness on her part, this embracing of the male values of mortal hazard, the Fortinbras values, which turns the scale. Now the King enters Helena's world, his surrender being marked by his first full-length speech in the full flood of rhyme, beginning:

> Methinks in thee some blessed spirit doth speak
> His powerful sound within an organ weak . . .
> (ii. i. 178)

Helena's weakness is throughout emphasized, by herself and others; but she is a channel for greater powers, and in that trust risks her life. The King recognizes that 'impossibility' may, after all, make sense; for such a girl so to hazard her 'youth', 'beauty', 'wisdom' and 'courage', he says, argues either 'skill infinite', or some form of desperation (ii. i. 184–7). He accepts her contract of healing or death; but, if successful, she asks in return for the hand of any lord it is in the King's 'power' to give (ii. i. 197). The King, now wholly under her influence, speaks a rhymed speech, in high excitement, almost triumph; and so this extraordinary scene, offering probably the most skilful dramatic use of rhyme in Shakespeare, closes.

That the healing is, as near as may be, or at least to science appears, a miracle, is re-emphasized by the subsequent dialogue of Lafeu and Parolles, with Bertram significantly both present and tongue-tied:

> *Lafeu* They say miracles are past; and we have our philosophical persons to make modern and familiar things supernatural and causeless. Hence it is that we make trifles of terrors, ensconcing ourselves into seeming knowledge, when we should submit ourselves to an unknown fear.
>
> *Parolles* Why, 'tis the rarest argument of wonder that hath shot out in our latter times.
>
> *Bertram* And so 'tis.
> (ii. iii. 1)

We have recently found blank verse catching fire, as it were, and blossoming into rhyme; now we circle back to prose, used to mark the appallingly realistic, near-distance, non-visionary, impact of the miracle. Perhaps nowhere else in Shakespeare are such stylistic variations so effective. Observe that Parolles is genuinely interested, while Bertram remains perfunctory and unimpressed. Knowing Helena so well as a humble retainer in his mother's house, he probably finds it impossible to see her as a person of importance. He may be jealous, or just uninterested; but the fact remains that throughout the subsequent dialogue he says no more. This is most important, and should be underlined in production: his silent presence on the stage should speak volumes.

The more Lafeu expatiates on the miracle, the more keenly Parolles tries to draw level, finding phrases or pretending that he would have found them. Comedy is used, as Bernard Shaw uses it in *Saint Joan*, as a bridge towards reception of an event so utterly beyond the normal, beyond the ken 'of all the learned and authentic fellows' who gave out the King as 'incurable' (II. iii. 14–16). But Lafeu's phrases are themselves weighty enough, and deeply significant: a 'novelty to the world', 'a showing of a heavenly effect in an earthly actor', 'the very hand of Heaven' (II. iii. 24–38). The personal weakness of Helena as merely the medium, the purified channel, of the transcendent, or cosmic, powers, is rightly stressed:

> In a most weak and debile minister, great power, great transcendence: which should, indeed, give us a further use to be made than alone the recovery of the King, as to be generally thankful.
>
> (II. iii. 40)

That is, Lafeu thinks that such powers should be more widely developed. Helena functions as a medium only; but this function is one with her poetic, Shakespearian, insight, born of love (p. 140); and both may be related to her virginity. We may seem to have moved far from social considerations, and yet they, too, are contained. This speech marks a fine extension of our former thoughts regarding the relative merits of virtue and rank: it is found that Heaven works directly through a simple girl, of humble origin.[1]

This is the girl whom Bertram, who shows no interest in

---

[1] This is an obvious example of a well-known, and sometimes disturbing, problem. There is a natural human tendency to expect such powers to work only through a person in high office, as in the old belief that English monarchs had the power of healing 'the King's evil' (see *Macbeth*, IV. iii. 146–59); or to suppose that they should act best through a minister of the Church. But the powers concerned do not appear to recognize such limitations.

There is, moreover, no suggestion in *All's Well that Ends Well*, as there is in *The Winter's Tale*, that the miracle may be by some regarded as the work of evil powers, of 'black magic': the issue is left simply as one between human learning and the invasion of the greater powers.

the miracle, rejects on grounds of birth: and Parolles, who does at least try to show interest, has told us that 'he's of a most facinorous spirit that will not acknowledge it to be the ——': he breaks off, and perhaps gestures to Bertram to complete his sentence; but it is Lafeu who continues with 'very hand of Heaven' (ii. iii. 35). Any able producer would make full use of Bertram's silent, sulking, presence.

Such an invasion of the story by an event beyond normality is nothing strange among Shakespeare's greater plays. We have only to think of the ghosts and other supernatural phenomena of *Julius Caesar*, *Hamlet*, and *Macbeth*, the inflated naturalism of *King Lear*, the symbolic and semi-transcendental tempests in work after work, the magical powers of Cerimon, the resurrections of Thaisa and Hermione, the visionary appearances of Diana and Jupiter, Queen Katharine's vision in *Henry VIII*. Some of these events, such as the *unusual* storms in *King Lear* and elsewhere, are poetic fabrications, for a purpose; nor need we ourselves believe in Jupiter as our god. But much of what happens in *Macbeth* can be paralleled among the phenomena of spiritualism; and the resurrection of Hermione may be allowed to shadow a truth regarding death which no Christian should find strange. What, however, is so remarkable in *All's Well that Ends Well* is the more near-distance, immediate and detailed, treatment of transcendence, the dramatist labouring hard to convince us of its reality; a quality driven home by Lafeu's exquisite prose comments, the more effective in that they follow our earlier poetic excitement like a douche of cold water, which nevertheless merely awakes us to the amazing fact. We are faced with an example of spirit-healing of a kind which anyone who chooses can witness in the public demonstrations of our own day. This is not the same as faith-healing, but rather the release, through a medium, of cosmic powers which so reinforce the organism that the obstructing element is dissolved. Such is the 'miracle', if so we choose to call it, of *All's Well that Ends Well*. No one who has read, and taken to heart, the New Testament, need be surprised, either at Helena's, or for that matter Cerimon's, powers. Certainly if we do not respond properly to Helena's achievement—if we regard it merely as an impossible fiction—we shall receive little of importance.

We shall merely rank ourselves beside Bertram as one who fails to recognize the transcendent when he meets it; and there is probably no more dangerous error than that.

True, we need not wish to be married to it, and a difficulty remains. But then Helena is herself no more than a medium. She is a very ordinary, if exceptional, girl: that is her paradox. However we look at it, Bertram's rejection is to be regarded as a great sin, given weighty theological expression. When, after her supposed death, he claims to have come to love her, the King comments:

> That thou did'st love her, strikes some scores away
> From the great compt, but love that comes too late
> Like a remorseful pardon slowly carried
> To the great sender turns a sour offence,
> Crying, 'That's good that's gone'.
>
> (v. iii. 55)

Who is the 'great sender'? King or God? Perhaps the lover is being imagined as carrying God's royal and redemptive pardon to the loved one; and failure incurs wrath. As in the Final Plays, the human drama is regarded as sacramental.

Much depends on our understanding of Helena as a channel, or medium, for the divine, or cosmic, powers. She is drawn directly as a medium, in contrast to Paulina whose function as miracle-worker is less realistically strutted. Like that of Cerimon, another such medium though a thumb-nail study only, Helena's miraculous powers grow from, or through, her own, personal, qualities. They are one with her virgin 'honour', her calling as Diana's 'knight' (i. iii. 122), her beyond-good-and-evil, Shakespearian and Nietzschean, insight (p. 140), her purified and all-embracing love. Such are Shakespeare's steps towards his conception of what might be termed a 'Renaissance sainthood'. Sainthood cannot be fully explained; but each of us can, in his own way, use his own best gifts as an approach to an understanding, and Shakespeare seems to have done so here, using his own inward experience of love, the creative bisexuality, and the ranging poetry born from it, to conceive his Helena; using that wholeness of his own poetic experience for which Helena is, as we have seen (p. 138), a voice. For poetry may be allowed to have functioned as his 'third eye', the expression of a unity beyond, and yet including, the male and female principles, a faculty of purity, perception, and power.

V

We have from time to time referred to the Sonnets, and indeed there are many correspondences. All our emphasis on simple truth and integrity as against showiness; on the new generation out of touch with old pieties; both in detail and in general conception, and in the handling of values, much, except for the miracle, is sonnet-stuff. This does not mean that *All's Well that Ends Well* was written at the same period, though there may have been some overlapping; what it does suggest is that the drama comes from the same intimate centre of the poet's creating soul as do the Sonnets; and, that granted, we may regard the miracle as corresponding in some sense to the miracle of Shakespeare's poetry. All miracles are the tapping of cosmic powers; and what else is the greatest poetry?

In the Sonnets Shakespeare's love becomes a vast conception over-arching world affairs: it is 'hugely politic', beyond all matters of 'state' (124); and when Shakespeare's consciousness, clarified by love, is offered its vision of human splendour, he tells us with some pride how his 'great mind most kingly drinks it up' (114). So too Helena speaks of 'imperial Love' (II. iii. 81), and is herself given imperial comparison as 'a maid too virtuous for the contempt of empire' (III. ii. 33). We may say that Helena very closely corresponds to that in Shakespeare's soul which loved the Fair Youth. And here we find another parallel. Bertram is not unlike that youth: both are handsome, noble, and in danger of being led astray by a false and decadent society. When Shakespeare complains 'thou dost common grow' (Sonnet 69) he is seeing his loved youth very much as Helena may be supposed to have seen Bertram. The young man in *A Lover's Complaint* is a more satiric portrait than either, but much of the poem, written from a woman's viewpoint, offers analogies to *All's Well that Ends Well* (e.g. remembering Bertram's wooing of Diana, 148–329; and see *The Mutual Flame*, p. 196).

We can accordingly understand why Shakespeare found himself able to pour so much of his most cherished feeling into the creation of Helena. And there is more to say. Helena's miracle is not merely a miracle of healing; it is, pre-eminently, a *healing of the King*. Now, if we read 'king', as I have elsewhere read it in Hamlet's 'catch the conscience of the King' (*Hamlet*, II. ii. 642; '*Hamlet* Reconsidered', *The Wheel of Fire*, enlarged edn., p. 303), and as indeed it must be read throughout Shakespeare, as denoting the very soul of the body politic, we have an analogy to Shakespeare's royalistic drama, so closely and continuously concerned with infusing health into his community. Great as is Helena's 'miracle', Shakespeare had himself experienced the like, using the 'third eye' of poetry.

Helena is advanced to social favour through her art, as was Shakespeare through his. Whether or not Shakespeare himself ever expected a return of love from his Fair Youth, or some other, as a result of his work, we cannot precisely say. It is, however, clear that in a general sense Shakespeare must have known what it was to value fame as a means to raising himself in the eyes of a loved one; and to that extent *All's Well that Ends Well* may be called autobiographical.[1] All this may appear trivial, and, whether true or not, unimportant. But it points on.

For it helps us to see why such vast issues can be felt bulging through this at first sight unsatisfactory plot. What is our main opposition? A sharply personified condensation of an opposition insistent throughout Shakespeare's work regularly concerned with the wrestling of male and female principles; here feminine love in virgin purity set against male values of prowess linked to sexual laxity. All Shakespeare's women, bad or good, are conceived as units, but his men are divided; here the contrast is rendered explicit, is part of the dramatic thesis. Helena is a unit, Bertram in pieces. Helena has spiritual, Bertram merely human, worth; she preserves piety to the past, using her father's legacy to noble effect, whereas he gives away his ancestral ring for a temporary infatuation. To risk, for the moment, a very rough simplification,

---

[1] For my earlier remarks on the autobiographical element in *All's Well that Ends Well*, see 'The Shakespearian Integrity', p. 219 below; also *Christ and Nietzsche*, pp. 123-4.

we can say that she, under symbolic expansion, becomes—
though this is not the *whole* truth of her—a representative of
the medieval world, of Christian faith, and he of the new
Renaissance, with no sure positive values but male honour on
the field of battle, and with no sexual principles, or even
understanding, since he can speak the most urgent love-poetry
and repudiate it soon after. Of this contrast we find traces
also in the contrast of Trojans and Greeks in *Troilus and Cressida*. The implications are vast: for this is the contrast of
Church and State; more, of East and West, since Helena's
sanctity channels occult powers drawing our thoughts back to
New Testament times, and earlier, and to be associated rather
with the esoteric traditions of the East and the various spiritualistic movements of our own day than with the official learning, the scientific, or theological, learning, of the West.[1] All
this is implicit in our central passages contrasting Helena's
miraculous cure with the learning of the established schools
(pp. 148, 150, 154 above).

And yet, once again, Helena is not herself to be limited to
one side of the opposition: she is, through love, inclusive. She
stands at the very heart of that complex of which the Clown
and Parolles are the two opposing extremes. She alone escapes
the Clown's condemnation and she alone refuses to condemn
Parolles. Her life is bound by no doctrine, but is rather a way,
a mode of being, expressing love and honour at their best. In
her, life aspires to art, to poetry; and that is why her consciousness functions on the poetic level.

One peculiarly interesting thought, to us of the twentieth
century, may be drawn from the play: we watch the male,
humanistic, values proving themselves only really positive in
war, whereas the female, spiritualistic values have another
office, healing; more, the healing of a sick king. We may again
notice that Helena, like Christ himself, yields no whit to the
soldier in point of initiative and courage: she voluntarily risks
torture and death in the cause of love.

Two last questions remain. One is this: if Helena be, as
she seems, a creature of bisexual and virgin integration, how
can she marry? Shakespeare met the difficulty, in part, by

[1] A similar contrast is developed in my article 'The Scholar Gipsy: an Interpretation'; *The Review of English Studies*, Jan. 1955.

carrying on the emphasis on virginity and the goddess Dian into the affair with the girl Diana; and certainly in spirit Helena remains throughout Diana's 'knight' (i. iii. 120). For the rest we may say that, though in our era men or women of perfected, or near-perfect, integration appear to be better without a sexual partner, yet perhaps a state may be reached where the virtues of virginity and of marriage are, as Helena as good as tells us they can be (p. 136), identified; and if so, it is this which Helena aims at. In her sanctity aspires to sexuality. True, it is hard to see Bertram as an apt partner, but this is an old story, and we feel the same about other of Shakespeare's young heroes. Our second question is this: after reading the story of so masterful, yet humbly feminine, a woman, so busily, and even more convincingly than other Shakespearian heroines, putting male confusions in order, we may ask whether it points us to some new form of society where the female values will be in the ascendant? To that new 'Aquarian age' which esoteric thought today is never tired of prophesying, and to which the feminine insistencies of so much modern drama, of Shaw, O'Neill, and O'Casey point? Perhaps. If so, Helena's assumption of the male prerogative of marriage-proposal, however strange to us it may be, makes perhaps a necessary emphasis, and one germane to the whole. To discuss such a society here, or even offer any suggestions as to its nature, would be beyond our purpose, though we may hazard the thought that the feminine, which includes the religious, spiritualistic, and poetic attributes, would assume greater prominence in the handling of affairs: a state we can, should we so choose, understand to be forecast by Byron's 'man-queen' in *Sardanapalus* (i. i), and even feel to be darkly symbolized in the queenship of Shakespeare's age, and of Pope's and Tennyson's, our three ages of poetic harmony; and in ours, too, for that matter, though the harmony eludes us.

What's in a $\mathcal{N}$*ame?*

———◆———

What's in a name? That which we call a rose
By any other name would smell as sweet.
(Romeo and Juliet, ii. ii. 43)

I

Henry V's 'Crispin' speech may serve as a starting-point for an inquiry into Shakespeare's use of proper names.[1] It contains examples of two main literary uses: (i) a good list of place-names to make a poetic cluster, though these are, it is true, personal titles; and (ii) a single personal name 'Crispin', acting as a verbal talisman, in which 'more is meant', as Milton says of the old myths in *Il Penseroso*, 'than meets the ear'.

Place-names in literature are generally more exciting if they denote foreign parts, as in Bassanio's

> Hath all his ventures fail'd? What, not one hit?
> From Tripolis, from Mexico, and England,
> From Lisbon, Barbary, and India?
> And not one vessel 'scape the dreadful touch
> Of merchant-marring rocks?
> > (*The Merchant of Venice*, iii. ii. 268)

In the use of such glamorous names Shakespeare is scarcely pre-eminent: he is always more vitally engaged by persons than by places; even here, and it is one of his best pieces, the names are carelessly listed rather than imaginatively charged. Shakespeare does not pursue a fine name for its own sake as does Marlowe in *Tamburlaine*:

> 'And ride in triumph through Persepolis'!
> Is it not brave to be a king, Techelles?
> Usumcasane and Theridamas,
> Is it not passing brave to be a king
> 'And ride in triumph through Persepolis'?
> > (*1 Tamburlaine*, ii. v. 50)

[1] Except where explicitly stated I follow the spelling of the Oxford Shakespeare, since a continual reference to Quarto or Folio is likely to prove more confusing than helpful.

The triumph exists as much in the name as in the conquest. Milton, in his different fashion, is similarly entranced:

> . . . and what resounds
> In fable or romance of Uther's son
> Begirt with British and Armoric knights;
> And all who since, baptiz'd or infidel,
> Jousted in Aspramont or Montalban,
> Damasco, or Marocco, or Trebizond,
> Or whom Biserta sent from Afric shore
> When Charlemain with all his peerage fell
> By Fontarabbia.
>
> (Paradise Lost, I. 579)

Such Marlovian and Miltonic characteristics are, of course, well known, and in comparison Shakespeare might at first appear rather dull. His exotic names do not in this way assert themselves; they do not stick out; but their unobtrusive functioning may be nevertheless important. *Othello* has a goodly assortment: Sagittary, Anthropophagi; Pontic, Propontic and Hellespont; the Egyptian 'charmer'; Mauretania, 'the base Indian' (or 'Judaean'), Arabian trees, Aleppo (I. iii. 115; I. iii. 144; III. iii. 454–7; III. iv. 57–8; IV. ii. 229; V. ii. 346–51). These are the less assertive in that they grow from a soil which delights in wonderful words such as 'coloquintida' and 'mandragora', and is, in conception, throughout colourful and exotic. They are mostly extensions of Othello's personality, with a personal reference not apparent in our examples from Marlowe and Milton, who tend to love exotic names for their own sake. Shakespeare's best effects will always be determined by the human drama.

To Shakespeare the Orient exerted a magical appeal. Arabia, the land of the Phoenix, is an accepted marvel, and India is magical with wealth and merchandise of spiritualized significance. The Fairies of *A Midsummer Night's Dream* come from India, but they can also talk freely in terms of Greek mythology:

> Did'st thou not lead him through the glimmering night
> From Perigouna, whom he ravished?
> And make him with fair Aegle break his faith,
> With Ariadne and Antiopa?
>
> (A Midsummer Night's Dream, II. i. 77)

Mythology provides Shakespeare with a fine storehouse of personal names, throughout the 'In such a night' duet of Lorenzo and Jessica (*The Merchant of Venice*, v. i. 24), and elsewhere.

Once in *Antony and Cleopatra* Shakespeare appears to neglect with a strange insensitivity a chance which Marlowe or Milton might have seized on with fervour. Caesar is speaking of Antony and Cleopatra:

> His sons he there proclaim'd the kings of kings;
> Great Media, Parthia, and Armenia
> He gave to Alexander; to Ptolemy he assign'd
> Syria, Cilicia and Phoenicia. She
> In the habiliments of the goddess Isis
> That day appear'd.
>
> (III. vi. 13)

The style is cold. Again, with a number of personal names:

> He hath assembled
> Boccus, the King of Libya; Archilaus,
> Of Cappadocia; Philadelphos, King
> Of Paphlagonia; the Thracian king, Adallas;
> King Malchus of Arabia; King of Pont;
> Herod of Jewry; Mithridates, King
> Of Comagene; Polemon and Amintas,
> The Kings of Mede and Lycaonia,
> With a more larger list of sceptres.
>
> (III. vi. 68)

We are glad to be spared the 'larger list' from this perfunctory account. But the lines are spoken by the coldly efficient and practical Caesar in a scornful mood, and the effect is in character: it is as purely factual as the list of an unimpressed civil servant. Again, though the list shows no overtones, no sensuous revelling, its sharp, consonantal practicality is one with a certain glitter; and if the glitter be superficial, that, too, may be dramatically appropriate, since we get the effect of a number of minor regalities of slight stature compared to our mighty Romans, Antony and Caesar.

Egypt itself has, however, a certain, general, dignity, especially in the phrase 'the Serpent of Old Nile' (I. v. 25). Cleopatra, as queen, stands up well against the Romans, and here again the finest effect is in the simple use of 'Egypt' as a term of address in Antony's repeated, and re-echoing, words, 'I am dying, Egypt, dying' (IV. xiii. 18, 41); or Caesar's marvellous entry-line, 'Which is the queen of Egypt?' (v. ii. 111).

Shakespeare's best successes are likely to be simple and to involve persons. Spiritual values are for him housed in the words 'Rome' and 'Roman'; and in Latin place-names. So we have Antony's 'a Roman by a Roman valiantly vanquished' (*Antony and Cleopatra*, IV. xiii. 57). *Julius Caesar* is full of relevant material; and so is *Coriolanus*, where indeed the very name 'Coriolanus', won by the conquest of Corioli, is exquisitely handled in truly feminine and maternal fashion by Volumnia, as she marvels at the strangeness of her own son's personal name changing to a place-name, which will now, in its turn, be suffused with his own personality:

> My gentle Marcius, worthy Caius, and
> By deed-achieving honour newly named——
> What is it?——'Coriolanus' must I call thee?
> (Coriolanus, II. i. 191)

Ancient Rome is itself so saturated with human values that any suggestion of it rings with nobility, as when Portia is 'nothing undervalu'd to Cato's daughter, Brutus' Portia' (*The Merchant of Venice*, I. i. 166), or Antonio called

> one in whom
> The ancient Roman honour more appears
> Than any that draws breath in Italy.
> (The Merchant of Venice, III. ii. 295)

So, too, Horatio, whose name is a Roman derivative, can proudly, at the last, claim a spiritual descent: 'I am more an antique Roman than a Dane' (*Hamlet*, v. ii. 355). At a similar moment at the end of *King Lear* (v. iii. 285) the disguised Kent, who has been functioning as a personification of manly virtue, lets us know that, even in a play otherwise restricted to names of British or Anglo-Saxon type, his assumed name has been 'Caius'; though why the doctor in *The Merry Wives of Windsor* should bear the name is less clear.

Shakespeare's only place-name of directly symbolic fabrication is—it comes from his 'source'—'Belmont' in *The*

Merchant of Venice, used to establish a spiritual contrast with waterlogged Venice (*The Shakespearian Tempest*, pp. 127–37).

And then, there is England. It is comparatively easy to strike fire from 'Christendom', 'Agincourt', and 'Harfleur', but what is so remarkable is Shakespeare's ability to use English or Welsh names, with all their lack, at least to us, of exotic colour and appeal, in such a way as still to entrance us: an excellence found pre-eminently in the first part of *Henry IV*. Scottish place-names attain a high dramatic intensity in *Macbeth*. In such instances the personal, or spiritual, even *moral*, powers seem to be present within the places themselves; each separate place is, as it were, no less richly charged than the one word 'Rome'. The simple words 'England' and 'English' are obvious powers. Examples abound. We may point simply to Henry V's

> And you, good yeomen,
> Whose limbs were made in England . . .
> > *(Henry V*, III. i. 25)

The poet relies, simply, on emotions, or powers, which are assumed; and somehow he always succeeds. It is the same with that remarkable cluster in his 'Crispin' speech:

> Then shall our names,
> Familiar in his mouth as household words,
> Harry the King, Bedford and Exeter,
> Warwick and Talbot, Salisbury and Gloucester,
> Be in their flowing cups freshly remember'd.
> > *(Henry V*, IV. iii. 51)

Apart from the name 'Harry', the power here seems to radiate less from thought of the persons concerned than from that of the places. Why are they so effective? It is as though the places have become themselves, as places, personal. We could say that, in time of war, if this simple grouping of names, as Shakespeare handles it, does not raise a flutter of patriotic feeling, nothing will.

Throughout the Histories English place-names are exquisitely handled, either in themselves—as in the immortality given by Falstaff to 'Shrewsbury clock' (*1 Henry IV*, v. iv. 151) —or as titles, where the places are one with the people. When Richard, Duke of Gloucester, refers to 'the faultless blood of

pretty Rutland' (*Richard III*, I. iii. 178), words typical of
Shakespeare's feeling for the pathos of slaughtered youth,
'Rutland' gathers to itself all the warmth of a Christian name.
But there is a personal dignity, or sovereignty, in the title too;
as when Buckingham in *Henry VIII* bitterly comments on his
loss of the ringing title 'Duke of Buckingham' and his return
to simple 'Edward Bohun' (II. i. 103). The material is too rich
and obvious for detailed comment.

We might, however, note how strangely Dover appears
through much of *King Lear* to be impregnated with a kind of
gracious power, at once an escape and a rendezvous, where
saving, sea-borne, forces gather. This may be reading too
much into what is a necessary plot-mechanism, but certainly
another port, Milford Haven, the very word 'Haven' playing
its part, exerts some such effect in *Cymbeline*. Imogen speaks:

> O! for a horse with wings! Hear'st thou, Pisanio?
> He is at Milford Haven; read, and tell me
> How far 'tis thither . . .
>
> (III. ii. 49)

Again she asks

> how far it is
> To this same blessed Milford; and, by the way,
> Tell me how Wales was made so happy as
> T'inherit such a haven.
>
> (III. ii. 59)

I do not say that it functions so clearly as Dover in *King Lear*
as a place of saving powers, but at this moment it seems to
Imogen to do so, and elsewhere exerts a strangely potent
appeal as an opening on to a wider world, on the outskirts of
the action.

In *Henry VIII* two names are exquisitely used by Griffith
in his eulogy on Wolsey as the founder of the short-lived
Cardinal's College, Ipswich,[1] and of Christ Church, Oxford:

> And though he were unsatisfied in getting—
> Which was a sin—yet in bestowing, madam,
> He was most princely. Ever witness for him
> Those twins of learning that he rais'd in you,

---

[1] To be distinguished from Ipswich School. See the full account given in *Ipswich
School* by I. E. Gray and W. E. Potter (*Ipswich*, 1950).

Ipswich and Oxford!—one of which fell with him,
Unwilling to outlive the good that did it;
The other, though unfinish'd, yet so famous,
So excellent in art, and still so rising,
That Christendom shall ever speak his virtue.

(*Henry VIII*, iv. ii. 55)

Observe the exquisite placing of the names in firm vowel contrast within this gracious and quiet speech: change their order, and part of the quality is lost.

II

We have seen how Shakespeare's place-names tend to involve persons. We now turn to the second type of name found in our 'Crispin' speech; that is, names following the type of 'Crispin' itself; personal names which, without being exactly 'labels', yet carry undertones of significance, and often of a certain personal dignity, or royalty, which repay study. The play on 'Crispin' working up to the climax of 'Crispin Crispian' most excellently suggests, without forcing, the word 'Christian', and this is why it can function so well as the pivot-mechanism of Shakespeare's key-speech in delineation of Christian warriorship; the very fact that it suggests, without asserting, the word 'Christian', subtly underlining a recognition of the complexities and difficulties involved: 'Christ' or 'Christian' would not, in such a context, have done so well.

The other personal name of importance here is 'Harry': 'Harry the King, Bedford, and Exeter' (*Henry V*, iv. iii. 53). This is to Shakespeare a talismanic name, as in that strange phrase 'a little touch of Harry in the night' (*Henry V*, iv. Chorus. 47). But its force is felt most vividly in an earlier speech addressed by the King to his brothers and also, in effect, to the Lord Chief Justice, who had had cause to correct him before he became king, and is, on his accession, terrified of what may now be in store for him. The new king disabuses them all, not by argument, and with no fine sentiments, but in these simple words:

Brothers, you mix your sadness with some fear:
This is the English, not the Turkish, court;

Not Amurath an Amurath succeeds,
But Harry Harry.

(*2 Henry IV*, v. ii. 46)

There, in two lines made of two names, we have the whole
story of what England, throughout the centuries, stands for,
or what at least we should like to think that England stands
for: what, anyway, Shakespeare's England stands for. Henry
is its personification: 'We are no tyrant, but a Christian king'
(*Henry V*, i. ii. 241).

From now on we shall discuss Shakespeare's more general
use of personal names. The suggestions of these are drawn from
a wide range of languages, and used, for the most part, with
point and precision.

He normally avoids obvious labels. Minor persons, such
as the servants and musicians of *Romeo and Juliet* (i. v; iv. iv),
the members of Dogberry's watch in *Much Ado About Nothing*
(iii. iii), the press-gang recruits in *2 Henry IV* (iii. ii) and the
fishermen in *Pericles* (ii. i) may be given labels according
to calling or appearance. Here is a selection, one from each
group: Potpan, Hugh Rebeck, George Seacoal, Ralph Mouldy,
Patchbreech. There are sometimes labels for more important
people. We have 'Antony Dull' for the constable in *Love's
Labour's Lost*; 'Speed', a name intrinsic to the conception
throughout, for the messenger-servant in *The Two Gentlemen
of Verona*; Slender and Simple in *The Merry Wives of Windsor*;
Justice Shallow, Justice Silence, Mistress Quickly—a name
which assists our reading of the part as a brisk and energetic
woman—and Doll Tearsheet, in *2 Henry IV*; Sir Toby Belch
and Sir Andrew Aguecheek—which I take to suggest cowardice after the manner of Macbeth's 'cream-fac'd loon' and
'lily-liver'd boy' (*Macbeth*, v. iii. 11–17)—in *Twelfth Night*;
Sir Oliver Martext in *As You Like It*; and Mistress Overdone
and Kate Keep-down (iii. ii. 215) in *Measure for Measure*.
But there are no double-barrelled labels such as Ben Jonson's
'Sir Epicure Mammon' or Etheredge's 'Sir Fopling Flutter';
where such labels are in question, Shakespeare's respect to the
royalty of the individual allows each his personal right to a
sensible Christian name, maintaining the balance which Sheridan preserves in 'Sir Anthony Absolute' but departs from in
'Sir Fretful Plagiary'. For the rest, our labels are usually

masked, as in 'Proteus' in *The Two Gentlemen of Verona*, where a knowledge of ancient myth is needed to recognize the meaning; 'Ford' for a man who has to cross the swollen waters of sexual jealousy, a name lending itself organically to a pun on Falstaff's equally symbolic ducking (*The Merry Wives of Windsor*, III. v. 36); or 'Touchstone', for one whose wit serves as a criterion—a label certainly, but one which, like the probably related name 'Bassanio' (p. 177), demands and challenges thought.

Even with low-comedy characters significances may be submerged or complex. Those of Bottom's companions in *A Midsummer Night's Dream* are indirect: 'Quince', traditionally played as a small and wizened old man, for one whose office it is to correct the illiteracy of the others (III. i. 86–107), though his scholarly equipment is meagre and his talk scarcely as *acid* as the name might imply; 'Snout', jingling with 'spout', for a tinker; 'Flute', ironically, for the *bellows*-mender, who is to speak 'as small as you will' (I. ii. 53) as Thisbe; 'Snug' for a home-repairing joiner; and Starveling cast for Thisbe's mother, the tailor. Sometimes there is point in a contrast of Christian and surname. 'Christopher Sly' in *The Taming of the Shrew* makes a pretty paradox of the fine and the mean which delicately suits the man's dual role of drunken sot and grandee; and a comparable paradox gives us 'Launcelot Gobbo', 'Launcelot' carrying on from his ancestor Launce in *The Two Gentlemen of Verona*, and 'Gobbo' because he is a 'huge feeder' (II. v. 46), in *The Merchant of Venice*; and also 'Pompey Bum', a device offering a fusion of nobility with indecency—the name 'Bum' being explicitly interpreted in terms of bestiality at II. ii. 235—organically relevant to the thought of *Measure for Measure*. Bottom's name, apart from suggesting 'a bottom of thread,' for a weaver, is similarly meaningful. He is a stupid, earthy, man, and his union with Titania comically symbolic, the more so for his ass's head, on which he comments: 'It shall be called Bottom's dream, because it hath no bottom' (*A Midsummer Night's Dream*, IV. i. 223). The 'dog' of 'Dogberry', itself the name of a bush, carries an equivalent import, suggestion of animals often being present in Shakespeare's human thinking, as when Katharina the Shrew is compared with a pun on her name to a wild cat (*The Taming of the Shrew*, II. i. 271), or Polonius' spying servant in *Hamlet* is called 'Reynaldo'; though 'Rinaldo' is also the name of the thoroughly admirable, though astute, steward and adviser in *All's Well that Ends Well* (III. iv. 18–42); where, too, we have another animal in the Clown's name, 'Lavache', which appears to have an important bearing on our reading of his philosophy (p. 104). Dogberry's companion, Verges, the 'headborough' or petty constable, has a name derived from 'verge', a staff of office; and 'Borachio' is a Spanish derivative, meaning 'wine-skin' and so 'drunkard' ('I am no Borachio'; Middleton's *The Spanish Gipsy*, I, i). 'Costard', originally 'apple' but used with comic or rough-house (as at *The Merry Wives of Windsor*, III. i. 14 and *King Lear*, IV. vi. 248) overtones for 'head', as the name of the country simpleton in *Love's Labour's Lost*, denotes 'bullet-headed' or 'thick-head'; it is a word for the head *solidly* conceived. Such names are not overruling; both Bottom and Dogberry have their own humorous dignity, and Costard wit: they are not definitions, they just point affinities. So, though 'Feste' suits the pivot-person in a play composed for a festive occasion, it must not preclude our recognizing his strain of irony and melancholy. 'Moth' in *Love's Labour's Lost* is a pretty diminutive; and so, for a different reason, is 'Nym' in *The Merry Wives of Windsor* and *Henry V*. No one will complain of 'Pistol' for what is mainly a contemporary satire in *2 Henry IV*.

One exquisite use of an abstract label occurs in *Henry VIII*, where the name 'Patience' for Queen Katharine's loving attendant is exquisitely relevant to the suffering martyrdom and Christian charity suffusing this noble play.

Generally name-meanings are the finer if half-veiled through the use of words of foreign origin. Don Adriano de Armado is an outstanding Spanish concoction of obvious point in *Love's Labour's Lost*; a work, by the way, which contains two names, 'Sir Nathaniel' and 'Holofernes', of a Biblical background suited to pedants, but otherwise of a non-committal type which does not recur. In more serious vein the French gives us 'Fortinbras', the strong of arm, in *Hamlet*, and 'Parolles' in *All's Well that Ends Well*, a name directly related to 'word' (v. ii. 42), for one who apes a courtier's words and phrases, with perhaps an overtone of 'parole' as 'word of

honour', here ironically affixed to a liar and a coward. 'Lafeu'
fits an old man in whom the spirit of youth and wit burns still,
and whose nature is reflected in his own speech on dancing
'Canary' with 'spritely fire and motion' (ii. i. 77). Latin or Latin-
Italian gives us 'Benvolio', for the friendly well-wisher, and
'Malvolio' for the reverse, one tainted, if not with malevolence,
at least with rancour;[1] and 'Benedick' and 'Beatrice' for
creatures of light, respectively blessed and blesser. Greek
or Greek-Italian gives us the two 'Antipholuses' suiting the
antiphonal quality of the rapid alternations of their balanced
appearances, and also the two 'Dromios' to underline the
breathlessly *running* (Greek, *dromos*) farce, as when Dromio of
Syracuse enters 'hastily' (iii. ii. 70–2)—we may remember
'Speed' (p. 170)—in *The Comedy of Errors*; 'Petruchio', for
a man of rock-like determination, in *The Taming of the Shrew*;
'Philostrate' for a master of revels and ceremonies in *A Midsummer Night's Dream*; and 'Philario' for a friend in *Cymbeline*.

Some names come direct from Shakespeare's sources, and
sometimes he changes a name for one that pleases him better.
For my present purpose, I follow my usual method of studying
the result *irrespective of the source*. Provided that exact history
was not in question, Shakespeare enjoyed full liberty to change
his names; and even when history was involved, he was capable
of saddling his Macbeth with the crime of Donwald, for at
least two sound reasons: since Macbeth was the murderer of
James I's ancestor, and since the name 'Macbeth' jingles with
death, 'Macduff' coming as a neat balance, just overweighted
on the last syllable, to define the Thane of Fife's role as victorious avenger. A name found in a source may already hold
imaginative implications and so do much to inspire or assist
delineation, as with the three ladies of *Coriolanus*, Volumnia,
Valeria, and Virgilia, slightly drawn in Plutarch but exquisitely
developed by Shakespeare on the wavelengths of each particular

---

[1] Leslie Hotson, who takes Malvolio to be a satiric portrait of Sir William Knollys,
Comptroller of the Queen's Household, offers the dual meanings: (i) *Mala-voglia* = ill
will or evil concupiscence, and (ii) *Mal-voglio* = 'I want Mall' (i.e. Mary Fitton).
'Aguecheek' he interprets as *Agu-chica*, 'Little-wit', shortened from *agucia chica* or
agudeza chica (*The First Night of Twelfth Night*, 1954; pp. 108, 115). Hotson denies
any suggestion here of physical weakness; but it is hard to see how English ears could
fail to register such a suggestion, especially when the name comes at the end of Sir
Andrew's absurd challenge (iii. iv. 190).

name. If any name is effective, that effect is constituent to the art‑form, whether it be due to Shakespeare's invention or to his acceptance; or merely to his infusing of vitality into what was a given part of his material, as in his richly emotional and reiterated development of the name 'Richard' in *Richard II* (*Richard II*, I. iii. 32, 40; II. i. 15; II. iv. 17–18; III. iii. 54, 61, 62; III. iv. 83, 89; IV. i. 108, 118, 218–20; v. i. 12–13, 26; v. ii. 6, 22, 28; v. vi. 33; *1 Henry IV*, I. iii. 175), in sharp distinction from the name's comparatively colourless use in *Richard III*; and in the emotional and intimate warmth carried by the Roman names in *Julius Caesar*.

A remarkable effect is gained by 'Rousillon' (Folio, 'Rossillion') in *All's Well that Ends Well* in a fine speech where Helena's love creates, as it were, before our eyes young Bertram's potential excellence and dignity by a repeated use of the young man's title, which is nevertheless a derivative from the 'source '(III. iii. 104, 123; see p. 142 above). The 'source', you see, need not function as the negation of art.

That granted, we may study any of Shakespeare's names, irrespective of their particular source, which can sometimes be actually misleading, as miniature works of art, as creations, made, after the manner of the poet's own reading of creation, human or artistic, of a blending, or marriage, of elements, spiritual and material (*The Wheel of Fire*, enlarged edn., p. 265). When a name is a true creation, the conceptual or spiritual significance will not dominate as it does in the 'label'; but neither will the name be a haphazard conglomeration of syllables.

A good example of such a name is Congreve's 'Millamant' in *The Way of the World*. True, it has a label basis in the idea of 'a thousand lovers', but there is more to it than that, since it carries a sense of militancy at the start and a ringing note at the end. It is the right name for a woman who stands up for her sexual rights against the man; and in contrast we have 'Mirabell', with its peculiarly feminine suggestion, for her lover. There is thus a pretty sexual criss-cross, organic to Congreve's purpose. Throughout literature we find such names occurring; as in Belinda and the exquisitely named sylphs of Pope's *Rape of the Lock*; Sterne's 'Smelfungus'; Bernard Shaw's 'Bluntschli', and many others; T. S. Eliot's 'Prufrock', suggesting prudishness and a frock coat; and elsewhere. In this kind Shakespeare is pre-eminent. That his contemporaries were well aware of such potentialities is clear from Lussurioso's interest in the name 'Vendice' in Tourneur's *The Revenger's Tragedy* (iv. ii.), which contains other, more cumbrous, attempts, the name 'Lussurioso' being one of them.

Here are some early samples from *The Two Gentlemen of Verona*. 'Panthino', if we remember the Greek *'pan'* meaning 'all', may be allowed to suit a family retainer whose responsibilities appear to go well beyond that of a normal servant. The thick and colourless brevity of the name 'Thurio' well fits the foolish lord who serenades Silvia, the overtone of 'thurible', or incense-vessel, matching his adoration. Especially interesting is the chivalrous and virtuous gentleman vowed to a life of chastity after loss of love (iv. iii. 21), whose name 'Sir Eglamour', blending *église* and *amour*, holds connotations both ecclesiastical and romantic; and when he plays a part similar to that of Friar Laurence in *Romeo and Juliet* by assisting Silvia to join Valentine, the rendezvous is appropriately 'Friar Patrick's cell', and the setting an abbey (iv. iii. 43; v. i. 3). 'Silvia' is certainly the right name for a heroine destined to be captured by outlaws in a forest; and so is 'Valentine', in fine contrast to 'Proteus', for the especially *virile* young *lover* who is to protect her and bring all to a happy conclusion.

Let us glance at the names in *The Merchant of Venice*. 'Shylock' appears, according to F. E. Halliday's *A Shakespeare Companion*, to derive from the Hebrew *shalach* or cormorant. 'Shalach' was said to be the name of Shem's grandson (*Shylock*, H. Sinsheimer, 1947, p. 87). Possibly the English syllables tend to mark the Jew's progress from outcast diffidence to legal brutality involving imprisonment, as in the scene with the jailers and Antonio, while the name's rather pleasing sound also tends to qualify our sense of his cruelty: we are probably right not to regard him as a simple stage villain. He has a well-named daughter, 'Jessica', the first syllable pointing our thoughts to the 'jesses', or strings attached to a captive falcon, as in Othello's

> Though that her jesses were my dear heart-strings,
> I'd whistle her off and let her down the wind
> To prey at fortune.
>
> (iii. iii. 261)

Which exactly fits Jessica as captive (II. iii. 2), and the emotional implications of her escape from Shylock's view. There is another well-named lady, 'Nerissa', which sounds like a diminutive of nurse, admirable for a young confidante. If 'Gratiano' comes from the Italian *'grazia'* for 'grace' the name may be too pleasing. Perhaps we should admit a hint of the quality implied by our word 'ingratiating', with its suggestion of superficiality, of being on the winning side, as when he engages to marry Nerissa provided that Bassanio succeeds with Portia; and certainly Gratiana in *The Revenger's Tragedy* is just such a person. 'Grates' is used for 'disturbs' in *Hamlet* (III. i. 3) and *Antony and Cleopatra* (I. i. 19); and there is certainly something irritating about Gratiano. Of Antonio's 'ancient Roman honour' (III. ii. 296) we have already spoken. He is introduced at the play's opening by two similarly named gentlemen, *The Merchant of Venice* being unique in possession of three unindividualized persons with name-variations on a single syllable: Salanio, Salarino, and Salerio.[1] Possibly 'sal' contains suggestion of the Latin for 'open sea '*(salum)* and 'safety' *(salus)* to suit their introductory chorus concerning the dangers of navigation on the high seas; with a further hint of 'salute', or perhaps even 'salaam', to match their rather exaggerated, courtier-like, poetry (I. i. 8–40) with respect to the 'royal merchant' (III. ii. 240; IV. i. 29) Antonio.

There are other royalties. Besides our 'royal merchant', there is the Duke of Venice; and Portia, who is herself conceived pretty nearly as a princess, is wooed by two princes. One is the Prince of Morocco with his noble bearing and speech, the word 'Morocco' with its three o's itself realizing that 'shadowed livery of the burnish'd sun' (II. i. 2) of which he speaks. The other is the Prince of Arragon, generally, and rightly, performed as a man of *arrogance* matching his title and words. But what, in this play of royalty, of Bassanio? He is central, loved by both Antonio and Portia, and a rival to princes. How are we to view him?

'Bassanio', with its suggestion of 'bass' and its two a's, gives him a certain weight and dignity. If we recall that the Turkish military title 'bashaw' is spelt 'basso' by Marlowe (*1 Tambur-*

---

[1] In the original texts Salerio enters later (III. ii). See the *New Variorum* edition (1888), pp. 1–2, 159–60.

laine the Great, III. i. 1) we may, knowing that Bassanio is a soldier (I. ii. 122), begin to feel that he is no inadequate rival to Morocco, who boasts that he carries a scimitar

> That slew the Sophy and a Persian prince
> And won three fields of Sultan Solyman.
>
> (II. i. 25)

'Basilisk' was a name used for a certain type of Elizabethan cannon. True, a soldier is not necessarily royal. But we must remember that the name 'Basil' comes from the Greek *'basileus'*, meaning 'king', and that the good prince in *Titus Andronicus*, so firmly contrasted with his bad and appropriately named brother 'Saturninus,[1] is called 'Bassianus'. That this particular name was regarded by Shakespeare as peculiarly telling is clear from the dramatic emphasis of Portia's first breath-catching use of it, 'Yes, yes, it was Bassanio—as I think he was so called'. This comes directly after Nerissa, who later ends a scene (II. ix) with the equally telling line 'Bassanio, lord Love, if thy will it be', has described him as 'a scholar and a soldier' (I. ii. 122-6). Bassanio is naturally one to complain that 'Gratiano speaks an infinite deal of nothing' (I. i. 114); his own speech is pre-eminently scholarly (e.g. at III. ii. 73-107); and Portia thinks herself 'unschool'd' in comparison (III. ii. 160). He travels with the Marquis of Montferrat (I. ii. 123), and is clearly to be regarded as a man of intellect, worth, and even splendour. His financial difficulties were originally caused not by riotous living but by the attempt to preserve a 'noble rate', or station equivalent to his rank, by showing a 'more swelling port', or outward display, than his means could stand (I. i. 128, 125); and we begin to understand why he is regularly referred to as 'Lord Bassanio'.

There is another possibility, to which my attention was drawn by my brother. The Greek word *'basanos'* is defined in Liddell & Scott's Lexicon as meaning (i) 'a dark-coloured stone on which pure gold, when rubbed, leaves a peculiar mark'; and (ii) 'the use of this as a test'; or, in general, 'a test, trial, whether a thing be genuine, solid, or real'. We have derivatives in the Latin *'basanites lapis'*, mentioned by Pliny,

---

[1] This contrast has recently been well analysed by Mr C. Alan Sommers in his treatment of the play. See my note on p. 75 above.

M

and the English 'basanite', not however found before the eighteenth century. If we compare our definition with Bassanio's speech before the caskets, 'So may the outward shows be least themselves . . .' (III. ii. 73–107), we find that it very exactly covers all that is implied by his crucial choice.

That Portia herself, 'nothing undervalued to Cato's daughter, Brutus' Portia' (I. i. 166), should respond as she does to the description of Antonio's 'Roman honour' (III. ii. 293–303), is natural; and that she alone among Shakespeare's comparable ladies should bear a name of such weighty and historic import further underlines the part she is to play in *his* cause, descending from her romantic Belmont and deputizing for the powerfully named Bellario—remember Bellarius in *Cymbeline*—as 'a young doctor from Rome' (IV. i. 53) to infuse, as in her weightily phrased and royalistically toned speech on 'the quality of mercy' (IV. i. 184), the specifically feminine and Christian values of Shakespeare's romantic heroines into the very strongholds of male, Roman, law. She can, as it were, meet them on their own terms; and she does so.

Some of these readings may be questioned, but it is clear that Shakespeare's names can be interesting, and even important, without being exactly labels. A name cannot help being meaningful, though Juliet seems not to think so:

> What's in a name? That which we call a rose
> By any other name would smell as sweet.
> So Romeo would, were he not Romeo call'd,
> Retain that dear perfection which he owes
> Without that title.
>
> (*Romeo and Juliet*, II. ii. 43)

I doubt it. Try 'Iachimo': the romance withers. 'Romeo' contains a handsome set of hints: the nobility of 'Rome' or 'Roman', the *romantic* connotations of 'rom-'; a sturdy suggestion of 'roaming', as when Leontes calls Mamilius 'my young rover' (*The Winter's Tale*, I. ii. 176); and yet, since it is a lover, a lighter, falling, quality in the penultimate 'e', countered by a strong rise on the final 'o'. It is a suitable name for a sturdy young man whose role is that of a lover, and, despite Juliet's argument, it is necessary. Shakespeare was right to accept it without further question.

We have mentioned Iachimo. Both 'Iachimo' and 'Iago' clearly suit bad persons. Iago, Spanish for James, was, it is true, the name of the patron saint of Spain, invoked in her national war-cry; but even so both the religion and the war-cry of Spain would be evilly toned for Elizabethan and Jacobean ears. Apart from this, the vowel-sounds inevitably suggest evil, recalling Machiavelli, the evil connotations of whose name in Shakespeare's time need no emphasis: we need only point to Roger Ascham's fear of all things Italian; to the importance of Machiavelli, who speaks the prologue to *The Jew of Malta* in Marlowe; and to 'the murderous Machiavel' of *3 Henry VI* (iii. ii. 193). 'Iago', 'Iachimo' and 'Machiavelli' all have over-tones of evil, 'Machiavelli' suggesting devilish *machinations* as well. If it be argued that Machiavelli was in fact a profound and balanced thinker, and that the aura of evil since gathered by the term 'Machiavellian' does him a gross injustice, we can answer simply that no injustice whatsoever has been done since, had he wished to be regarded by posterity as a good man, he should not have allowed himself to be called 'Machiavelli'.

'Mercutio' is good, as good as 'Millamant' and in the same style. Its suggestion of the 'mercurial' well suits the quick-silver quality of the man's wit. But the word's latter half derives from the Latin '*cutio*' meaning 'I strike', a meaning forcefully used in 'the thunder-like percussion of thy sounds' to denote a great soldier's anvil blows in *Coriolanus* (i. iv. 59). There is less thunder in Mercutio; but there is a strong, manly, English—in Shakespeare's sense—fighting quality of the kind which despises the new-fangled tricky sword-play of a Tybalt 'that fights by the book of arithmetic' (*Romeo and Juliet*, iii. i. 107; and see ii. iv. 20–38). All Mercutio is in his name.

As for 'Tybalt', this, with its variant 'Tybert', was the name of the cat in the medieval *History of Reynard the Fox*, of which a Flemish version was translated and printed by William Caxton in 1481. So Mercutio calls Tybalt a 'rat-catcher' (iii. i. 80) and drives home the association:

> *Tybalt* What would'st thou have with me?
> *Mercutio* Good king of cats, nothing but one of your nine lives . . .
>
> (*Romeo and Juliet*, iii. i. 81)

I once saw Tybalt played with feline suggestion, the hands used as claws. But this is probably going too far: the second syllable of his name, suggesting a sudden blow, the blow from a staff, bolt, or catapult, suits the crisp, almost decapitated, rapped-out, quality of Tybalt's phrases, matching his sword-play—'one, two, and the third in your bosom' (II. iv. 24); and the sharp challenge of his personality, as he flashes on the stage, is the reverse of feline. No: his name applies, not to his hands, or general behaviour, but to the hidden subtleties, as of claws unsheathed, of his new-fashioned rapier-play:

> *Mercutio* 'Zounds, a dog, a rat, a mouse, a cat, to scratch a man to death! A braggart, a rogue, a villain, that fights by the book of arithmetic!
>
> (*Romeo and Juliet*, III. i. 105)

'Cat' comes in last, as a climax, and is followed by 'scratch'. The reference to 'cat' in 'Tybalt' accordingly directs our understanding less of his total personality than of his sword-play.

We have another fiery person with an important name: Hotspur in *1 Henry IV*. This is a good example to demonstrate the fallacy of supposing that because a name, or indeed any other imaginative effect, was already to hand, given in the source, it cannot be richly meaningful in the work in which it appears. Sometimes Shakespeare makes a name to suit a conception; here the conception derives from the name. Either way, artistic harmony is preserved.

In 'Hotspur' two rich vowels are so contained by soft consonants that we receive an impression of power together with the especial *chivalry* with which Hotspur is associated (at III. ii. 109–11 and v. i. 85–100). He is also *impetuous*; he is called 'hot' (III. ii. 108 and v. iv. 114) and his 'heat of blood' related to his name (v. ii. 16–19). 'Chivalry' derives from '*cheval*', the French for 'horse', and here the medium of action is to be *riding*, physically and realistically indicated by 'spur'. Horses are impregnated with high imaginative sympathy in Shakespeare, as in the lines on 'roan Barbary' in *Richard II* (v. v. 78–94): other horses with names are Richard III's 'White Surrey' (*Richard III*, v. iii. 64) and Sir Andrew's 'grey Capilet' (*Twelfth Night*, III. iv. 318). So, finding the name 'Hotspur' given him, Shakespeare builds a dramatic personality around it:

> *Hotspur* Hath Butler brought those horses from the sheriff?
> *Servant* One horse, my lord, he brought even now.
> *Hotspur* What horse? a roan, a crop-ear, is it not?
> *Servant* It is, my lord.
> *Hotspur*   That roan shall be my throne.
>   Well, I will back him straight: O, Esperance!
>   Bid Butler lead him forth into the park.
>   (II. iii. 72)

When asked by Lady Percy what carries him away, he answers: 'Why, my horse, my love, my horse' (II. iii. 81). He is conceived as, pre-eminently, a horseman, and the realization is close and exact; you feel his horses *near* you. He speaks 'terms of manage to his bounding steed' in his sleep, and will love his wife infinitely well—when 'on horseback' (II. iii. 54, 106). He thinks naturally in such terms, interpreting an earthquake as a kind of colic, a horses' disease; comparing poetry to 'the forc'd gait of a shuffling nag', and finding Glendower 'as tedious as a tired horse' (III. i. 28–31, 134, 158).

The emphasis on riding and horses implicit in Hotspur's name sends ripples, in Shakespeare's usual manner, throughout the play. And here we find a fascinating contrast. Our comic scenes show us the obverse of the chivalric, horsemanship, values. They are, in various ways, mocked. So Prince Hal thinks of Hotspur as killing 'six or seven dozen Scots at a breakfast' and giving orders for his 'roan' to be cared for (II. iv. 117–21), and Falstaff of Douglas as one 'that runs o' horseback up a hill perpendicular' (II. iv. 382). Here Falstaff makes especial fun of Douglas' *perpendicular* ascent, countering all those laws of gravity which bear so heavily on Falstaff himself, the especial volatility of horsemanship being driven to a comic extreme. In direct contrast we find Falstaff himself conceived as one at the mercy of gravity who regularly has to go *on foot*. The robbery he engages in with Hal and Poins is planned with much talk of horses (I. ii. 142, 195, 197), and this is followed by the scene at the inn-yard in Rochester involving the Carriers and Ostler, with talk of 'stable' and 'gelding' (II. i. 39, 105–6); again, the horses are *near* to us.

But before the robbery Falstaff's horse is stolen; he is 'un-
colted', and calls out for it; and is later told that it is behind the
hedge (II. ii. 12, 45, 33, 76). The comedy derives from his
lumbering weight. Walking is a peculiar labour to him (II. ii.
27–9). He is locked to earth, earth-bound. Told to lie down
and put his ear close to the ground to listen, he asks if they
have any 'levers' to get him up (II. ii. 36–9). When the
travellers arrive, they have their horses led down the hill
(II. ii. 87): the scene is conceived largely in terms of horses,
mainly to show Falstaff as a comic contrast to Hotspur, and
to Hal as he is to appear later. Falstaff is too heavy for the
chivalric, volatile, ethereal values, and so called 'this bed-
presser, this horseback-breaker, this huge hill of flesh' (II. iv.
272). The nearest he gets to horsemanship is to 'snort like a
horse' when sleeping behind the arras (II. iv. 586). The
comedy is carried on into the final warring when Prince Hal
announces that he has procured for him 'a charge of foot' and
Falstaff replies disconsolately: 'I would it had been of horse'
(III. iii. 207–9). His supreme moment of comedy is his falling
to the ground and lying there, in pretence of death, after fighting with Douglas; Prince Hal 'spies Falstaff on the ground'
(direction, V. iv. 102); and this is followed by the comedy of
his lumbering rise (V. iv. 111). His name suggests 'falling' and
a 'staff', recalling the 'levers' already noticed, for support. He is
conceived physically as a slow, lumbering, earth-locked person,
in contrast to Hotspur. For all this Hotspur's name seems to
have acted as a release mechanism.

The play is accordingly rich in horses; it aptly enough opens
with the King's thought of the 'armed hoofs' of civil war
bruising the 'flowerets' of the English countryside (I. i. 8), and
before the final battle of Shrewsbury Vernon and Hotspur
discuss their various contingents entirely in terms of the fresh-
ness or otherwise of their horses (IV. iii. 19–27). It is natural
enough, indeed all but inevitable, that the climax to which the
play's main action moves should be defined in terms of horsemanship. Prince Hal and Hotspur are to meet in battle and
both are, in contrast to Falstaff, exponents of chivalric excellence. But there is also a subtle difference. Hal is first characterized, within a speech of buoyant 'i' sounds and aerial and
youthful imagery, in terms of an idealized, spiritualized, horse-

manship directly pointing on to the Dauphin's exaggeratedly
spiritualized praise of his horse in *Henry V* (III. vii. 1–44):

> I saw young Harry, with his beaver on,
> His cuisses on his thigh, gallantly arm'd,
> Rise from the ground like feather'd Mercury,
> And vaulted with such ease into his seat,
> As if an angel dropp'd down from the clouds,
> To turn and wind a fiery Pegasus
> And witch the world with noble horsemanship.
>
> (IV. i. 104)

To this Hotspur responds, on a deeper note of rounded o's
suited to his name and personality, threatening to sacrifice his
foes, 'all *hot* and bleeding', to the goddess of '*smoky* war'
(IV. i. 97–115). His own horsemanship is far from spiritual or
symbolical; rather is it again most realistically conceived; more,
it is shown as a physical desire, almost lust, a greed first for
the physical contact of the horse's *warm* body, and next for the
impact of horse on horse. Notice again the word 'hot' and the
thundering o's:

> Come, let me *taste* my horse,
> Who is to bear me like a thunderbolt
> Against the bosom of the Prince of Wales:
> Harry to Harry shall, hot horse to horse,
> Meet and ne'er part till one drop down a corse.
>
> (IV. i. 119)

Hotspur's poetry is his personality, and both an expansion of
his name. Such is the subtle contrast, conceived in terms of
horsemanship, of Hal and Hotspur.

The name 'Falstaff' was presumably first suggested to
Shakespeare by Sir John Fastolfe in *1 Henry VI*, and used with
a significant modification to replace the original 'Oldcastle' in
Henry IV; and it has since proved satisfactory enough to our
ears. We have already observed its connotations of falling and
walking, in association with physical weight; but why, we may
ask, should it *sound* so light? Is it aurally inapposite? Surely not.
Probably 'falsity' is implied also, and 'staff' might refer to
fighting, the two syllables together suiting one who appears,
superficially at least, a coward and a braggart. Again, Falstaff

is, whatever his attractive qualities, in the last resort an unreliable 'staff', or support, to a young prince, after the thought
of 'two props of virtue for a Christian prince' (*Richard III*,
III. vii. 95); and that is why he is eventually rejected. In these
respects Falstaff is a lightweight. Besides, though physically
heavy and earth-bound, he is mentally, and herein lies the
grand paradox of his personality, most agile, indeed volatile,
according precisely to the terms indicated in his own speech in
praise of sherris sack (*2 Henry IV*, IV. iii. 92–136). The name
seems to hold a positive portmanteau of possible meanings;
and that this should be so is certainly appropriate.

'Owen Glendower' seems to have inspired Shakespeare to
build from it a personality and attendant atmosphere matching
its suggestion of fearsome glens, dour temper and glowering
eyes, all softened to a dark vowel-music, like the music which
his magic calls from the spirit-world. Very different is the other
Welshman, 'Fluellen' in *Henry V*, a name whose liquid syllables
are prettily correspondent to the continuous flow, without
pause, climax, or structure, of his chatter.

A name may sometimes do much, as we found with 'Tybalt',
to deepen or correct our understanding. It is so with the fairies
in *A Midsummer Night's Dream*. Though the name appears
to derive originally from continental folk-lore, the sound of
Shakespeare's 'Oberon', with its o's exerting the effect found
in 'Morocco' and 'Othello', certainly suits the powers of a
fearsome and dusky-featured deity 'from the furthest steppe
of India' (II. i. 69). His consort, 'Titania', a name which is
found in Ovid's *Metamorphoses* where it covers Diana, Circe,
and Latona and which inevitably suggests 'Titan', sounds no
less impressive than her consort. There is clearly more to them,
as Max Reinhardt's film, if I remember correctly, tried to show,
than tinsel. They contrast rather threateningly with the homely
little Greek community of Theseus, Lysander, and Demetrius,
where Greek names seem nearer to us than in any other play,
jostling naturally with Elizabethan artisans: in Theseus the
humanity and courtesy which this hero has in Sophocles'
Oedipus Coloneus is given a Renaissance tinge. Puck, developed
from English folk-lore, is different from them all; he is a law
unto himself; or perhaps we should say that he is a meeting-
point for the rest, the presiding spirit of this magical piece.

'Orsino' in *Twelfth Night* is another name made of 'o' sounds; and he, too, is barbaric. It was many years ago brought to my notice by the late Professor E. A. Dale of Toronto that the name is related to '*orso*', from '*ursa*', Latin for 'bear'; and Professor Hotson has recently discussed it in relation to a contemporary nobleman, Don Virginio Orsino, whose crest was a bear. Bears are in Shakespeare highly charged with suggestion of ferocity; but how then does such a name, which certainly *sounds* very powerful, suit a romantic lover who opens his play with the love-sick 'If music be the food of love, play on . . .' (*Twelfth Night*, i. i. 1)? Well, it might seem not to, but we must take it into account; and if we do so, we shall find that our original impression needs modification. For Orsino's passion for Olivia is a raging, almost animal, desire:

> And my desires, like fell and cruel hounds,
> E'er since pursue me.
>
> (i. i. 22)

His love 'is all as hungry as the sea, and can digest as much' (ii. iv. 102). Indeed, Romeo's words 'more fierce and more inexorable far than empty tigers or the roaring sea' (*Romeo and Juliet*, v. iii. 38) fit Orsino. His values are barbaric. When he thinks that Viola has betrayed him, he is half prepared to kill her:

> Why should I not, had I the heart to do it,
> Like to the Egyptian thief at point of death,
> Kill what I love? A savage jealousy
> That sometimes savours nobly.
>
> (v. i. 121)

Throughout the play, as I have shown in my *Principles of Shakespearian Production*, Orsino's passion for Olivia is contrasted with Viola's love for him and his own, dimly-recognized but gradually maturing, love for Viola. The contrast is close to that of the two love-experiences presented in the Sonnets.

What, then, is our conclusion? That, though there are undoubtedly 'romantic' qualities in Orsino, yet that he is in the main to be regarded as a barbaric figure, an oriental despot; and yet in his way, fine, noble, powerful, glamorous; at first restless in passion, but finally matured by a true love. In production, he will not be what is called a 'juvenile lead'. The hint given by his name, with its two heavy o's enclosing an 'i', is a sound pointer.

Both Olivia and Viola have good names. Olivia, conceived, as Professor Leslie Hotson has recently well observed, as a lady enjoying almost royal prerogative, is a serene and gracious person whose proper setting is a *garden*. She is accordingly a natural peacemaker whose pre-eminently civilized bearing contrasts with both Orsino's unruly passion and Sir Toby's caveman wrangling, as she cries, 'Hold, Toby, on thy life I charge thee, hold!' She sees him as one fit only 'for the mountains and the barbarous caves where manners ne'er were preach'd' (IV. i. 49–53). Rightly enough she bears a name recalling the 'olives of endless age' of Sonnet 107 and the symbolic 'olive' of *Timon of Athens* (v. iv. 82). 'Viola' carries suggestion of flowers and music. Both are natural feminine associations. 'Rosalind' in *As You Like It* starts with 'rose' but ends more strongly, contrasting with the 'Rosaline' of *Love's Labour's Lost* and *Romeo and Juliet* (II. iii. 44); and so, of course, it should. Ophelia and Perdita distribute flowers. Ophelia's name, with its rising vowel-sounds from 'o' through 'e' to 'i', implies a certain lightness, which underlines the traditional interpretation, favoured by Shakespeare himself in description of her madness in terms of 'prettiness' (*Hamlet*, IV. v. 188), and counters the tendency sometimes found nowadays to indulge in the wrong sort of originality by making her a tough girl. She is very different from Cordelia, whose name clearly indicates a stronger conception. 'Cord' might be said to point to her ugly death, but such an association would be of little value. More important is the suggestion of strength implied by the first syllable, to match variously the girl's emotional hardness, endurance and integrity; and we are aware of a relation to the Latin *cor*, *cordis*, meaning 'heart'. Emotional integrity is our key, emphasized by Albany's 'Speak what we feel, not what we ought to say' at the play's conclusion (*King Lear*, v. iii. 326). In contrast we have her sisters, Goneril and Regan. The names are important. The first contains undertones of an unpleasant disease; the second implies 'regality', which is not exactly 'royalty': there is a certain cold rigidity and cutting edge to it. In production Regan will be outwardly prepossessing, with the superficial and deceptive prettiness

which makes Lear, who is blind to the real issues, refer specifically, in contrast with Goneril, to her 'tender-hefted nature'
(*King Lear*, II. iv. 174). Bianca in *The Taming of the Shrew*
suggests a virtuous but colourless, because *white*, personality
to contrast with Katharina, who clearly wins at the conclusion
rather as Octavia is made to contrast with Cleopatra in *Antony
and Cleopatra* (III. iii).

In *Measure for Measure* we have two interesting feminine names: Isabella and Mariana. Here the warm vowels of
'Mariana' play against the colder sound of 'Isabella' to underline a vital contrast; and it is worth noting that the excessively
moralistic clown in *All's Well that Ends Well* is shown as
planning to marry a girl called 'Isbel' (I. iii. 25). The interpretation of *Measure for Measure* is greatly assisted by attention
to its names. Some of the lower-grade persons we have already
noted. There is also 'Froth', the foolish gentleman; 'Abhorson',
blending 'abhor' and 'whoreson', for one engaged in the
repellent profession of executioner; and 'Barnardine', whose
level sequence of three broad yet elongated syllables, the first
perhaps containing a hint of Barabbas in the Christian drama,
exactly matches the man's intransigent nature and his probably
expressionless, barn-door, face. As for the Duke, though he is
normally referred to in terms of his office, the name 'Vincentio',
containing hints of both *binding* (e.g. in chains) and *conquering*,
is in the background to remind us that he is 'a scholar, a states-
man and a soldier' (III. ii. 158), these qualities serving as a
necessary framework to his actions. He is one to bind or lose
the others at will and to emerge, on every level, victorious.

An interesting name is 'Angelo'. Since 'angel' derives from
the Greek for 'messenger' or 'ambassador', the name may be
referred to the Deputy's office as one wielding a delegated
authority. Angels are in Shakespeare always externally apprehended (*The Wheel of Fire*, App. B), and the name accordingly
points us to Angelo's peculiarly virtuous, and probably pleasing, appearance, a thought driven home by the Duke's

> Twice treble shame on Angelo
> To weed my vice and let his grow!
> O what may man within him hide
> Though angel on the outward side!
>
> (III. ii. 291)

Then there is Lucio. He is rather a problem. The fairly pleasing name appears at first to point the more attractive, because witty, elements in his personality. But there is much else, which leads Professor Nevill Coghill to regard him as a kind of devil within the pattern and to suggest a reference of 'Lucio' to 'Lucifer' ('Comic Form in *Measure for Measure*', *Shakespeare Survey*, 8). The name calls to mind so many confusing comparisons that decision is hard. Shakespeare seems to have been fond of the syllable 'Luc-'. Lucianus is certainly the villain of *The Murder of Gonzago* in *Hamlet* and Lucullus and Lucius false friends in *Timon of Athens*; and we have the punning on 'luce' and 'louse', perhaps with a hit at Sir Thomas Lucy, in *The Merry Wives of Windsor* (i. i. 16–22). But in *The Comedy of Errors*, which also has a servant 'Luce', little more than a voice, Luciana is sweet-natured and wise; Julia's witty servant Lucetta in *The Two Gentlemen of Verona* is happily conceived; and Lucentio in *The Taming of the Shrew* a normal romantic lover. Sir William Lucy in *1 Henry VI*, Lucius, father and son, in *Titus Andronicus*, Lucius and Lucilius in *Julius Caesar*, the young servant Lucilius in *Timon of Athens* (i. i. 112), and Caius Lucius in *Cymbeline*, are all sympathetic persons. Lucina as goddess of birth is honoured in *Pericles* (i. i. 8; iii. i. 10) and *Cymbeline* (v. iv. 43). Of course the archetype 'Lucifer' is itself ambivalent, with associations positive and negative.

Names continually serve as correctives. In *Hamlet* the pleasing Roman dignity of 'Claudius' directs us to recognition of those kingly qualities that must not be forgotten; so, too, 'Polonius', though it contains the thought of 'policy', a term negatively toned in Shakespeare's day, yet with its two weighty o's and Latinized form preserves a certain dignity which should at least prevent our interpreting the old man as a buffoon. Much the same can be said of 'Gonzalo' in *The Tempest*, the name perhaps hinting a variation of 'counsellor' loaded and drawn out to match the old man's slow and ponderous speech. 'Gonzago', the ill-starred hero of *The Murder of Gonzago* in *Hamlet*, possesses a similar, and greater, weight.

Hamlet is, indeed, unique in possessing a peculiarly varied assortment of names from many languages, giving a strange, yet studied, effect of diversity with universality stopping just this side of confusion: we could call it a *cosmopolitan* play. We have already referred to the Roman Claudius, the Romanized Polonius, the French Fortinbras, the Romance-form 'Reynaldo', and the delicately vowelled Ophelia. Gertrude is Anglo-Saxon; Laertes Greek; Rosencrantz and Guildernstern, with hint of effeminacy in 'rose' and either, or both, 'gilt' or 'guilt' in Guildernstern—they are meant to be flashy names—are Germanic. Marcellus is Roman, Bernardo and Francisco Italian-Spanish. Of 'Yorick' all I can say is it fits. Osric is Danish. There may be an overtone of 'joke': one *made* jokes, the other *is* a joke. Then there is the Frenchman, Lamond or Lamord, according to our text, the name reflecting either worldly valuations (*The Wheel of Fire*, p. 319) or the deadly action of the man's duelling.

Horatio, who calls himself 'more an antique Roman than a Dane' (v. ii. 355), bears a name blending ancient Roman with the Italian. And there is more to say of him. What is he, as a person in the play, for? After the Ghost scenes he is there mainly to 'feed' Hamlet. The one essential is that his should be a good name for Hamlet to use. The name, with the lightly carried deep notes of its two o's, is especially useful in the colloquial threnody of the Graveyard scene: 'I knew him, Horatio'; 'Prithee, Horatio, tell me one thing'; 'To what base uses we may return, Horatio' (v. i. 202, 214, 222). The effect can best be demonstrated by actual speaking. But indeed, Marcellus and Bernardo at the start (i. i. 42–53) and Hamlet continually (e.g. i. ii. 159–85) *reiterate* the name, so building up Horatio as a point of reference or silent court of appeal, reserved during the action but destined to sum up after it.

Of 'Hamlet' itself I can think of nothing whatever to say, unless we refer it to Shakespeare's son. It seems utterly non-committal. Perhaps that is the point. Nor can I say much of 'Lear', though it is clearly an improvement on 'Leir' and reiterated once with fine effect, 'O Lear, Lear, Lear . . .' (i. iv. 294) by Lear himself. Apart from the ladies there seems little to remark on in *King Lear*, except that it contrasts directly with *Hamlet* in preserving a reasonably correct, local and historic, tone: the names contribute to an atmospheric unity.[1] But there is more to say of *Othello*.

[1] Mr S. Musgrove has recently ('The Nomenclature of *King Lear*', R.E.S., July 1956) noted that the names of the main plot in *King Lear*, except for Oswald's, are

Apart from the general atmosphere of colourful proper nouns, the persons themselves are cleverly designated. The o's of 'Othello', as we found in 'Morocco', 'Oberon', and 'Orsino', serve to convey the dusky-mantled and power-housing quality which we want. The Moors were a people with noble traditions, and perhaps the more readily idealized in Shakespeare's day because of their traditional hostility to Spain. 'Desdemona' may be said to derive from the Greek '*dusdaimōn*', meaning 'unhappy in her guardian *daimon*'; or, more briefly, 'ill-fortuned' or 'ill-destined'.[1] The name on Othello's lips is poignant, paradoxically never more so than when, on the occasion of his worst descent into jealousy, he *omits* it, calling her 'mistress' (IV. i. 261). After that he recovers, using it with a controlled anguish: 'Ah, Desdemona; away, away, away!' (IV. ii. 40). The finest music of all is drawn from it in the last scene, where it sounds like a knell: 'Ay, Desdemona', 'Have you prayed tonight, Desdemona?', and last, 'O Desdemona, Desdemona, dead!' (V. ii. 23, 25, 280).

Iago we have already discussed. The syllables of his dupe, 'Roderigo', neatly suggest the young nit-wit's pusillanimous, wriggling, quality, caught as he is in Iago's meshes, in descent from the comic relationship of Sir Toby and Sir Andrew in *Twelfth Night*. There may even be an overtone of riding, recalling Sir Toby's 'I'll ride your horse as well as I ride you' (*Twelfth Night*, III. iv. 321). Brabantio sounds, and is, a vociferous opponent. The name would seem to be related to 'Brabant', a place-name; but in *Othello* it derives its peculiar dramatic suitability from 'brabble', which means 'a frivolous action at law', a 'paltry' or 'noisy quarrel', 'brawl' or 'petty war' (*O.E.D.*): brabble occurs in *Titus Andronicus* (II. i. 62), and Sir Hugh Evans speaks of 'pribbles and prabbles' in *The Merry Wives of Windsor* (I. i. 56). 'Ban' means a curse, with perhaps

British, and that those of the sub-plot, together with Oswald's, are Anglo-Saxon. In the glossary of William Camden's *Remaines of a greater Worke concerning Britaine*, which Shakespeare may have known (see *King Lear, Arden Edition*, 1952, ed. Kenneth Muir, Int., p. xxxvi), 'Oswald' is equated with 'house-ruler' or 'steward' and 'Edgar' given as the Saxon for 'happy (*or* blessed) honour (*or* power)'. Mr Musgrove observes that in the *Remaines* 'Edgar' and 'Edmund' occur as the names of Anglo-Saxon kings whose characters contrast similarly to those of their namesakes in *King Lear*.

[1] This derivation was first suggested to me by a remark of Henry Norman Hudson in the *New Hudson Shakespeare*. See also the *New Variorum* edition (1886), p. 336.

also a thought of 'forbidding the bans' of a marriage. All this has its counterpart in the street brawl and Brabantio's curses and charges against Othello. 'Cassio' suggests 'cassia', a fragrant shrub or plant, recalling the Duchess of Malfi's thought of being smothered to death with cassia (*The Duchess of Malfi*, iv. ii. 223); a happy name for one 'fram'd to make women false' (*Othello*, i. iii. 404). But there seems little reason to name a prostitute—if indeed she is one—'Bianca', unless, ironically, with some bearing on the contrast of appearance and reality which dominates throughout.

In his Roman plays Shakespeare's freedom was constricted, but they nevertheless show a sensitive handling, with a fine consistency of person with name, as in the three ladies of *Coriolanus* (p. 173). In *Julius Caesar* 'Casca' fits the man as he is depicted and 'Brutus' and 'Cassius' make a neat, if unobtrusive, contrast, the one deliberate and phlegmatic, the other more ebullient and temperamental; and as the contrast develops during the later scenes, the poet uses his freedom in choice of subsidiary persons to drive it home.

Especially important is his use of the name 'Messala' as a tragic overtone. See with what a reiterated and funereal stress it is used by the heavy-soul'd Brutus when he hears of Portia's death: 'Welcome, good Messala'; 'No, Messala'; 'Nothing, Messala'; 'We must die, Messala' (iv. iii. 162, 166, 181, 183, 189; and see iv. iii. 230; v. iii. 91); but the more fiery Cassius significantly uses it on *one* occasion only, countering its quality by opening with a sharp call and a couple of close and crisp repetitions before following up with a speech of foreboding toning with the tragic presence of his interlocutor, who is obviously there for this especial purpose (v. i. 71–3). But Cassius does not remain in this mood. The foreboding is mastered. When his death comes it is conceived buoyantly, almost optimistically, as a kind of *release*, and is accordingly associated with two appropriately named persons: one is the lightly-vowell'd 'Titinius', whose name is spoken four times by Cassius, who calls him his 'best friend', and twice by Pindarus, in this brief passage (v. iii. 1–35); the other is 'Pindarus' himself, a name of resilience suited to his new freedom:

> Far from this country Pindarus shall run
> Where never Roman shall take note of him.
>
> (v. iii. 49)

The dramatic atmosphere, felt from *within* the experience of Cassius, counters the tragic action with an impact of release.[1] But tragedy closes in with the re-entry of Titinius with Messala whose name again sounds the death-note, when Titinius, answering the question 'Is not that he?', says:

> No, this *was* he, Messala.
> But Cassius is no more. O setting sun . . .
>
> (v. iii. 59)

This is the note carried on into the scene of Brutus' death. His attendants in the Ghost scene (iv. iii) were Varro and Claudius, and now he enters (v. v) with 'Dardanius, Clitus, Strato, and Volumnius'. His step, you feel, is heavy: 'Night hangs upon mine eyes; my bones would rest' (v. v. 41).

And what of Antony? He is first addressed by Caesar as 'Antonius'[2] (i. ii. 3–6, 189), and then either as 'Mark Antony' or 'Antony', the former dominating. But when we turn to *Antony and Cleopatra*, we find a change. The Folio spelling in *Julius Caesar* was 'Antony', but in the later play we have 'Anthony'. Is there a reason for this?

The poetic atmosphere of *Antony and Cleopatra* sparkles. The Greek, Greek-Egyptian, or otherwise oriental names, Alexas, Mardian, Diomedes, Seleucus, Iras, Charmian, and Cleopatra herself, contrast with the Romans: Caesar, Lepidus, Agrippa, Domitius Enobarbus. Some of Antony's friends, such as Eros and Dercetas, are Greek, and the piratical Pompey has with him the Greek 'Menas' and 'Menecrates', two *minatory*, threatening names: Menas is clearly a rough, and even dishonourable—as a Roman would not be—adventurer. Antony's ambassador to Caesar, Euphronius, is Greek (*euphrōn*), indicating good-nature and perhaps less directly suggesting 'euphony' as a pleasing speaker (iii. x. 7–18); he is a pleasant man in contrast to Caesar's messenger to Cleopatra, 'Thyreus', sent to

---

[1] See my extended discussion in *The Imperial Theme*.

[2] The Folio 'Antonio' was rightly emended by Pope. Since the compositor had already met a number of 'Antonio's', but hitherto no 'Antonius', the mistake was not unnatural. It reoccurs at i. iii. 37.

try his 'eloquence' and 'cunning' (III. x. 26, 31) to win over the
queen, the name holding suggestion of the Greek for 'door',
'*thura*' (English style, *thyra*), and also, perhaps, with its thin,
soft, sinuous and gathering sound serving to point a probable danger with reference to his unctuous and flattering
speech. Antony's main *fighting* supporters, Ventidius, Cani-
dius, and Scarus, are necessarily Roman; but that the criticism
of Antony at the play's opening should be spoken by persons
with Greek names, 'Demetrius' and 'Philo', rather than
Romans seems a little strange, though they may be needed to
maintain the stage-grouping as a contrast to the messenger
from Rome. Anyway, it is certainly right that Antony's dying
should be supported by Greeks, Eros, Diomedes, and Dercetas.
The general contrast is, of course, historically forced, since the
play is dramatizing a clash of cultures.

Antony, the Roman, is being entrapped by the allurements
of a non-Roman, part-oriental and part-Greek, culture, and this
is caused by his surrender to Cleopatra's love. That Eros
should be his attendant and partner in suicide—we may recall
Cassius' death—is accordingly symbolic, his name being that
of the Greek god of Love.

In this play the original Folio text regularly uses the spelling
'Anthony'. The spelling was normal and may mean nothing
much. The crisp, clipped syllables of our earlier 'Mark Antony'
no longer appear. When anyone here tends to preserve the full
style by calling our new hero 'Marke Anthony', the words seem
a little awkward, though 'Marcus Anthonius', used on a single
occasion, for a purpose, by Enobarbus (II. VI. 116), has some
point. But even Caesar only once (IV. i. 13) departs from the
more intimate, single, name 'Anthony', which dominates
throughout and on Cleopatra's lips reaches an erotically
charged intensity at the close (IV. xiii. 11; v. ii. 314). The
name 'Anthony' is *visually* less Roman than Greek, since it
contains suggestion of the Greek '*anthos*', for 'flower';[1] and
our play is rich in fertile, and sometimes flowery, imagery,

---

[1] This was suggested to me many years ago by a commentary which I have unfortunately been unable to trace. There is, however, no such Greek name: according
to Plutarch the Antonii claimed descent from one Anton, supposed son of Hercules.
The flower-association could have been present to Shakespeare: 'anthos' occurs for
'rosemary' in 1585 (*O.E.D.*).

N

bearing directly on the theme of love. Antony is a Roman being
orientalized—for here the Greek and the oriental make a single
quality—and simultaneously being invaded by love and Elysian and flowery intimations:

> Where souls do couch on flowers, we'll hand in hand,
> And with our sprightly port make the ghosts gaze;
> Dido and her Aeneas shall want troops,
> And all the haunt be ours.
>
> (IV. xii. 51)

We are watching a move beyond Aeneas as symbol of imperial
Rome to some new, more flowery, yet still heroic, conception.
Such an understanding may cause us to accept the Folio text of
Cleopatra's

> For his bounty
> There was no winter in't; an Anthony it was
> That grew the more by reaping . . .
>
> (V. ii. 86)

instead of falling back on the emendation 'an autumn 'twas'
and running the risk of a second 'sermons in books, stones in
the running brooks'!

Of the other Roman names, little more need be said, except
that 'Dolabella' is good for the kindly listener to Cleopatra's
description of her dream, and 'Proculeius' magnificently
appropriate for a captain of the guard. And then there is
Enobarbus. You would not think much could be made of that,
and yet it is once used with most striking dramatic effect. As
his ruin crashes down on him, Antony hears that Enobarbus,
hitherto the very personification of loyalty in this play of loyalty,
has deserted him, crossing to Caesar's camp. The short scene,
where he hears the news from a soldier, ends as follows:

> *Antony* Go, Eros, send his treasure after; do it;
> Detain no jot, I charge thee. Write to him—
> I will subscribe—gentle adieus and greetings.
> Say that I wish he never find more cause
> To change a master. O! my fortunes have
> Corrupted honest men. Dispatch. Enobarbus!
>
> (IV. v. 12)

There is a pause after 'Dispatch'. Then the hushed, drawn-out
syllables of the name 'E-no-bar-bus', lifting on 'Eno' and fall-

ing on 'barb', are made to speak volumes. They express in one
agonized word Antony's realization of his own impending
disaster; even more, his grievous sense of personal loss; and
finally, and strongest of all, a shocked realization of human
frailty. Again, this is an effect which can only be properly
demonstrated by actual speaking.

Roman names are used regularly with obvious delight
and a sense of Roman nobility. But, as we have seen, Greek
can also play its part. Greek names are well enough handled
in *Troilus and Cressida*, though probably the subtlest name-
effect there is gained by a poignant use of the reduced form
'Cressid', for the semi-Greek 'Cressida' (as at i. i. 104 and
v. ii. 143). That *Timon of Athens* should rely so heavily as it
does on a number of Roman names for subsidiary persons
might seem illogical unless we recognize how much more suitable they are than the Greek for the effete and decadent society,
corresponding to that of Rome in its decline, with which our
three main persons, Timon, Alcibiades, and Apemantus, are
all jointly, though very differently, contrasted. 'Timon' itself
is fitting, if we remember the Greek '*timē*', for 'honour' or
'worth'. To be precise, *timōn*, present participle of *timao*, 'I
honour', would mean 'honouring'. The name itself seems to
have directed Shakespeare's emphasis both on Timon's *worth*
(e.g. i. i. 229–35, and throughout) and on his trust in that of
his friends; and in general on his glittering world. Timon is
contrasted with the worthless and valueless 'Apemantus', who
sees men as baboons and monkeys (i. i. 261), and later *apes*
Timon's prophetic hatred, offering him his own specifically
bestial philosophy, the relation to the beasts being underlined
for us (iv. iii. 221–378). The name's second syllable touches
'*mantis*', Greek for 'soothsayer' or 'foreboder,' suiting his
function as one who *warns* Timon of what is to follow. Shakespeare seems to have been inspired by the name—there is
little else—in Plutarch's *Antonius*.

The two courtezans, Phrynia and Timandra, are Greek.
Why the latter, which may suggest something like 'one who
sells herself to men', should be allowed to echo 'Timon' is not
clear, unless to hint a reflection of Timon's underself, rather
as Lucio's slanders against the Duke may be supposed to hint
a psychological truth in *Measure for Measure*.

Pericles has a number of showy Greek names, though without any obvious depth. 'Pericles', though itself Greek, does
well enough, if we think of the Latin, for one who is to endure
a succession of dangers; 'Thaisa' is wholly successful for a
delicately conceived heroine; the 'z' of 'Dionyza' does something to prevent so grand a name being inappropriate to so
unpleasant a person; but 'Leonine' is surely too good for her
servant-accomplice. 'Marina' conforms to the pattern of other
girls in the late plays. Perhaps the only really interesting name
is 'Cerimon', hinting 'ceremony', a word highly charged in
Shakespeare (as at *Henry V*, iv. i. 250–304; *Measure for
Measure*, ii. ii. 59), as a designation for one who is a nobleman
before becoming a saint and miracle-worker (see pp. 273–4).

The Winter's Tale, with Hermione for heroine, has a goodly
assortment from the Greek. 'Polixenes', suggesting 'the enter-
tainer of' or 'one entertained by' 'many friends' is appropriate
for one to whom Leontes indirectly refers as 'Sir Smile' (i. ii.
196); 'Leontes' hints a leonine nobility, underlined also by
Paulina's 'He is touch'd to the noble heart' (iii. ii. 222), which
might be missed; and Antigonus' kindly soul opposes tyranny
like that of his namesake Antigone in Sophocles. Autolycus is
interesting: 'auto' suggests an individualist, one who thinks
only of himself and 'lycus', from the Greek for wolf, '*lukos*', is
apt, as in the original to which he refers, to such a 'snapper up of
unconsider'd trifles' (*The Winter's Tale*, iv. ii. 24–6). 'Florizel'
is a fabrication from the Latin to suit a prince in a pastoral
and flowery scene recognizing the goddess Flora (iv. iii. 2),
but his assumed name 'Doricles' is Greek: both contrast with
the more traditionally pastoral names 'Corin', 'Silvius', and
'Phoebe' in *As You Like It*. We might suggest that the function
of Antigonus' wife, Paulina, as a personification of Leontes'
conscience is underlined by the New Testament association of
'Paul'. She thus contrasts with the Greek-pagan community
of the names around her; and so, for that matter, do the purely
Latin names of the two children, Mamilius and Perdita. Variations on the Roman and the Greek seem to occur with differing
significances in different plays.

The names in *Cymbeline* are difficult. 'Cymbeline' itself
serves to sound the right note of peaceful and purposeful
serenity to which the action moves, possessing a softly shining

quality which makes the word 'radiant' (at v. v. 476) a natural epithet. Names of both British and Roman cast, Cassibelan and Tenantius, give our story a hinterland of historical mystery and grandeur. The mystery converges on the carefully named Posthumus Leonatus, a personification of strange origin: 'I cannot delve him to the root' (i. i. 28). He is the son of Sicilius who had fought *against* Rome under Cassibelan and who was given the title 'Leonatus' by Tenantius; since his mother did not survive his death, and his father and brothers had been killed in action, he was adopted by Cymbeline, who named him 'Posthumus Leonatus' (i. i. 28–41). The names are mostly Latin or Latinized, even that of Britain's ancestral king, Mulmutius, whose laws Cymbeline asserts to have been 'mangled' by Augustus Caesar (iii. i. 47–62). Such names (for the sources, see J. M. Nosworthy's excellent *Arden* edition) perhaps underline the thought that both the British hero and Britain herself are to be regarded as a composite, in part Roman. Ancient Britain and Rome cohabit anachronistically with Renaissance Italy, which gives us 'Iachimo'; but the anachronism is purposive, considered, and subtly handled. Imogen once uses the name 'Richard du Champ' (iv. ii. 377). The jostling of periods is disturbing, yet purposive. That Shakespeare is here very seriously concerned with his names is made clear by the oracular tablet left by Jupiter and expounded by the Soothsayer, in which 'Posthumus Leo-natus' is the 'lion's whelp', and the 'piece of tender air' interpreted, through '*mollis aer*', as '*mulier*', or 'woman' (v. iv. 138–40; v. v. 444–50), meaning Posthumus' wife, Imogen, whose name had another form 'Innogen', perhaps indicating 'innocence'.

There is a doctor called 'Cornelius', perhaps with reference to some supposed medicinal properties in the cornelian stone.

A problem arises concerning the King's two sons, Guiderius and Arviragus. I have myself regarded the elder, Guiderius, as the more muscular and active, and Arviragus as the more artistic, of the two.[1] And yet the first name is a weaker word, though with suggestion of 'guiding', whereas the other at least sounds far stronger, with a central syllable 'vir', for strength.

---

[1] This reading was not new. Dr E. M. W. Tillyard had made a rather similar distinction; and it has probably been made before, following Bellarius' description (iii. iii. 86–98). For the names in *Cymbeline*, see also my study in *The Crown of Life*.

Should these names modify our reading of the contrast? Or are we being pointed to the supremacy of art over action? Or is there really no significant contrast at all?

Our understanding of *The Tempest* must take account of the name 'Prospero'. It is natural to regard Prospero as a kind of god-man holding within his dramatic context almost divine power, like the Duke in *Measure for Measure*, for whom Escalus offers a 'prayer' that his doings may prove 'prosperous' (III. ii. 258–9). That his name, which means, 'I prosper' or 'I favour', can hold divine associations, is clear from Timon's

> So I leave you
> To the protection of the prosperous gods,
> As thieves to keepers.
>
> *(Timon of Athens*, v. i. 187)

The names of the other three main people, Miranda, Ariel, and Caliban, are all interesting. 'Miranda' is composed on the pattern of 'Marina' and 'Perdita'. 'Ariel' is a direct pointer to the spirit's function as a being of the lighter elements, air and fire, and also perhaps of the poetic imagination which 'gives to airy nothing a local habitation and a name' (*A Midsummer Night's Dream*, v. i. 16). 'Caliban' is more complex. Is it an anagram of 'cannibal'?—but, even so, its real significance lies less in the thing anagrammatized than in the anagrammatical quality of the word, as though we were faced by something inorganic, gone wrong, lumbering, like the meaningless gestures of an octopus. We may recall that Othello's 'cannibals', the 'Anthropophagi', were juxtaposed to 'men whose heads do grow beneath their shoulders' (*Othello*, I. iii. 143–5), and that Caliban is described in the *Dramatis Personae* as 'a savage and deformed slave'. Prospero calls him a 'born devil', growing uglier in mind and body (IV. i. 188–92). He is, in part, infra-natural. 'Ban' means a curse, with overtones of religion or black magic, as in Edgar's 'lunatic bans' in *King Lear* (II. iii. 19); and Caliban has a fine store of such evil imprecations. We must not then regard him simply as a primitive, as a natural being; spiritual entities are involved, and some of them are evil. The disjointed quality of the name is pointed by the way it lends itself, indeed finds and realizes itself, in Caliban's own back-befront use of it—as when the Lord's Prayer is said backwards for black magic—in his drunken spluttering:

'Ban, 'Ban, Ca—caliban
Has a new master—Get a new man!
(The Tempest, ii. ii. 197)

Such considerations prevent our viewing Caliban merely as a simple, primitive nature-force: he is that, certainly, but there is more. We must not forget that his mother Sycorax was a witch in Algeria and that her god was Setebos, and that these names too are richly potent. The *New Variorum* notes (1892; p. 5) point to 'kalebon', Arabic for 'vile dog'; and Calibia, on the Moorish coast.

'Alonso' is vaguely suggestive, appropriate to a bereaved father, *disconsolate* and *alone* in his *loss*. Of Gonzalo we have already spoken. 'Trinculo' is good for an especially light-weight jester in contrast to the profundities of his setting.

Sometimes a name artificially given, or taken, within the action may be significant. In *Much Ado about Nothing* Beatrice's unkind name for Benedick as 'Signor Mountanto' (i. i. 30) must, if balanced with Leonato's witticism on his reputation as a 'rake' (i. i. 112) and the use of 'mounted' in *Cymbeline* (ii. v. 17), be allowed, it seems, a rather broader connotation than we ourselves should otherwise have applied to him. Both Viola's assumed name of 'Cesario' in *Twelfth Night* and Imogen's of 'Fidele' in *Cymbeline* are individually and exquisitely apt, and used to fine dramatic, or poetic, effect. Rosalind's taking of the name 'Ganymede' in *As You Like It* may—irrespective of sources—assist our reference of Shakespeare's girls-disguised-as-boys to the central theme of the Sonnets.

The study of Shakespeare's names raises some queer questions. Why are there two persons named Jacques in *As You Like It*? Why should there be a 'Gadshill' in *1 Henry IV* where there is also, most confusingly, a place of that name? Why in *2 Henry IV* is a comic character called 'Bardolph'—'dolph' conceivably hinting a reference to his swimming in liquor—when there is a Lord Bardolph in the same play?[1] Why are Shakespeare's two man-chasing women, in *A Midsummer Night's Dream* and *All's Well that Ends Well*, both called Helena? Why are two such different people as Philoten in *Pericles* and Cloten in *Cymbeline* given names ending in '-oten'? 'Cloten' may be related to 'clot-pole', a term used once to jingle

[1] A possible answer is given in the *New Variorum* Shakespeare, 1940, p. 3.

with 'Cloten' (iv. ii. 184); but 'Phil,' for friendship (iv. Chorus.
18–20), is pleasant. Finally, why are Shakespeare's two main
examples, in *The Merchant of Venice* and *Twelfth Night*, of
what we may call a favourably viewed homosexual passion—
that of Achilles in *Troilus and Cressida* is less ideal—called
'Antonio', whereas the third Antonio, in *The Tempest*, is a
villain? He, like the Antonio of *Twelfth Night*, has a Sebastian,
and the resemblance of the temptation scene to that between
Lady Macbeth and Macbeth may indicate an emotional relationship. Should we deduce that this Antonio, the lonely
enigma of whose personality is so emphasized throughout
W. H. Auden's *The Sea and the Mirror* (in *For the Time Being*),
is to be accorded a greater significance, and perhaps sympathy,
than we had supposed?

III

Before closing we might suggest that Shakespeare's own
name suits a poet so royally and chivalrously dedicated, who
so subtly steers his course between crude heroics and the
subtler values always, as we shall see (p. 205), in Lyly's exquisite
phrase blending 'letters' with 'lances': the 'spear' is 'shaken',
but does not pierce. The action, though militant, is spiritualized. We are not the first to read a significance into the
name. In his memorial verses printed in the first Folio of
Shakespeare's works Ben Jonson wrote of Shakespeare's 'true-
filed lines'

> In each of which he seems to shake a lance
> As brandish'd at the eyes of ignorance.

That may be a simplification, but one natural to Ben Jonson.

The subtle handling of names throughout Shakespeare's
works is an inevitable part of his creative method, of-a-piece
with the rest. He is a poet who avoids preaching, exact definitions, and labels. He bases his work on a stern realism, but he
does not stop there; he offers realism interpenetrated with
spirituality, with meaning. Such is the nature of his best
achievements always, in matters great or small, and that is
why his name-creations seem at first ordinary enough, until

you look more deeply. This is the way of poetry: it has its
'sources', its realisms; an account of an oriental monarch's
architectural exploits gives us *Kubla Khan*; the historical
Samarkand, Flecker's golden journey; Byzantium, Yeats' two
most weightily impregnated poems. Poetry is a kind of alchemy,
and names may be part of it, as when Viola questions the sea-
captain:

> *Viola*   What country, friends, is this?
> *Captain*   This is Illyria, lady.
> *Viola*   And what should I do in Illyria?
>   My brother, he is in Elysium.
>   Perchance he is not drown'd: what think you, sailors?
>   (*Twelfth Night*, I. ii. I)

We may say that Shakespeare, indeed that all poetry, all art,
starts, and must start, with Illyria; but that it does not leave us
there. Before we properly know what has happened, we are in
Elysium.

The Shakespearian Integrity

This essay first appeared in *The Burning Oracle*, published by the Oxford University Press in 1939. It is here given a surface revision, mainly a clarification of phraseology and a smoothing of syntax. One small paragraph has been omitted. The last paragraph is new, and so are the notes, though some of these restate acknowledgements which appeared in the original text.

Though in period stretching well into the reign of King James, Shakespeare's work is pre-eminently Elizabethan, rooting from the soil of *The Shepherds' Calendar* and *Endimion*. But *The Spanish Tragedy* is behind him too: that is, if he did not write parts of it himself. Its strong action, its pathos, its family sympathy, its use of dark personal symbols, such as Revenge and Andrea's Ghost, its melodramatic yet strangely human horrors, its nature-imagery, the surge and fall of its blank-verse modulations, are closely Shakespearian. Shakespeare includes both the graces and the horrors of his age, working to transmute by a significant action the murder and revenge motifs of *The Spanish Tragedy* into the actualized divinity of *Endimion*.

Alexander and Caesar stride colossal across the Elizabethan imagination, imperial prototypes prefiguring Elizabeth. Ancient Rome was as much a stately ideal as Hellenic mythology a lover's paradise. Both coalesce in the perfect sovereign of Lyly's *Endimion*, Cynthia, whose court searches truth 'not in colours but life' and claims virtues 'not in imagination but execution'; the ideal being, to quote a pregnant phrase of Alexander's in *Campaspe*, the 'joining' of 'letters with lances' (*Endimion*, IV. iii. 48–50; *Campaspe*, I. i. 82).[1] Shakespeare's drama gives us blood and murder: tales of pagan revenge—how else, indeed, can the widest problems of action in face of evil be better dramatized?—and political anarchy. A bloody theme may arrest our attention to a number of profound truths, as in Christianity itself, but the Shakespearian poetry aims also to reintegrate its world into some person of royal strength or some lady of sunshine love. Neither may be, in themselves, Christian symbols; but the process to which I refer has vital Christian analogies. Each movement aims to organize itself into a living stillness; the conflict builds a peace; from the

[1] The importance of John Lyly is discussed in my article on his work in *The Review of English Studies*, April 1939.

temporal is created the eternal. This is how the interplay of tempests and music becomes the axis of Shakespeare's world.

In all this pre-eminent among his contemporaries, Shake-speare becomes the consummate dramatist. But what is drama? First, it must rivet and hold attention, and at once. The economic pressure exerted on a poet-entertainer by this neces-sity is, within limits, good, since he is thereby forced to do the very things which are most helpful. And, second, it must convince with a truth: startling alone is of no use. The balance of significance and action has been struck by Shakespeare as by no other playwright. *Tamburlaine* has a levelled activity without true progress, and little meaning: what would it be, stripped of rhetoric? *Othello*, without its rhetoric, would still have a gripping plot. *Doctor Faustus* has spiritual significance, but the true conflict is ideological and static. *The Duchess of Malfi* holds deepest significances, but they are transmitted almost wholly by impressionistic language or events subdued to, or moulded by, the impressionistic plan: the story is weighted, clogged, stifled. Impossible as it may be to abstract finally plot from poetry, there remains meaning in the state-ment that Shakespeare gives us a good story. This is true of the parts as well as the whole, since each full-length scene has in isolation a significant dramatic value. Just think of what happens in *Richard III*, *Romeo and Juliet*, *A Midsummer Night's Dream*, in all the plays. Things move from the start and are kept going. Action rises on action, event scrambles over the shoulders of event; it is an attack. On what? On the audience's attention, for one thing; but, deeper, an onslaught on all fundamental negations in terms of human energy. In battering down inattention it also batters down a certain blindness. The action is not superficial: it is rather sacramental. Infinite subtle-ties are involved: irony, suspense, surprise, tempo-variation, climax, anti-climax; resolution in pathos or humour; channel-ling of subjective feelings of fear, hatred, horror, pride, and love; all are struts to build into us a lively sense of action shaped by some high-reaching intellectual and spiritual significance. At intensest moments we *are* the action. Shakespeare is the voice of an age which was in love with the various purposes and fortunes of men. He therefore helps to restore mankind's faith in its existence.

Action which is truly significant must be, however, or at least seem, natural. And the Shakespearian vitality is organic through and through: you get little feeling of artifice or mechanical schemes. His work is rooted in nature.

All great poetry is in part traditional. Shakespeare has the ghosts and witches of popular superstition, his Hellenic gods, the Christian colourings of his day's orthodox theology, the ingrained classical respect of the Renaissance, the national fervour of Elizabethan England. His stories are not usually invented, and often sink deep into some historic or mythical tradition. He uses various and often to us contradictory materials, blending a spontaneous contemporary Elizabethanism with a mythological Athens to make *A Midsummer Night's Dream*, and an essential Englishness with an Italian setting to create Mercutio. The range of selection is remarkable, and attempts at exact source-tracing variously easy, misleading, or impossible.[1] What, for example, is the exact relation of *Hamlet* to the *Oresteia* on the one side and *Mourning Becomes Electra* on the other? And what is the relation of this relation to the *Ur-Hamlet* or Holinshed? Our understanding must be comprehensive. In Shakespeare a common racial store of impressions rooted deep in antiquity echo from the fringes of consciousness their ancient significances. All are used with a most delicate feeling for their quiddity, their past, and are never transplanted without a goodly accompaniment of earth. There is a fine sense of the soil in word-derivation alone; and it is the same with historic atmosphere, the British, Roman, or Italian colourings, and the stories themselves. His Weird Sisters are three fateful women ('weird'='fate') as much as witches; and yet again they are furies of tormenting guilt; while the Scottish setting is intrinsic to the conception. Cleopatra may ask for her 'lace' (*Antony and Cleopatra*, I. iii. 71) to be cut, but hot Egypt is in her acceptation of the Messenger. The greatest poets are as receiving-stations for invisible messages across the ages; they express that 'life through the ages' of the Gospel phrase; and we need not invent boats that never existed. So, though secondary causes spawn themselves multitudinously from our study, no final cause can be isolated to 'account for' the

---

[1] Professor Kenneth Muir's recent study of Shakespeare's sources provides an important demonstration of the subtleties involved.

Shakespearian power. The Renaissance was a comprehensive period: in Shakespeare, its inclusive voice, tradition is one with originality, birth being by nature neither a copy nor a miracle, but both.

Shakespeare's impressionism is less conventional than Webster's. There is little over-emphasis on stock reactions which cannot bear a final analysis: to Webster a 'charnel' must be hideous, but the tomb of Hamlet's father 'wherein we saw thee quietly inurn'd' (I. iv. 49) has also its proper serenity. In Shakespeare many of Webster's negative associations are to be found, but they are not isolated and not dominating: they are used when needed. Moreover, Webster's more abstract and universal impressions date mostly from the medieval and Christian era: whether from orthodox religion, folk-lore superstition, or pseudo-science. Shakespeare has these, and indeed may be said to use the best of the two cultures, medieval and Renaissance, as Webster is attracted to the worst. But he is also as likely to overwing ten centuries and nestle his mind, temporarily, in a pre-Christian world altogether; or, thrusting forward, to forestall some discovery of modern psychology. His Christianity, as in *Measure for Measure*, may be closer to the Gospels themselves than to any Christian system. His classical mythology strikes one as a spontaneous flowering, as in Lyly's plays and Spenser, without the bookish, learned touch of *Euphues* and Marlowe. It is fresher than those; since, whatever the outward form, the human essence is primary. Each reference is selected not for itself but to meet a requirement on other, more human, grounds.

His work is thus traditional without being second-hand: similarly, though speaking directly from his age, he is not what is usually known as 'realistic'. We shall not normally find Marlowe's metallic extravagances nor his harsher mechanistic realisms; the 'casques' affrighting the air at Agincourt (*Henry V*, I. Chor. 14) are more typical than Webster's 'rusty' cannon flying in pieces; here death certainly does not go on 'strange geometrical hinges' (*The Duchess of Malfi*, III. v. 121; IV. ii. 227). Nor is there anything like the contemporary cockney realism of *Bartholomew Fair* and *A Shoemaker's Holiday*. You could accuse Shakespeare of an aristocratic romanticism. The middle class—stressed, though satirically, in

Webster—gets scant notice; the lower classes are, as a group, blockheads; though as *individuals* any one may be given a fundamental dignity beyond Tamburlaine. Marlowe, who set down Renaissance aspiration beside its ugly and perverted lusts, who saw the damnation awaiting Faustus and the hideous indecencies which may overtake a Bajazet or an Edward II; or Jonson with his stark stripping satire of ridicule butchering natural vices for a Jacobean holiday—these deliver the goods of which it might seem that Shakespeare had never heard. And yet he can always adapt his manner to the occasion. We find a mechanical or scientific twist in certain images of, significantly, *Troilus and Cressida*; and when we are concerned with a loveless and machine-made type of man or conflict, as in *Coriolanus*, we have harsh city imagery and metallic war, the body of man itself being described as a war-engine (v. iv. 20–3). Throughout Shakespeare references occur to professions of all sorts: the law, medicine—remember the Apothecary's stock-in-trade in *Romeo and Juliet*—seamanship, all are there. Indeed, his range of reference has led to his being considered a sailor, a lawyer, and so forth. But such more specialized references do not overweigh his characteristic naturalism. Nor does satiric realism have any final say. Since Shakespearian drama is heroically conceived, mechanic and city suggestion, or other such 'realisms', cannot illustrate the emotional directions involved, for man is part of nature just as machines are part of man, and to define human emotions in terms of machines is to explain the whole through the part. When Webster's Duchess compares herself to a rusty cannon (III. v. 121) the metaphor is the more striking for not being apt. This error Shakespeare tends to avoid. Images, events, persons, all are subordinated to a vital centre. Shakespeare is concerned first with positive, normally with noble, aspects, and selects and emphasizes accordingly. Where the realistic or sharply trivial or mechanic is found it is softened into its context, not sticking out, itself being felt as part of 'great creating nature' (*The Winter's Tale*, IV. iii. 88).

The country of Shakespeare's birth is continually recalled in his writing. His poetry is soil-rooted, nature-rooted. Flowers, weeds, trees, and woodland glades; birds of all sorts, animals kind and cruel; rivers and seas and sea-cliffs; winds and

o

weather in all moods; moon, sun, stars, shadowed or shining —they are on page after page, image after image. The elements of earth, water, air, and fire are dramatic persons on his stage of impressions, sometimes with an explicit, sometimes an unobtrusive and embedded, schematic interrelation among themselves or reference to plot and action; but always significant. Impressions of sunrise are peculiarly beautiful, suiting the upward and energic tendency of Shakespeare's work. The process of the seasons plays its part. Rivers and the sea, especially the latter, are symbols of strength and urgency. The only natural image under-emphasized is, perhaps, the mountain.

This vast mesh of naturalistic impressionism is enwoven throughout with human emotions and actions; as when at the close of *King Lear* the impressions become more spring-like to tone with Cordelia's re-entry. These emotions and actions in their turn are felt as sprouting from a natural context, so that man is known to be no stranger in his world. The synthesis Wordsworth pined for is related to all the complexities of human life, the inward and the outward worlds being felt as subtly interaffective. Where images from daily affairs are found, they are more likely to be drawn from the country than from the town; and natural images in general tend to show first-hand experience and observation. Even when the associations are of communal and traditional immediacy they strike us, nevertheless, as fresh rather than ready made. The traditional is, as it were, newly discovered at every moment. Appeal is to all the senses in turn. At any moment you may all but touch and smell, not so much by definite sensory provisions as by direct metaphoric contact with that whole situation of which the tactile or olfactory image is really our own, literary, abstraction. Shakespeare may often assume a comparison not explicit, though felt, his imagery involving an action or animal not directly named, the ladder he rose by knocked away; and one such, when his more complex manner is at work, may blend into another, the real change taking place behind the words, to give us the sense of vitality without its sight. Analysis of separate impressions only the more clearly silhouettes their nature: they are, like everything else, always parts of an organic whole, impelled by a central unseen, but felt, force. So Shakespeare's language, even when no naturalistic impression is involved, is charged with a vital non-bookish energy; the speech coheres, in one organic rhythmic indissolubility, without either the assertive intellectual agilities of Donne—since the transferences, however swift, never outpace the already gathered momentum of their context—or the studied mosaic of Milton. Even the best beauties of Shakespearian verse are, as it were, carried on the rising and subsiding swell of the main flood, and you are conscious primarily of that psychic whole behind, calling them into being and calling them back at will. They relate not to each other so much as to this whole, on which their life and meaning depend. A Shakespearian speech is a microcosm of both his own poetic universe and creation in general, where all these qualities inhere.

Moreover, style varies from play to play: you have the unmetaphoric lucidity of *Julius Caesar*, the double phrase-coinings of *Hamlet*,[1] the Miltonics of *Othello*, and so on. But such effects are organic to the plays concerned: with the most startling, to Shakespeare, of all historic themes in *Julius Caesar* there is the less need of a metaphoric richness; the dualistic quality of *Hamlet* blends with its reiteration of twinned-phrases; the style spoken by Othello is part of his tragedy. Shylock has his own cast of phrase; and Richard III, for a reason, swears always by Saint Paul, who is reputed to have been lame. It all comes like a natural growth; but this does not preclude idealization. There is richness and colour. Riches themselves, crowns and sceptres, rich jewels, gold and silver, dominate over all but grand naturalistic and universal splendours, though they are not allowed any Miltonic assertion. Of the middle-class professions merchants are conceived with a glamour touching that of soldiers and kings, whereas man's mechanic and scientific genius is, comparatively, slighted. My emphases are, of course, comparative only: look long enough and you will find pretty nearly every sort of reference. I do not suggest a romantic naturalism with either nature's ferocity or human disease forgotten; nor a limited naturalism ignoring the divine significances of Christianity. But all these, and more, are dominated by a sense of natural and human vitality, and possess always their own organic cohesion and necessity.

[1] These were first, I think, observed in George Rylands' *Words and Poetry* (1929; pp. 179–80).

Certainly, whether in word, speech, symbol, or human action,[1] Shakespeare has a unique ease and grace, the wheeling of a bird, or spring of a cat, especially at a crucial and testing moment. So, though the social problems that worry us today may seem to be neglected, yet when he does touch them he says more in short space than many sermons; witness Romeo and the Apothecary, or King Lear in the passage which makes Bradley, not unjustly, worship him.

Shakespeare's human drama is organically related to widening circles of society and nature. A central person or persons will normally, in the greater plays, be shown involved in some subjective conflict widening out to a family interest; filial in *Hamlet* and *Coriolanus*, paternal in *King Lear*, matrimonial in *Othello* and *Macbeth*, romantic in *Romeo and Juliet* and *Antony and Cleopatra*. The family psychology is penetrating. Next, there is the community; most strongly felt in *Romeo and Juliet*, *Julius Caesar*, *Troilus and Cressida*, *Macbeth*, *Coriolanus*, and the Histories, where citizens may be used as choric and communal voices. The tragic hero being normally a king or some equivalent the social implications of his fortunes properly go deeper than we, today, at first suspect; and his faith in kings clearly gives Shakespeare an advantage in dramatic condensation which succeeding generations have lacked. In each greater play you get a tight social unit of hero, family, and community in reciprocal action, with body-metaphors applied to the state and continual thought of social disorder as a disease, the well-known dialogue in *Coriolanus* (i. i. 92–169) being the most elaborate example of a normal tendency. You cannot here uproot the protagonist's psychology from his communal soil: disorder-effects in *Macbeth* apply equally to both. The implied metaphysic corresponds to the Pauline doctrine of the 'body' of Christ. The individual is, in a sense, the community, and therein lies the dramatic advantage of a king-hero, since in him most clearly personal and general significances coincide. The internal rottenness of Denmark hands over the state to Fortinbras, whose name waits, as a threat, from the start, and serves to frame the play's peculiarly meditative and personal problems with the flash of steel.

[1] Caroline Spurgeon has observed that impressions of the human body in action are frequent.

Beyond social limits we may advance to nature: the action is not merely accompanied by natural imagery but is rather entwined with it. Trees are a usual organic metaphor, and may be used to denote family descent. A kingdom may be a garden gone to riot in weeds (*Richard II*, III. iv. 29–66). The life of bees is adduced to support a long speech on communal order in *Henry V* (I. ii. 187–213). Animals may be used to raise certain stock reactions of liking or disgust, but may also be presented with an inward sympathy and vital apprehension to point human analogies; and other natural impressions are regularly involved. The interplay and procession of seasons is integral to imagery and sometimes, as in *The Winter's Tale*, plot. Belief in cosmic disruptions corresponding to political disturbance is continual; sun and stars may be blacked out for a murder in *Macbeth*, but shine for love in *Antony and Cleopatra*; the music of the spheres accompanies a mystic resolution in *Pericles*. Man and his actions are felt as a microcosmic reflection of a macrocosmic whole; or perhaps I should put it the other way round, since to Shakespeare man's experience is central. But it is never isolated. Each person is, poetically, the universe: 'What observation mad'st thou', is an eager question in *The Comedy of Errors*, 'of his heart's meteors tilting in his face?' (IV. ii. 5). The elaborate equating of Antony with the universe in Cleopatra's dream is therefore a logical act pointing ahead to the creation of the god-man Prospero.

Shakespeare's contemporaries accomplish less. The family interest in *Tamburlaine* is unconvincing, and the hero isolated; and *Doctor Faustus* shows a man at grips with God and Devil, family and nature alike overleapt in his star-grasping desire; though in *Edward II* we draw nearer Shakespeare. Webster in *The Duchess of Malfi* has a strong family interest, but communal and princely references are mostly satiric. Ben Jonson in the great comedies appears to present an aggregate of isolated individuals mechanically combined rather than the close-tissued body of a play: action is invented for the persons, not of equal rights with them; whereas even the Shakespearian comedy tends to preserve the balances which we have noticed. Parolles and Ford are one with a richly humorous action, but Bobadil and Kitely are left to provide a large part of their own, keen, analysis. And because the Shakespearian art-form has at once an organic indissolubility and compact universality, all that happens within it appears natural. Any error gains re-adjustment from its context. Each word derives peculiar force from its speech, each speech from personality and situation, situation from action, action from play, and every play from the collected works. The focus of each greater whole being right, no details can go far wrong.

The stress is primarily on man. Shakespeare's universe is naturalistic: a science of elements in ascending grades is some-times explicit in statement and continually implicit in imagistic management, but angelic hierarchies play no great part. Much of Spenser's *Heavenly Hymns* is excluded. Both transcendental flights and sordid realisms are, on the whole, avoided.[1] And yet the Christian values and sentiments are often found more sensitively and inwardly conceived than by professional pro-pagandists. Friars dominate action, and love, as in Lyly, is religiously haloed. Portia is almost a Christian symbol. The interplay of church and state in the Histories may be power-fully dramatized, and the feeling which accuses an Archbishop of becoming an 'iron man' of war (*2 Henry IV*, IV. ii. 8) is as deep as that which admires Hotspur and glorifies Henry V. Shakespeare is not anti-Christian; nor even, except perhaps for a speech in the Graveyard scene of *Hamlet* (v. i. 262–4), anti-ecclesiastical. *Macbeth* reveals an orthodox opposition of grace and evil in verbal suggestion, however naturalistically the larger symbols and actions are conceived. But the main issues are fought out in terms of a humanistic conception setting man between subhuman tempests of nature and a superhuman music blending with the universe and thence the divine. The Christianity of *Henry VIII* is thus, in its dramatic, as opposed to imagistic and philosophic, stress, new.

The Shakespearian art-form reflects both the queen-centred nationalism of its birth and that organic stability claimed by the British constitution today. All the swarming resources of this most holistic period are at Shakespeare's call. No aspect is quite neglected—quotations could be adduced against any one of my statements—but the stresses are his own. He is always in masterly fashion recognizing the significant, winnowing it from

---

[1] I say 'on the whole'. See my essay on Shakespeare's angels, *The Wheel of Fire*, enlarged edition, App. B.

the chaff: not only his kings, but those most important symbols, his sea-tempests and music, are beautiful dominant abstractions from the Elizabethan world. His recognition of the significant, the apparently romantic, directions, is one with his nature-quality, since he uses mainly, and with an unswerving insight, only what has positive strength and survival-value. That is, he is prophetic. To recognize, explore, and express what was most significant in England during the medieval-Renaissance transition was necessarily to be prophetic, since we still, as a nation, as men, move by the momentum then generated.

II

The central thrust is thus positive and creative; indeed, a love. This love is both an outward sensuousness and an inward sympathy. The sensuousness is not Marlowe's. Marlowe's descriptions in *Hero and Leander* are sensuous to danger-point, and the danger will be found to lie in his abstracting tendency. His sensuousness is mental and therefore limited. In *Venus and Adonis* we have an even stronger sensuousness, and yet it appears, because not so limited, healthy in the sense that D. H. Lawrence is, or tried to be, healthy. Marlowe's poem concentrates externally on Leander's beautiful body, the erotic ornamentation of Venus' temple and the lascivious approaches of Neptune. Pictorial art[1] may be by itself a too facile way to sensuous description; and, for the rest, the poem's territory is both mentalized and narrow; and there are touches bordering on the lascivious, charged with poetic approval but with ever so faint a sense of sin to increase the delight. Shakespeare's physical descriptions work outside the sin-consciousness altogether: they apply equally to flowers, animals, and man, and do not expand the superficially desirable any more than he elsewhere descends to the superficially ugly. In *Venus and Adonis* the beauty of Adonis, seen through Venus' mind, is indeed most lusciously felt; but so also is the horse, restless with hot instincts, his stallion magnificence, buttock and all, finely

[1] Compare C. S. Lewis' discussion of artificial metal-work in Spenser's 'Bower of Bliss' (*The Allegory of Love*, pp. 324–33).

described; there is an inclusive purity together with a fine and sympathetic realization of animal vitality, as in descriptions of the horse and 'poor Wat', the hunted hare; the hound's baying 'to the welkin', the snail's withdrawn antlers, the 'angry-chafing' boar (259–318, 679–708, 921, 1033–8, 662).

Everything is inwardly conceived: the poet even imagines the darkness closing over the frightened snail in his tiny shell-house. Adonis' blood-life is felt through his physique; he is, as it were, a body lighted from within, and you get more of a real physical existence than in Marlowe's description of Leander's nakedness. Shakespeare is inside one object after another and this is, paradoxically, the one condition of being properly outside it and able to show it in convincing action, the famous description of 'poor Wat' being only a peculiarly obvious example of a general sympathy. In *Venus and Adonis* and *The Rape of Lucrece* Shakespeare gets his main poles of reference clear, his later intensities of love and evil being already implicit. The subjectively conceived agony of Venus predicts the later tragedies, and a study of *Venus and Adonis* alone reveals the psychological centre of Shakespeare's work: a love which, though powerfully physical, is not merely a lust; a vital identification rather than a confined sense-suggestion of eye or touch, as in Marlowe's Leander; and this not limited to the beautiful, and thence by a rebound to the ugly, as in the plays of Marlowe, but dispassionately universal. Exact differentiation is hard, since every one of the opposite qualities is contained: lust, sense-perception, beauty. The difference is one of inclusion. All is so trusted, as Marlowe seldom trusts, that each object expands, dissolves, into a universal particularity where inward and outward are not distinct; and this is perhaps what the Gospels mean by being 'pure in heart'. Thence everything becomes sacramental. The difference is analogous to that between marriage-love and flirtation, between a dynamic adventure and a static enjoyment. Shakespeare is continually *married* to whatever he is treating, accepting it as itself and as a whole. His animals and people are thus neither ideal nor realistic, but real; the vital principle of each is apprehended and their actions therefore powerful.

This integrity is a matter not of unique instincts but rather of an orderly arrangement of a kind which cannot be achieved whilst a sin-sense of the Marlovian type blots the actual with a fear. It might be rash to press any charge against so beautiful a work as *Hero and Leander*, but the nature of the difference will be clearer if we take a wider field of inspection. There are passages in both Marlowe's *Edward II* and Greene's *James IV* where schemes are laid to influence an idle king with sensuous and artistic delights; there is a set-piece of Renaissance exuberance concerning delights offered to a lady in *James IV*, associated with callous wrong; there are the Helen and Homer passages in *Doctor Faustus* related to moral damnation; and we have Jonson's satire on Sir Epicure Mammon's projected sensuous pleasures. There is nothing of this in Shakespeare. Positive impressions are never impregnated with an admittedly evil force or association; except, indeed, for Claudius in *Hamlet*, where the problem is clearly faced and a necessary part of the conception. The induction to *The Taming of the Shrew* has passages of the kind with no shred of evil suggestion, and we find them expanded through the early acts of *Timon of Athens* with a similar, and even more powerful, impact of essential good, their critic being, significantly, the puritanical Apemantus. Natural human pleasure such as good food and fine clothes are, unless foreign fashions are the comic argument, creative forces. Consider Katharina's punishment: not to eat, not to have pretty clothes. On such fundamental simplicities the Shakespearian imagination works, echoing the Gospels. Shakespeare's greater works use feasting, child-symbols, sex-impressions with a fine integrity. His villains tend to the puritanical: deformed Richard sneers at the 'lascivious'—a word entirely dependent on the sin-morality sex-complex— pleasures denied him; Iago is a Manichean moralist worse than Bosola; Lucio in *Measure for Measure* is as much a study in puritanism gone wrong as vice gone right. Shakespeare can present wicked lust with evil tonings, as in *The Rape of Lucrece*; laugh at it in *The Merry Wives of Windsor*; can cram his pages with sex-neurosis; and point a moral in *King Lear*. But there is a central artistic sanity never disturbed which prevents his presenting with positive tonings an evil which he distrusts or distrusting as evil any essence demanding positive associations. His metaphysic and ethic ultimately obey rather than dictate to imaginative law. A speech of Tamora in *Titus Andronicus*

(II. iii. 10–29) is, I think, the only possible exception. Shakespeare's finest 'set-piece' of the kind which we are discussing is the description of Cleopatra on Cydnus; and notice how, and at what supreme moment in his work's development, this occurs. Though *Antony and Cleopatra* is almost an expansion of Spenser's Bower of Bliss, since in both soldierly honour is shown as disgraced by a sensuous fascination, and though there may be disgrace, yet nevertheless the disgrace, if it be one, is shared by forces of nature beyond personal failings. A vital and energic principle is touched which releases power: Shakespeare exploits the dynamic within an experience which if static, when limited, as in Spenser's Bower of Bliss, to the visual-sensuous in abstraction, is immoral. Such vital recognition renders the creation of a Falstaff possible, the humour of Falstaff being ultimately dependent on a simple, yet deep, recognition of ultimate physical being. Falstaff is a precise and universal *embodiment*. He is himself humour, and his weakest wit more significant than the brilliances of lesser creations. He is always, in one grand sense, right, his 'honour' speech (*1 Henry IV*, v. i. 128–43) serving as an approach to a conception formulated in deadly poetic earnest two hundred years later by Byron. Jonson, who freezes himself in firmly on the other side of puritanism, knows where he is, as Marlowe does not, and his comedy is therefore satiric: the ruling ethical direction of his mind forbade the Shakespearian sympathy, and therefore power.

The originating source of such creation should be already, in its general nature, clear. If one were to press for a personal and less valuable deduction there is some evidence. The Sonnets express a tortured heterosexual desire and idealize a homosexual love. *Venus and Adonis*, more likely to be in this sense revealing than any play, is written from the woman's view and the sensuous attractiveness is all male. *The Two Gentlemen of Verona* celebrates the victory of a masculine friendship over sexual love; and the Antonio-Sebastian drama in *Twelfth Night* is a miniature *Othello*. Antonio in *The Merchant of Venice* loves Bassanio as warmly as does Portia, and indeed their loves are once finely compared by Antonio, with perhaps a touch of jealousy (IV. i. 277–8); and we feel that everyone would be most uncomfortable were a wife, instead of ships, found for him at the end. It has been suggested that Mercutio was in love with Romeo, which might explain much, including both his love-ridicule and flare-up at the word 'consort' (*Romeo and Juliet*, III. i. 49). Cassius is a fervent lover: of Brutus, of Titinius. *Timon of Athens*, a play whose artistic cumbersomeness joined to titanic power might well present an imperfectly objectified experience, displays a universal love of man to men with, outside the dance, no feminine persons except, significantly, two prostitutes.[1] The one play which seems to need a key which we have not got, *All's Well that Ends Well*, dramatizes a woman's terrifically sincere tracking down of a young man; and an obscure speech of Helena (I. i. 181–92) goes nearer than anything in Shakespeare to characterize the sweet, almost feminine, abandon, the seeing into persons and forces generally, which is the essence of Shakespeare's art.[2] The admiration of masculine action and the heavy stress on loyalty throughout, as in Enobarbus, might derive from some especially fiery centre of a man-to-man love or admiration. Such a tendency would be for the most part expressed dramatically in heterosexual terms, whereas a normal nature would scarcely have left these hints. The boys who turn out to be girls in many of the plots may be in this regard deeply significant. Of course, 'lover' to an Elizabethan can denote a relationship at once less than sexual and more than friendly, and the Sonnets probably reflect a complex of love and social worship similar to that of love and allegiance in *Endimion* which we, in a less aristocratic and royalistic age, cannot quite understand. I have no desire to stress a point which some might find disconcerting. There is, however, further evidence of what might be called a 'bisexual' temperament, as I shall shortly indicate. But whatever the personal facts there is no unhealthiness; by which I do not mean no perversions. Rather the reverse: a nature not afraid of, and serenely able to create from, whatever so-called perversions it possesses. Sadism, such as you get in *Hassan*,[3]

---

[1] The psychology of Shakespeare's hero might be called an expansion from Plutarch's brief account of Timon in his life of Marcus Antonius.

[2] The thought here provides the needed 'key', which was subsequently used to make my essay on *All's Well that Ends Well*.

[3] No adverse criticism of this fine play is intended. See my article on it in *The Wind and the Rain*, Winter, 1944.

is quite absent, since cruelty is not presented with pleasing associations. The whipping incident in *Antony and Cleopatra* is precisely used to meet a correct demand, nor do the horrors of *Titus Andronicus* or eye-gouging in *King Lear* come under the meaning of the term.

The first half of Shakespeare's work concentrates on two primary emotional positives: (i) the normal romance interest of human love, and (ii) royalty, with especial reference to martial action. Both are approached with a profundity too easily missed. The two are related imagistically as eros-charged symbols: love may be compared to a kingly presence (pp. 66, 275), and both love and kings are associated with the sun, repeating age-old religious associations.

Shakespeare's love-understanding goes deeper than Lyly's, with emotions more rounded and convincing. The Comedies have deep tragedy-contacts and smiles play through tears. *A Midsummer Night's Dream* has nightmare fears, and *Twelfth Night* a melodic pathos. In *As You Like It* melancholy and bitter satire, as in Jacques' speech on the Seven Ages of Man (II. vii. 139–66), are interspaced with happiness, all toning with the shadowed glades of the forest to make a dappled world. Feste is a wistful figure, so is Touchstone, and both are deep, some-times trenchant, thinkers. But most depends on the heroines. They are sunshine, laughing women in touch with a wisdom and happy mockery unknown to men. They are conceived as superior beings, with Christian sympathies, able to teach their men like children, as at the conclusion of *Love's Labour's Lost*; or to right the plot gone wrong through masculine error as in *The Merchant of Venice*. Both Rosalind and Viola show a maturity of love, almost maternal in wisdom, yet paradoxically half on the brink of tears, sunshine and rain together as in Cordelia (*King Lear*, IV. iii. 20), which contrasts with the more gaudy passions and petulant jealousies of the men. Of Venus and Helena we have already spoken. Shakespeare shows a less inward sympathy for masculine love. Orlando, Orsino, Bassanio, and Romeo are, as lovers, weak, often rhetorical, figures compared with their ladies. What actor of Romeo has not felt instinctively that something, not all his own fault, has gone wrong during the Balcony Scene? Yet again, when tragedy thickens, what Romeo can fail to gain a new lease of life? Shakespeare's men become grandly and purposively tragic as his women do not. Then at once he is within them. They endure conflicts unknown to the singly purposeful heroines, and the specifically tragic resolution is theirs. Compare Romeo's death with Juliet's, Othello's with Desdemona's. The women may be allowed to show fear (p. 134), but not the men, except in face of the supernatural, and then only temporarily. The greatest of his women miss *tragic* stature at their end: Lady Macbeth dwindles off somnambulistically, and Cleopatra inverts death to life. Even Queen Katharine's end is rather weak in self-pity. Compare Romeo's set purpose in the tomb; the grandeur of Lear and Timon; the almost heroic self-pitying, because less than self-condemnation, of Othello and Macbeth; the noble reserve of Buckingham and Wolsey. Shakespeare is most within his men when tragedy overcomes them, lending them strength to overcome tragedy.

Yet he is not really then so much inside his heroes as inside the whole ritualistically conceived tragic sacrifice of which normally men are the protagonists. This sacrifice, in its reversal of material action, might again be called feminine. Those heroes Shakespeare seems most 'within' for a long period, such as Richard II and Hamlet, tend to the philosophic and the feminine, the death-shadowed. And yet the word 'within' begs the question, since it is really we who feel ourselves 'within' certain sorts of writing, and not others: finally, love and death are bound to hold a subjective appeal over fine action. In making women strongest in love and men in action, Shakespeare is the voice for a deep truth. But in tragedy you get a union, and so we have the eternal marriage and archetypal sacrifice of Cleopatra's self-immolation for Antony, a woman at once becoming and conquering that whole destiny whose maternal presence encloses earlier heroes. We can hazard at least this: a certain feminine or masculine-subjective strain, in Shakespeare, or in us, or, still better, in creation, is to be associated with love and death; a certain masculinity with action of a more superficial sort. These wrestle for mastery. Full of action as Shakespeare's stage is, it yet continually works to transmute action to a peace. That peace is in his heroines from the beginning: notice how the women in *Richard III*, *King John*, *Richard II*, *Henry IV*, and *Julius Caesar* suffer from

man's political conflicts, sometimes pathetic, sometimes de-
nouncing, as from a deeper wisdom, man's schoolboy quarrels;
and how the heroines of the later plays, Ophelia, Desdemona,
Cordelia, Hermione, Imogen, Queen Katharine, suffer instead
from man's psychological conflicts. Moreover, ultimate forces
of evil and love, negative and positive, flow most directly from
two women, Lady Macbeth and Cleopatra. These tap, without
conflict, the universal energy, good or evil, as the men do not.
The sunshine fun and deep unrhetorical love of his ladies
suggest, as does also the humour of Falstaff, some universal
force beyond man's philosophy or ethic. Shakespeare's three
most rounded and complex figures are Falstaff, Hamlet, and
Cleopatra: the non-ethical mountain of fleshly enjoyment and
keen satire on all manly ideals and action; the figure of man
and all his problems shadowed by the mothering nearness of
death; and woman in her unmoral, cosmic fascination, over-
arching empires and transmuting death to life. Within the
dramas feminine love is, like that of Shakespeare himself in
the Sonnets, the 'star to every wandering bark', unshaken
by tempests (Sonnet 116). It is a deep, unlustful, marriage-
consciousness: witness Katharina the Shrew's final speech on
marriage; or Portia's equally lovely surrender to Bassanio. I
emphasize the deep conception of marriage here: it is implicit
in Shakespeare's drawing of the snail (p. 216); a perception of
the self-hood's integrity, its inward music. There is a metaphysical depth, a totally non-moralizing yet Christian profundity about it. I point again to Helena's 'Not my virginity
yet . . .' (*All's Well that Ends Well*, i. i. 181–92).

It is the same with Shakespeare's more masculine themes.
There is any amount of nobility, but not tinsel glitter, in his
perception of soldiership or kings. Kingship is presented as a
burden. Kings may be saintly as Henry VI, villainous as
Richard III, weak as Richard II, practical as Henry V: all are
human individuals as well as sacred symbols. Indeed, the
dualism of sacred office and human character is, especially in
Richard II, pregnant, the balance struck dramatically forecast-
ing the balance of constitution and monarchy which England
enjoys today. From the poetic rhapsodies on divine authority
in *Richard II* we pass to problems of political order in *Henry IV*,
and so on to the all-but-perfect king *Henry V*, where kingship

functions in direct alignment with both religion and comrade-ship. Outwardly Shakespeare's world is often intensely selec-tive, if you like romantic, as in his sublimation of soldierly valour and honour, but his inward realism is unmatched. There is no superficial sense of glory such as we find in *Tamburlaine*. Shakespeare's mind is married to, while Marlowe has an affair with, valour, honour, kingship; he takes each and all for better or worse with their rooted tentacular relationships, sins, and responsibilities. So kings are conceived tragically. The three burdened soliloquies of Henry VI, Henry IV, and Henry V might be said to reflect the spiritual royalty of Shakespeare's mind; since he too aims to hold vast conflicting forces in a peaceful balance. Himself a king of one sort, he sees and feels into kingship of another. Indeed, kingship is always a dramatic intensification of personality, raising to the highest power the wider significances inhering in all men. The king is the objectified super-self of each subject, from ancient ritual to modern times holding an especially dramatic office. So Shakespeare's kings have an inward dignity and the sequence of their stories an epic, if tragic, power which we find nowhere else in our literature. In them there beats, as a heart in a body, a deep romantic yet spiritual perception, reaching to the inward music of man and community alike.

Having so felt into the essence, Shakespeare recreates the externals with full yet never assertive splendour; having recog-nized the suffering passivity in all things, he can infuse into them the energies of action. The rough English type of a Faulconbridge is as typical as Richard II. Shakespeare's martial splendours and kingly sceptres, his deeds of turmoil and battle, never appear materialistic, since they are fed from deeper levels. Any one person or event, as we saw with any one image, is a provisional expression only, pointing to a greater whole. As before, we are drawn to think of a rather feminine nature, yet only in the sense that Christ might be called 'feminine', because cosmic, in comparison with Alexander or Caesar: in other words, creative. Whatever it be, this love gives us an exposition of princely action and communal insight which levels all other English poets but Byron on the plain beneath, their differences unnoticed, and charges the Shakespearian stage with ever new creative significance, working not from the outside, but from the inner springs. Again, the inwardness is one with the objectivity; the feminine strain in man's nature being the condition, paradoxically, of any masculine achievement that shall last. So passive and active blend. Henry V, the hero-king, must be apprenticed, not to arms, but to the satiric humour of a Falstaff. Shakespeare is the poet of national action not deceived by its surface glory; the prophet of kingship never forgetting the pygmy stature of kings; the poet of active life, remembering death. The working out of this sequence leading to the accomplishment of Tudor supremacy was a task far greater than is usually supposed, dependent on a unique insight into social forces, in order and disorder alike, and a central honesty of love, human and thence national, intrinsically outside the range of any other poet of his, or our, day. Shakespeare writes, as it were, the Old Testament of the Elizabethan age; and, alone joining perfectly 'letters with lances', shows the slow resolution of discordances towards that high, if temporary, harmony of which his own art is the sovereign flower.

If Shakespeare's kings are men, so all his men are, in their way, kings.[1] All are conceived with native force, direction, and wholeness. Each, with whatever faults, asserts himself in his own right. Hotspur is typical. Bottom has his own royalty, and the humour which he radiates is one with our recognition of it, as when we enjoy his boldness before Theseus. When Shakespeare comes near ridicule, as with Malvolio—and we may observe that excessive puritanism is here in question— the man's dignity is handed back at the end, with a fine exit. Shakespeare's humour is eminently sympathetic. Parolles, his braggadocio ludicrously exposed, remarks to himself that, if his heart were great, it would crack; but it is not, so 'simply the thing I am shall make me live' (*All's Well that Ends Well*, IV. iii. 373). Each, however dishonourable, is himself, and neither man nor God can take that from him. Autolycus needs no advertisement: the humour is one with our admiration. So, too, with the protagonist villains: Aaron and Iago, the worst, do not repent, and they at least have the virtue of consistency.

---

[1] The tendency can even lead to the attribution of royalty to persons with no right to it. See my remarks on Antonio in *The Merchant of Venice* and Olivia in *Twelfth Night* (pp. 176, 186).

The villainy of Richard III is subtly motivated in terms of inferiority, and his integrity, though weakened during the Ghost scene, is magnificently recaptured; while Shylock is in danger not of despisal but of excessive sentiment. At the extreme Caliban has *spiritual* dignity. The poet sees each, not perhaps precisely as he sees himself, since rationally one may be seriously deluded about oneself, but with an objective conception taking into full account all subjective and emotional profundities. He knows all men with that sympathy which each feels for himself. To complain of Shakespeare's aristocratic sympathies and lack of interest in other social strata would be superficial; whenever he is dealing with an individual from another class—and he has little interest in men in the mass except through symbolisms of order or kings—he crowns him before our eyes; as, for example, with the gravedigger who outwits Shakespeare's most profound hero, Hamlet, with a profundity; or the Messenger's 'I have done my duty' (II. v. 88) in contrast to the childish petulance of his most showily regal figure, in *Antony and Cleopatra*.

His fondness for kings and dukes is one with his fondness for lovers. The equating of kingship with successful love occurs throughout the Sonnets; and it is, indeed, a universal association. Aristocratic themes are used partly as the cinema today shows the heroine in a fine dress; and what hard worker, having paid for a seat, would wish it otherwise? Shakespeare exploits dramatically the kingship in every man, as, indeed, does the kingly office itself, being a communal possession. Therefore his greater heroes are not 'characters' known as we know acquaintances, but aspects of our own, kingly, selves; just as his love-themes are our own fine love-affairs, not the rather silly business of our neighbours. Such identification is the quintessence of the properly dramatic. A significant moment occurs between Falstaff and Doll Tearsheet: from a sordid background, with a fat drunkard and a prostitute as principals, and a few prose utterances, is created a romantic intensity in comparison with which Milton's Eden pales. Why? Falstaff and Doll may seem very different from a Romeo and Juliet, but not to themselves, at that moment. Shakespeare here allows himself music. He is indeed always recognizing and objectively dramatizing the inward music, the deepest self-hood, the very

P

'I'-ness, so to speak, of his persons. This is precisely what is meant by love. And, since people do not always know their own self-hood, one of his major themes, from Benedick, Orsino, and Katharina the Shrew through King Lear to Enobarbus, Leontes, Coriolanus, and Wolsey ('I know myself now'; *Henry VIII*, III. ii. 379), is the gradual recognition by his heroes of their own deepest selves; which is, normally, a kind of love; a kind of eros-music, at once a humility and a royalty. And for a similar reason we too read Shakespeare, to dig deep enough to recognize ourselves. The dignity of human personality is thus central throughout. His people are therefore, unless of the type of Sir Andrew Aguecheek, nearly always courageous, Parolles not excepted: indeed, he is perhaps the bravest.

In this sense Shakespeare is profoundly Christian, though it is important to remember the total acceptance conditioning such integrity. Many passages and many persons, especially Friar Laurence and Cerimon, tone with traditional religion. Moreover, Shakespeare shows properly no conflict of the sexual-romantic and the Christian: indeed, Christian sanctities are consistently invoked in the cause of dramatic love, conceived as an enduring emotion. His ladies are allied continually with Christian associations. New Testament references and half-conscious reminiscences often witness a coincidence of the human with the archetypal and the Christian; as when Othello's bearing towards his armed retainers recalls Jesus' dignity in face of arrest; or when Antony's tragedy[1] has its 'last supper' and the desertion of Enobarbus is patterned on that of Judas. Timon and Richard II are impressionistically related to Christ himself. But I point rather to that even more deeply embedded and instinctive Christianity in the very conception of human personality. In both Christianity and Shakespeare you have a central humility and passivity violently creative, radiating action, a process, as it were, of continual incarnation; and both finally reach, through this, the farthest death illuminations of the Western world. But Shakespeare is too truly a dramatist and a Renaissance artist, and perhaps also too good a Christian, to place his sole trust in poetry or religious

---

[1] As has been observed by Mr J. Middleton Murry, in his essay on *Antony and Cleopatra* (*Shakespeare*, 1936; pp. 362–7).

meditation. His studious princes, as in *Measure for Measure* and *The Tempest*, must take up their burdens again; Fortinbras brings his name and army to cure Denmark of its mentally insoluble disease; and the last play of the whole sequence is *Henry VIII*. Perhaps Theseus comes nearest to Shakespeare's ideal of manhood, slight sketch though it be. See how, after the moonlit night of fears and fancies, he enters with the rising sun, to wake the lovers from their dreams.

III

This self-identification with all human positives is not presented uncritically. Mercutio is set beside Romeo, Falstaff's honour-speech beside Hotspur's; Feste is there to criticize Orsino's love, Jaques to criticize Orlando's. Lust is presented as a nightmarish evil as early as *The Rape of Lucrece*; and indeed the second and third parts of *Henry VI* and *Titus Andronicus* have passages of black intensity unequalled again until the great tragedies.[1] Profundities are in Shakespeare's imagery, and often more than that, from the start. Advance is mainly through exploitation and rearrangement of old resources, an ever-deeper penetration of himself. At the turn of the century the darker elements gain force. Disloyalty and ingratitude had for long been emphatic revulsions, to which that supreme giving of himself which Shakespeare's works reflect may have rendered him quiveringly susceptible; and these revulsions are now expanded. His other main negation, apart from death itself, is a blackish lustful evil such as you get in *The Rape of Lucrece* and *Macbeth*, the tonings of those two being imaginatively identical. From such disturbances the great tragedies arise.

Two main issues are involved: sex and death. With the first an inward integrity had already made possible an achievement beyond that of Spenser or Marlowe, and similar to, though richer than, Lyly's. Webster's human feeling is not incomparable with Shakespeare's, but with death he, if not his Duchess, fails. Against extremes of ingratitude, marital infidelity, sex-nausea related to jealousy, all evil and death, the

[1] See Appendix D, below.

Shakespearian trust is now advanced. The very sympathy which sees so deep into the human essence that it creates with equal ease and sureness Juliet and her nurse, cynic Mercutio and romantic Romeo, forces the creation of Iago, Regan, Apemantus, Lady Macbeth. The Shakespearian love is challenged by its own children, like King Lear, and we get a universe in self-conflict.

Hamlet is harshly confronted with infidelity and death. His play turns on the baffling problem of action, thus questioning Shakespeare's most profound sense of human reality. Hamlet's is precisely the dramatist's normal problem: to find an action which can objectify the unrestful and groping intuition. In this Shakespeare's normal success is due to an inward integrity and correct balancing of imaginative material, but here the balance is, for once, gone. Aesthetic positives of feasting and music, kingly dignity, and love, are aligned with Claudius, the murderer; negatives of death and cynicism with Hamlet, the philosopher-hero. *Hamlet* is thus a self-questioning, as is no other play, of the central principle within Shakespeare's creative art. Not only the goodness, but the very dynamic, of life is being questioned. What strong action can be, to a sensitive intelligence, inherently poetic? The situation demands coarse, material revenge, and Hamlet, the poet-hero, is at a loss. But static drama is, for Shakespeare, impossible, and the conflict is resolved by an oscillating action. When in the fourth act natural loveliness aligns itself with Claudius, or at least against Hamlet, we have Shakespeare fighting beside his villain to preserve that cosmic, human, and natural trust which he, as Hamlet, is losing. The result is indeterminate but satisfactory; the crisis is objectified, and afterwards the sense of human force and direction never wavers; the imaginative balance is not again unsteady. But meanwhile *Hamlet* has pointed on to the especially inward conflicts, the spiritualized action, of the great tragedies.[1]

Troilus and Cressida is satirically concerned with both sex and war, though the hero survives madly idealistic and active, with a most impressive romantic force, at the end. Earlier,

---

[1] The problem of *Hamlet* will be the better understood if we can see that the relation of Claudius to Hamlet bears certain important similarities to that of the King to the three tragic persons in *Henry VIII*. See *The Crown of Life*, p. 314.

Ulysses' order-speech sums up the cosmic trust that is felt to be shaking. The material is carefully ordered. *Measure for Measure* analyses the inherent difficulty of practical government to a sensitive mind, while also unfolding a deeply Shakespearian sexual ethic, close alike to Gospel teaching and modern psychology, and bearing directly on my present arguments, since pharisaic righteousness is shown as superficial and natural instinct treated with sympathy. In *Othello* Renaissance villainy attacks a romantic faith, the opposition of cynicism and love found in Mercutio and Romeo repeated to darker purpose; in *Macbeth* ultimate evil, supernatural, nightmarish, medieval, with strong tonings of folk-superstition, is a rampaging force of murder; in *King Lear* a world of agony, related to a broken love, writhes towards a purgatorial resolution with the world of the comedies trailing behind pathetically in the Fool, just as Hamlet's words on Yorick's songs recall Feste. In *Timon of Athens* loss of love starts a torrent of curses against all false shows of decency and order.

The greater tragedies develop aspects of *The Duchess of Malfi*: a thought which increases our respect for that massively crammed work. But the human contacts are closer and more vivid, usually concerned with excruciating suffering at some sense of blank desertion, the ingratitude-*motif* driving the play now to the borders of sanity. Yet there is no Websterian paralysis of pain. Thought and imagery are carried easily, thrown up by but never clogging the action. Protagonists are never inwardly conquered, are never passive sufferers: they remain kings in a deeper than the obvious sense. There is an energy which, indeed, Webster comes near to matching in *The White Devil*. Othello's love endures; Macbeth accuses himself before others accuse him, and ends with an honest relation to men, fighting bravely, unrepentant though self-condemned. The force and felt optimism within *King Lear* are generally recognized; and I have written with fervour of *Timon of Athens* as a positive document. The balance of human freedom and outward coercion is carefully maintained, destiny, or chance, urging equally Macbeth to crime and Cleopatra to nobility. The theme of indomitable aspiration running from Marlowe through Milton to Goethe, Byron, and Shelley is here more closely defined in terms of human limitation, and consequently more compressed and explosive. Our sense of victory finally derives from a tough, unburstable, instinctive grip on the human essence and its native invulnerability; barks may be tempest-racked but cannot be lost; the personality, the 'I'-ness of the universe and its creatures, is felt as indivisible; and death cannot enclose the life which contains it. The 'I' cannot, indeed, recognize death, which is known only through the mediation of another: a thought relating to Shakespeare's final plays. Every hideous evil is thus felt to be purified by man's native, though constricted, royalty, every sting of satire subdued to a non-satiric direction in the whole. Pride and humility are, in that whole, one. The negative forces are dramatically related and objectified, and never exert an unconditional and suffused mastery. The evil in *Macbeth* is associated consistently with the unreal and the infra-human, and dispelled at the end; death's macabre mockery comes too late to prevent Cordelia's reunion with Lear; the curses of Timon are not those of an Apemantus. The prevailing energy is related to courage, the hero always being, or having been, a soldier. This is again the joining of 'letters with lances', the warrior-ideal now contributing to intense psychic and spiritual conflicts in brave dramatic action. These conflicts concern mainly that romantic and energic faith central in Shakespeare; the opposition of love and cynicism implicit in *Othello* is explicit in *Timon of Athens*; and *Hamlet, Troilus and Cressida*, and *King Lear* show related essences. You can feel the poet asserting his central faith against apparent hostilities. Though Iago is certainly part of Shakespeare's mind, Othello's lost and recaptured faith is the emotional heart of his work, while Thersites knows himself the universal deformity, 'in everything illegitimate' (*Troilus and Cressida*, v. vii. 19).

The Shakespearian strength arises equally from an inward profundity and a generous sensuousness. Both are as necessary to a universal as to a human marriage; both are needed to grapple with tragedy and death.

Remember how the animals in *Venus and Adonis* are so created that sense-impression is one with an inward sympathy. Such an intuition accepts experience whole, and with a love which induces a harmony, seeing things precisely as they are, as their dynamic selves, rather than blurred by subjective and static associations. Though Shakespeare's world is crammed with all kinds of evil, loathing, horror, it is not itself evil, because ordered; and it could not have been ordered without first being, all of it, understood and therefore loved; and it could not have been loved if it were not, in essence, vital, and therefore good. A crime in *The Rape of Lucrece* or *Macbeth* may be compared to a foul smell, but neither the inward reality of moral evil nor the sensuous reality of foul smells necessarily meets Shakespeare's final, that is artistic, condemnation. They are felt as similar, that is all; as vital forces of unhealth to the communal and individual organisms respectively. Marlowe's equation of wicked lust and bright joy is seen, on this level, merely as an untidiness; nor would Shakespeare allow Webster's association of murderous horror and ritualistic dignity (*The Duchess of Malfi*, iv. ii. 180–97). These could not happen because they are false to human existence as he knows it; but such a perfect organization, which is one with correct ethical associations, depends on a clarity impossible without love. That is, you can never properly distinguish good from evil whilst you are hating either, still less if you are fearing either; and indeed must love both before you are in a position to prefer one. Such a consideration goes far to remove certain obstructions to an understanding of the ultimate evil, death. Webster's horror is largely sensuous: cords and coffin, cold corpses, mouldering bones, earth, worms. Much of it you get, too, in *Hamlet*, the ultimate evil appropriately emphasized in that crucial play. The part played by such impressions in our horror at another's death is probably larger than we think. Yet a wide enough extension of sensuous acceptance and inward sympathy will love earth and worms too, as did Blake, recognizing sense-horror to be a trivial reaction on a limited human and biological plane, since the scent of rotting seaweed or leaves seems healthy enough. Such acceptance cannot come without an embracing of all negations, spiritual and physical, which involve each other. Shakespeare's matchless ordering of his material shows such an acceptance.

My argument is adumbrated in *The Tempest*. Prospero's art is a drawing towards him of evil, at once a mastery and a forgiveness of it. So, having as it were everything in its right place, Shakespeare's sense of human and cosmic energy, or life, does the rest. Since he is not clogged and hampered by ultimate taboos, power breathes through. Milton seems to be hampered at the first, sexual step; but until the mind is integrated there it will be powerless with death. In each of these two disturbances we find that physical disgust and a sense of sin may be twin hindrances: the horror dramatized in Claudio's death-speech (*Measure for Measure*, III. i. 116–30) shows both.

The interdependence of deep spiritual understanding and wide sensuous receptivity is intrinsic to poetry, since depths of individual being in the unseen world of human personality are therein to be expressed through a vital and energic language born of sensory perception; and it is too common an error to think that we can explore the Shakespearian profundity without close attention to his surface. Such poetry must be weighty to balance the 'ponderous and substantial' (*Measure for Measure*, III. ii. 298) essences which it weighs; and to match what is organic and natural it must itself have nature-quality and organic, fibrous strength. Poetry, we are told, sees into the 'forms of things unknown' to re-create them in sensory 'shapes', and both art and love show a similar penetration to the 'heart' of their objects (*A Midsummer Night's Dream*, v. i. 12–17; II. ii. 104–5). In Shakespeare's greater plays the process is apparent not only in language but also in action and organization. The unveiling and the re-expressing of psychic depths which characterize all poetic drama is here found in action and symbol on a wide front. The poetry tears away the superficies of human affairs, penetrating essence; re-creates, not copies, from sight of the source. The ship's engine-room is shown us, we hear its clang and hiss. My remarks on Shakespeare's orderly world, or feminine and passive nature, must not be misread. These qualities are—have been all along, but especially are so now—a transparent medium for projecting terrific conflicts. Action was always Shakespeare's strength, a sense of human, or other, energy. In the greater plays violent forces are let loose, often related to those energic sources of life which we call sexual; a stormy and wrenching agony is his theme. Whatever feminine gentleness conditioned his art, a masculine agony of conflict is its material.

This clash of forces, both communal and psychological,

he reveals, naked. A veil is lifted in *Julius Caesar* disclosing disorder-portents drizzling blood over Rome, the life-blood of the community exposed; Hamlet is confronted by death's naked terror and his mind flayed by a hideous revelation of sexual unfaith in a mother; in *Macbeth* nature's surface is blasted to show infra-natural horrors, weird sisters, ghosts, apparitions, nightmarish things, while a woman's mind sinks shafts into bottomless evil; in *King Lear* a madness-phantasmagoria dances mirage-like, a capering grotesquerie of unreason led by naked Tom. There is a tearing-off of a covering, an exposure. Timon goes naked to his sea-shore tomb, willing that all superficies of orderly life be destroyed; and the resolution of these conflicts comes through the sensuous and burning fascination of hot sun-bred instincts in *Antony and Cleopatra*. Through all, even as the outward is sloughed off, a new structure of inner experience forms, clouds being puffed away to reveal a vaster, numinous, substance of the quality which Nietzsche in his study of tragedy called 'Dionysian'. Analysis reveals significance on significance in this structure.

I have often analysed the logic within Shakespeare's symbolisms: the subtle impressionism, especially the interchange of moonlight and dawn, in *A Midsummer Night's Dream*;[1] the deep unity of *The Merchant of Venice*, pound of flesh, three caskets, and the conflict of Shylock and Portia all contributing to a single, profound statement;[2] the balanced handling of disorder and central authority in *Julius Caesar*; the baffling opposition in *Hamlet* of an ethical good associated with death against an evil apparently backed by forces of life. The tempest which was used mainly as a symbol of adverse fortune in the Comedies and more subtly, though only imagistically, in the Histories, becomes from *Julius Caesar* onwards violent in effect and meaning, closely in-knitted in the whole. A usual construction is: order and music; thunder of conflict; plaintive or broken music, a backwater of momentary peace following the pattern of the New Testament drama; and then the tragic impact, rounded off by a ceremonial conclusion. Various symbols grow and form from the poetic soil. In

---

[1] My detailed examination of *A Midsummer Night's Dream* is given in *The Shakespearian Tempest*, III.

[2] See *Principles of Shakespearian Production*, IV.

Othello the handkerchief focalizes and universalizes the action; in *King Lear* the storm is the occasion for a dramatization of both passion and pathos, with a purpose forming on the fringes of consciousness from the tempestuous pain, if only through the wedding of man's agony with cosmic turmoil. In *Macbeth* the miniature conflict of death and life in the three thunderous apparitions contrasted with the creative harmony symbolized by the procession to music of future kings is an especially fine example of a revealed and optimistic pattern bursting through, interpreting, and binding the main surface action of nightmarish evil. But there is nothing schematic or mechanical. Symbolism blends with iterative imagery and that with the persons of the play themselves, so that there is scarcely an isolated or isolatable heart to the organism, though the apparitions in Macbeth, the handkerchief in *Othello*, the tempest in *King Lear*, might provisionally be called so. For the *King Lear* tempest, in expressing the relation of protagonist to environment, reflects the conflict, that is the action, and therefore the whole play, as does no one person; and the organic heart must sometimes be known rather through these symbols than in the tragic hero. Such symbols are not added to the story-action: they contribute to it, are at once thrown up from the depths by it, are part of it, and urge it on. The play's deepest inwardness expands and encloses it; in *King Lear* the unveiled and psychological almost bursts the apparent universe, almost *is* the objectively natural and cosmic. And, indeed, these symbolisms which we have considered inward must be equally regarded as evidence of an action not so much seen deeply into as widely expanded. A human story is given its full and proper context of society, nature, the universe. The action is shown in its context of the whole of life, and to do so much, in so short a space, demands the shorthand statement of symbolic extravagance. The inward and the outward, as so often in our study of Shakespeare, are found to coincide, while all intermediary appeals of imagery, characterization, historic authenticity and so forth, are contained.

Shakespeare's symbolism is, like his imagery, based on a feeling for nature-forces, life-forces: the child, feasts, music on the one side; ghosts, ill portents, thoughts of disease on the other. The implied metaphysic is optimistic in so far as it regards the created world as good and in the main, certainly in the long run, victorious. Moral law is observed, but only as an aspect of a greater, more universal, whole. The apparent disasters of Macbeth and Antony derive not from any especial condemnation, but simply from understanding of the way things happen, and a deeper ethic matures from a more careful inspection. *Macbeth*, being concerned with evil, is crammed with ghosts and semi-realities, whereas *Antony and Cleopatra*, being concerned with love, has the most realistic surface of the great plays, love tuning, as it were, with creation. But the evil also throws up more life, denying itself, as in the child-apparitions of *Macbeth*. And the worst conflicts are never depressing: they reflect a health and sense of energic being denied to the horror-paralysis and nightmare harmonies of *The Duchess of Malfi*. Lear's 'No, I'll not weep' (*King Lear*, II. iv. 286) is a key passage in the Shakespearian victory. Moreover, spiritual conflict tends to objectify itself into armed opposition and the wound contributes to its own closure. But that wound is itself creative: from it the passionate and naturalistic poetry swells out and the whole action is inspired. The poet's task is, indeed, easier in *Macbeth* than in *Antony and Cleopatra*, since artistic intensities are often happiest with evil. An inrush of power is shown attending conflict. Only then do Romeo, Macbeth, Lear, and Timon become truly powerful. The agony *is* poetic definition, their suffering felt as of no greater discordance than nature's tempests. The energy and the meaning exist in this very effort of reconciliation, and poetic mastery is often the more evident, indeed easier, the more wild the conflict to be resolved. Finally, we must always remember what the plays are, not only what they say; what they say appearing sometimes merely as dust which obscures the poetry's ultimate direction. Yet also their artistic structures, though only a medium for power, a wire white with electric heat, have their own inevitable, because organic, precisions. There is formal pattern as well as action. In the middle, usually, is our climax, with sense of the swing and leverage of existence; at the end, there is peace. The plays work up to a wild un-studied ritual, with pictorial and sacrificial quality: the star-crossed Romeo and Juliet in the tomb; Hamlet carried off to a dead march, with cannon; the tragic loading of Desdemona's bed; Cordelia limp under the white hairs and burning eyes of Lear; the trailing pikes and dead march of *Coriolanus*; Cleopatra's self-dramatized immolation, guided and guarded by her two girls in their dying loyalty. In close relation are reminders of the community's continuance. The purgatorial conflicts hurl themselves up to these almost formal and ceremonial conclusions, recalling the equally positive, yet equally unforced and naturalistic, beauty in agony of the Crucifixion. The protagonist is happily withdrawn from the front line of a terrific and painful, yet creative, action. A relation to the Christ-tragedy is sometimes suggested, and to a sensitive understanding always embedded, not so much by direct, or even unconscious, influence, but because the same piece of work is being done according to the laws of the same universe: the steady generation from instinctive energy of spiritual power.

We are left with a feeling of both power and peace; of a rhythm, deep as winter or night or sleep necessary to the pulses of existence; of emotional depths which therefore are not finally thwarted; of a thunder which is but a part of some universal music. Shakespeare's naturalistic quality lends itself only provisionally to metaphors from any human art: the structure of verse and symbol certainly creates what we may call a musical-tempestuous design, but it is a breathing organism, one living whole; so that, remembering that a passivity and a psychological harmony were the conditions of the play's creation, we can say that we find them also to be mysteriously the reward of our reading. Action and inaction, conflict and peace, tempest and music are, in the completed whole, one. And, just as the generated emotion of a Shakespearian speech out-distances its own expression, as each person and event aims not to assert but to submerge itself in the whole, since all and each live entirely on the central creative energy; so some power greater than the play itself, which, as in all greatest art, you feel to be no finished and polished finality but rather a rough approximation and provisional expression only, is felt calling each separate work into being and back at will, like the heave and subsiding of a wave, the ocean mass itself profoundly undisturbed. By its very accepted limitations—it is their especial office—each tragedy throws up the shadowings of some mysterious otherness, a something behind, which is also the inmost vitality of its own poetry, rooted like that in the depths of *personality*; which is, too, felt within the play's symbolic direction and ritualistic conclusion, its whole-searching quality. Towards a further inclusion beyond tragedy the sequence accordingly moves.

IV

Macbeth, *King Lear*, and *Antony and Cleopatra* are toned respectively as experiences of Hell, Purgatory, and Paradise. In *Antony and Cleopatra* all natural elements intermesh for celebration of a sovereign love. That love, though backed by impressions of sun and fertility, is, however, shown in conflict with the social order and needing death for its proper consummation: 'Husband, I come' (v. ii. 289). Death is here dynamically conceived as an entrance into the cosmic harmony, the autonomy of human instinct creating, through Cleopatra, its own paradise. The organization and balance of materials are delicate. Nor is realism slighted. Indeed, the often harsh phraseology would seem to be labouring to drag back the aspiring theme, which wins in its despite, a tendency especially clear in the fine adulation of Cleopatra spoken by the critical Enobarbus. Shakespeare's dramatization of the final mystery is established in terms rich in physical sex and, for once, a barbaric regality; yet also deep in conception of personality, as when Cleopatra's dream-lover becomes himself the universe, the strongly sensuous and authentically spiritual being once again found to be interdependent. If, however, we want a more directly idealistic treatment of similar penetration we can turn to *The Phoenix and the Turtle*, a poem which matches the work of Donne in the delicate refinement of a style recalling Donne's own phrase, in *A Valediction forbidding Mourning*, 'like gold to airy thinness beat'.

The resurrection and reunion plots which logically follow stand alone in our literature.[1] Regarding them as a further

---

[1] I say in 'our literature'. The correspondences with the Inca play *Apu-Ollantay*, probably an earlier work, are striking. A translation appears in Sir Clements Markham's *The Incas of Peru*.

exploitation of the mysterious power generated through the great tragedies and *Antony and Cleopatra*, we can say that they dramatize a victory over death. Their nature is, nevertheless, foreshadowed in certain earlier romances, and indeed the Comedies, with their mistakes and discoveries, their untying of tangles and ceremonious conclusions, often contain, as do also the plays of Lyly, hints of a universal. Shakespeare's work develops through a reorganizing and re-penetration rather than a change of material. In his last period favourite poetic impressions tend to present themselves as dramatic actualities; as persons, or events, or both. Poetry is itself the solution, its power the revelation.

There is, however, no dissolution of the individual into nature, or a world-soul. Personality must, in the Shakespearian art, remain one certain term of reference. So Hermione is restored as herself, and the restoration is presented as a natural fact; there is no black magic, she is 'warm', Leontes' embrace as 'lawful' as 'eating' (v. iii. 89–105, 109–11). We may observe that the hero does not himself die; it is his experience of another's death that is dramatized. Leontes' repentance and 'faith' (v. iii. 95), Paulina acting as his *conscience*, condition the resurrection. In *Pericles* and *The Winter's Tale* the final discovery of the child either born or lost under conditions of tempestuous conflict reflects nature's creative onwardness as the resurrections of Thaisa and Hermione represent the victorious eternity of love. Gods—Diana, Neptune, Apollo, Jupiter—have, variously, significance, especially Jupiter in *Cymbeline*. In *The Winter's Tale*, apart from the resurrection, we have country scenes, golden comedy, and young love set against tragic nausea, bitterness, and death, with final emphasis on creation and peace. *The Tempest* is both an artistic auto-biography and a universal pattern of man's relation to the divine, the final identity of the individual and the universal soul being reflected into the very structure of its symbolic action. Prospero's 'cloud-capp'd towers' speech (iv. i. 148–58) magnificently sees creation as ephemeral in a way which does not appear pessimistic, a similar positive being implied to that otherness always felt behind Shakespeare's own poetic impressions, plots, persons, and plays. The language of this last group may be far from smooth; often abstract, elusive, twisted; at the bitter passages reaching an explosive compression even greater than in the Tragedies. The final period of composition marks not so much a changed approach to human existence as a new totality of comprehension within which death is itself annulled, while the inherent Elizabethan pastoralism, and that positive human, and especially feminine, trust, which have vitalized the whole progress, are found the resolving elements of its close.

Prospero's return to Milan is balanced by Shakespeare's writing of *Henry VIII*, which completes the series ending with *Henry V*. The play is massive and epic with three personal tragedies; the usual ingratitude-*motifs*, self-discovery through disaster, and a newly emphatic Christianity. The vision and miracle quality of other late plays recurs in Queen Katharine's vision of the immortal life. *Henry VIII* recalls the early *King John* in balance of a national and royal ascendancy against individual suffering, its last movement celebrating both the rise of the king and the birth of Elizabeth. In Cranmer we find humility contrasting with the more normally Shakespearian pride of the three tragic persons, and to him Shakespeare entrusts the final prophecy. Such an acceptance of the contemporary and the national is not strange. We tend to pass over the national feeling evident in the show of kings in *Macbeth*, and of which there is even a trace in *King Lear*. *Cymbeline* works out a studied union of Britain and Rome, and indeed things Roman, of central positive importance to all Elizabethans, are especially so to Shakespeare, and hence the archetypal significance of his theme in *Julius Caesar*. Though capable of sharpest social and militaristic satire, Shakespeare concludes his lifework in praise of England's destiny.

This last series corresponds to the Tragedies as does the resurrection to the crucifixion in Christian belief. It is the inevitable and proper fulfilment of Shakespeare's genius, since his ghosts were from the start more alive than other dramatists' men. As in Goethe's *Faust*, the solution comes through the more feminine element, as opposed to nationalism and soldier-ship, among the Shakespearian values, including a most vital feeling for the marriage bond and family issues generally, though this leads back to the spiritualized historic conception of *Henry VIII* with, however, its strong feminine sympathies. The theme of wronged women is found from beginning to end of Shakespeare; the extreme agony induced by suspicion, or proof, of their unfaith is proportional to the sense of their importance; and, at the last, they are redeeming forces. That is why the final act of *Antony and Cleopatra* is of so pivotal a significance.

Shakespeare's last works are written from a consciousness of the eternal which reflects itself into a new emphasis on arts of design, such as embroidery, carvings, and Hermione's living statue; with religious impressions of oracles, chapels, temples, sacrifice, and incense; and, too, an especially sacramental approach to nature, as in the emphasis on the 'fire-robed god' (iv. iii. 29) Apollo and his plot-directing oracle, together with the fertility-festival, in *The Winter's Tale*, and the pagan sun-worship of Guiderius and Arviragus in *Cymbeline*. To withhold the mystical sympathies demanded is to shirk the first duty of interpretation. Eventually the resurrection of Hermione must be considered the most strikingly conceived, and profoundly penetrating, moment in English literature.

Our various conflicts of romantic emotion and critical cynicism, order and disorder, soldierly honour and feminine devotion, life and death, all from a final view dissolve into the opposition, especially strong in the last plays, of his dominating symbols, tempests and music. These apply in turn to conflicts psychological, communal, and cosmic; to the inter-activity of dynamic rhythm and formal pattern in the art-form itself; and to the blend of male and female, active and passive, elements in the poetic mind. The Shakespearian poetry grows from an integrity responding directly to the wholeness of creation, with all opposing tendencies allowed to mature in fullest freedom under the final synthesis, which in turn becomes a medium for an almost god-like power. That power is personified in Prospero, to whose 'so potent art' (*The Tempest*, v. i. 50) even graves are obedient. Such an imaginative and holistic medium alone can crash the barriers of human death. So Shakespeare's universe is fundamentally poetical, not philosophical; nor, in our usual, but limited, sense, exactly dramatic. In it we finally meet no negation, but listen rather to a vast breathing, a rhythmic pulse, the surge and sob of a great ocean, which may remind us of Keats' last, and best, sonnet.

The organic indissolubility of Shakespeare's art may be seen from the way his life-work expands the pattern of a single Shakespearian tragedy: from realism, through impassioned imaginative conflict, to mystic intimations, for of these each tragic hero in turn had his share; and finally, in *Henry VIII*, a ritual conclusion. Such is the organic harmony, resembling rather the works of nature than the works of man.

Some Notable Fallacies

Before closing my thirty years' work of Shakespearian interpretation, I wish to counter what appear to me to be certain dangerous misunderstandings.

My interpretations have from the first relied on what I call the 'spatial' approach to poetic drama, the viewing and elucidation of atmosphere and pattern; and this has led certain critics to see them as a reduction of Shakespearian drama to the static. But surely they should never have given such an impression, since they are so obviously impregnated throughout by a strong awareness of the dynamic. They have regularly been marked by a sense of what might be called the 'positive direction' of Shakespearian tragedy.

How this comes about will be clearer as we proceed. First, however, we may observe that it is certainly true that many of those who have followed the trail blazed by the new method have indeed tended to constrict the plays by a static philosophizing. This tendency I have already discussed at length in my 'Prefatory Note' to the 1953 reissue of *The Shakespearian Tempest*, where I argue that the heavy emphasis laid on the philosophy of 'order' in the academic studies of our time has its dangers. There are many different kinds of order: divine, cosmic, political, social, and psychological. These may, in various ways, conflict with each other, and only an elastic interpretation, responsive to such variations, will do justice to each conception in turn. Indeed, every disorderly action may be regarded as undertaken in the cause of some variety of order, as when there is a clash of orders personal and communal.[1] For the rest, we can say that it is in the very nature of such drama as Shakespeare's to show us a protagonist challenging some settled system. We must, clearly, be aware of the symbolisms and other effects asserting external order; but to see no more in the play than a misguided and unsuccessful challenge by the protagonist is to reduce tragedy to a moral tract. To put

[1] See my essay 'Brutus and Macbeth', especially the note on Bergson (*The Wheel of Fire*, enlarged edn., p. 137).

it bluntly, when Romeo cries, 'Then I defy you, stars!'
(*Romeo and Juliet*, v. i. 24), we are not shocked. On the contrary, it is his business as a dramatic protagonist to speak like
that, and we are glad to hear it: it is what we have paid our
money for.

Not only are our sympathies channelled. Our final sense
of tragic resolution and harmony derives from a dimly apprehended recognition that the hero has been both vanquished
by and withdrawn into some vast indefinable which is far
more mysterious than any conceivable 'order', and which has
itself in part ratified the challenge. This is, in essence, the
solution advanced by Nietzsche in his *The Birth of Tragedy*
(XVI, XVII, XXII). So again, I insist on the positive direction,
the achievement, not only of the Shakespearian tragedy as a
whole, but even of the Shakespearian protagonist as a person.
He is doing something, and getting somewhere, even if we
can't precisely say where. We may even hazard the suggestion
that, since the action of *Macbeth* shows a steady quieting of
unrestful and possessing spirits through acts of blood, we
cannot be sure how far the deeds of the protagonist might be
supposed to have served a beneficial purpose if viewed from
dimensions outspacing our earthly computation. Much the
same happens in *Hamlet*: in both plays we watch the gradual
dissolution of the unrestful powers, which are at first objective
and seen by all, later subjective and seen only by the protagonist, and finally dispelled. Our suggestion is pure guess-
work; but even so it at least serves to indicate the kind of
possibility of which the student of tragedy should be aware.

Nothing is more deeply ingrained in the Shakespearian
art than the mystique of growth. You find it in all the long
Shakespearian speeches. They are more than a succession of
analysable statements, however subtle, though that is how they
are usually spoken. They proceed in waves; there is at least one
cusp, or climax, and often two, and we normally sink back to a
quiet conclusion, as after the breaking of a wave. This is a
quality which can best be demonstrated by actual speaking,
though the failure to recognize its presence leaves much of the
speaking of Shakespearian verse today inadequate.[1] Examples

---

[1] I plan to leave a few records of my own Shakespearian speaking with my various
dramatic papers (p. 9) in the Shakespeare Memorial Library at Birmingham in order

of such speech-structures abound. John of Gaunt's speech on England (p. 28) must start with the voice of an old, sick man; the repetitions accumulate; power breaks through; he rises from his chair or couch; the impact of the later thundering lines depends on contrast with the opening; but the end, though bitter, is quiet, as he sinks back. So, too, Henry IV's sleep-speech (p. 33) starts with the realistic accents of a sleepless man, but, as the poetry swells, the vast sea is realized, the inward emotion taking charge. It is often a contrast of poetry with realism; the one is silhouetted against the other, as again in Henry V's Crispin speech, after the manner already discussed (p. 43). But observe that the climax need not be marked by an increase of volume: 'Crispin Crispian shall ne'er go by' will be given full rhetorical force, but a new kind of power follows in 'We few, we happy few, we band of brothers', spoken softly (*Henry V*, iv. iii. 57, 60). It is all done by contrast.

Henry's Crispin speech will, of course, only be effective if the other persons react: they are at first surly, but as the power grows, their eyes light; they live the unfurling, the flowering, the blaze; and indeed the quality I emphasize is as much a characteristic of the whole play as it is of every long speech.

I have often described these greater unfurlings, like the opening of a blossom, or the splaying of a fountain. The start will be realistic, but as the action gathers, the surface is split open disclosing portents and powers. A new access of energy takes charge in the middle action, and a new and less constricted technique is needed in both acting and production. Production after production fails, in both scope and detail, from a sad blindness to this positive movement, this gathering, sweeping, and over-sweeping power. The producer may think that he has it, but I maintain that he has not. Where thunder is required, I have never yet heard it so orchestrated and interspaced that it comes with the impact demanded. As for ghosts, apparitions, and so on, the failure is disastrous: one receives the impression that neither the producer nor the actors seriously believe in anything of the sort. We need not pause to discuss whether they are right or wrong, since all that I am

to demonstrate this quality for those who may, in years to come, find the matter of interest.

arguing is that this is the impression left on us, and that the Shakespearian essence has accordingly been by-passed. So at the best we watch a pathetic story of noble but unhappy people tormented by unconvincing spooks as they sink to a sad end. That is not Shakespeare.[1]

Of this access of power mysteriously growing in assurance as the plot becomes more grim, the protagonist, as a person, has his share. He, too, grows in power and stature. A simple and obvious example is Richard II. From weakness and irresponsibility he moves, as disaster falls on him, to kingly confidence and kingly power; at one time he becomes a saint in sorrow ('I'll give my jewels for a set of beads' . . . , III. iii. 147); at the deposition he compares himself to Christ, and, rising in all the poetry of his lost kingship, assumes a tragic stature dwarfing his enemies; and at his death knocks over his assassins like ninepins, crying

> That hand shall burn in never-quenching fire
> That staggers thus my person.
>
> (v. v. 109)

This is Shakespeare's weak protagonist. The conception is diametrically opposed to that of Marlowe's *Edward II*. Marlowe's plays give us flamboyant assertion countered by pitiful tragedy; Shakespeare's, grandeur and assertion in and through tragedy.

Such developments of spiritual power must, however, be realized without forgetting their obverse. External failure and spiritual advance variously alternate and interpenetrate, and all this must be reflected in the speaking and the acting; without a firm basis of realism on which to play the poetry lacks relevance. It is pre-eminently a question of performance, and it is from actual stage experience that understanding can best mature. The actor of Romeo has a poor enough time at first; everything is against him; but from his banishment onwards, things improve. At the news of Juliet's death the part becomes really enjoyable; and as he strides into the tomb and speaks to Balthazar with accents worthy of a Timon, inches are added to his stature. This is what the actor feels, or should feel.

---

[1] A similar complaint was registered by Edward Gordon Craig in *On the Art of the Theatre* (1911).

King Lear and *Timon of Athens* provide grand and obvious examples of this tragic achievement.[1] It is not simply a moral advance, though moral issues may be involved. Macbeth enjoys it as surely as anyone: he opens neurotically with a spasmodic, nervous verse; but the rhetoric grows more rotund as he proceeds tyrannically; and he ends on a pinnacle of whatever it is that is expressed in his three supreme pieces of poetry in the fifth act. Our tragic hero has attained to self-knowledge and an honest relationship; and though he is not shown as repenting, we may recall that Wolsey, who in the comprehensive pattern of *Henry VIII* represents the power-quest as Buckingham the old theme of betrayal, is redeemed by no penitential act of his own, but rather finds his 'heart new open'd' and enjoys 'a still and quiet conscience', simply through an unveiling by others and an acceptance by himself (III. ii. 367, 381; *The Crown of Life*, pp. 285–6). It is as though salvation comes not through repentance but by recognition and acceptance; and in these there lies a spiritual achievement.[2] Play Macbeth in the last act merely as a criminal run to earth, and you fail, however well you do it; indeed, the better you do it, the worse your failure. Play him as a man who is all that, but with in addition the spiritual stature of one who has gone through Hell and emerged with both courage and honesty intact, at once unrepentant yet self-condemned, and then, however badly you do it, you at least act Shakespeare. We may recall our early pointer: 'Though his bark cannot be lost . . .' (I. iii. 24). Sometimes it almost seems as though Shakespeare knew what he was doing.

However that may be, each tragic hero in turn attains to some variety of eternal insight: as in Macbeth's time-spurning nihilism, Timon's Nirvana-like longings, Lear's *sub specie aeternitatis* politics, Antony's Elysian expectation, and the imperial love-dreams of both Romeo and Cleopatra; each is lifted, as it were, above his own drama. From the start my

---

[1] For an excellent recent account of the tragic 'achievement' in *Hamlet*, see 'The Meaning of the Graveyard Scene in *Hamlet*', by N. J. Marquard; *Theoria*, Pietermaritzburg, VII, Nov. 1955.

[2] 'Repentance' is a difficult concept. It is doubtful whether 'repent' as we use the word at all adequately corresponds to the Greek *'metanoein'* of the New Testament, which may be allowed to cover not only 'repentance' but also what I have here designated as 'recognition'.

interpretations have taken all this into account. In *The Wheel of Fire* I was at pains to insist that all Shakespearian tragedy, including even the most dangerous essences, should be interpreted 'in a spirit positive and dynamic'.[1] Throughout the insistence has been maintained. Difficult questions are, of course, raised, since the moral order appears to be slighted. To put it bluntly, though I have (p. 237) compared *Macbeth*, *King Lear*, and *Antony and Cleopatra* to experiences of Hell, Purgatory, and Paradise, it makes no sense, within my field of study, to say that Macbeth is damned: the Hell has been experienced during the action. What happens afterwards we are not told, but the whole tendency of Shakespearian humanism counters the doctrine of Hell as a state of lasting torment after death.

This is not to say that there are not many references to it. Shakespeare wrote with the medieval tradition behind him, and his thought and imagery are often drawn from it; but the tendency today to allow such thought-forms to dominate our response is dangerous. The intellectual patterning may be, to some extent, medieval, but the dramatic action is not. The works of Marlowe, Shakespeare, and Webster could not have been composed and acted in the age of Chaucer; the vast outpouring of Renaissance drama variously assimilates, counters, and interprets in terms of dramatic action the settled worldview of the preceding centuries. It is true that in both *Troilus and Cressida* and *All's Well that Ends Well* Shakespeare appears to contrast old and new ways of life to the advantage of the old. But what most distinguishes him from his contemporaries and successors is the subtlety of his interpenetrations, his delicate balancing of the two worlds, and, at the happiest moments, his harmonizing of them. Though his drama is no passive reflection of Christian dogma it certainly does very often, in matters both infernal and paradisal, demonstrate, not indeed the truth of the dogma, but the truth of THAT the truth of which the dogma itself exists to establish. The orthodox teaching of damnation may be factually wrong and yet symbolize a great truth. There are similarities both superficial

---

[1] 'On the Principles of Shakespeare Interpretation', *The Wheel of Fire*, enlarged edn., p. 11. The gist of this essay had appeared two years before the first publication of *The Wheel of Fire*, in the year 1928. See Appendix E, below.

and profound between the conclusion of *The Winter's Tale* and the dogma of the Resurrection, but there is a danger of concentrating on those which are superficial and passing over those which are profound. *Measure for Measure* is a work of close New Testament affinities; but, like the New Testament itself, it exists more nearly as a challenge to orthodox morality than as an advertisement for it. In that subtlest of plays, *All's Well that Ends Well*, the exponent of the religious viewpoint driven to an extreme is the significantly named Clown, 'Lavache', Helena herself being a personification of what we have called, by paradox (p. 156), 'Renaissance sainthood'. So we do Christianity itself little service by regarding Shakespeare's plays as no more than pendants to the religious tradition, since in so doing we inevitably end by slighting that human insight and spiritual penetration through which alone the Shakespearian impact exists and what might be called the corroboration of Christian truth in Renaissance terms is accomplished.

It would, indeed, be strange were Shakespeare's poetry so orthodox as is sometimes supposed.[1] He writes at a moment of balance between two world-views, sharing both; and we have only to point to what follows to see how inevitable it was that his work should hold not merely a teaching but a challenge. What I have said, here and elsewhere, of *Macbeth* falls directly into line with the literature of the next three centuries, which shows a succession of such, and far more uncompromising, challenges. Milton's life-work, following Marlowe's, is such a challenge, and the problems raised by his Satan, and in a lesser degree by his Comus, point on to Goethe, Blake, the Romantics, to Ibsen and Nietzsche. There is, indeed, on the main issue, no room even for argument. We may deplore the movement, but it exists. The two primary myths of Renaissance Europe, functioning during the last three centuries precisely as did the myths of the ancient world, are the *Faust* myth and the *Don Juan* myth. On these many variations have been played, in England and throughout Europe, Goethe's *Faust* and Molière's

---

[1] I would ask those many modern commentators who have written sensitively on the Christian affinities of Shakespeare not to assume that this statement constitutes an attack on their work. My remarks are intended as a necessary warning; but I am thinking rather of a climate of opinion than of any particular articles or books.

Don Juan, or *Le Festin de Pierre*, being perhaps the most distinguished foreign examples. These myths represent two main challenges levelled respectively against (i) the established theological system and (ii) sexual morality. The protagonist may end unhappily, as in Marlowe and Molière, or happily, as in Goethe and Shelley's *Prometheus Unbound*; for the *Faust* myth is, or can be seen as, a variation on the archetype of the *Prometheus* myth. We can detect a movement from pessimism to optimism. The development of modern science and modern psychology is part of the same movement, the same challenge. We could say that our poets and dramatists, with their myths, are at work interpreting the movement.

But only two, at least to my knowledge, have succeeded in holding the balance steadily: Shakespeare and Byron. Of Shakespeare I need say no more. Byron very exactly balanced guilt with self-assertion. Hell was deep-planted in his mind from youth: conviction of sin was ingrained; but he fought steadily against the doctrine of eternal damnation, with an insistence pointing on to the humorous treatment accorded it by Ibsen in *The Pretenders*, and by Bernard Shaw in *Man and Superman* and *Saint Joan*. Such is the conflict adumbrated in his early tales and most perfectly expressed in *Manfred* and *Cain*, the former compactly fusing the myths of *Prometheus*, *Faust*, and *Don Juan*. In Byron's own *Don Juan*, and also in his *Sardanapalus*, we have, as it were, a conquest, a coming through, into light. But *Manfred* and *Cain* best represent the balance. Manfred, though guilt-stricken, will not submit to the devils; Cain, the God-condemned, suffers for his gentleness. The balances are held, as they are in Shakespeare, with an almost inhuman reserve. I say 'inhuman', since it is all too human to pretend to know the whole truth when, in fact, you do not. In these terrible matters only the greatest know when, and how, to preserve silence.

We can accordingly regard Shakespeare's greater plays as a fusion of Renaissance action with medieval thought. But it would be an error to regard these elements of his drama as finally distinct, or even for long distinguishable, since each at every instant interpenetrates and modifies the other. And since my interpretations have always been aware of this, and of other such, interpenetrations, it would not be correct to equate what I have called the 'spatial' element in the plays with medieval thought and the 'temporal' element with Renaissance action. The 'spatial' qualities have often had nothing to do with medieval thought at all, and when they have had, they have always been handled with full recognition of the moment-by-moment fusion; they have been seen in relation to the new whole into which they have been incorporated, and not in terms of that other whole, the medieval thought-system, from which they have been derived.

So we must beware of regarding Shakespeare's work as dominated by any easily definable system. Philosophies of order certainly play their part; but the challengers of order are no less, and probably more, important. Nor can we say that Shakespeare's whole life-work culminates, at the conclusion of *Henry VIII*, in a vision of 'order', unless we make some important reservations. The concluding ritual crowns a play in which the adverse challenge of three personal assertions has been given a sympathetic, if tragic, hearing; it is itself performed before, and partly for the sake of, the unruly, disorderly, London mob, who are thus constituent to the effect; and we watch the celebration, not of some abstract concept, but of an exactly located, specific, personal, royalty, the christening ceremony of the child Elizabeth, together with the prophecy spoken over her about England, both together regarded, or so we may suggest, as defenders not merely of 'the Faith', but of all the humanities, sympathies, and profundities of Shakespearian drama.[1] The emphasis is not on any intellectual concept, scheme, or system, but is rather, in the way of great poetry, specific, human, and localized, with full dramatic immediacy and contemporary impact, resembling the conclusion of Aeschylus' *Oresteia*.

It must be confessed that the attendant theory of what I have regularly, for want of any better terms, called 'spatial interpretation' remains extraordinarily difficult. This is partly because our distinctions between 'space' and 'time' are insubstantial, both 'space' and 'time' being abstractions from the real. The reality may be called 'space-time'. All art is its language.

Literature, as an art, exists through the fusion of the

[1] See below, p. 277; also *The Shakespearian Tempest*, 1953; Prefatory Note, p. xxiii.

kinetic and the static. It is, certainly, a sequence; a sequence of thoughts, images, events. But this sequence is also composed of units of mental solidity, such as images, or words of weighty sound; and the whole accumulates to make a work which possesses symbolism, unity of atmosphere, structure and form. The result is, mentally at least, both dynamic and solid; it exists in space-time; the two elements are only by abstraction distinguishable. That this is so may be seen by watching their interaction; each detail in the sequence can only be fully received with some knowledge of the whole, the pattern, the form; and yet that form is entirely made from the sequence. Each is the other. Again, it is only by getting what might be called the structure, the flowering, the fountain-splay of speech or dramatic action that we realize, as has already been demonstrated, the vital essence, the growth-quality, the access of power, in the Shakespearian art. If you get only the sequence as a sequence, the result is, paradoxically, dead, static. We are brought up against a paradox: sequence alone is static, while understanding of the formal, and in that sense static, entities, conditions our sense of the dynamic.

We may turn for assistance to Nietzsche's *Birth of Tragedy*, with its emphasis on the Dionysian otherness, or dimension, as the true source of dramatic power.[1] In contrast, he regarded epic as an Apollonian art, like sculpture, its horizontal movement lacking the Dionysian upthrust which he finds in great drama. This may be unfair to the greatest epics, but we can see what he means by turning to Marlowe's *Tamburlaine*, which, despite its narrative array of world-shaking events, offers merely a repetitive sequence of actions which leaves a sense of the static and the superficial, and precludes any significant unfurling, any growth. Being too purely horizontal, it lacks dramatic immediacy, tension, and dynamism. Now Nietzsche's 'Dionysian' element may be equated with my 'spatial' element; they are both dynamic elements, with a thrust to be regarded as *vertical* rather than *horizontal*, the moment-by-moment up-thrust from the unseen which is the very essence of dramatic speech and action, of dramatic immediacy, the dramatic 'now'. So the 'spatial' understanding of

[1] Relevant passages will be found in *The Birth of Tragedy*, IV, V, VI, XII, XVI, XXIV; and indeed throughout.

literary art will always tend to reveal things *in depth* as existing simultaneously within the story and yet also apart from it, in their own right; and in so doing it introduces what we may call 'the spiritual', a new dimension, vertical rather than horizontal, of time, movement, and energy. That is why my interpretations, which have concentrated so consistently on the 'spatial' elements, have necessarily been characterized also by a sense of the dynamic and the dramatic. But the dynamism is not sequential: it is vertical. We see how Nietzsche's system, by bringing in the vertical, or spiritual, dimension, resolves our paradox. Finally, we must observe that the viewing of effects in symbolic depth reacts on our understanding of the story, the resolving elements existing not on the surface, but below.

The complexities remain baffling enough, and it is perhaps natural that the new theory, even after thirty years, still gives rise to many misunderstandings and misrepresentations. A usual criticism observes that I collect images irrespective of their context. I say, for example, that the young man of the Sonnets is compared on a number of occasions to 'gold'; and I am told that, since each reference is subtly different, I must not say this. But that argument would negate thinking, which depends on generalization, at its source. You could equally well dispose of the word 'tea-pot' by insisting on the quiddity of each example, since no two tea-pots are the same. It is, of course, true that it would be fatal to use a reference in a way, or sense, which its original context contradicts; but this has not been done. Those who try to follow my method up to a point, and yet insist on treating every minute particular contextually and as part of a sequence, trying to show how everything in turn points on or back to this or that, end by composing unreadable essays. Such attempts land us in complexities of doubtful relevance; and indeed you could not start doing this without first being aware of the group as a group irrespective of sequence. Such commentators are, in fact, adding little except confusion to what has already been done by the poet, who has already done all that can be done in terms of sequence, and if we are to remain tied to that we can do no better than return to the original text. The only perfect way of keeping everything in its context is to remain silent.

The 'spatial' approach, on the other hand, performs a necessary function *beyond* what has already been accomplished by the poet. It is not content with what the poetry *says*; it attempts to reveal the meaning of what it *is*. It tends to see effects in depth, as significant in their own right, and not merely as logical or narrative links, though, once attained, the new insight reacts sharply on logic and narrative. It may be a question of impressionism and atmosphere, or of separate symbolic solids, as when we gave our interpretations in depth of the Child apparitions in *Macbeth* (*The Shakespearian Tempest*, pp. 192–3) and the Dome in *Kubla Khan* and throughout romantic poetry (*The Starlit Dome*, pp. 90–7),[1] allowing them a metaphysical solidity and meaning previously ignored. And now we have been doing just the same with Shakespeare's names. The difference is that between a play read and a play produced: we all know what startling and unsuspected effects may be realized by the spatial projection of a good production. Interpretation *produces* the play or poem in the mind's theatre, and once recognized these new meanings become fixed. It is the same with the more general, more suffused, atmospheric groupings: by showing the tone, the colour, of the whole, we are really doing for the reader what stage-setting and costuming does for an audience. A new depth, or dimension, is revealed.[2]

'Spatial' interpretation thus covers a number of possible approaches. Sometimes, as in my account of *All's Well that Ends Well*, it will be convenient to take two main sequences with reference to the two leading persons, and group them side by side; sometimes, as in my work on *Antony and Cleopatra*, I have devoted one essay to atmospheric effects and a second essay to persons and events, though at every instant preserving awareness, throughout each analysis, of the implications of the other; sometimes an event may be viewed in turn from different points, as in Browning's *The Ring and the Book*; and indeed all drama does this, a peculiarly good example being provided by Shakespeare's *Julius Caesar*, with the dif-

---

[1] See my statement in *Essays in Criticism*, Oct. 1954; also the preceding controversy, Oct. 1953 and April 1954.

[2] Compare Mr Aldous Huxley's reference to stage productions in developing his theories of vision in his recent *Heaven and Hell*.

ferent views of the assassination as it appears to Brutus, Cassius, and Antony. Then there is my chart of Shakespeare's dramatic universe given in the Prefatory Note to the 1953 edition of *The Shakespearian Tempest*, which reduces to clarity on one sheet what would take a long argument to develop in words. None of this is really new: I recently saw it stated that biography in the ancient world paid higher regard to qualities than to narrative, the emphasis on the latter being a modern development. Milton employed a 'spatial' approach to the New Testament in his *De Doctrina Christiana*. My use of the word 'spatial' really means just this: we must not let ourselves be *limited* by the temporal approach. In all thinking this is necessary: the words of the simplest sentence can only be meaningful in so far as we grasp the whole. The unit of stage-speaking is not the word but the phrase, or clause; if these are clear, the constituent words will be clear too. You get, so to speak, the phrase before you get the words from which it is made. Paradoxes abound. All thought exists in space-time.

With a major work of art the same holds good; and the more richly it is composed, the more truly it is impregnated from the Dionysian, vertical, dimension, the more necessary it will be to force our minds to include much that is passed over by a normal, horizontal reading. Of course, some works contain little that is not at once assimilable; the sequence, as a sequence, does all that is needed. Such lesser, more purely Apollonian, works we shall leave alone; to attempt to interpret would merely be putting in our own words what the poet has put better in his. Interpretation will not make such blunders.

That the implications of what we may call 'the new interpretation' have not as yet been grasped may be seen from the extraordinary lack of readiness to distinguish properly 'interpretation' from 'criticism'. This distinction, which was clearly stated from the first in the introduction to *The Wheel of Fire*, is rarely understood. We live, certainly, in an age where fine distinctions do not receive much attention; and yet this is, surely, a broad distinction. Even those who sensitively follow my work are always anxious to call it 'criticism'; but I would ask, can my treatment of the Phoenix in *The Mutual Flame* or my pages on the Crown in this volume, both typical of

R

my work, be properly called 'criticisms' of the Phoenix and the Crown? You might as well call the science of Christian theology a criticism of the New Testament, or the average sermon a criticism of Christ. Criticism aspires to a judgement, a valuing, of symbolic statement; interpretation aspires to an understanding of it. Criticism brings its own ethical or aesthetic standards to the judgement of literature; interpretation goes to literature to discover standards for use elsewhere. Each may, of course, employ the other; it is a question of which dominates. But the question as to which dominates is a matter of considerable importance, and those whose minds are responsive to necessary distinctions and the proper *nuances* of language will not confuse them.

For many years now it has been my assertion that in our age, where writers of classic standing are concerned, there is this mental action to be made which I call, for want of a better word, 'interpretation', and which must be made before 'criticism', if it is our aim to criticize, can be profitably undertaken; and this truth I have demonstrated again and again, as good an example as any, since its findings so directly reveal the limitations of contemporary criticism, being my essay on *The Scholar Gipsy* in *The Review of English Studies* (January 1955). It is, you see, a quite definite act of mind for which I contend. I would even assert that all art of highest quality *demands* interpretation. Recently, in the section called 'Symbolic Eternities' of my book *Laureate of Peace* (1954), I argued that each art is limited by its peculiar nature; some arts are locked to space, and some to time; some appeal to the eye, some to the ear. The more complete reality would be that which is recognized by all the senses acting in unison; it would be simultaneously spatial and temporal, sound and colour, sense-perception and thought; and of course we have no reason to suppose that the whole in all its richness would, even so, be fully perceived.[1] Art is, however, an adumbration of it, and so we find the spatial arts always aspiring to motion and the temporal arts to structure. Each tries to transcend itself. Poetry and drama go far towards attaining the inclusion and the fusion which we want, but they cannot do so completely, since they are, in fact, strung out in temporal sequence.

[1] See, in this connexion, my article 'Spiritualism and Poetry' in *Light*, March 1956.

This sequence must be allowed to transcend itself, and this is the work of interpretation. We accordingly conclude, as I have already stated and more fully argued in *Laureate of Peace*, that art demands a specific act of interpretation; that interpretation of the spatial arts will tend to concentrate on the temporal elements of vitality, suggestion, and narrative; and that of the temporal arts on symbolic solids, atmospheric unity, structure, form. Each works to help the art in question to transcend the limitations of its peculiar medium; and it is only through such acts of interpretation that the deepest significances of the art in question can mature. It is a matter not of passive receptivity but of active co-operation; and through such interpretative co-operation we touch, however insecurely, the fringes of reality.

Appendixes

Literature and the Nation

I offer a brief list covering my work in this kind. It might be said to have started with the opening section of *The Imperial Theme*, 1931. This was followed by the passages on *Henry VIII* and the concluding section of *Principles of Shakespearian Production*, 1936; the concluding section of *Atlantic Crossing*, 1936; and the relevant passages in 'The Shakespearian Integrity' (p. 204 above) in *The Burning Oracle*, 1939. During the war there appeared a small booklet *This Sceptred Isle* (on Shakespeare), 1940; 'Britain as a Dramatic Artist', *The Times Literary Supplement*, 5 April 1941 (reprinted under the title 'The British Genius' in *Hiroshima*, 1946, and at Appendix B, below); 'Four Pillars of Wisdom' (on Shakespeare, Goethe, Byron, and Nietzsche), in *The Wind and the Rain* (Winter, 1941–2, pp. 133–44); *Chariot of Wrath* (on Milton), 1942; 'A Great National Poet' (on Tennyson), in *The Times Literary Supplement*, 10 October 1942 (reprinted as 'Excalibur' in *Hiroshima*, 1946); *The Olive and the Sword* (composed, except for the second section, in 1940; p. 12 above), 1944; *The Dynasty of Stowe*, 1945; *Hiroshima* (on literature and the Atomic Age, together with essays as noted elsewhere in this list, and also essays on Hardy's *The Dynasts* and Francis Berry's *The Iron Christ*), 1946; and the concluding section (composed 1940) of *Christ and Nietzsche*, 1948.

Lecture-recitals of the Shakespearian statement were given during both 1940 and 1941 in London, in collaboration with Miss Nancy Price at the Tavistock Theatre, to the Poetry Society, and at the Institut Français and The Polish Hearth; and also at Cheltenham and Torquay (reviewed in *The Herald and Express*, Torquay, 17 January 1941), and to The University College of the South West of England, Exeter. Others were given on the dramas of Tennyson. These recitals, in which acting was interspersed with lecture-commentary, culminated in my production of *This Sceptred Isle*, under the patronage of Lord Queenborough as President of the Royal Society of St George and of Sir Archibald Flower, at the Westminster Theatre, London, from 21 to 26 July 1941 (reviewed in *The Times*, 23 July 1941).

This Shakespearian theme was also developed in lectures and broadcasts. There was a University lecture at Oxford in 1940; a B.B.C. broadcast of Cranmer's prophecy in *Henry VIII* in 1941; a talk 'Shakespeare's World' (printed in *Hiroshima*, 1946) on the Overseas Service of the B.B.C. in 1943; a lecture and a broadcast through the British Council, in Jamaica, 1951; public lectures under the auspices of the University of Cape Town, the University of the Witwatersrand, Johannesburg, and the University of Pretoria, 1952; a public lecture at the University of Leeds and a lecture to the English Association, during the Coronation Year, 1953; and a lecture at the University of Munich in 1957.

A full account of these activities, including part of the lecture commentary to *This Sceptred Isle*, is lodged, under the title *A Royal Propaganda*, in the library of The British Museum and in the Reference Library at Birmingham (the concluding section of it is printed as Appendix C, below). Other material, including press-cuttings and programmes, together with the prompt copy of *This Sceptred Isle*, may be seen among my *Dramatic Papers* (p. 9 above) in The Shakespeare Memorial Library, the Reference Library, Birmingham.

The Westminster Theatre production was arranged in three acts, as follows. Act I, 'St George for England', was composed of Faulconbridge's lines in *King John*, John of Gaunt's speech in *Richard II*, the Ghost scene in *Richard III* and the heroic speeches of *Henry V*. Act II, 'Patriotism is not Enough', started with a couple of soliloquies from *Hamlet*, continued with the central soliloquy and much of the Cauldron scene from *Macbeth*, and concluded with some long extracts from the falling action of *Timon of Athens*, including Timon's meetings with Alcibiades and his army, the Bandits, and the Senators. Act III, 'The Royal Phoenix', was limited to Buckingham's farewell and Cranmer's prophecy from *Henry VIII*, and Elizabeth I's prayer before the Armada. Act II was given a more elaborate production than the rest, with settings and a free use of 'voices off' to support the actor. Here the lecture-commentary was read for me by Henry Ainley. It will be seen that by far the heaviest emphasis fell on *Timon of Athens* as a critique of patriotism, before returning to the national prophecy of *Henry VIII*.

The British Genius[1]

What we call literature is a living record more vital than history, and by inspection of certain great writers who speak for imperial Britain we may explore the soul-force from which her power and influence have grown. A thousand and one historical details are, of course, ready enough to crowd in and fog the clarities of great poetry; and these must be refused entrance. Here, however, I intend to offer no detailed examinations nor any deeply considered list of writers, but merely a few suggestions which may point, as it were, the proper direction of such a study. Especially we should be willing to regard the balanced oppositions of dramatic poetry as the only true, because inclusive, national record, whereby the total of any situation is imagined by the total, that is the fully integrated, man; in which kind of poetry England enjoys a clear pre-eminence.

The genius of Great Britain is inherently Christian without ceasing to be imperial. The tyrannical and militaristic find no final sanction in English poetry, from Shakespeare onwards. Tybalt, Hotspur, Coriolanus are exquisitely diagnosed. More, they are laughed at, and no comprehensive treatment of our national literature must omit that characterizing humour which has, since Chaucer, been one of its greatest strengths. Similarly, British imperialism is faced with some 'Lest we forget' reminder at every major turn of our literature. Just as Shakespeare's kings are conceived inwardly, with depths of burdened responsibility, promptings of conscience, and finally a continual complementing of world-ceremony by some tragic and religious insight, so, in the wider unfurling, is England's

---

[1] Originally published in *The Times Literary Supplement*, 5 April 1941, under the title 'Britain as a Dramatic Artist', and again, with its present title, in *Hiroshima*, 1946.

nationhood itself felt by its authentic voices as deeply engaged in some eternally valid, world-wide purpose. The glittering, the glory, the ecstasy of power are never endued with excessive rights, except by Marlowe and, though very differently, by Milton; and are, moreover, always liable to be brought to the bar of humour. The continual interplay of temporal and spiritual authorities within the conflicts of Shakespeare's Histories functions throughout later writers, though often without that happy use of kingship which renders the Shakespearian art-form so compact. Justice and mercy, glory and tragedy, man and God, are balanced.

The assurances of Cranmer's prophecy in *Henry VIII* and Pope's *Windsor Forest* are more remarkable forecasts of British imperial achievement than we today at first sight realize. Whether our history has exemplified that spirit of justice and benevolence so urgently demanded by our own poets may be questioned. In support or attack one after the other seems certain that Britain is falsifying her destiny in so far as she fails to be an international and moral force; and many complaints today regarding her actions since the War of 1914–18 are such as would not normally be applied to other nations, and, even in a most hostile critic, assume that she should rise above the level of current international morality. It would indeed seem that Great Britain has some appointed destiny which she is always in danger of falsifying, either in one direction or the other, and our repeated yet varying literary reminders may be taken as a steady calling of her back, from one unaltered and single standpoint, to the straight and narrow path avoiding extremes; all being written, if the truth were known, from an identical position, though facing differently according to circumstances. However that may be, the impression so strong, until recently, both on the Continent and in America, that Great Britain has failed to live up to some supreme responsibility was not new.

Often, it is true, subsequent history tends to prove complaints unjust. Byron's criticisms of Castlereagh and Wellington in *Don Juan* are not, I believe, the normal historical judgements, and it is likely that recent criticisms of Neville Chamberlain will meet a similar rebuttal. None of this is, however, of primary importance. Something has been working itself out

through England and her strangely accumulated imperial influence which can stand independently of any possible criticisms of motive in any individual instance. Her own safety
may well dictate a more than selfish European policy, and
business competition further a colonial penetration which
later assumes some other and deeper significance.

Not only is Great Britain's soul-history beautifully reflected in her poetry: that history is, in itself, quite remarkably
akin to poetry, especially dramatic poetry. This is at first sight
very far from obvious. But when Italy or Germany assert their
rights to colonial possessions one may, with all sympathy, yet
feel that so idealistic, self-conscious, a national ambition differs
in quality from the more gradual, unobtrusive and subtly
organic expression of British imperialism. The very fact of
some vast good, if we admit so much, having matured from a
myriad individual virtues and vices falls into line with creative
activity in general: the process is, as it were, both so large
and so strange as to seem miraculous and therefore a natural
rather than a human accomplishment.

Remembering Keats' advice 'that if Poetry comes not as
naturally as the leaves to a tree it had better not come at all'
(to John Taylor, 27 February 1818), can we not diffidently
apply the thought to Britain's growth in power and prestige?
Is that imperial power not rather, today, a collaboration?
Even in India, prestige surely does the greater part. England
can, indeed, no longer defend, or force unity on, her wide-
flung empire. Keats' definition of poetry in *Sleep and Poetry* as
'might half-slumbering on its own right arm', a phrase clearly
applying rather to the Shakespearian than the Marlovian type
of writing, strikes a note to which many incidents in our history correspond. Both Shakespeare's Hal and Byron's Sardanapalus typify the English temperament, as does Drake on
Plymouth Hoe, in time of danger. Before each of her recent
wars England must, to others, have appeared to be 'half-
slumbering'; and yet this tendency is not unrelated to what
Keats called 'negative capability' (to George and Thomas
Keats, 21 December 1817); the ability, akin to humour, to
be in doubt without too violently grasping for precise and
immediate solutions, together with a reliance on ocean forces
beyond man's direct and daylight understanding; a waiting,

when complexities become intolerable, for solutions to work themselves out.

For years many shades of political thought, communist, pacifist, and imperialist, have agreed on one issue: that our inter-war government was inefficient. Events have justified many adverse criticisms, our country certainly appearing to fall between two stools on every possible occasion; and yet perhaps there was no dignified alternative. Moreover, very similar objections will always be raised against any great, because comprehensive, thinker: he is blamed for being neither one thing nor the other, when his whole purpose is rather inclusive, working towards assimilation of opposing viewpoints. Great Britain instinctively moves towards a middle position in her desire to include both sides of any opposition; and, like Pope or Byron, two such eminently inclusive and holistic poets in all matters of human relationship, she is, at any one moment, likely to be vilified by her contemporaries, though the later results of her policy, as of such poets' experience, are often enough prized.

Our traditional system of government by opposing parties and administration of justice by rival counsels for prosecution and defence both rely on a balance of conflicting opposites such as is rooted in the nature of drama, thereby conjuring into existence an impartial wisdom. That wisdom is, however, more usually realized on earth through alternations, like the psychic alternations in us all from season to season, or from morning to night; and hence the rhythmic flow and undulation of liberal and conservative principles, corresponding to the alternating emphases of Dryden as against Milton, of Johnson against Pope's satires, Blake against Burke; seen likewise in the single development of Wordsworth, the prophetic reach of Tennyson, and, finally, the inclusiveness of a Byron or a Shakespeare; while the disrupted quality of Milton's work and life is a record of a titanic will to synthesis on every plane, communal and personal, in the age of England's greatest internal disturbance. Now the strength of the British Constitution, itself reflecting those Shakespearian art-forms to which it enjoys blood-relationship, is one with its organic growth and truly poetic elasticity and stability, whereas more arbitrary schemes recall Pope's strictures on critics who 'write dull receipts how poems may be made' (*Essay on Criticism*, 115). Great Britain's importance across the globe remains organically continuous with the balance, or union, of opposites in her internal structure, and no understanding of the British Constitution which does not respect its traditional and organic, rather than schematic, nature will prove adequate.

In both court of justice and parliament central persons, with proper emblems of authority, are used to hold the necessary balances and symbolize the super-personal wisdom generated, or called down, by the dramatic conflict. Within the nation this function resides in the Crown, itself of infinitely greater importance, because less humanly limited, in our constitutional system than in a tyrannic absolutism; and indeed corresponding more closely to the symbolic heart of a Shakespearian play, the child-apparitions in *Macbeth* or tempest in *King Lear*, than to the protagonist-king. Itself passive, it reinstates our political complexities in the realms of that poetic art whose action obeys the silent laws of creative life and, as Pope tells us, in comparing poetry with 'nature', always, like a heart in a body, 'works without show and, without pomp, presides' (*Essay on Criticism*, 75); which is, again, the 'mild majesty and sober pomp' whereby Burke once, in his *Reflections on the Revolution in France*, characterized the British Constitution. The Crown is a mystic symbol, rising dome-like above those harsher energies it at once nurtures and dominates, as an almost maternal presence above childish arrogance; and I often wonder that the recurrence of national assurance in our literature should so neatly accompany the presence of a feminine sovereign on our throne. I am thinking of Shakespeare and Queen Elizabeth; Pope and Queen Anne; and Tennyson and Queen Victoria.

I do not think Britain has advanced through any missionary genius or individuals of outstanding intelligence; while her more prosaic thinkers often remain sublimely unconscious of her own deepest nature. Her empire-builders and soldiers have been men of a reserved, almost foolish, confidence, with courage and a sense of justice; without sentimentality, but also without hatred or cruelty; and with very often a sense of humour. These have done the work of a nation of 'shopkeepers' at home; and neither the one nor the other group show, as individuals, any profundity, nor any real artistic sensibility. Yet they have contributed to the making of a nation pre-eminent in literature.

We must, however, realize that poetry is itself the most practical of the arts. Whereas painting and sculpture reflect physical manifestations in unnaturally static, though significant, design, and music does precisely the opposite, expressing the dynamic and abstract-transcendental, poetry, in combining the two, in fusing the mystical with the concrete in closest dramatic reference to human problems, performs, if not a higher function, at least one more useful for life's actuality as we know it. It draws near to Christianity in its persistent refusal to forget either this world or the next; to shirk, or be abased before, the test, or thrill, of action.

Now this vigorous and on occasion profound, almost mystical, common sense, which is yet not unaware of its own limitations, works as well in the English business man or soldier as in Chaucer, Shakespeare, or Doctor Johnson. A certain ethical compulsion results from it, however various the shapes taken. The 'good form' of the gentleman is an unwritten ethic; 'sportsmanship' and 'fair play' involve recognition of a viewpoint opposite to one's own; and the whole Puritan tradition of money-making as a test of character is not utterly misguided, as one realizes when up against anyone of erratic temperament whose lack of money-sense, which is really a lack of the time-sense, shelves personal responsibility. Political responsibility is ingrained in the British temperament. You can see therefore how, from this not very promising general level of good-hearted humanity whose wisdom is a wisdom far beyond their own comprehension, a Shakespeare or a Byron—let alone a Wordsworth or a Hardy, the more obvious types—may start up, fully aware, poetically, of those qualities dormant in their less spectacular brethren, while also checking all visionary impulses by a stern, tough, reasonableness. So, too, we find leaders and statesmen whose value lies precisely in their inability to be too dangerously and personally forceful, British politics normally avoiding like the plague men of originality and vision.

Britain's geographic position has done much to create her unique strength, and also her poetry. An intermixture of Celt,

Saxon, and Norman, thereafter closed and compacted by her islanded and fortressed history, provides the initial stamina, felt in the variety and flexibility, yet highly compressed power, of her language; and, next, affected closely by the Continent, but not of it, and also touching America, Africa, Australia, and the East by her sea-power and trade, she has been peculiarly able to exercise a steadying influence. She is, indeed, herself, as Addison saw, the fulcrum of the world's scales, and her policy of working for a balance of power, however selfishly dictated, has actually forced her into the position of a dramatic artist, pointing a direction from preliminary indecisions, and aiming to build from conflicts peace. Without contraries, said Blake, there can be no progression. The policy of Great Britain has been one of pacific inclusion to which the militarisms of other nations have played their contributory parts.

I have suggested some of Great Britain's national attributes; her balancing of opposites, her wavering, unplanned, yet seemingly almost predestined course; also the humour, tragic acceptance, and traditional, almost superstitious, compulsions of the British temperament; and its ethical common sense. Against these new forces rise on the Continent of Europe. From this conflict Great Britain will, we assume, emerge successful, but the success cannot be easy and the more profound difficulties will remain. Their solution seems to lie in some further assimilation, by Britain and the Empire, of ideas and energies at present alien to her conscious, and often insular, thinking. These will force her back to reconsideration of her own as yet fitfully understood poetic heritage, and to an acceptance, at once more imaginative and more sincere, more bold because more truly humble, of her imperial destiny.

APPENDIX C

A Royal Propaganda[1]

The emphasis falling on such words as 'royal' and imperial' in my writings on literature and Great Britain have always been in danger of misunderstanding, though a cursory reading of my earliest statements in *Atlantic Crossing* (1936) and the booklet (p. 7 above) *This Sceptred Isle* (1940) should suffice to show that from the start my aim was, in the best sense, liberal. What there was in it of nationalism was always being pointed, through royalism and empire, towards supernationalism. It is perhaps easier today, after a lapse of years, to isolate the core of my meaning and explain its independence of any so limited a concept as 'patriotism'. What I was really trying to do was to define the total and potential meaning of the Crown in a modern constitutional system, whether national, imperial, or supernational, in alliance with an established Christianity; or for that matter with 'religion' in the broadest sense. That had not been previously, so far as I know, attempted; nor could it be done except by a poetic, and primarily Shakespearian, approach. It is not surprising that the task has often proved, and still proves, difficult.

Our Sovereign functions as the head of our established church; or perhaps we should say that the Crown functions variously as 'state' and as that which subsumes both state and church. The ambiguities are probably unavoidable. The Archbishop crowns the Sovereign, and the Sovereign appoints the Archbishop: we are reminded of the age-old problem of the hen and the egg, and the one problem is as deeply rooted and mysterious as the other. In obedience to the royal principle, Shakespeare's three male conductors of divine power—the Duke in *Measure for Measure*, Cerimon, and Prospero—are

[1] See p. 264 above.

men of worldly place before becoming saints; and as for Helena in *All's Well that Ends Well*, though herself humbly born, she from the start subscribes, and even aspires, to the aristocratic valuations. In the men, anyway, the usual process is reversed, sainthood flowering from nobility; and the two rulers return to re-engage their sovereignty. In primitive societies king and priest were one person, and they may be so again, if the prophecy of Ibsen's *Emperor and Galilean* holds any truth. Meanwhile Crown, and not Mitre, symbolizes our *final* and *active* authority. And yet what exactly is that authority? Though particular decisions, including the appointment of bishops, appear to be made entirely by ballot-papers, members of Parliament and cabinet ministers, it is fatal to assume that this is the whole story, and it would seem almost as fatal to attempt to say what the 'whole story' is. The Crown is not part of our system; it encloses it. It is both heart and aura of the nation's body, at once soul and whole. It belongs to a category, or dimension, notoriously difficult to define, and indeed scarcely susceptible of any but a poetic and dramatic treatment, whereby it is defined (i) positively in terms of poetic imagery and symbolism and (ii) negatively in terms of persons failing under the burden of active kingship. That is why we can do no better than work through the many variations played on kingship throughout Shakespeare's dramatic poetry, which is, it seems, the only comprehensive definition of our, or perhaps any, time. We have watched kings falling in country after country, and it is likely that the works of Shakespeare have themselves done much to preserve our own intuition and understanding of royalty. This, then, is what I was doing throughout my war-time labours: *using Shakespeare to define the meaning of the Crown, for us, today.*

And so, too, with 'empire'. My use of the term from *Atlantic Crossing* onwards derived not from any exclusive belief in the destiny of Great Britain, but rather from a conviction that the word held promise of developments outspacing any local origin. Though what used to be called the 'British Empire' has become much depleted since the war, the Shakespearian message lives independently of such surface changes, and that is precisely why the word 'empire' was often for my purpose preferable to 'commonwealth', since the greater concept, in descent from the Roman '*imperium*' and carrying overtones of both Vergil and Dante, sinks its origins deeper, expands wider and aspires higher, than the lesser. It carries, indeed, as has already been expounded by the eminent historian, Sir Ernest Barker, religious connotations gathered from the past, as the other does not. That it is a spiritualized concept may be felt from Shelley's words in his *Defence of Poetry* on 'that imperial faculty whose throne is curtained within the invisible nature of man', and from Shakespeare's own use of it, as in Helena's phrase 'imperial love', Romeo's dream of himself as love's 'emperor' beyond death, and Cleopatra's cosmic vision of 'an emperor Antony' (*All's Well that Ends Well*, II. iii. 79; *Romeo and Juliet*, v. i. 9; *Antony and Cleopatra*, v. ii. 76). 'Commonwealth' alone, though it can be recognized as one part of the royal whole, as in *Richard II* (III. iv. 35), lacks authority: we may recall the handling of Jack Cade in *2 Henry VI* and how in *The Tempest* (II. i. 150–65) Gonzalo's idea of a Utopian commonwealth is shown, by a neat stroke of ironic dialogue, to be parasitic on sovereignty.

When I was invited in 1954 to send a message on Shakespeare's birthday to the University of Peshawar, it was with no sense of disharmony that I repeated, in short space, the old theme, addressing them as follows:

> I send the English Literary Club of the University of Peshawar my very good wishes for its Shakespeare Festival Day. It is a great pleasure to know that, though the world is so unsettled, yet Shakespeare lives more vividly than ever before, not only in England, but in countries far from his own land. Empires come and go, and politics change, but great literature offers a gift more lasting and of more worth. What is the secret of Shakespeare's appeal? It is, I think, a kind of royalty, a golden thread of excellence, nobility, and grace, not limited to any one country or any one way of life; a deep, spiritual nobility, or royalty. It is this that the human race recognizes, and responds to, irrespective of belief or race, wherever Shakespeare is read or acted.
>
> These are high, some would say romantic, imaginings. But I am the less nervous in offering them since I have noticed that, though we in England are a little reluctant to face, or at least to speak of, the richer meanings within great poetry, other nations are more ready; and among those other nations, one of the most ready is, surely, the great sub-continent to one of whose universities this message is

addressed. For you, in the East, with your long spiritual and philosophical traditions, appear often to be able to see more deeply into our English literature than we ourselves. It is true that, though 'a nation of shopkeepers'—and critics—we have produced a number of great poets, including Shakespeare; and I often wonder how we did it. But this is certain: Shakespeare is no longer ours; he is yours, just as much, perhaps more.

In this 'golden thread' of which I have spoken lies a great power, a great good, and a great gift. Though spiritual, it is tough; though subtle, it is strong; strong enough, as I sometimes think, to 'put a girdle round about the earth', binding it in service to the destinies, not of nations, but of Man.

The old theme was being expanded, but the expansion was no more than a simple, and perhaps obvious, development in direct descent from my earlier statements.

We are moving inevitably towards world-unity. But of what pattern shall that eventual order, unifying and stabilizing the millions of East and West in all their diversities, be? The terms 'communism' and 'commonwealth' suggest little beyond an equitable enjoyment of some satisfying *status quo*; they are counters which sound well in a small context, but tinkle weakly in the greater. 'Democracy' is a word which says more than it means, since in the present state of humanity no people, as a people, can in effect *be*, though it may contribute to, its own government; and hence the word lands us in a marsh of imprecision, systems so different as those of the United States of America and Communist Russia laying rival claims to its support. Both Milton of the Commonwealth and Dryden of the Restoration use 'democracy' as a term of abuse; and we may doubt if such a word is one to stand the stresses of world-government in the centuries to come. But cannot Shakespearian England, or Great Britain, offer as rough prototype some royal conception more finely tuned to the issues? Indeed, even were communism first to inundate the world, must not some royal, or imperial, pattern, in descent from the great traditions of the past, and sinking its foundations, as is demonstrated throughout that necessary work, A. M. Hocart's *Kingship*, to the earliest beliefs and practices of man, reassert itself? For the Crown is necessary: within it opposites are contained; community and individual, justice and mercy, church and state, this party and that party; in, and through, it we live a doubleness, at once making and renouncing all personal claims. The Crown is the personification of the impersonal. Politically it is the supreme paradox. The royal prerogative certainly exists, but is rarely exercised, the final source of authority and power being lodged in one *who has no power*, who may not even cast a vote, and is really less free than any subject. In and through the symbolism, the poetry, the extreme of power is thus equated with the extreme of service; and it is to this sovereign paradox that those who lead the nation, and who wield, provisionally, a modicum of actual power, must bow. Here our various conflicts are imaginatively surmounted, given a higher, symbolic and yet intensely human, synthesis; through the drama, the fiction, in which we *collaborate*, we are, like an audience at a play, *compelled to be free*. By such thoughts we may approach the final mystery of royalty and freedom in reciprocal action as poetically defined for us in Byron's *Sonnet to George IV on the Repeal of Lord Edward Fitzgerald's Forfeiture* (p. 89).

And it is towards such a consummation that Shakespeare's total drama labours, to reach its conclusion in *Henry VIII*. For we may say that all Shakespeare's work, his weak kings and his strong ones, even those challengers of royalty, Falstaff and Macbeth, and the anarchical Timon, contribute to the final ritual of Elizabeth's christening and Cranmer's prophecy before the turbulent London crowd; which is, as I have shown elsewhere (*The Crown of Life*, pp. 333–6), conceived as a *comprehensive* scene, while nevertheless forming part of 'a specific and exactly located harmony', at a definite point in history, with the royal child Elizabeth as 'defender not only of "the Faith", but also of all the humanities and profundities of Shakespeare's world' (*The Shakespearian Tempest*, 1953, Prefatory Note, p. xxiii). If we want one, single, human figure incarnating this ideal of magnanimous sovereignty, I point, once again, to the thumb-nail sketch of Theseus in *A Midsummer Night's Dream* (*The Shakespearian Tempest*, pp. 167–8).

Such complexities were contained in my national thinking from the start; allowance was made, again and again, for every opposite. The Crown is the enemy of all one-way propaganda, and so of all 'propaganda' as the word is usually understood;

and therefore propaganda in its cause is really propaganda against propaganda. It raises man above party, above himself and all his most cherished intellectual schemes; it attunes his political and social being to a greater, more complex, more courteous, impersonal, yet strictly personified, wisdom; at the limit to the divine. Always in Shakespeare royalty aspires to be a Christian power; it is, or symbolizes, Christ *in* power.

Humanity must, indeed, beware of letting any one man wield absolute power as the 'deputy elected by the Lord' (*Richard II*, iii. ii. 57). But in this there is nothing new. From earliest times, as Hocart demonstrates, king and constitution have been expected to act in just interplay, tyranny being not natural, but an intruder; so that our modern 'constitutional monarchy' differs rather in degree than in kind from the monarchies of the past. And it is also certain that there should be, in any truly human system, some visible 'figure of God's majesty' (*Richard II*, iv. i. 125) on earth, if only to safe-guard our freedom, since in the last resort freedom depends on royalty, and anything else is merely the way to either barbarism or tyranny, or both. Rightly, the true opposite to tyranny is not 'freedom' which may mean anything or nothing, but rather royalty, symbolizing, as it does, a wisdom over-arching the ephemeral, and often self-delusory, choice. Such royalty, as Bernard Shaw's King Magnus explains to us in a notable passage of *The Apple Cart*, functions in terms not only of the present, with which elections are mainly concerned, but of the distant past, and of futurity; and again we see its kinship with poetry, which Byron defined as 'the feeling of a former world and future' (Journal, 28 Jan., 1821). Throughout the human story, the Crown acts as not only 'defender of the Faith', but as the defender of many faiths. It is the one safe-guard of the artist. It links the body communal to spheres beyond earthly sight; it preserves our faculty of vision; it is a window for ever letting in God's air to the sick room of human politics. If all this is true of a nation, it will be found appallingly more true of world-order; and it is precisely this truth which we are, consciously or unconsciously, recognizing whenever we praise, or enjoy, the works of Shakespeare.

It would seem, then, that, all things considered, I was, for my purpose, right to refuse any central and final emphasis on such comparatively flat and flattening concepts as 'democracy' and 'commonwealth'; though it may be that only those who have experienced the best in what is covered by these great words can properly understand why they do not, alone, go far enough. The world today endures two opposing compulsions: there is (i) an inevitable drive towards world-order countered by (ii) a stronger and more widespread nationalism, in big and little states, than has hitherto been known on earth. Where can we search out a scheme to point the way towards the harmonizing of these apparently incompatible compulsions? Only, it would seem, by taking as an analogy, or rough prototype, our own royalistic democracy. No supernationalistic order can function justly apart from that self-surmounting which we associate with royalty. This much at least is needed if we are to lay foundations for the greater life on earth, and if that is to reflect the hierarchies beyond; for Heaven, or so we have been told, is, not a commonwealth, but a kingdom.

The Second Part of
'King Henry VI' and 'Macbeth'[1]

I do not think it is generally recognized that Shakespeare's earliest tragedies contain a wealth of poetic passion of a kind we do not find again until the *Macbeth* and *King Lear* period. One play in particular, *2 Henry VI*,[2] shows an ambitious and sometimes, though not always, immature attempt at the expression in words of those tense moments where the mind is stretched almost to breaking by a passionate apprehension.

In the earliest plays there are already the far-fetched analogies that 'knit heaven and earth together' (*2 Henry VI*, v. ii. 42); and an unbalanced mind is seen in *Titus Andronicus*, as in *King Lear*, to have penetrated more deeply than those around it into a serene truth, and, I think, to have found a moment's rest there:

> *Marcus* Alas, my lord, I have but killed a fly.
> *Titus*　But how if that fly had a father and a mother?
> 　　　　How would he hang his slender *gilded* wings
> 　　　　And buzz lamenting doings in the air!
> 　　　　Poor, harmless fly,

[1] Originally published in *The New Adelphi*, September 1927.

[2] The three parts of *Henry VI* are now, thanks to the labours of Professor Peter Alexander, generally accepted as authentic Shakespearian originals of the early 90's, when they were performed. The correct texts appeared first in the 1623 Folio, and we cannot be sure that there was not some slight revision during Shakespeare's maturity; but since all the events and so many details of language, including a number of those used in this essay, are shadowed by the pirated versions of Parts II and III published in 1594 and 1595, there appears to be no need to confuse our present argument by such a supposition (1956).

> That, with his pretty buzzing melody,
> Came here to make us merry! And thou hast killed him.
>
> (*Titus Andronicus*, III. ii. 59)

Compare with this *King Lear*, where in a very similar state of mind King Lear says:

> Thou shalt not die: die for adultery! No:
> The wren goes to 't, and the small *gilded* fly
> Does lecher in my sight.
>
> (IV. vi. 114)

It is not strange that Shakespeare should have started writing on these lines; nor that he should deliberately, perhaps in deference to someone's criticism, leave this kind and put himself to a process—we see it developing in *King John* and *Richard II*—of making more objective, more metrically meticulous, and, at the same time, less passionate and personal plays; a process destined to culminate in the perfect differentiation of character in *Henry IV*, to be disturbed by a new unrest in *Julius Caesar* and *Hamlet*, and to reach another perfection in the classic mould of *Othello*.

What is strange is that at times the poetry of those early plays reaches an intensity not very different from that of *King Lear* and *Macbeth*. What they lack is just what the practice of the middle period produced: restraint in matters of blood and death, clear characterization, and unity of design in the whole. But their great moments seem to have been neglected by critics. Nor have I seen it noticed how often the forms of character and incident in the great tragedies are foreshadowed in these early plays. The similarity in theme and treatment of *Titus Andronicus* and *King Lear* is obvious; and here, too, Aaron is the precursor of Iago. The tragic movement of the last acts of *Richard III* is in parts an exact forecast of the declining action in *Macbeth*. We have a love tragedy in *Romeo and Juliet* balancing a love tragedy in *Antony and Cleopatra*; and the introspective *Richard II* reminds me of *Hamlet*. Both periods end with a fairy play.

Nor is this similarity confined to themes. The parallels of incident and phrase in *2 Henry VI* and *Macbeth* are, to say the least, curious; and I think that the fact that in *King Lear* and *Macbeth* Shakespeare was treating incidents and themes already

directly foreshadowed in *Titus Andronicus, Richard III,* and
2 Henry VI, may partly account for the peculiar intensity and
spontaneity of those two, according to some critics, most
powerful of Shakespeare's tragedies.

In the preface to the Arden Edition of *2 Henry VI,* Mr H.
C. Hart says: 'I leave it to my notes to point out a continu-
ously running series of Shakespearianisms in *2 Henry VI.* It
is interesting to see how many times parallels appear from
Lucrece, from *Venus and Adonis,* and, oddly enough, from *King
Lear.*'

My purpose here is to show that this is not really odd;
that *King Lear* and *Henry VI* were written at periods of composition artistically akin. And still more striking than parallels
with *King Lear* are those with *Macbeth.* In *2 Henry VI* we have
the spirit-raising scene (I. iv), with the spirit's 'Have done,
for more I hardly can endure' (I. iv. 41), reminding us of
'Beware the Thane of Fife. Dismiss me; enough' (*Macbeth,* IV.
i. 72). Compare

> . . . and Gloucester's show
> *Beguiles* him as the mournful crocodile
> With sorrow snares relenting passengers;
> Or as the snake, roll'd in a flow'ring bank,
> With shining chequer'd slough, doth sting a child
> That for the beauty thinks it excellent
>
> (*2 Henry VI,* III. i. 225)

with

> . . . To *beguile* the time,
> Look like the time; bear welcome in your eye,
> Your hand, your tongue; look like the innocent flower,
> But be the serpent under 't.
>
> (*Macbeth,* I. v. 64)

This is an interesting example of compression of phraseology
in the later play. Again,

> Not resolute, except so much were *done,*
> For things are often spoke and seldom meant;
> But that my heart accordeth with my tongue . . .
>
> (*2 Henry VI,* III. i. 267)

resembles

> The flighty purpose never is o'ertook
> Unless the deed go with it. From this moment
> The very firstlings of my heart shall be
> The firstlings of my hand. And even now
> To crown my thoughts with acts, be 't thought and *done*
> > (*Macbeth*, IV. i. 145)

and

> Words to the heat of deeds too cold breath gives.
> > (*Macbeth*, II. i. 61)

York's soliloquy in Act III has a Lady Macbeth ring:

> Now, York, or never, steel thy fearful thoughts,
> And change misdoubt to resolution:
> Be that thou hop'st to be, or what thou art
> Resign to death; it is not worth the enjoying.
> Let *pale-faced* fear keep with the mean-born man
> And find no harbour in a royal heart.
> > (*2 Henry VI*, III. i. 331)

For 'pale-faced fear' compare Macbeth's 'That I may tell pale-hearted fear it lies' (IV. i. 85). Again, compare

> *Suffolk*   Now, sirs, have you *dispatch'd* this thing?
> *First Murderer* Ay, my good lord, he's dead. . . .
> > (*2 Henry VI*, III. ii. 6)

with

> *Macbeth* 'Tis better thee without than he within.
>   Is he *dispatch'd*?
> *Murderer* My lord, his throat is cut; that I did for him.
> > (*Macbeth*, III. iv. 14)

King Henry's words are an admirable comment on Macbeth:

> Thrice is he arm'd that hath his quarrel just,
> And he but naked, though lock'd up in steel,
> Whose conscience with injustice is corrupted.
> > (*2 Henry VI*, III. ii. 233)

But the nearest parallel I can call to mind is Malcolm's:

> . . . and the chance of goodness
> Be like our warranted quarrel.
> > (IV. iii. 136)

Perhaps the most remarkable of all is the death in delirium of
Cardinal Beaufort, a scene (iii. iii) of great power, exposing
the workings of guilt in the mind. The conception and phraseology are similar to the sleep-walking scene. It is, indeed,
remarkable how, whenever there is a similarity of incident, the
early phraseology tends to recur in the later play. We hear that

> . . . sometime he calls the king,
> And whispers to his *pillow*, as to him,
> The secrets of his over-*charged* soul.
>
> (iii. ii. 374)

Compare the Doctor's 'The heart is sorely *charged*' and 'In-
fected minds to their deaf *pillows* will *discharge* their secrets'
(*Macbeth*, v. i. 58, 79). At the conclusion of the scene we have
the King's 'Forbear to judge, for we are sinners all' (iii. iii. 31),
corresponding to the Doctor's 'God, God forgive us all' (*Macbeth*, v. i. 82). Here, too, we have 'Disturb him not. Let
him pass peaceably' (iii. iii. 25), recalling *King Lear* (v. iii.
315).

The death of the villainous Suffolk at the hands of Walter
Whitmore (iv. i) reminds me of Macbeth's final meeting with
Macduff. Both Macbeth and Suffolk find a prophecy realized,
and are thereby struck with terror, seeing in their antagonist
the foretold instrument of immediate death.

Mere parallels of words and phrases are frequent. We
have 'gallow-glasses and stout kerns' (iv. ix. 26) corresponding
to the 'kerns and gallow-glasses' of *Macbeth* (i. ii. 13). 'Burns
with revenging fire' in *2 Henry VI* (iv. i. 97) balances Men-
teith's 'revenges burn in them' (*Macbeth*, v. ii. 3). 'Like to
the summer's corn by tempest *lodg'd*' (iii. ii. 176) is paralleled
by Macbeth's 'Though bladed corn be *lodg'd* and trees blown
down' (iv. i. 55; and the expression recurs at *Richard II*, iii. iii.
162). 'If not in Heaven, you'll surely sup in Hell' (v. i. 216)
recalls: 'Hear it not, Duncan, for it is a knell that summons
thee to Heaven or to Hell' (*Macbeth*, ii. i. 63). The characters
of both the Duchess of Gloucester and Queen Margaret
show the conception of Lady Macbeth in the germ. In *Macbeth* alone of the great tragedies is a head brought on the stage:
that, too, comes from *2 Henry VI*.

And finally we have the magnificent first fifteen lines

of Young Clifford's soliloquy after seeing his dead father,
beginning

> O! let the vile world end,
> And the premised flames of the last day
> Knit heaven and earth together;
> Now let the general trumpet blow his blast,
> Particularities and petty sounds
> To cease!
>
> (*2 Henry VI*, v. ii. 40)

Compare

> Had I but died an hour before this chance,
> I had liv'd a blessed time; for, from this instant,
> There's nothing serious in mortality;
> All is but toys; renown and grace is dead,
> The wine of life is drawn, and the mere lees
> Is left this vault to brag of.
>
> (*Macbeth*, ii. iii. 98)

The association of sudden death with the 'last day' occurs, too,
in Macduff's 'Up, up, and see the great doom's image!' (*Macbeth*, ii. iii. 84).

I have concentrated on *Macbeth*, where parallels to this
play are most numerous, but there are other parallels in
2 Henry VI with the later plays, of which I would quote one
which is peculiarly interesting:

> *Suffolk* If I depart from thee I cannot live;
> And in thy sight to die, what were it else
> But like a pleasant slumber in thy lap?
> Here could I breathe my soul into the air,
> As mild and gentle as the cradle babe,
> Dying with mother's dug between its lips.
>
> (iii. ii. 388)

Compare *Antony and Cleopatra:*

> . . . and it is great
> To do that thing that ends all other deeds,
> Which shackles accidents, and bolts up change,
> Which sleeps, and never palates more the dug,
> The beggar's nurse and Caesar's.
>
> (v. ii. 4)

The parallel helps to support the reading 'dug' in *Antony and
Cleopatra* in face of the Folio's 'dung'. Possibly, one can see

something of the future Antony and Cleopatra throughout the
loves of Suffolk and Margaret. The whole play is a seething
mass of diverse tragic power; a young writer's premature
attempt not at a tragedy, but at all tragedy, and the wealth of
terrible experiences huddled successively into these five acts
is amazing.

Some of these comparisons would not be, in themselves,
more than interesting; but taken together, they, and especially
those referring us to *Macbeth*, must, I think, have some further
significance. It is possible that, whilst Shakespeare was treating
a theme which had some similarity of incident with a previous
play, other incidents and phrases from the former play were
set in motion in his mind by laws of association; and I think
this to be the truth, but not the whole truth.

Mr John Masefield, in his *Shakespeare and Spiritual Life*
(The Romanes Lecture, 1924), has said: 'I have no doubt that
at least half of *Macbeth* was written at a sitting.' I do not
know how many people would agree. Though that must remain doubtful, I think most of us feel a certain fiery cohesion,
a lack of artifice, almost of art, in the rush and whirl of movement that makes *Macbeth* especially, and also *King Lear* and
Timon of Athens, appear peculiarly as spontaneous, wild, un-
trimmed growths of the mind in a sense that the earlier plays
of the great period, *Julius Caesar*, *Hamlet*, *Othello*, and the
later ones from *Antony and Cleopatra* to the *Tempest*, are not.
I do not suggest that these three are greater plays than those
preceding or following; merely that they are different, a trilogy
of unique personal intensity, unlike both the impersonal projection of *Othello* and the transcendent vision of *Antony and
Cleopatra*. If, as Mr Masefield implies, *Macbeth* is in respect of
intensity and spontaneity the supreme creation in what he
considers Shakespeare's most 'glorious' creative year, it is not
surprising to find these parallels to what was probably Shakespeare's first tragedy. Images, characters, and events which
have the most immediate and personal influence over a writer
will probably predominate in his earliest work; and will come
back to him with unusual rapidity and power of expression
when in his maturity he allows himself to treat similar themes.
Both *2 Henry VI* and *Richard III* went to the making of
Macbeth.

APPENDIX E

The Principles of Shakespeare Interpretation[1]

I offer some suggestions for the interpretation of Shakespeare: for some new method such as I outline here is called for and imminent in contemporary literary thought. This method has in actual practice the merit of disclosing fresh beauties and of reconciling old discrepancies.

It is remarkable that the existing mass of Shakespeare criticism [2] should have accomplished so little of positive value in proportion to its bulk. Critic after critic, from poets to academic scholars, has returned to the attack: and reader after reader returns, wisely, not to the critic but to Shakespeare himself, in the theatre or the library. And yet I believe that there has been much waiting for the critics and left undone. This I attribute in many instances to a complete neglect of the poetic quality of the plays; in others, to an easy contentment with, if not overstated, certainly useless, paragraphs of rhetorical and amateurish praise. Swinburne's *Study of Shakespeare* is a case in point. That is, critics have either analysed the plays as naked prose narrative deducing facts of characterization from the apparent acts and rational sentiments of the heroes, whilst wholly neglecting the pulse and throb of passionate life which makes those acts and sentiments of any permanent interest; so that much of what has been written of Hamlet or Brutus could have been applied with as much absolute value in its

[1] This, my first published 'manifesto', appeared in *The Shakespeare Review*, September 1928. The essay contained a footnote acknowledgement which ran: 'I would express my indebtedness to the critical work of Dr A. C. Bradley, Mr John Masefield, and especially Mr J. Middleton Murry: to whom the criticisms of my article do not apply'.

[2] At the time of writing this essay I had not started to emphasize the distinction, first theoretically discussed in the Introduction to *The Wheel of Fire*, between 'criticism' and 'interpretation'.

result to Hieronimo or the Brutus of Plutarch, that which differentiates Shakespeare's figures from lesser writers being always exactly what is passed over in silence by critics who stress characterization at the expense of poetry. Or, realizing the all-importance of the poetry and finding themselves confronted with a seemingly impossible task, they have fallen back on vague paeans of idolatry. And today there is also a tendency to neglect the deeper significances of the plays for an insistence on the dramatic nature of their composition, a tendency to find easy reasons for all difficulties of interpretation, in the taste, or lack of taste, of the period and the audiences for which they were composed. Again the main issue is shirked. And yet all agree as to the fundamental grandeur of the plays. But what is it which renders these plays of deep interest from whatever point of view they are approached? What is their essential reality which we apprehend intuitively but cannot afterwards express in terms of intellect and reason? These questions we ask too seldom. Little has been done in the way of analysis of the imaginative quality of the plays: critics have done too little towards an interpretation of their poetic meaning.

It is worth asking what exactly is the usual critical and analytical process. One is confronted with a play that moves one intensely, say *Macbeth*. *Macbeth* leaves us with a sense of positive accomplishment. It is good, not ill, and we are the better and the happier for having read it. Now this sense of a positive and happy experience remains with us, and next we try to explain the nature of the work that aroused it. We begin to reason. But the purely poetic quality, which first aroused our interest, does not easily lend itself to analysis: so we deliberately start to analyse just as much of the skeleton of the plot and the superficial appearance of the characters as is readily tractable to reason. We see in it, perhaps, a moral problem, and immediately apply our own system of ethics to it, and find ourselves writing at length, not on *Macbeth*, but our own ethical philosophy. Any murder story would have done as well. We have abstracted from the unique reality a small fraction, whereas we should have considered the play as an individual poetic whole. Thus the usual conclusion is that *Macbeth* points the lesson of the blackness and hatefulness of crime; that it shows us the miserable end of a murderer; that in watching the hero we will see clearly how dangerous it may be to take the wrong path, and in watching his wife will learn what kind of woman to avoid. Such criticism concentrates, in tragedy, always on the unpleasant potentialities of its subject, forgetting that the original experience, which it purports to interpret, was pleasant; and surely in our valuation of a spiritual experience the quality of pleasure, well-being, or sense of good is quite fundamental and must under no circumstances be lost in process of translation from one order of consciousness to another. Such criticism, again, is all negative, whereas our original experience was positive. So tragedy continues to baffle us. By what concepts, then, can we express rationally our unrational yet positive joy in tragedy? Certain words come inevitably to the mind: grandeur, pathos, destiny. And such indeed point the way of a sound interpretation. But they have been worn dull with use, and we are not content with single words. It is necessary to consider how, without degenerating into rhetoric and sentiment, we can delve deeper into the poetic and unrational meaning of Shakespeare's tragedy. I suggest five main principles.

I. We should observe absolute loyalty to our aesthetic reaction to the poetry. In matters of sexual immorality or crime, the themes of two of Shakespeare's greatest tragedies, we must banish all extraneous considerations of shame and ethics, except in so far as a reference to the moral order may be implicit in the play and our enjoyment of it. The poetic consciousness, in poet or reader, itself knows no shame and is quite unmoral. But how many critics have been true to the fact that, as we read, *Macbeth* points the grandeur of the soul meshed in crime rather than the ignominy of it, and that *Antony and Cleopatra* points the supreme excellence of the erotic impulse even though unsanctified by that expedience and convention and worldly success which is so large a part of formal morality? Shakespeare is not at pains to show us what to avoid, nor what to imitate. The poetry goes deeper, and exposes the essence of human reality. Great tragedy is a statement, not a persuasion. And though the statement may persuade us, as real life persuades us, that some things are profitable and some unprofitable of imitation, the tragic poet does

T

not bend to teach. He leaves us to draw a moral, if we choose, and we have a perfect right to do so. But let us not claim that we are interpreting Shakespeare by so doing, for we are merely interpreting ourselves. *Macbeth* has more to tell us than that sin brings retribution. Its total significance is so powerful, so positive, so pleasant: our interpretation, in its total effect, should be so, too. We must, then, be absolutely true to our individual and personal experience, for by so doing only can we criticize truly that outside ourselves which gave us that unique experience.

II. We must start our interpretation from the thing to be interpreted. That is, we must concern ourselves primarily with the perfected result of literary creation without letting our immediate understanding be hampered and clogged with irrelevant considerations. The value of 'sources' is very slight, though the time hitherto spent on the tracing of them must have been excessive. A knowledge of sources—in itself, as is all knowledge, praiseworthy, though necessarily often guess-work—adds practically nothing to the philosophic and aesthetic import of a work of art. Modern psychology will show us, too, that sources are not so simple as many past critics have supposed. A friend of Shakespeare's may well have played a more important part in the creation of Brutus than did Plutarch's *Lives*. And it is exactly that differentiating quality of personal sympathy and insight which endows Shakespeare's creation with a significance of which Plutarch's is sterile, and which causes us to devote our detailed attention to the one and not to the other. Again, an insistence on the necessity of considering at every turn the limitations of the manners and taste of Shakespeare's time, and the commercial nature of his work, is dangerous to a true critical outlook. Such knowledge is, of course, interesting. But it has little to say compared with our immediate and personal experience derived from the text. Within the limits of his age and profession Shakespeare has created works of positive and lasting significance. To suggest at any important point that had those limits been other than they were, Shakespeare might have done this or that, is critically, though not necessarily untrue, certainly uninteresting and often distracting. All artists work within the limits of their materials, but what is important is the positive nature of their creation within those limits. That is, in Shakespeare's case, apparent to the ordinary educated reader who knows little of Elizabethan stage history, and nothing of 'sources'. And under this heading I would also deprecate the hypothetical attribution of intentions and personal bias to Shakespeare. One should not say that he meant to show Brutus as the finest character of *Julius Caesar*, and Cassius as the villain of the play. Many people today feel the reverse. One can say nothing of Shakespeare's intentions, or his feelings towards his own characters. Nor can one do more than hazard vague guesses of Shakespeare's 'personal' religion as distinct from those essentially religious experiences transmitted by a reading of the great plays, and such guesses are of little interest; for one can only speak with authority of one's own response to Shakespeare's creations. So that in using the word 'Shakespeare' we should not mean some imaginary person who likes the characters we like and dislikes those we dislike, and who holds our own views on ethics and religion, but rather see that its meaning for us must necessarily stand for that creative impulse behind the text which is responsible for the experience which each play, as a whole, gives us. Again, I would assert that we must start our interpretation with the thing to be interpreted, and beware of losing ourselves in a morass of hypotheses and abstractions.

III. We should give more detailed attention to the individual peculiarities of style in each play.[1] The imaginative and intellectual atmospheres of Shakespeare's greater plays call for minute examination. For the greater plays have each a unique atmosphere which harmonizes with the theme—intellectual or moral, as in *Troilus and Cressida* and *Measure for Measure* respectively, or passionate, as in the great tragedies —which the play presents. It will be found that each play thus expresses a particular and peculiar vision of human existence, and that this vision determines not alone the choice of the main plot, but the selection or invention of subsidiary scenes and characters, the matters brought up for discussion within the scenes, and the very fibre of the language in allusion, choice of imagery, metaphor and general cast of thought. Each of the

---

[1] My original note here ran: 'The method employed by Dr A. C. Bradley in *Shakespearian Tragedy* may be extended to nearly all the plays from *Julius Caesar* to *The Tempest* with a corresponding pregnancy of result.'

greater plays from 1599 onwards turns on a single theme, which is often reflected in the minutest details of thought and language, and the minute details of thought are often of a metaphysical significance as yet unrecognized. Thus more careful paraphrases should be attempted, expanding and explicating the condensed and often highly-charged metaphorical language in terms of rational rather than associative thought. Attention to these considerations will reveal the possibility of analysing the warm flesh and pulsing blood of Shakespeare's plays, and of so coming nearer towards plucking out the heart of their mystery; whereas hitherto we have too often either been content with an unintellectual adoration of the living body or, turning scientific, have attended only to the bones.

IV. The plays from 1599 (*Julius Caesar*) to 1611 (*The Tempest*) must be regarded not only individually, but also as a succession forming a closely consecutive relationship in which groups of plays and single plays shed mutual light on each other.[1] The sequence is impressive and compelling, and evidences clearly some purpose in the creating power which we name 'Shakespeare'. *Julius Caesar* stands alone. Then the first group reflects a mind in intellectual trouble, with a recurrent and clearly expressed antithesis of the two dynamic mental acts, faith and reason, or intuition and intelligence. 'Two truths are told' in the problem plays, but they are unreconciled and the dualism persists until in the second group we have a sublime vision of human grandeur, the immanence of the Great Spirit in man, the swelling act of the soul's tragedy. And the third shows us a purely mystic view of life born, it would seem, out of tragic contemplation, the imperial theme of religious peace culminating in the mystic symbolism of *The Tempest*.[2]

[1] At this point I had a note: 'Here especially I must express my debt—both direct and indirect—to the writings of Mr J. Middleton Murry.' I should, however, state that this note did not apply to my reading of the Final Plays, concerning which Mr Murry held the traditional view. I was referring rather to the general tendency of Mr Murry's writings in *Discoveries* (1924) and elsewhere to search for spiritual truth within the works of literature, and in particular to certain general and unformulated emphases on Shakespeare's spiritual development. For some relevant facts regarding my early work, see my preface, pp. 8–9 above; also *The Imperial Theme*, 1951, pp. v–vi.

[2] It will be seen that at this period I had not begun to survey the importance of *Henry VIII* as the concluding work of the sequence.

William James, in *The Varieties of Religious Experience*, traces exactly this progress of the spirit from mental pain and division to unrational unified acceptance of suffering, and thence to a serene and mystic assurance. He draws on many instances, including one who comes probably nearer to Shakespeare in creative power than any other European writer, Tolstoy. To what extent the imaginary Shakespeare of our own minds, which many people would call 'the real Shakespeare', was at all times in his uncreative as well as his creative moments fully aware of this sequence need not concern us. Such a Shakespeare is, at all events to a critic of the poetry, a pure abstraction. Moreover, to say that this sequence is a matter of chance proves nothing. We know little of the basis of artistic creation; and we know still less of chance. If such a choice of themes, if such a movement of the poet's mind, be 'chance', then that chance-movement is worth our deepest attention and analysis.

V. Lastly, I would insist on the value of an examination and correlation of Shakespeare's poetic imagery throughout his work. The association of certain ideas and images throughout Shakespeare is remarkably consistent, and many of the hitherto easily dismissed 'fancies' hold a deeper significance when related to other similar images than has yet been expected.

I think that the significance of the plays from 1599 to 1611 as revealed by such a critical method will not lead to a chaotic and dangerous view of life, but will rather justify Mr Middleton Murry's words on Shakespeare: 'The perfection of his faculties was such that he succeeded in creating an organic synthesis, an act which held in solution a psychology, an ethic, and a metaphysic'.[1] Especially do the plays demand and provide the now necessary synthesis of religious and aesthetic experience.

[1] Quoted from 'Towards a Synthesis', *The Monthly Criterion*, June 1927.

Additional Note (1958). Turning over the pages of my Folio facsimile, I find that the names Euphronius and Thyreus, discussed on pp. 192–3 above, cannot properly be attributed to Shakespeare, since they do not occur in the original text.

Indexes

by
Patricia M. Ball

The indexes cover the volumes *The Wheel of Fire*, enlarged edition (WF), *The Imperial Theme* (IT), *The Crown of Life* (CL), *The Shakespearian Tempest* (ST), and *The Sovereign Flower* (SF), in the editions published and reissued by Messrs Methuen & Co. between 1949 and 1958. A few important references to *The Christian Renaissance* (Macmillan, 1933), *The Principles of Shakespearian Production* (Faber & Faber, 1936; Penguin Books, 1949), *Christ and Nietzsche* (Staples Press, 1948), and *The Mutual Flame* (Methuen & Co., 1955) are added to Indexes A and B, under the letters CR, SP, CN, and MF.

Entries referring to notes or appendixes are not distinguished. A single entry covering a series of pages, e.g. '129–44', does not necessarily indicate either the continuity of the subject or a reference to it on every page. In Index B, references to passages quoted in the text are only included when they are the immediate subject of commentary.

P. M. B.

Index A

Shakespearian Works

All's Well that Ends Well: WF 158; IT 13–15; CL 48, 61–3, 70, 74, 78, 82, 96, 127–8, 152, 162, 218; ST 23, 31, 45, 50–3, 58–60, 65–6, 74–5, 101–2, 105, 121, 134, 279, 296, 303; SF 8, **95–160,** 172–4, 187, 199, 213, 219–26, 250–1, 256, 274–5; MF 54

A Lover's Complaint: IT 348; ST 23, 30–1, 66; SF 133, 157

A Midsummer Night's Dream: WF 63, 254, 258, 265, 286, 330, 336–40; IT viii, 8, 14, 104, 325, 332, 354–5; CL 51–2, 68, 72, 82, 94, 110, 192, 204–11, 215–19, 246–7, 250, 265, 285, 314; ST xv, xxi–xxiii, 32, 40, 75, 90, 98, 104–6, 130, **141–69,** 263, 267, 270, 273, 279, 298–301, 307, 310–12, 317, 322, 327–330; SF 47, 91, 140, 164, 171–3, **184,** 190, 198–9, 206–7, 220, 224, 227, 232–233, 277; CR III

Antony and Cleopatra: WF 8–9, 53, 68, 84, 118, 140, 149, 173, 179, 210–11, 236, 245, 256, 262, 265–7, 287–8, 292, 296, 307, 336, 339; IT vi–viii, 3–5, 19, 23–31, 40, 44, 58, 83, 90–2, 116–17, 123, 134–5, 142, 148–50, 154–9, 168, 189–91, **197–350,** 358–60, 366–7; CL 12–13, 16–19, 34–6, 39, 57, 64, 69–71, 89, 102, 106–7, 110, 119–20, 123, 131, 135–7, 146, 153, 160, 165, 168, 175, 191, 194–5, 203–5, 209, 214–16, 220, 227, 245, 262, 269, 273, 281, 286, 289–92, 296, 303, 310, 314, 317–21, 324, 327, 334–5; ST vii, xi–xiii, xx–xxi, 8–14, 29, 40, 48, 53–5, 58, 64–5, 76, 88, 103–4, 118, 121–5, 130, 135, 163, 173, 176, 179, 202, **210–17,** 226–7, 234–6, 239, 259, 262, 266–8, 271, 278, 307–21, 324–5; SF 65–9, 75, 97–8, 123, 129, 133–4,

137, 150, 165–6, 176, 187, **192–5,** 207, 212–13, 218–22, 225–6, 229, 233–40, 249–50, 256, 275, 281, 285–6, 289

As You Like It: IT 9–10, 13–14, 26, 290, 294; CL 42, 67, 70, 100–2, 111, 128, 147, 153–7, 192, 195–6, 205–6, 210, 214–17, 298; ST 18, 35, 44, 71, 74–5, **83–7,** 93–4, 99, 139–41, 194, 201, 235, 263, 272, 327; SF 10, 55, 111, 123, 133–4, 147, 170–1, 186, 196, 199, 220, 227

Coriolanus: WF 287; IT 18, 25–7, 30, 44, 118, 135, **154–98,** 269, 302, 366; CL 34, 118, 166, 186–9, 197, 211, 221, 260–1, 267, 286, 289, 303; ST xi, xii–xv, xviii, 31, 40, **206–10,** 215–17, 239, 250, 293–4, 296, 308; SF 17, 20, **65–8,** 71, 75, 134, **166,** 173, 179, 191, 209, 212, 226, 236, 266

Cymbeline: WF xviii, 63, 256–8, 263–5, 305, 334–6; IT 42; CL viii, 9, 16, **19–22,** 23–6, 30, 42, 47, 58, 72, 83, 92, 117, **129–202,** 203–9, 216–21, 248, 257, 270, 284, 296–8, 306–8, 319–24, 334–5; ST x, xv, xviii–xix, 2, 20, 31, 40, 83–5, 123, 135, 176, 197, 218, **234–41,** 243, 248, 254–7, 263, 268, 301–2, 308, 318, 321–3, 327; SF **73–80,** 86, 102, 131–3, 155, 168, 173, 178–9, 188, **196–200,** 222, 238–40

Hamlet: WF v–viii, 2–5, 11–15, **17–46,** 65, 69, 74, 120, 140, 159, 173–4, 180, 188–9, 198, 222–3, 231, 235–6, 240–5, 248, **253–5,** 257–65, 269, 281, 284–9, 292, 296, **298–325,** 326–43; IT ix–x, 2–4, 16–18, 21–8, 31, **96–124,** 125, 137, 176, 181–2, 198, 240, 263–5, 278, 285, 289–90, 303–4, 309, 316, 332, 340, 344, 355, 359, 362, 365–6; CL 10–12, 17, 20, 29, 34, 40, 73–7, 82–4,

96, 103, 110–14, 118, 124, 130–1, 147, 152, 165–70, 187, 191–2, 205–7, 214, 217–25, 243–4, 257, 262, 269–71, 276–7, 283, 298, 306, 314, 319, 324, 330, 336; ST vii, xviii–xxi, 44, 58, 122–3, 131, 150, 160, 164, 169, 174, **176–9**, 200, 217, 238, 242, 272, 294, 305–6, 311, 316–19, 324, 327; SF 47–50, 54, 64, 73, 81, 96–7, 121, 124, 155, 158, 166, 172, 176, **186–9**, 207–8, 211–14, 217, 221–2, 225–35, 246, 249, 264, 281, 286–7; SP III (e)

Julius Caesar: WF 7, 15–16, 51, **120–39**, 140, 180, 206, 253, 256–7, 261, 286, 292, 306, 314, 328–31, 339; IT viii, 2, 9, 16–22, 25–31, **32–95**, 102, 155, 176, 190, 226–7, 237, 243, 366; CL 11, 18, 83, 191, 195, 205–6, 211, 221, 224, 233, 303 , 334; ST viii, xi–xiii, xviii, 38, 54, 137, 171, **183–7**, 189–91, 194, 201, 217, 250, 294, 310; SF 8, 47–8, 65, **73–5**, 133–4, 155, 166, 174, 188, **191–2**, 211–12, 219–21, 233, 239, 245, 256–7, 281, 286–7, 290–2

King Henry the Fourth, Part One: WF 44, 287, 312, 319, 334; IT 3–9, 25, 72, 214; CL 100, 112, 140, 146–7, 187, 203, 217, 258, 297, 305–7, 324, 335–6; ST ix, xv, xxiii, 23, 26, 38, 41, 50, 56–60, 106, 298, 318; SF 20, 25, **32–6**, 37–9, 43, 47, 53, 67, 81, 117–23, 167, 174, **180–4**, 199, 214, 218, 221–4, 227, 266–8, 277, 281

King Henry the Fourth, Part Two: WF 265, 287, 340; IT 2–3, 7, 10–11, 15, 333; CL 100, 112, 133–5, 140, 203, 209, 217, 220, 258, 285, 288, 297–8, 305–7, 324, 329, 335–6; ST ix, xv, xxiii, 20–1, 24–6, 35–43, 46–7, 50–3, 57–60, 106, 182, 312–14; SF 20, 25, **33–6**, 37–8, 43, 47, 52, 81, 118, 121–2, 169–72, 184, 199, 214, 221–5, 247, 268, 277, 281

King Henry the Fifth: WF 44, 323, 334–340; IT 2–11, 32, 149, 214, 332; CL 36, 110, 147, 162–3, 203–5, 208–10, 219, 256–8, 274–6, 285, 298, 306, 318, 324, 329, 333–5; ST 14, 25, 32, 38–42, 47–52, 55–6, 63–4, 67, 72, 104, 212, 225, 244, 285, 310–16; SF 20, 25, **36–47**, 55, 72, 77, 81–3, 87, 163, **167–72**, 183–4, 196, 208, 213–14, 222–4, 239, 247, 264

King Henry the Sixth, Part One: WF 340; CL 203, 206, 255–6, 306, 321; ST 23–5, 31, 41–3, 47, 56–8, 70, 74, 294, 297–300, 317, 320–2; SF 14, 18–25, 32, 40, 70, 183, 188, 222, 280

King Henry the Sixth, Part Two: IT 16, 250, 348; CL 86, 197, 203, 206, 211, 247, 255–6, 303, 306, 321; ST xix, 26, 34–42, 52, 56, 66–9, 174, 296–7; SF **14–20**, 21–5, 32, 70, 78, 222, 227, 275, **280–6**

King Henry the Sixth, Part Three: IT 2–3, 15, 363; CL 136, 197, 201–3, 206, 211, 219, 255–6, 270, 286, 292, 306, 321, 335; ST 22, 25–9, 34–8, 43; 46, 50–2, 70–1, 107, 269, 294, 320–1; SF **14–20**, 21–5, 32, 46, 70, 78, 86–8, 179, 222–3, 227, 280

King Henry the Eighth: WF 323–4, 337; IT 367; CL viii, 30, 50–1, 72, 93, 97, 137, 162, 167–8, 172, 190–1, 196–7, 202, 223, 255, **256–336**; ST xi, xiv–xv, xviii, xxii–xxiii, 2, 46, **241–6**, 254, 268, 294, 322; SF 38, 47–9, 63, 73, 78, **80–8**, 121, 155, 168–9, **172**, 214, 221–2, 226–8, 239–41, 249, 253, 263–7, 277, 292; SP III (c)

King John: WF 274, 305, 329, 340; IT 5–7, 11, 14, 42; CL 59, 130, 134–7, 140–1, 146–7, 165, 172, 194, 201, 205, 209, 256–8, 270, 285, 289, 296–7, 306–7, 335; ST 20, 23–7, 30–7, 40–6, 49–51, 54, 295; SF 20, 24, **25–7**, 44, 55, 76–7, 81–6, 221–3, 239, 264, 281

King Lear: WF xix, 2–6, 9–15, 19, 32, 41–4, 50–1, 60, 84, 97–105, 108, 118, 138–40, **160–206**, 207, 210, 219–23, 235–6, 252–4, 257, 261–3, 266–70, 274–8, 281–3, 286–7, 290–2, 296, 307, 330, 340; IT 16–18, 22, 26, 116–17, 141, 155, 199–201, 204, 210, 227–9, 237, 240, 251–2, 259, 263–6, 278, 282–3, 288–90, 303, 309–12, 316, 324, 332–4, 338–42, 356–9, 362, 365–6; CL 11–12, 18, 24, 35–6, 41–4, 50, 53, 57–60, 63–5, 69–71, 75, 81–2, 87–8, 96–100, 110, 123, 130–2, 136, 142, 146–7, 152–3, 167, 173, 179–80, 183, 191–5, 201, 205–6, 210–11, 214, 217–22, 234, 257, 268–9, 276–7, 285–7, 296–8, 324–6; ST xx–xxi, 7, 15–16, 31, 36, 58, 69, 83–5, 105–7, 130–2, 176, 183, **194–201**, 204, 227, 235, 239–40,

250, 255, 268, 302; SF 10, **58–60,** 64,
71–3, 77–81, 88, 97, 121–3, 134, 155,
166–8, 172, 186–90, 198, 210–12, 217,
220–2, 226–30, 233–9, 249–50, 270,
280–6; SP III (App.)

King Richard II: WF 8, 117, 257–9, 260,
265, 305, 308, 329, 339; IT 2–11,
143, 250, **351–67;** CL 30, 40, 44, 47,
82, 89, 136, 149, 166, 194, 205–6,
222, 246–8, 256–8, 270, 275–8, 281–8,
294–6, 306–7, 329, 335; ST xxi, 20,
24–6, 32–4, 37, 43, 51–4, 57–9,
69, 235, 271, 294, 298–302, 310–11,
331; SF 20, 25, **28–32,** 33, 36, 56,
70–6, 88, **174,** 180, 213, 221–3, 226,
247–8, 264, 275, 278, 281, 284; CN
132–3

King Richard III: WF 140, 154; IT 7;
CL 57, 85–6, 129, 137, 146–7, 165–7,
205, 211, 257, 281, 284, 287–9, 306–7;
ST xix, 23, 26–7, 32–6, 40, 45–6,
67, 105, 252, 300, 307, 321; SF 20,
21–5, 29, 32–3, 36–7, 49, 60, 71, 168,
174, 180, 184, 206, 211, 217, 221–2,
225, 264, 281–2, 286

Love's Labour's Lost: WF 263–5, 339–
340; IT 13–15, 332; CL 95, 100–2, 109,
147, 203, 209, 297–9, 327; ST xiii,
xxi, 26, 58–60, 73, **75–83,** 86, 94,
98, 130, 133, 138–9, 262, 272, 295,
301, 309, 312–14; SF 141, 170–2, 186,
220

Macbeth: WF 2–13, 16, 32, 42–5, 51, 88,
97–105, **120–59,** 160, 177–80, 187–9,
196, 205–7, 210, 221–2, 240, 243,
249, 253–69, 277–83, 286–7, 296,
329, 333–7; IT viii–ix, 13, 16–18, 22–
30, 33, 40–2, 46, 57–61, 81, 94–5,
102–3, 107–9, 119–23, **125–53,** 155–9,
166, 176, 191–2, 200, 204, 227–9, 234,
237–40, 252, 263–4, 268, 288–90, 301,
307–10, 316–17, 324, **327–42,** 343–4,
359; CL 11, 18, 24, 36, 39, 42, 59–60,
67, 80–7, 91, 96, 113, 120, 124, 130–1,
140, 165–8, 172–3, 179, 187, 191–5,
208, 211–13, 216–21, 235–6, 240–2,
257, 270, 284–7, 296, 300–1, 317, 327–
328, 335; ST viii–ix, xiv–xv, xviii–xxiii,
5–7, 10, 15–17, 27–8, 34, 40, 55, 65,
91–3, 112, 118–20, 129, 137, 142, 146–
153, 156, 160–1, 171, 176, 183, **187–94,**
201–2, 205, 215–17, 223, 238–9, 250,
254–9, 266–72, 284, 288, 293, 298,

303–11, 315, 319, 323, **326–32;** SF 10,
20, **58–65,** 68, 71–3, 80, 86, 97, 113,
134, 154–5, 167, 170, 173, 200, 207,
212–14, 221–2, 227–39, 245–6, 249–51,
256, 264, 270, 277, 280–90; SP **IV (3);**
CN **85–6;** CR III

Measure for Measure: WF 2–5, 12, 15, 43,
51, 55, **73–96,** 97, 173, 192, 242, 245,
252–3, 259–60, 279–81, 296, 309,
315, 321, 324, 333, 336–7, 341; IT
12–20, 82–90, 109–10, 331, 355,
358, 366; CL 10–11, 61, 152, 179, 188,
201, 207–8, 221, 224, 235, 288–90,
298, 324–6; ST xv, 40, 154, 169,
174–6, 189, 197, 272; SF **51–2,** 57, 69,
72, 81, 88, 95, 102–7, 111, 134, 139,
146, 170–1, **187–8,** 195–8, 208, **217,**
227–9, 232, 251, 273, 291

Much Ado about Nothing: WF 289,
338; IT 9, 12–14, 26, 234, 290, 298;
CL 43, 70, 73, 140, 146–7, 150–2, 204–
207, 211, 217–19, 298, 327, 333; ST
xxiii, 40, 52, 71, 75–6, **87–93,** 94,
104–6, 138–40, 154, 214, 236, 296,
299, 307–10, 317; SF 101, 112, 123, 126,
133, 170–3, 199, 226

Othello: WF 3–6, 9, 12–15, 28, 43, 48,
53, 63, 69, **97–119,** 140, 147, 152, 165,
169, 177, 211, 219–22, 235–6, 245,
249–54, 257, 262–5, 269, 273, 282–3,
287, 290–3, 329, 339; IT 17–22,
25–7, 139, 147, 154–7, 160, 200–4,
214, 240–1, 259, 264, 278, 281–3, 288–
290, 301–3, 309–10, 316–18, 332; CL
10–11, 17, 20, 36, 49, 59, 74, 79–85,
96, 101, 123, 130, 140–2, 145–7, 152,
165, 191, 203–5, 213–15, 221–2, 249,
277, 290–1, 295–6, 301; ST xxi, 7–8,
15, 40, 65, 123, 126, 131, 152, 165,
179–83, 185–7, 191, 194, 198, 201,
221, 263, 311; SF 64–6, 78, 96, 123–4,
127–9, 134, 164, 175, 179, 184, **189–91,**
198, 206, 211–12, 217–18, 221–30, 234–
236, 281, 286; SP III (d)

Pericles, Prince of Tyre: WF xviii–xix,
236, 256, 265, 305, 337, 342; IT X, 11,
263; CL 9, 13, **14–17,** 18–19, 22–5, 29,
32–75, 76, 92, 96–9, 103, 107, 110,
116, 122–31, 147, 153, 156, 162, 165–
174, 183–96, 200, 203–4, 207, 216, 220–
222, 231–2, 235, 242, 250, 257, 268,
284, 293–4, 312, 318–20, 327, 333–5;
ST xv, xviii, 1, 32, 53, 114, 120, 123,

136, 174, 213, **218–29**, 230–1, 234, 239–40, 248, 263, 268, 310, 327; SF 69–71, 96–102, 108, 132, 146–7, 155–6, 170, 188, 196–200, 213, 226, 238, 273

Romeo and Juliet: WF 60–5, 245, 258, 263–5, 333–4, 339–40; IT 8–9, 12–13, 42, 225, 244, 276, 325, 332; CL 42–3, 47–50, 54, 64, 69, 73–4, 96, 102–3, 110–111, 119, 123, 146, 150–2, 169, 187, 203–4, 207–9, 216, 265, 296–303, 327; ST X, xviii, 39, 42, 45–7, 53, 61–3, 72–3, 148, 151, 298, 303–7, 316–19, 322–3; SF 36, 55, 66–7, 95, 133–4, 170, 173–5, **178–80**, 184–6, 206–9, 212, 219–221, 225–9, 235, 246–9, 266, 275, 281; SP **III (b)**

Sonnets: WF 63, 211, 258, 263, 327–9, 337, 341; CL 38, 64, 83, 102, 110, 131, 194, 240, 284, 334; ST 21, 39, 54–5, 59–60, 65, 71–3, 136–7, 199, 269, 273, 305, 324; SF 102, 109, 125–6, 129–41, **157–8**, 185–6, 199, 218–19, 222, 225; MF throughout

The Comedy of Errors: WF 261; IT 11; CL 36, 70, 131, 204; ST 40, 54, 75, **113–20**, 121, 138–41, 242, 307; SF 173, 188, 213

The Merchant of Venice: WF 63, 75, 119, 258, 262, 265, 282, 333–5; IT 8–15, 29; CL 39, 48, 67, 70–3, 147, 150–2, 155, 165, 179, 188, 204, 210–11, 215, 283, 288, 291, 298, 324–6; ST xiii–xv, xxi, 28, 41, 50, 56, 60–1, 75, 98, 117, 121–3, **127–37**, 138–41, 148, 154, 174, 252–3, 258–60, 278, 289, 303, 323; SF 50–1, 66, 81, 131–3, 163–7, 171, **175–8**, 184, 190, 200, 211, 214, 218–25, 233; SP **IV (2)**

The Merry Wives of Windsor: WF 289; IT 13; CL 70, 86, 96, 112, 140, 205, 211, 215–20, 297; ST 7–8, 75, **99–103**, 104–6, 125, 139–40, 154–6, 168, 260; SF 121, 166, 170–2, 188–90, 213, 217

The Passionate Pilgrim: ST 58, 62, 302

The Phoenix and the Turtle: IT 349–50; CL 170, 210, 250, 321; ST xxiv, 278, 293, **320–5**; SF 112, 136–8, 237; MF Part II; CR XII

The Rape of Lucrece: WF 259–60; IT 16, 133, 333; CL 39, 212; ST 21–6, 29–30, 34, 40–1, 45, 50–1, 59, 64–5, 72, 153, 293–5, 305, 309–11, 322; SF **216–17**, 227, 231, 282

The Taming of the Shrew: CL 70, 131, 211, 215, 219, 327; ST 23, 40, 75, 94, **103–12**, 117–20, 126, 134, 139, 154–6, 297, 300, 303; SF 133, 142, 171–3, 187–8, 217, 222, 226

The Tempest: WF ix, xx, 15–16, 49, 74, 144, 241, 256, 289–90, 315, 320, 324, 330, 334–7, 340–2; IT vii, 15, 136, 199, 308, 325; CL 13, 16, 23, **24–8**, 43, 46, 51, 54–5, 65, 72–4, 77, 92, 108, 124, 131, 149, 172, 185–96, **203–55**, 256–7, 260, 263, 268, 276–8, 288, 291–7, 300, 304, 307, 311, 319, 322–4, 327, 333–6; ST xv, xviii, xix–xxiii, 9–13, 98, 101–2, 105–7, 117, 122, 156, 163, 168, 241, **247–66**, 268, 274, 277–9, 283, 319, 322; SF 9, **69–72**, 73, 77, 80–1, 88, 121, 134, 188, **198–200**, 213, 225–7, 231, 238–40, 273–5, 286, 291–2; MF 54–6

The Two Gentlemen of Verona: WF 63, 245; IT 11, 14, 26, 332; CL 32, 152, 157, 203–6; ST 52, 58, 68, 75, 83, **94–9**, 100, 117, 139, 194, 299, 317; SF 131, 170–1, **175**, 188, 218

The Winter's Tale: WF xviii, 256, 265, 270, 282, 289–90, 333; IT 11; CL 14–19, 22–3, 29, 37, 43–5, 49, 53–9, 65, 69–72, **76–128**, 129–30, 140, 149, 156–9, 164–167, 170, 173–5, 183–6, 189–91, 196, 200, 203–6, 212, 215–22, 229–32, 235, 242, 245, 248, 257–63, 267–8, 273, 286, 289–92, 296–7, 310–13, 319, 324, 327, 332, 335–6; ST xv, xviii, xxi, 40, 123, 131, 218, **229–34**, 239–40, 243, 262–3, 268, 273–4, 300; SF 69–71, 89, **98–102**, 106, 131–2, 135, 148–149, 154–5, 178, 186, **196–8**, 209, 213, 222–6, 238, **240**, 251

Timon of Athens: WF 2, 5–6, 9–13, 43, 50, 84, 97, 140, 147, 165, 168, 175, 178, 189, 201, **207–39**, 242–57, 262–3, 269, 281, 287, 315, 320, 340; IT 14, 18, 22, 26–7, 31–2, 35, 44, 49, 83, 120, 135, 146–8, 155, 189–91, 199–204, 217, 221, 233, 240, 259, 262–4, 278–9, 282–3, 288, 302, 305, 309, 316, 324, 357–61, 364–6; CL viii, 12, 18, 23, 34, 47–8, 51, 54, 61, 69, 70–4, 82, 89, 96, 117, 162, 172, 206, 211–12, 216, 219, 222–3, 248, 256, 276–9, 283–8, 292, 295–6, 300–1, 326–7, 333; ST viii, xv, xviii–xx, 2, 18, 83–5, 104–6, 109, 112, 131, 152,

171, 191, **201–6**, 212–14, 217, 235–6, 241, 280, 297, 314, 321; SF **53–7**, 59, 64, 70–2, 78, 81, 88, 138, 186–8, **195,** 198, 217–21, 226–30, 233–5, 248–9, 264–5, 277, 286; MF 54; SP **VI** (1949 Penguin); CN **223–7**

Titus Andronicus: WF 170; IT 16, 250; CL 131, 166, 188, 203; ST X, 1, 23, 26, 30, 33, 39, 42, 52, 71, 114, 130, 295, 302; SF **75–6**, 177, 188–90, 217–220, 224, 227, **280–2**

Troilus and Cressida: WF 3–5, 43, **47–72,** 107, 140, 165–7, 180, 189, 194, 222, 235–6, 242–5, 252–4, 257, 261–5, 269, 281, 289, 318, 335–41; IT xi, 8–9, 15–18, 26–7, 200, 250, 264, 278, 283, 288–290, 303, 309–12, 316, 332–3, 348–9; CL viii, 10–11, 17, 20, 36, 49, 98, 120, 131, 139–40, 161, 165, 194, 200, 205–211, 235, 256, 276–7, 296, 324–6, 335;

ST ix–x, xx–xxii, 125, 169, **170–4,** 186–8, 202, 269, 279, 303, 309–10, 316, 322; SF 10, **52–4,** 57, 66, 78, 95, 102, 123, 159, 195, 200, 209, 212, 228–230, 250, 291

Twelfth Night: WF 245, 263–5; IT 8–14, 26–8, 115–16, 244–5, 297; CL 36–7, 62, 65, 70, 96, 100–2, 129–33, 140, 152–5, 194–5, 201–5, 210–11, 217–19, 234, 275–6, 294, 298; ST 7, 44, 53, 66, 75, 99, 120, **121–7,** 136, 139–41, 154, 174, 180, 188, 194, 228, 237–8, 251–3, 295–6; SF 123, 129, 133–4, 137, 170–2, **173,** 180, **185–6,** 190, 199–201, 218–220, 224–9; SP **III** (a)

Venus and Adonis: IT 213, 243, 250, 333; CL 91, 103, 209, 212, 219; ST 23, 26, 29, 32, 60, 64–5, 70, 74, 98, 104, 107, 154, 263, 298–301, 306, 322–5; SF **215–18,** 220–2, 230, 282

Index B

Shakespearian Themes

I. LITERARY THEORY

Interpretation: 'spatial' theory, etc.: WF
v–ix, 1–16, 24, 33, 59, 71, 104–5, 109,
120–1, 129–30, 141, 158, 206–7, 210,
244, 255–6, 260, 270–97, 308, 324–5,
331, 337–8, 343; IT v–xiii, 1, 19–25,
28–30, 91, 108, 204–5, 255–6; CL vii–
10, 15–16, 19, 26–9, 66, 79, 83–4, 120,
166–7, 192, 195–6, 202, 224–31, 241–6,
250–3, 269, 281, 319, 336; ST vii–xxiv,
1–19, 63, 97, 269–92, 304, 326, 332;
SF 7–14, 56–7, 90, 95, 103, 156–60,
201, 206–7, 228, 232, 235, 240, 245–59;
MF 109; SP I, II; CR I. *See also II,*
'Creative or poetic imagination', 'Spatial
and temporal arts'.

Unpublished material: SF 9–10.

Early articles: SF 8–9.

First statement of principles of interpretation (1928): SF 287–93.

Summary of main principles: WF 14–16.

Chart of Shakespearian universe, with
commentary: ST xiv–xxiii; SF 257.

Interpretation and criticism: WF 1–3, 16;
SF 257–8, 287.

'Sources': WF 7–9, 128, 134, 282, 331,
337–8, 343; CL 9, 28–9, 227–30; ST
xxiv, 8–13; SF 173–4, 180, 199–201,
207, 290–1.

Biographical factors and artist's 'intentions': WF 6–7, 240–2, 277–9, 324–5,
337–8; CL 28–9; ST 3, 9, 325; SF 291–3.

Ethical, philosophical, and 'character'
criticism: WF 9–13, 120, 152, 158,
270–97; IT 1, 19–25, 221, 255–6, 264;
ST vii–xiv, xix–xxiii, 3–7, 16–17; SF
245, 253, 288–91.

Interpretation and the theatre: IT 21–2.

Theatrical technique, effect and purpose:
WF vi, 13, 300, 309–10; CL 96, 192,
196, 331; SF 28, 154–5, 186, 246–8,
256; SP throughout.

Obligations: WF v–vi, 2, 16, 137; IT
v–ix, 30; CL vii–viii; ST xxiii; SF 287,
292; *and see* Index C, under Masefield,
Murry, Spurgeon, etc.

Textual problems, authenticity: WF 214,
239, 312, 317, 326–43; IT X, 145, 188,
250, 258, 267, 291; CL viii, 16, 19–21,
26, 32–54, 74–5, 168–202, 258–73,
277–8, 283–5, 292, 297, 300–1, 319;
ST 2–5, 31–2, 191, 201, 218, 235, 240,
305–6, 320, 325–32; SF 14, 58, 80,
96–102, 136–8, 194, 280, 285.

Anachronisms: CL 129, 142, 150–1,
165–6; SF 78, 197.

Style of theophanies and gnomic speeches:
WF 79–80; CL 42–51, 57, 74–5, 192–6;
ST 326–7, 332; SF 96, 146, 151–3.

Shakespeare's vision, technique and development: WF 15–16, 31, 43–4, 48–52,
84, 97–105, 118–20, 138–40, 149,
160–1, 178–9, 221–3, 236, 239–48,
252–69, 286, 308–9, 324; IT 1–31, 196,
199–200, 204, 225, 255, 261–5, 269–70,
278, 282–90, 302–11, 316–18, 324–6,
343–67; CL vii–37, 54, 57, 64–5, 69–73,
96, 99–102, 128–30, 138–9, 146–52,
157, 166–8, 172–3, 183, 187–96, 201–
226, 241–3, 253–8, 276–8, 285–91, 296–
298, 306–7, 317, 320, 324–36; ST xiv–
xxiii, 5–6, 14–19, 33, 40, 44–5, 57, 75,
81–6, 93, 105–7, 114, 117–19, 127,
131, 139–40, 164, 169–71, 183, 189,
193–4, 206, 213, 216–18, 247–92, 297,
300, 308, 319, 324, 331; SF 8, 16, 19–21,
25–9, 43, 46–7, 50, 53, 57–8, 63–5,
69–91, 95, 132–4, 140, 147, 155–60,
200–1, 205–41, 246–53, 280–6, 291–2;
SP I; CR III.

Vision and technique of the Final Plays: WF 16; CL 9, 13–31, 36–40, 47, 51, 70–2, 98, 102, 142, 172–5, 186, 189–91, 201–4, 257, 318–22; ST 218, 229–30, 240–1, 247, 266–8; SF 69, 84, 87, 101–2, 147, 155–6, 237–41, 292–3.

Poles of Shakespearian vision: IT 23–5, 327–42; ST xiv–xxi; SF 216.

Discussion of symbolism: CL 226–30, 246–251, 336; ST 13–17, SF 87–91, 233–6.

Universality of Shakespearian symbolism: ST 270–92; SF 210–11, 234–5.

Symbolic personification: WF 73–4, 83, 96–7, 105, 109, 167–8, 177–8, 182, 235, 249–56, 276, 284–93; IT 19–25, 227, 259–60, 278, 290, 300–4, 308–25, 338; CL 24–7, 73–4, 125–6, 140–2, 163–4, 201, 208–12, 220, 232–40, 318; ST 257–60; SF 84–5, 88, 159, 222–3, 238.

Psychological realism: WF 73, 96–7, 105; IT 263, 289, 324–5; CL 51, 59–60, 96, 142, 296, 302; SF 216, 222–6. *See also* 'Ethical, philosophical, and character criticism', 'Symbolic personification', above.

Plot-controllers: WF 74, 79, 89; CL 73, 207–8, 220–1, 232; SF 69–72, 134. *See also V*, 'Supernormal persons'.

Choric figures and speeches: WF 135, 163–6, 182, 195–7, 207, 216, 330; IT 95, 175, 238, 269–73, 316–18; CL 37, 52, 62, 74, 99, 279, 315–16, 319; ST 200; SF 37–8, 41, 81, 176, 212.

Positive direction of Shakespearian play or tragic hero: WF 11, 49–51, 155–9, 232–3, 243–4; IT vi, 24–5, 29–31, 116–17, 122–4, 153, 199–350; CL 11–13, 25, 34, 127, 222, 335; ST viii–ix, xiv, xx–xxiii, 192, 257, 268, 288–92; 312; SF 56–7, 66, 69, 86, 229–37, 241, 245–50, 289–90; SP I, V.

Tragedy: WF 220; CL 30, 35, 126–7; ST 169–71, 176, 217; SF 221.

Tragedy and comedy: WF 19, 60–1, 160–76, 203; IT 14, 203, 253–4, 307–8, 325, 345; CL 51, 69–70, 86, 99–100, 112–13, 129–30, 170, 297, 307, 314–17; ST 82, 86–7, 105–7, 113, 119, 126, 140, 145–6, 153–6; SF 220, 229, 238. *For comedy see III*, 'Humour'.

Literature and the nation: SF 12, 214, 266–279.

Summary of work on 'Literature and the nation': SF 263–5.

Drama and royalty: SF 89–91.

Drama and religion: WF 294–7; CL 12, 23, 30–1, 35, 79, 227.

Drama and ritual: CL 35, 70, 79, 227, 319–20, 331, 336; SF 91, 235–7, 241; *and see II*, 'Ritual and ceremonial'.

Greek drama: WF 294–5; CL 30, 35, 49, 128, 227; ST 278; SF 89.

Morality drama: WF 294; CL 36–52, 57, 70, 73–4, 80, 226–7, 272, 306; SF 146.

Drama and romantic love: CL 30, 79, 149.

Drama and madness: WF 284–7, 300.

Elizabethan and Renaissance literature: WF 104, 170; CL 29–31, 35, 79, 96–7, 128, 149, 227, 241–6; ST X, 19; SF 47, 205–9, 213–19, 227–31, 250–2.

Revenge themes: WF 324.

Romantic poetry: WF viii; CL vii, 228, 251; SF 251, 256; *and see Index C*, under individual poets.

Poetry and prose: SF 123.

Satire: WF 55–62, 69, 76, 214, 314–15, 320–1; IT 26; CL 10, 13, 29, 44–5, 61, 98, 101, 111–13, 150, 218–19, 247, 254, 270, 297–8, 303, 326, 335; SF 35–7, 54, 59, 86, 116, 119, 123, 126, 157, 172–3, 208–9, 213, 217–20, 224, 239.

Irony: IT 173, 192; SF 54, 124, 127, 172–3, 191, 206.

II. ARTS

CL 51–2, 58–9, 62–4, 73, 241–2; ST 104–7, 271; SF 232, 236, 258–9, 271.

Spatial and temporal arts: SF 253–4, 258–9, 271.

Creative or poetic imagination: WF viii, 8, 241, 244, 258, 265, 276, 285, 300, 308–11, 340, 343; IT 29, 332–4, 351–5, 361–2; CL 22–3, 27–8, 34, 79, 208–12, 221–35; ST 153, 280–92, 310–15; SF 72, 90, 138–40, 146, 155–60, 174, 198–201, 215–19, 223–32, 235–41, 253–9, 289–93; CN 132–3. *See also III*, 'Bisexuality'.

Artistic temperament: IT 82; CL 158–60; SF 197–8.

Art and life: WF 207–11, 286, 310–16, 319–25; IT 76, 257–60; CL 122–8, 235, 240–4, 252, 319, 336; ST 167–8, 280–292, 313; SF 72, 159. *See also I*, 'Literature and the nation'.

Art and nature: CL 104–5, 117–28, 184, 336; SF 207, 215–18.

Art and society: WF 300–3; SF 50, 56, 160. *See also I*, 'Literature and the nation'.

Music: WF viii, 61, 71, 76, 97–104, 112, 116–19, 127, 175, 198, 203, 208–11, 272, 296; IT 6, 12, 20–2, 28–30, 44, 47, 61–4, 71, 77, 81–3, 107, 116–17, 135, 153, 164, 169, 181, 185, 196–200, 220–1, 227, 236, 244–6, 252, 257–9, 280, 297–8, 323, 335, 347, 360–6; CL vii, 13–25, 38–9, 47, 50–1, 55–8, 62–3, 67–8, 73, 108–9, 122–4, 133, 155, 160, 168–71, 181, 191–2, 196–8, 204, 208–211, 216, 219–22, 233–5, 238–44, 251, 270, 275, 290–1, 294–6, 320, 336; ST throughout; SF 47, 68, 89, 139, 186, 206, 214–15, 228, 233–6, 240; SP II (2); CR VII. *See also IV*, 'Tempests'; *V*, 'Supernatural music'; *and VI*, 'Order and disorder'.

Songs and singing: WF 108, 182; IT 12, 22, 77, 114–17, 221, 244–5; CL 26, 62–3, 100–2, 109–11, 133, 160–1, 169–70, 173–4, 181, 189, 192, 218, 233–6, 246–7, 270, 290–1, 327, 333, 336; ST 57–61, 74, 78, 82–6, 91–4, 98, 102–3, 117, 124–7, 131, 141, 146–7, 155–8, 161–8, 176–80, 187, 200, 212–213, 226–7, 235–8, 242–3, 251–2, 262–3, 272, 277–9, 290, 301–2, 326, 329; SF 80, 229.

Sound effects: WF 15, 42, 89, 110–11, 178, 182, 194–5, 322–3; IT 135, 157, 173, 196–7; CL 299, 320, 329–30; ST xvi–xviii, 160–1, 206–7, 210, 217; SF 68, 117, 235; SP II (2).

Dancing: CL 21, 47, 50, 58, 62, 73, 109, 120, 196, 216, 245–7, 300, 327; ST 61, 74–5, 80, 87, 91–4, 117, 144, 165–8, 202, 213, 232, 243, 252, 263–6, 277, 326; SF 173, 219.

Masques: WF 209, 213; CL 171, 185, 190, 195, 221, 245–6, 300–1, 311, 327; ST 77, 80, 129, 162, 166, 263–4.

Ritual and ceremonial: WF 211, 322–4; IT 7–8, 12, 17, 64, 83, 107, 136, 281; CL 14, 17, 20–1, 47, 51, 68–70, 73, 116, 124, 160–1, 168–9, 181, 190, 196, 226–7, 232, 246, 251–2, 257, 294, 306, 318–36; ST xvi–xviii, 239–43, 246; SF 41–2, 85–7, 91, 146, 196, 221, 233–7, 241, 253; SP V; *and see I*, 'Drama and ritual'.

Statues, plastic and sculptural impressions: WF 97–105, 115–19; IT 46, 60; CL 64–5, 73, 117–27, 175, 184, 248, 319; SF 240.

Monumental and architectural effects: WF 103–4, 119; CL 64–5, 73, 107, 123–4, 175–6, 246, 251; ST xv–xvi; SF 201, 240, 256.

Arts of design (including needlework, tapestry, metalwork): WF 108; CL 58–9, 62–3, 73, 174–6, 251, 318; ST 112, 226, 235; SF 215, 240.

Painting and painters: WF 207–9, 213–14; CL 64, 117, 248; ST 104–6.

Heraldic devices: CL 47.

Renaissance art: CL 176.

Poetry: WF 207–9, 214, 219–20; CL 58; ST 62.

Acting and play production: WF 300–2, 310–13; IT 107; CL 233, 243.

Stage directions: WF 49, 172, 180, 292; IT X, 245; CL 20, 47, 51, 56–7, 63, 68, 73, 168, 171, 186, 190, 319, 325–30; ST 17, 66, 171, 226, 239, 243, 329.

Sports and games (including hunting, fencing): WF 322–3; IT 253–4, 281, 345; ST 89–90, 104, 160, 164, 297–9, 309; SF 39–40, 47, 77.

Bell-ringing: ST 61, 164, 219.

III. HUMAN THEMES AND VALUES

IT 1–2, 19, 149; ST 131, 267–92; SF 20–1, 27, 30, 103–4, 107, 126, 139, 156–60, 166, 206, 209–14, 226, 230–6, 240, 253.

Spirit of life, life-force: WF 84, 149, 156–7, 212, 220, 296–7, 308–15, 319, 323–5, 342; IT 1, 24–31, 34–5, 39–40, 44–62, 80–1, 90–2, 96–153, 197, 200, 219–22, 229, 232, 240, 248, 260–2, 304, 316–18, 329, 336–50, 360; CL 17, 30–1, 34, 57,

66, 120–8, 306, 310, 314–17, 329; ST 192–4, 210–16, 280–92, 331–2; SF 16, 20, 89, 206, 210–11, 215–18, 222–6, 229–38.

Kingship, royalty, nobility: WF 148–51, 154–5, 167, 172, 199, 209–25, 234–9, 249–56, 269, 318; IT 2–19, 25–7, 30, 55, 61–71, 80, 92–6, 102–6, 112–14, 120–6, 129–33, 147–53, 198, 205–16, 221, 235, 244–50, 257–62, 296–8, 307, 320–1, 336–42, 363–7; CL 48–51, 64, 71–2, 86, 96, 106–8, 111, 116–21, 130, 134, 138, 153–67, 188, 197–201, 204–5, 248, 252–8, 275, 285–6, 289–96, 306–21, 327–36; ST xii, xv–xvii, xxi–xxiii, 34, 46–52, 70–6, 131, 154, 160–1, 166–8, 192–4, 212, 216, 244, 254, 294–5, 299,| 308, 315–16, 322; SF 8, 12–91, 105–6, 113, 126–8, 139, 142–6, 154, 157–60, 169, 176–8, 184–188, 194–7, 200, 205, 211–15, 219–30, 237–9, 248, 253, 273–9; MF III, and 129–34; SP V. See also I, 'Literature and the nation'; IV, 'Sun', 'Gold'; and V, 'Supernormal persons'.

Aspiration, ambition: WF 58, 62–72, 124, 140, 152–3, 179, 210–13, 221, 234, 245, 340–2; IT 86, 154–5, 159, 172, 177, 356–8; CL 12, 52, 239–46, 250–2, 257–8, 272–3, 278, 281, 287–9, 296, 316; ST xix, 280–325, 330; SF 13, 20, 24, 37, 60, 65, 70, 83–4, 107, 126, 139, 159, 209, 229, 237, 274–5. See also 'Pride', below.

Idealism: WF 85–90, 117, 201–2; IT 75–6; ST 171, 176; SF 48, 66–8, 108, 138, 211, 216, 222, 228, 237.

Love and romantic values: WF 15, 20–31, 34, 40–3, 47–8, 52–5, 58–72, 84–9, 92–6, 107–19, 154, 162, 165, 168, 174–175, 179, 185–6, 198–206, 209–39, 245, 248–56, 261–9, 287, 292–3, 309, 314, 320–2, 340–1; IT 1–3, 6–30, 34–5, 39–40, 44, 48–9, 58–63, 66–96, 101–5, 114–23, 126–7, 132–3, 137–8, 142, 147, 154–5, 163–6, 170–3, 177, 181–4, 189–350, 366–7; CL 10–22, 26–31, 34, 42, 49–52, 57–9, 65, 72–3, 76–9, 91, 99, 103–10, 116, 122, 139, 147–9, 154–7, 209, 214–16, 222, 244–5, 299–301, 317, 321, 327, 333–5; ST ix–xviii, xxi–xxiii, 17–18, 52, then throughout; SF 32, 53,

59, 65–8, 75, 78, 103, 108–13, 116–18, 123–6, 129–50, 154–60, 174–8, 185, 193–4, 205–6, 213–32, 235–40, 249, 275, 281, 286.

Feminine principle, femininity: WF 107–111, 152, 307–8, 336–7; IT 14, 18, 194, 197, 202, 235, 269, 290–324, 327–30, 333, 336, 366–7; CL 130–2, 152–7, 164, 167, 199–201, 233, 289–96, 299–302; ST xii, 154–5, 277–8; SF 64–8, 78, 109–13, 118, 126, 131–4, 142–3, 160, 178, 220–4, 232, 239–40, 270; MF throughout. See also 'Bisexuality', below.

Beauty: WF 25, 28, 39, 58, 61, 70–1, 110–16, 203–6, 336–7, 342; IT 114–17, 213; ST 79–80; SF 17–18, 80, 110, 139, 153, 215–16.

Grace and gentleness: WF 82, 95, 127; CL 159, 163–4, 200–1, 233, 288; ST 306–7, 315, 322; SF 15, 21, 59, 64, 77–8, 232, 252.

Sexual themes: WF 65, 74–96, 200–1; IT 218–29; CL 143–9, 223, 297–300, 303–6, 327–9; SF 21, 66, 78, 104–43, 150, 159–160, 174, 217–20, 226–33, 237, 252, 289. See also 'Love', above; 'Morality', 'Lust' and 'Physical revulsion' below.

Bisexuality: SF 132–4, 138–40, 149–50, 156–60, 219–24, 232, 240; MF throughout; CN 123–5.

Homosexuality: WF 211; SF 200, 218–19; MF throughout; SP III (a); CN 123–5.

Innocence, purity and impurity: WF 18, 74, 79, 82, 86–95, 115–16, 174, 192; IT 14, 17, 20, 77, 114–15, 150, 310; CL 11, 61–2, 108–9, 148–9, 220–1, 244–246, 316, 333–4; ST 40, 45, 174, 226, 276–9, 306–7, 315, 319, 323–4; SF 61, 72, 108, 112, 135, 146, 197, 216.

Virginity, chastity, asceticism: WF 85–7, 91–5, 211–13; CL 50, 57, 244–6, 306; SF 105–12, 118, 122, 126, 133, 136–141, 145–6, 154–60, 175, 222.

Marriage, procreation, birth and themes of creation: WF 55, 109–11, 265, 296, 309; IT 26, 62, 90–1, 125, 140–4, 149–53, 159, 171, 248, 336–7; CL 17–20, 38–9, 52–3, 59, 66–8, 76, 79, 86–91, 98–9, 108, 119–20, 127, 139, 149, 164–166, 172–3, 195, 244–6, 296, 303–6, 312, 316–18, 329; ST 59–61, 82, 85–6, 92, 109, 119–20, 153–4, 166–8, 175, 179–180, 183, 192–3, 217, 220–2, 225–8,

231, 239, 246, 252–3, 263–4, 268; SF 61, 77–80, 85, 98, 103, 108–16, 121, 131, 136, 141–2, 159–60, 216, 222, 230, 238–239. *See also IV*, 'Great creating nature'.

Babies, childhood, and youth: WF 159; IT 77, 131, 141–4, 149–53, 250, 320, 327–8, 337–9; CL 77–81, 86–91, 96–9, 107, 120, 158–63, 220, 233–5, 330–5; ST xv–xvii, 74, 192–3, 221–34, 241, 246, 268; SF 18, 59–61, 64, 69, 77, 85, 90, 153, 168, 173, 182, 217, 234–5, 238, 253, 256, 270, 277, 285.

Children and parents, the family: WF 62, 163–6, 169, 185; IT 47, 96–9, 102–105, 126–7, 140–4, 164–5, 170–4, 177, 181–4, 190–6; CL 14–19, 25, 49–51, 77–80, 87, 90, 115; ST 59, 115, 118–19, 199, 229; SF 15, 18, 58–9, 66–71, 77–8, 98–9, 113, 127–31, 147, 157–8, 205, 212–13, 239.

Domesticity: WF 107–9, 117–18, 161; IT 35–6, 40, 81, 135; CL 102–3, 291, 296.

Illegitimacy: WF 169.

Incest: WF 18; CL 38–40.

War, glory, and heroic values: WF 33, 47–51, 58–63, 70–1, 105–7, 110–12, 115–20, 150–1, 237–9, 253, 263, 293, 301, 304–8, 317–24; IT 1–19, 25, 75, 89–90, 96–8, 111–12, 125–9, 147–9, 154–98, 204–6, 210–16, 235, 246–8, 266, 269, 280–6, 297–306, 323–4, 327, 347, 366; CL 49–50, 136–40, 145–7, 158–9, 163, 166, 171–2, 242, 255–7, 289, 321–2, 329, 335; ST xii, xv–xix, 17, 22, 25, 34–9, 56–7, 64–6, 87, 91, 125–6, 166, 179–81, 188–9, 196, 206–211, 215–16, 244, 265–6, 298, 315–19; SF 13–49, 53–6, 64–8, 73, 77–9, 82, 103–6, 110–12, 116–21, 126–7, 133, 139, 142–4, 152, 158–60, 169, 177–83, 187, 193–4, 200, 208–11, 214, 220–4, 227–30, 239–40, 266.

Honour: WF 52, 55, 58, 61–2, 71–2, 317–21; IT 3–10, 14–21, 25, 30, 44, 49, 60, 68, 71–81, 85–7, 94, 98, 111–12, 123–9, 134, 149–50, 166–9, 190–1, 194–8, 211–12, 266–7, 286, 296, 306, 338, 366; CL 47–8, 137–8, 148, 171–2, 281, 333–4; ST xv–xix, 41, 65, 171, 187; SF 35–6, 48–9, 53, 56, 65–8, 104–133, 143–5, 156, 159, 173, 195, 218, 223, 227, 240.

Cowardice: SF 48, 103, 107, 112, 119–24, 173, 183. *See also* 'Honour', above.

Masculinity: WF 111, 307–8, 336–7; IT 298–303, 324, 327, 366–7; ST 109, 318–19; SF 65, 78, 109–13, 118, 126, 131, 142, 178, 221–4, 232. *See also* 'Bisexuality', above.

Strength, power and the power-quest: WF 76–9, 82, 95, 201; IT 159–65, 171, 178, 184–90, 194–8, 321; CL 163–4, 201, 218–20, 238, 278–88, 296–7, 311, 334–336; ST 175–6, 185–6, 207–9, 216; SF 32–7, 41–2, 51–3, 60–5, 73, 77–83, 88–9, 104, 141, 187, 197, 248–9, 267–72, 277–8.

Weapons: IT 157–8, 168, 196–7; SF 119–20, 179–80.

Pride, egotism: WF 47, 55–9, 71, 85–8, 92–3, 124–5, 161–2, 166, 186, 190, 198–200, 206; IT 64–6, 78, 81, 154–98; CL 273–95, 315–16, 334; ST xii, 207–10, 293–300, 306–7, 323; SF 20, 23, 37, 65–8, 75, 82–4, 104, 112, 115–16, 139–41, 176, 230.

Individualism: IT 17, 363–6.

Stoicism: WF 171, 179, 191, 195–9; IT 76, 341, 356, 361; CL 10–11, 29, 180; ST 57.

Government and state themes, English nationalism: WF 33, 78–9, 303–4; IT 167–8, 172; CL vii, 167, 201, 253–8, 307, 315–21, 324–36; ST xxiii, 20; SF 13–14, 21–32, 38–9, 47–59, 63, 66–91, 104, 157–60, 167, 170, 187, 207, 212–15, 222–4, 229, 239, 253; MF 129–35. *See also I*, 'Literature and the nation'.

England and the Continent, Britain and Rome: CL 130–52, 157, 164–7, 172, 195, 297–8; ST x–xiii; SF 24–7, 36, 73–80, 166, 197, 205, 239, 272. *See also I*, 'Literature and the nation'.

Politics or society and the individual: WF 35–8, 47, 57, 72, 122, 132–8, 149, 153–156, 186, 215, 223–4, 236–9, 300–3, 314–17, 321–4; IT 9–10, 18–19, 28–9, 42, 45, 53–6, 61–73, 84–5, 91–5, 126–7, 134, 174–80, 184–5, 189, 194, 197, 363–7; CL 136, 164, 206–7, 280–2, 291–4, 306–7, 310–12, 321–2, 333; ST x–xvii, 45, 51, 58, 64, 137, 189; SF 13, 32, 47–8, 65, 74–5, 81, 88–9, 103–4, 157–8, 212, 222–3, 239, 245, 270–1.

Civil wars, treachery, insurrection: WF
37, 150; IT 6, 10, 16, 47, 54–6, 60–3,
67–72, 78, 112–14, 126, 176–9, 182–5,
197, 241, 266–8, 304–6, 310; CL 51,
87, 205–6, 213, 216, 238, 246–7, 254,
272–8, 282–3, 296, 308, 313; ST 24–5,
28, 34–6, 39, 50, 54–8, 90, 94, 137,
176, 183–8, 248–9, 259–60; SF 14–15,
19–26, 29–37, 40, 46–8, 58–9, 65–6,
73–6, 82, 120, 182, 205, 213, 249.
Loyalty and disloyalty: WF 18, 39–40,
62, 68–70, 91, 115, 218, 227–8, 253;
IT 14, 79–81, 86, 124–6, 241, 262–78,
285, 349; CL 17–19, 108, 205, 287–9,
292, 295, 315; ST 244; SF 20, 26, 67,
77–8, 83–4, 194–5, 199, 219, 226–9, 236.
Tyranny: CL 85–96, 110–11, 126, 216–19,
238, 257, 281, 333–5; ST 133, 197;
SF 13, 21–4, 37, 52, 60–5, 73–4, 170,
185, 196, 249, 266, 270, 278.
Freedom: CL 118, 126–7; SF 47–8, 65, 73,
88–91, 191–2, 229, 277–8.
Church and state: CL 254–8, 312–36; SF
25–7, 51, 84–5, 159, 214, 273–9.
Utopia: CL 247–8, 254; SF 275.
Common people, mob: CL 303–6, 317,
320–2, 328–36; ST xii–xvii, xxii–
xxiii; SF 209, 225, 253, 277.

Evil and destructive vision: WF 3–4, 19,
23, 29–32, 38, 41–3, 87–8, 112–17,
120–59, 174, 223, 239, 253, 257–69,
279, 287, 315–16, 321; IT 15–30, 39–40,
47, 57–63, 70–1, 77–8, 81, 94–5, 101–
111, 114, 122–53, 199, 263–5, 268, 290,
300, 304, 309–11, 316–18, 325–44; CL
24–5, 29, 38–41, 52, 58–62, 73, 76–
96, 124–7, 130–2, 142–9, 165, 177,
206, 211–17, 220–2, 235–42, 248, 335;
ST xiv–xix, xxii, 33–4, 73, 87, 90–1,
137, 146–53, 156, 160, 174–5, 187–93,
217, 226, 254–62, 267, 270–6, 280–2,
288, 293, 302–5, 308–12, 323, 326–32;
SF 20–4, 36, 58–64, 76, 120, 130, 140,
144–5, 154, 179, 198, 205, 209, 214–
217, 222–35, 246, 249, 288–9. See also
'Hate, the hate-theme', below; IV,
'Tempests'; V, 'Hell, damnation'; and
VI, 'Order and disorder'.
Chaos and disintegration: WF 19–20, 38,
43–5, 50, 116–22, 127–38, 147, 150,
153–6, 192, 201, 221–5, 230–3; IT 18,
47, 57, 61, 70–2, 80, 102, 129–30,

137–40, 144–53, 178, 330–1, 342; CL
82–3; ST 151, 171, 187–94, 201–6, 280–
292, 330–1; SF 20–4, 53, 58–60.
Guilt and sin: WF 26, 35–9, 45, 82, 87–9,
93–6, 126–7, 151–6, 194–5, 237–9,
258–9, 316; IT 28, 81, 101–2, 105,
128–30, 133; CL 40, 73, 76–9, 83–4,
99, 113, 121, 126–7, 212–14, 233–4,
248, 282–3, 317; ST 51, 67–8, 190,
255–7; SF 33–4, 42–3, 50–1, 72, 81,
111–12, 115–16, 143–5, 156, 200, 207,
215–18, 223, 232, 252, 284, 289–90.
Hate, the 'hate-theme': WF 15, 43, 58, 70,
97, 112–14, 120, 140, 165, 168, 172,
199, 214, 217, 221–39, 244–8, 252–7,
261–9; IT 15, 73, 131, 167–8, 174, 263,
277–8, 290, 304–5; CL 10–12, 20, 23–4,
29, 212, 222, 238, 279, 285; ST 106,
201–3, 209; SF 21, 54, 57, 195, 206,
231, 270.
Death and death-consciousness: WF 3–4,
15–46, 65, 68, 74–6, 83–4, 129, 140,
173–5, 180, 198–201, 204, 226–7,
230–3, 243–7, 253, 262, 269, 296–9,
304–11, 315–20, 323; IT 12, 15–16,
25–30, 35, 48, 60–2, 66, 79–81, 90–6,
99–125, 129, 134, 137–40, 145–53,
160, 167, 173, 180–1, 185, 190, 194,
197–9, 232, 236–42, 248–50, 259–62,
266, 273–4, 283–9, 302, 307–25, 328–9,
336–50, 355–67; CL 10–22, 31, 34–5,
38–9, 53–9, 63–70, 73–7, 89, 94–7,
107, 120–8, 131–2, 160–1, 169–71,
179, 204, 212–13, 231–3, 252–3, 288,
292–5, 306, 314; ST xiv–xix, 14, 33, 37,
41, 45–7, 53, 61, 66–8, 71, 93, 117–19,
131, 145–6, 150, 153–4, 160, 178–9,
182, 187–94, 201, 204–6, 210, 217–45,
252–4, 267–8, 282–6, 292, 300, 320,
323–4, 328–32; SF 15, 18, 26, 32, 35,
66, 69, 81, 84, 100–2, 129, 134, 147–9,
152–5, 159, 173, 186, 191–3, 208,
221–40, 248, 281, 284–5; MF IV.
Murder: WF 18–19, 26–7, 31–9, 42–5,
120–38, 149, 153–4, 315; IT 39, 45–8,
55–60, 68–9, 81, 93–5, 108, 121, 128,
134–6, 146; CL 58–9, 212–13; ST 190,
225, 258; SF 22, 32, 42–3, 49, 60, 63,
73–4, 173, 205, 213, 228–31, 257,
288–9.
Suicide: WF 20, 129, 174–5, 196–8,
305–9, 323; IT 78, 106, 328; CL 169;
SF 193.

Spiritual sickness, madness—'the sick soul': WF 17–32, 37–46, 103, 161–75, 181–4, 187, 190–2, 195–205, 221, 240–8, 252–4, 261–3, 286–7, 300, 307, 321; IT 98–111, 114–19, 182–3, 332–4, 357, 365; CL 10–11, 29, 40, 80–96, 206, 314–15; ST xvi–xvii, xxi, 57–8, 150, 153, 164, 167, 177–9, 198–200, 310; SF 48–50, 58–61, 81, 186, 228–9, 233, 280–1, 293.

Spiritual division: WF 120–39, 154–8, 315, 323; IT 56, 70–83, 94–5; SF 47–8.

Disillusion: WF 168, 191; SF 30.

Cynicism: WF 15, 22–30, 38–41, 47–8, 57–62, 69–71, 97, 111–19, 212–14, 225–7, 249–56; IT 26, 35, 123, 316; CL 11, 20, 29, 91, 142–7, 214–16, 222, 302; ST 171; SF 228–30, 240.

Psychic instability: IT 264–325.

Doubt, surprise and question: WF 141–6, 149, 153.

Fear: WF 83–4, 88, 93, 121, 126, 138, 146, 149–50, 153–8, 180, 196, 257–61; IT 40, 56–8, 61–4, 84, 94–5, 102–3, 125–9, 142, 186; CL 231, 308, 313, 333; ST 142, 145–6, 150–3, 160–1, 329; SF 43, 61, 85–6, 134, 142, 206, 220–1, 227, 283.

Cruelty: WF 26–9, 38, 45, 165, 169, 172–4, 179, 185, 201, 204; IT 109–11; ST 133–4, 195–201, 204, 258–62; SF 15–17, 20, 37, 40–1, 53–5, 59, 77, 175, 219–20, 270.

Jealousy and envy: WF 108, 256; IT 28, 80, 85–7, 131–2; CL 58, 79–96, 140, 149, 155, 205, 244, 279; ST 117–18, 140–143, 152, 167, 183; SF 153, 171, 190, 218–20, 227.

Anger, quarrels: WF 161, 168, 199, 221, 225–7; IT 74–6, 87–9; CL 292–3; ST 23–4, 30–2, 39–42, 56–8, 63, 94, 107–110, 117, 142–4, 162–7, 172, 184–7, 244; SF 190–1.

Curses: SF 81, 190–1, 198, 229–30. See also 'Hate, the hate-theme', above.

Suffering, tears, and grief: WF 32, 82, 101–2, 176, 219, 238; IT 29, 43–4, 53, 63, 88, 109, 114–15, 118–19, 173–4; CL 11–12, 19–20, 29–31, 42–3, 63, 95–6, 121–3, 153–7, 161, 189, 222, 231–2, 275, 289, 318, 331, 335; ST 21–30, 34, 40–1, 44–5, 52, 59, 69, 80–3, 94–8, 107, 113,

119, 130–1, 137, 172, 176, 183, 189, 200–1, 206, 213, 224–9, 234–7, 242, 249–56, 262–6, 273, 276, 280; SF 15–18, 27, 38, 71, 81, 107, 131, 140, 172, 199, 220–3, 229, 232–5, 239–40, 248, 293.

Purgatorial suffering: WF 161–2, 177–206, 292, 296; IT 31, 366; ST 196–201; SF 229, 235–6.

Conscience: WF 88, 128–9, 305–6, 315; IT 16, 110, 124, 128; CL 84, 88, 92, 95, 127, 179, 213, 309–10; ST 242, 310; SF 22–3, 49, 59, 196, 238, 249, 266.

Self-deception and self-knowledge: WF 78, 85–90, 93–5, 144, 164, 196–7, 201–2, 286–7; IT 79, 116, 128, 272–3, 276, 366; CL 252, 286, 293–4; ST 198, 245, 265; SF 67, 89, 116–17, 120–9, 139, 144, 224–6, 229, 239, 249.

Integrity: IT 8, 83–4, 87–8, 94, 181; SF 44, 57–8, 62, 78–80, 109, 119–31, 139, 146–8, 157, 186, 216–17, 222–32, 240–1, 249.

Honesty: WF 94–5, 228, 235. See also 'Integrity', above.

Redemption: ST 197–9, 204; SF 81, 145, 240.

Remorse and repentance: WF 35–7, 82, 94, 173–4; CL 95–6, 113, 126–7, 145, 179, 182, 273, 285, 288; ST 265; SF 33, 142–3, 224, 229, 238, 249.

Mercy, forgiveness: WF 75–6, 83, 90, 93–6, 197, 237–8, 280; IT 124, 188–90, 194; CL 155, 179, 252, 275–7, 317–19; ST 264; SF 47, 50, 68, 76, 81–2, 89, 140, 178, 231, 267, 276.

Faith: WF 212–14, 217–18, 222, 227–8, 236; SF 230, 238.

Patience: CL 65, 107, 153, 293; SF 99, 172.

Gratitude and ingratitude: ST 83–5, 195–6; SF 40, 54, 70, 227–9, 239. See also 'Civil wars, treachery', 'Loyalty and disloyalty', above.

Charity: CL 41–2, 52–5, 234, 274–5, 284, 289, 292–7, 317–19, 326–7, 335; SF 82–4, 172.

Humility: WF 199–201, 322–3; IT 3, 175–6; CL 48–52, 72, 166, 220, 239, 244, 273–8, 284–97, 315–18, 334; SF 36–7, 40, 45, 77, 82–4, 117, 126, 131–4, 139, 145–6, 150–4, 160, 226, 230, 239.

Pity: WF 44–5, 148; IT 53, 143, 149, 170, 330; SF 15, 18–20, 76.

Acceptance: IT 79, 100–1, 121–4; SF 82, 132, 140, 159, 226, 230–2, 249, 272, 293.

Peace: CL 258, 273, 293–4, 319–22, 328–336; ST 57, 162, 165, 168, 187, 198–9, 210–16, 226–8, 235–46; SF 21, 24, 27, 33, 40, 45–6, 56, 63, 77, 80–2, 85–7, 186, 196, 205, 221, 233–8, 272, 293–3. *See also II*, 'Music'.

Happiness: ST 39, 48–9, 53, 61, 80–6, 89, 112, 115, 119–20, 123, 126, 131–2, 141, 161, 166–8, 227–8, 234, 238, 252, 264–266, 273, 300–2; SF 220, 231.

Wisdom: WF 51, 55, 341–2; IT 3, 8; CL 248–53, 288, 296, 313, 331–5; ST 160–161, 167–8; SF 57, 65, 69–72, 127, 131, 138–9, 149, 153, 220–2, 269–71, 278. *See also V*, 'Transcendent vision', 'Supernormal persons'.

True and false values: WF 58–9, 70–2, 116, 119; CL 48–9, 55–7, 71, 105, 111–112, 146, 157–8, 161–2, 205–6, 244, 254, 282; SF 57, 107, 115–32, 144, 157, 186–7, 191, 229. *See also* 'Self-deception and self-knowledge', 'Integrity', above; *and IV*, 'Nature, creation and natural behaviour'.

Commonsense, worldly, or 'normally accepted' values: WF 33–41, 44, 51, 81, 304, 318–22; IT 96–101, 124, 269–73; CL 88, 98–9, 307–15; ST 142; SF 25–6, 31–2, 35–6, 49, 69, 72, 124, 130, 141, 188–9, 270–2.

Morality, ethical ideals: WF 10, 73–96, 139, 153, 181, 184, 187, 190–2, 223–4, 297–301, 315–16, 322; IT 17, 20, 80–3, 92, 97–8, 123–4; CL 38, 49, 62, 148–9, 317, 324, 329; ST 174–6; SF 14–15, 71, 91, 103–5, 111–12, 120–5, 128, 132, 139, 145, 159, 187, 217–18, 222, 231–5, 249–52, 267, 271–2, 288–91. *See also I*, 'Ethical criticism'.

Renaissance and Elizabethan ideas and values: WF 48, 62, 317–23, 336; CL 29–31, 79, 110, 118, 149, 228, 241–6, 249, 253–4, 333; ST vii; SF 13, 47, 58–9, 65, 73, 78, 126, 156, 159, 184, 207–9, 215, 226, 229, 239, 250–3.

Revenge: WF 20, 29–30, 36, 40, 43–5, 113, 136, 155, 191–2, 201, 225, 263, 317–24; IT 60–2, 109–10, 124, 144, 186–8; CL 35, 177; SF 48, 67, 76, 205, 228, 284.

Justice, law, and trials: WF 50, 73–99, 178–9, 187, 190–5, 199–201, 315, 324; IT 74–5, 356; CL 20, 41, 92–6, 176–9, 182, 190–2, 217, 233–4, 258, 274, 280, 283–4, 289–91, 307–10, 313, 320–6, 335; ST 196–7, 240; SF 13, 32, 36–8, 50–1, 56–9, 81, 90, 104, 175, 178, 267–70, 276.

Civilization and humanism: WF 50, 74, 89–90, 182, 192, 200–1, 207, 210–17, 229–32, 237–9, 245–7, 287, 292; IT 26, 156; ST 41, 48, 83, 194, 201–6, 235, 280–90; SF 53–9.

Social status: CL 44–8, 105–13, 238; SF 83, 98, 103–6, 113–16, 125–6, 131, 135, 141, 153–5, 208–9, 225.

Simplicity and sophistication: WF 62, 118, 167, 182–4, 199, 292; SF 90, 104, 121, 131.

Hypocrisy: WF 214–15; CL 60, 281; SF 21.

Sincerity: IT 82–3, 176; SF 57–8, 120, 131.

Sentimentality: WF 53, 117, 162, 293; IT 68; SF 270.

Righteousness: WF 74–6, 79, 82, 85–7, 96; SF 21, 37, 229.

Chivalry and chivalric society, courtliness: WF 318–24; CL 51–2, 163; SF 13, 29, 37, 44, 47, 53, 175, 180–2, 200.

Towns and buildings: IT 35, 155–7, 189–91, 197; ST 48, 98–9, 209, 212; SF 68, 209–10.

Body and spirit, especially physical-spiritual conflict: WF 8, 54, 65–8, 74, 205–7, 210–12, 220–5, 228–9, 262–9, 286–90, 336–7; IT 15, 35, 42–70, 74, 79–81, 93–5, 118, 132, 139–40, 200, 204–6, 210, 217–29, 238, 243–50, 259–263, 281, 325, 331–41, 347; CL 10–12, 23–6, 31, 64–5, 119–28, 200, 208–12, 219–23, 228–40, 248–9, 252, 306–17, 329–30, 335–6; ST 90, 100–8, 134, 139–40, 154–6, 161, 167–8, 197, 217, 259–62, 277–93, 307–8, 312–14, 319, 329–32; SF 32, 57, 69–71, 75, 111–12, 125–6, 140, 158, 171, 174, 182–4, 198, 218, 222, 231–2, 237.

Virtue, spiritual good: WF 58, 82, 85–96, 124, 148, 154–6, 177–9, 194–5, 198, 201–2, 211, 239; IT 81; CL 296; SF 59–64, 105–7, 120, 126–8, 131, 154–6, 187, 248, 274. *See also* 'Innocence, purity', etc., 'Virginity, chastity', etc.,

'Morality', above; *also V*, 'Supernormal persons', 'Religious mystics', 'Saints'.

Reason and intuition, the intellect and emotions or instinct: WF 3, 47–72, 88–9, 111–12, 123–5, 149, 162, 184, 218, 222, 245, 265, 317, 338–43; IT 2, 8–9, 16–17, 73–6, 80–1, 85–8, 101, 201, 271–3, 285, 301, 328–9, 354; CL 120, 210; ST ix–x, xvi–xvii, 6–9, 16–17, 51, 125, 157, 171–3, 277, 308–14; SF 20, 59, 64–8, 71, 90, 103, 124–5, 288, 292.

Lust and sexual licence: WF 59, 62, 69–71, 88, 192–3, 226, 280, 289–90; IT 132–3, 204, 219, 222–5, 248, 263, 278–279, 333; CL 37–9, 61–2, 211–12, 218–222, 236–41, 244; ST 34, 100–3, 260; SF 53, 59, 103, 106–13, 116, 121–32, 158–159, 185, 191, 195, 215–9, 227, 231.

Physical or sexual revulsion: WF 15, 23–8, 87, 93, 172, 192, 212–13, 223, 245–8, 262, 289, 309, 314–15; IT 17; CL 10; SF 217, 227, 232, 238.

Human appearance and physique: IT 35–44, 53, 85, 93–4, 178–9, 189, 192, 226–7, 257–9, 325; CL 90–1, 118–27, 154, 303–6, 329; ST 30, 34; SF 17–20, 74, 98, 135, 173, 209, 212, 215–16.

'Eroticism' in *Julius Caesar*: IT 44–53, 58–95.

Nakedness: WF 167, 173, 181–4, 287, 292; SF 215–16, 233; SP VI (1949 Penguin reprint); CN 227–8.

Clothes: WF 108, 184, 299; IT 68, 130–2, 148; CL 219, 231, 241–2, 252, 297–8, 330; SF 119–21, 126, 217; CR VII.

The senses, sense-forms: WF 54, 67, 207–212, 222–5; IT 129–32, 146–8, 199–206; ST 106, 201; SF 141, 149–50, 210, 215–218, 230–2, 237.

Eyes: IT 37–9; CL 39, 48, 83, 109–10, 114, 118, 199–200; ST 26, 68, 312–13; SF 150.

Perfume: IT 257.

Bad smells: ST 101–2; SF 121, 231.

Blood: WF 58, 123, 130–3, 137–9, 147, 150–1, 234, 261; IT 45–60, 67, 133, 159–60; ST 25, 145–6, 186, 190–2; SF 15, 18, 233.

Food and drink, feasting: WF 208–13, 221; IT 26–7, 39–40, 62, 81–3, 96, 125, 134–41, 149, 177, 185, 188–9, 204, 219–23, 243–4, 248, 266, 279, 323, 336–8; CL 47–9, 52, 66, 102–3, 159, 215–16, 248, 279, 294, 299–301, 304–6,

327–9, 333; ST xviii, 27, 61, 106, 112; 120, 133, 166–7, 191, 201–2, 208, 212–14, 255–7; SF 217, 226–8, 234, 238. *See also II*, 'Ritual and ceremonial'.

Generosity, bounty: WF 210–39; CL 276–7, 279, 287–8, 299; SF 54, 57.

Greed and meanness: WF 214–15, 225–8, 234.

Drinking and drunkenness: WF 340; IT 26, 39–40, 135–6, 204, 219–21, 243; CL 217–20, 237–8; ST 104–5, 125, 156, 259–60, 312–14; SF 171, 198–9.

Idolatry: CL 237.

Bestiality, degradation, physical indulgence: WF 116, 186, 200–1; CL 211–12, 217–20, 235–41, 246–8, 254, 297; ST 100–8, 134, 139, 154–6, 168, 258–60, 307–8; SF 15–17, 57–9, 70–1, 76, 121, 171, 195.

Stupidity: WF 47, 55–9, 71; ST 139; SF 172, 190, 209.

Coarseness and vulgarity: WF 47, 74, 89–91, 288–93; CL 283–4.

Ribaldry: WF 29, 55, 95; CL 109, 298–9, 304–5.

Humour, comedy: WF 19, 29, 41, 60–2, 72, 91, 95, 160–76, 214; IT 5, 13–14, 121, 174–5, 253–4, 298–9, 307–8, 325; CL 44–5, 51, 61, 76, 86, 98–102, 111–13, 154–6, 170–1, 217–20, 234, 258, 297–307, 315–19, 324, 336; ST xv, xxii, 85–7, 105, 124–6, 139–41, 146, 155–6, 162, 174–5; SF 35–8, 43, 47, 101, 111, 132, 149, 154, 171–2, 181–2, 190, 199, 206, 213, 218, 222–4, 238, 252, 266–72.

Wit: WF 58, 74, 89–91, 169, 300; IT 14, 39; CL 10, 134–6, 153, 209–10, 214–15, 299, 335; ST 76, 81, 87–92, 138, 174, 295, 309–14, 317; SF 35–7, 118, 121, 171–3, 179, 188, 199, 218.

Sleep: WF 83, 126–7, 146–7, 154, 203, 266; IT 35, 39–42, 77, 81, 125, 134–5, 147–9, 239, 312, 339–40; CL 52, 63–7, 123, 153, 160, 168–70, 190–2, 212–13; ST 46, 51, 106, 131, 142, 150, 159–61, 165, 187–9, 198–9, 239, 254; SF 22, 181, 236, 247. *See also V*, 'Dreams'.

Disease: WF 223; IT 6, 18, 25–7, 35, 40–2, 48–54, 65–6, 176–80, 186; CL 236; ST 17; SF 103, 152, 155, 186, 211–12, 231, 234.

Physical pain, torture: WF 169–72; IT 224; SF 18, 134, 152, 159.
Cures and healing: SF 100–3, 112–13, 131, 141, 146–59; 197. *See also V,* 'Cosmic powers'.
Age: CL 103–4; ST 76–7, 87, 119; SF 28, 173, 247.

Voyages, ships and shipwreck: WF 49, 63, 67; IT 116, 119; CL 18, 25–6, 36–7, 42–3, 48, 52–4, 63, 66–8, 72, 76, 98–9, 186, 203–4, 222, 231, 254–5, 288, 292, 318; ST 29–30, 33, 42–53, 64–73, 86, 95, 99–100, 109–37, 145, 172–84, 188–9, 203–5, 211–66, 269–78, 281–6; SF 222.
Themes of dispersal and separation: IT 9; ST 33, 62–3, 69–70, 94–5, 114–15, 119–23, 140–1, 157, 181, 224, 234, 242, 248–9, 253–4, 263; SF 77.
Loneliness: WF 121, 126, 129, 154–6, 259; IT 28, 87; SF 84.
Imprisonment: CL 177–8.
Reunion and restoration: CL 14–18, 21–2, 30, 57, 66–70, 73, 116, 123–7, 165, 189, 204, 335; ST 59, 113–15, 119–20, 123, 126, 141, 165, 227–31, 234, 238–40, 252, 263–6; SF 66, 69, 77–8, 100, 230, 237. *See also I,* 'Vision and technique of the Final Plays'.
Geographical location: IT 206, 322–3; CL 249–50.
Lands of the East, Indies, etc. WF 63; IT 133, 324; CL 215, 304, 318; ST 73–4, 99, 115, 125, 130, 142–5, 172–3, 183, 188, 216, 233, 241, 246, 254, 262–3, 269; SF 159, 164, 184–5, 190–4, 199–201.
Merchants, merchandise, and riches: WF 63, 207–10, 220, 228, 233–7; IT 8, 27, 49, 132–3, 205, 217–18, 279, 296; CL 48–9, 54–7, 71, 162, 333; ST 72–5, 96, 99–100, 110–12, 123, 127–45, 172–3, 202–5, 214, 226, 229, 233, 241–6, 252–4, 262; SF 54–7, 164, 211, 218.
Finance: IT 74–6; SF 28, 271.
Avarice: IT 132; SF 56–7.
Capitalism: SF 56.

Proper names: CL 129, 132, 142; ST 106; SF 43–4, 142–3, 163–201.
Professions: SF 209–11.
Philosophers, study and learning: ST 76,

79–81; SF 51, 69–72, 88, 148, 154, 172, 177, 187, 208, 221, 227–8.
Foreigners: CL 142, 147–50, 297–8, 330. *See also* 'England and the Continent', above.
Pirates: IT 119; CL 59, 98; ST 66, 100, 126, 174–5, 179, 199, 225; SF 192.
Braggarts, swaggerers: CL 136, 142–9, 218–20, 298; SF 36–7, 103, 107, 118–21, 126, 183, 224.
Flattery, flattering persons: WF 214, 225–6, 234; IT 89; CL 142–9, 333.
Fools: CL 132–4.

IV. THE COSMOS

SF 16, 20, 57, 72, 211–14, 229, 236–40.
The universe, space: WF 28, 50–2, 98–9, 118, 178, 189–90, 224–5, 229–33, 245, 249–52, 292–3, 297, 326–31; IT 25, 56–60, 156, 165, 191, 200, 208–10, 240–3, 251–2, 258–62, 313, 337–8, 341, 347–8; CL 22, 82–3, 89, 109–10, 115, 174, 245, 248, 334; ST xi–xiii, xvi–xvii, xxi, 136–7, 171, 185–6, 190, 215, 234, 265–92; SF 213, 234–7.
Nature, creation and natural behaviour: WF 103, 154–7, 179–95, 200–6, 225, 228–30, 246–7, 267, 277–88, 292, 314; IT 25–6, 115–16, 125, 134, 140–53, 163–5, 192–3, 196, 199–200, 210, 251–2, 257, 260–2, 334–44; CL 54, 89, 206, 212, 222–3, 226, 233–51, 306, 317; ST xvi–xvii, 75, 83–5, 94, 143–4, 158, 192–201, 204–6, 210–14, 235, 258–66, 277, 306–7, 315, 330; SF 16–17, 20, 30–1, 46, 61, 64, 77, 85–6, 97–100, 131, 140–1, 152, 155, 198–9, 209–15, 228, 234–41, 270.
'Great creating nature': IT 26, 141–53, 192, 224, 229–32, 236, 259–62, 286, 336–9; CL 82–3, 87–110, 117–28, 157–164, 173–6, 303–6, 328–36; ST xiv, 158, 192–3, 212–13, 263–4, 271, 280–92; SF 98, 209, 238.
Nature disrupted: WF 133–8. *See also III,* 'Chaos and disintegration', *and VI,* 'Order and disorder'.
Nature-spirits: CL 237, 247.

Tempests: WF viii, 10, 49–52, 63, 109–11, 128–39, 146–7, 164–8, 180, 183–5,

189, 199–202, 205, 224, 245, 272, 290–291, 296; IT ix, 6, 9, 22, 28–30, 55, 71, 147, 234, 237, 251, 330–1, 340, 360, 365–6; CL vii, 11–14, 17–18, 23–7, 36, 42–3, 51–9, 63, 68–72, 76, 97–8, 124, 169, 186–94, 203–6, 210–11, 217–24, 229–34, 240–1, 249–51, 303, 318–20, 328; ST throughout; SF 47, 139, 155, 206, 214–15, 222, 230, 233–6, 240, 284; CR VII. *See also II,* 'Music,' *and VI,* 'Order and disorder'.

Thunder and lightning: WF 131–2, 147, 164–5, 183, 189, 202, 340; IT 56, 84, 144, 153, 164, 244, 258–9, 332; CL 17, 186–94, 216–17, 221, 229–34, 251, 320; ST xi, 30–4, 38, 58, 66, 151, 175–6, 185–91, 195–200, 206–10, 213–15, 228, 232, 238–40, 247–50, 254–7, 260–2, 265–6, 274, 283, 326, 329, 332; SP II (2).

Eclipses: WF 12, 163, 188, 269, 326–31; IT 102–3; ST 54; SF 213.

Sun: WF 14, 98–9, 118, 188–90, 224, 227–35, 249, 252, 292–3, 326–30, 337; IT 25, 59–60, 102–3, 127, 144, 147–9, 156, 165, 193, 197, 224, 229, 232–6, 240–4, 258–62, 274, 313, 323, 337, 341; CL 49, 83, 92, 102, 106–11, 115, 157, 163, 166, 173–6, 180–1, 184, 221, 227, 235, 245, 318, 334; ST xi–xiii, 18, 31, 34, 38–9, 54–5, 58–9, 64–5, 73–8, 88–9, 94–5, 113–14, 137–9, 159–60, 171–2, 188–90, 194, 201, 205, 209, 215, 236, 242, 265–6, 270–3, 280, 284–5, 295, 301–2; SF 30–2, 41, 52, 68, 77–80, 84, 90, 97, 210, 213, 220, 227, 233, 237, 240; MF III.

Moon: WF 98, 118, 189, 224, 227, 230, 249–52, 292–3, 327–30; IT viii, 3–4, 25, 102–4, 127, 156–8, 239–42, 258–9, 272–3, 313, 337; CL 102, 106, 109–10, 227, 235–6, 247; ST xi–xiii, xxi–xxiii, 18, 33, 54–5, 65, 75–7, 130, 134–8, 142, 146–8, 157–61, 194, 201, 205, 209, 215, 232, 270–2, 280, 301–4, 317, 327–8; SF 210, 227, 233.

Stars, planets, etc.: WF 81, 98–9, 104, 118, 131, 134, 185–8, 251, 326–30, 339; IT 25, 47, 58–60, 64–5, 118, 126–7, 149, 165, 193, 240–2, 320, 324, 337, 347–8; CL 49, 88–9, 116, 176, 334; ST xi–xiii, xxi, 17–18, 27, 33, 54–5, 65, 91, 136–9, 142, 146–51, 163, 171, 198, 219, 233, 270–2, 280, 299, 328; SF 68, 210, 213, **222.**

Sky, heavens: WF 28, 100–1, 171–2, 183, 189; CL 82–3, 89, 109–10, 157, 174–6, 221, 245; ST 130, 242, 265–6; SF 77, 140–1.

Darkness: WF 84, 98–9, 130–5, 139–40, 144–9, 156, 190, 268; IT 22–3, 58–60, 96, 102–4, 108, 146–8, 151, 241–3, 273–4; CL 161; ST 18, 61, 93, 119–20, 137, 142, 145–54, 159–61, 167, 190, 270–2, 280, 284, 302–5, 311, 328–9; SF 192, 227, 236.

Dawn: WF 65; IT 60, 103–4; ST 63, 93, 159–64, 235, 252, 293, 298–305; SF 210, 227, 233.

Light: WF 77, 104, 148–9, 156–7; IT 22, 103–4, 108, 241–4, 274; CL 82; ST 18, 93, 119–20, 190, 270–1, 276, 280–5, 293, 300–5.

Air, breezes: IT 26, 142, 208, 227–9, 232, 236–42, 251–2, 256–62, 320, 330–1, 334–5; CL 58, 164, 197–201, 208–12, 233, 249; SF 17, 55, 58, 63–4, 77–8, 104, 123, 135, 144, 173, 176, 194, 211, 214–16, 236–9, 262–6, 272; SF 78, 197–8.

Winds: WF 164–7, 180–3, 193, 196, 202, 205; IT 147–9, 163, 238, 256–7, 330–1; CL 88, 198, 221; ST 22, 26–9, 33–40, 43–4, 48, 64, 71–2, 83–7, 94–5, 108–9, 116, 127, 130, 133–5, 165, 170–2, 176, 184, 188–92, 195–6, 200, 207–9, 216, 225, 231–3, 236, 255–7, 260–6, 272–6; SF 139, 209.

Clouds and fog: WF 130, 139, 145, 183, 189, 329; IT 144, 208, 212, 237–9, 251–2, 261, 283, 323, 330, 335, 341; ST 17, 26–7, 32–7, 65, 73, 86–7, 90, 95, 143–4, 148, 176, 188, 203, 213–14, 254, 270–2, 275, 328–9, 332.

Rain and dew: WF 149, 164, 205; IT 144, 237–8, 328; CL 161, 174–6, 245; ST 17, 26–31, 34–5, 40–1, 64–5, 87, 90, 94, 107, 111, 127, 145, 158–9, 163–6, 172, 176, 188, 195–6, 200–3, 210, 213, 236–8, 242, 270–2, 275, 301; SF 97, 220.

'Dews of blood': WF 326–31; SF 233.

Rainbow: ST 276.

Snow, frost, ice: WF 104, 229; IT 237, 261, 347–8; CL 109: ST 40, 80–3, 108–9, 119–20, 204, 233, 272–3.

The four elements: WF 99, 183, 189–90, 276; IT 200, 207–8, 214, 227–45, 251–2, 260–2, 320, 323, 330–1, 335–8; CL 53, 208, 212, 223, 226–9, **233,** 240–3,

249; ST 17–18, 58, 63–4, 160, 171, 190, 211, 313–15, 319; SF 198, 210; MF 46.

Fire: WF 130, 133, 139, 147, 167, 190, 200, 203–5, 327–30, 339; IT ix, 27, 34–5, 44–5, 50–61, 91–3, 156, 188, 196–7, 227, 236–44, 251, 320; CL 14, 55–7, 87–8, 198, 208–12, 224, 232–3, 247; ST 32, 58, 63–4, 77–8, 108, 185–6, 249–50, 271, 275, 285, 312–19, 324; SF 198.

Sea: WF 49, 63–5, 99, 109–11, 170, 180, 224, 230–3, 245, 304–5, 320, 330; IT 2–4, 25, 119, 199, 206–10, 228–9, 232–235, 258–9, 274, 282–3, 313, 324, 331, 347–8; CL 14, 18, 25–6, 36–7, 42–6, 52–7, 64–9, 73, 107–10, 184, 194, 206–8, 221–2, 231–3, 247–9, 252–5, 285, 288, 291, 310, 318, 330; ST xv–xx, 10, 14–15, 18–55, 65–76, 83, 86, 91–2, 94–9, 107–35, 144, 160, 163, 171–266, 269–70, 274–86, 291, 319, 325; SF 57, 69–70, 185, 209–10, 215, 240. *See also* 'Tempests', above, *and III*, 'Voyages, ships and shipwreck'.

Sea-shore and sands: WF 67, 228, 245; IT 236; CL 14, 26, 43, 59, 97, 184, 194, 206, 231, 245–7, 285; ST xv, 20–2, 37, 74, 92, 97–8, 110, 117, 135, 144, 172, 204–6, 209, 213, 224, 229, 240, 244, 251–2, 256, 263–6, 269–70, 277; SF 54, 68–70, 233.

Cliffs: WF 170–2, 179–80; ST 200, 235; SF 209.

Islands: IT 234–5, 258–60; CL 24, 91, 194, 214–15, 247–51; ST 235, 263, 283–4; SF 69–72.

Land, earth: WF 98, 224, 228–31, 249–51; IT 108, 146, 207–10, 217, 227–36, 240–2, 245, 250–1, 258–62, 312–13, 331, 335, 341, 347–8; CL 83, 89, 106, 109–10, 115, 160–1, 170, 173, 208, 212, 223, 236–40, 245–7; ST 58, 63–4, 70, 203, 264, 277, 280; SF 54, 182, 231.

Rivers, running water: WF viii, 222, 289; IT 26, 116–17, 156, 208, 214, 224, 227–240, 251, 256–61, 298, 323, 334–7; CL 195, 245, 251, 285, 318; ST 18, 23–6, 41, 44, 50, 58, 89, 96–7, 100, 104, 107, 131, 137, 143–4, 172, 176–8, 183–6, 204, 211–16, 244, 275; SF 209–10.

Ponds, still or calm water: WF 181, 289–290; IT 233–4, 256–8; CL 80, 149, 154, 198, 211, 218–19, 235, 239, 247; ST xxiii, 55, 101–2, 105, 117, 147–9, 179, 194, 212–16, 227, 235, 260, 265–6; SF 121.

Mountains: IT 25, 47, 64, 118–19; CL 157–158, 173, 206, 290; ST 19, 36, 39–41, 108, 133, 181, 246, 317–18; SF 77, 186, 210.

Stones and rocks: IT 27, 53, 155–7, 165, 191; CL 87; ST 29–30, 40, 44–5, 68–9, 96–8, 137, 207–10, 235, 244, 289; SF 68, 177–8.

Gold, jewels and metals: WF 10, 63, 98, 118, 187, 208–9, 233–7, 293; IT 8, 27, 34–5, 51–2, 94, 130–3, 155–65, 191–7, 205, 217–18, 236–7, 240–2, 248, 256–7, 260, 296; CL 38–9, 48–9, 54–7, 64, 68, 71–3, 99, 115, 143–4, 159, 174–6, 183–186, 194, 203, 318–21, 325–8, 331; ST 17–18, 29–30, 65–9, 72–4, 84, 89, 96–9, 106, 112, 115–20, 125–6, 130–1, 136–141, 147–9, 158–61, 172–3, 183, 202–3, 206, 209, 214–18, 222–3, 226–7, 230, 251–4, 263, 297–8, 301; SF 54–7, 60, 90, 132, 139, 177, 197, 209–11; MF 66. *See also III*, 'Merchants, merchandise, and riches'.

Deserts: ST 129.

Earthquake: WF 146–7; ST 17, 27, 171, 258, 274–5, 283.

Pastoral life, the countryside: WF 179–83, 189, 194, 202, 205; CL 88, 98–113, 247, 333, 336; ST 84–5, 163–4, 273, 301; SF 19–20, 29–31, 46, 85–6, 98, 106, 182, 196, 210, 238–9.

Seasons: IT 231–2, 259, 340; CL 76, 88, 99–106, 109, 115, 120–1, 173–4, 284–5; ST 17, 21–2, 26, 31, 40, 75–87, 90–1, 94, 108–9, 119–20, 139, 143–4, 158, 184, 194, 200–3, 232–5, 242, 261–4, 271–4, 277–9, 284, 300–1; SF 194, 210, 213, 236, 269.

Grain, fruits and harvest, fertility: WF 92; IT 147, 156, 163, 177, 189, 223–4, 229–232, 251, 259, 337; CL 91–3, 98, 103–10, 119, 173, 244–9, 303–6, 329–35; ST 33, 85–7, 158, 209, 212–14, 246, 263–4, 271–2, 313; SF 193–4, 237, 240, 284. *See also* 'Great creating nature', above.

Milk: ST 143, 149; CL 93, 108.

Trees, woods, shrubs: WF 136, 149, 156, 181, 225, 232, 237, 246; IT 140, 144–7,

U*

150–2, 163–5, 229–30, 251; CL 87, 160–
161, 164, 169–70, 197, 201, 221, 224,
237, 247, 284, 318, 334–5; ST 17–19,
26, 36, 39–40, 79, 84, 87, 108, 119–20,
133, 137, 142, 145–8, 152–3, 161–4,
170–1, 175, 181, 185–6, 193–6, 202–4,
207–9, 214, 236–9, 242–3, 246, 260–2,
265–6, 273, 277, 289, 301; SF 61, 64,
68, 78, 86, 175, 186, 191, 209, 213, 220.

Flowers: WF 149, 172, 180, 184, 189, 203,
292; IT 26, 64, 114–18, 141, 144, 151,
194, 197, 229–30, 234, 238, 256–7,
328–30; CL 39, 58, 102–6, 113, 121,
127–31, 154, 159–63, 169–70, 173–6,
194–5, 198, 245, 293, 319, 328; ST 17,
21, 55, 61, 77–82, 88–9, 103–11, 123,
156–62, 165, 178, 194, 216, 223–4,
232, 237–8, 272–3, 297–8; SF 88,
97–8, 182, 186, 193–6, 209, 215, 282;
MF 60.

Gardens and gardening: WF 18, 28; CL
44; SF 186, 213.

Spices: CL 54–5.

Animals: WF 12, 174, 180–6, 189, 192–4,
200–2, 205–6, 209, 232, 276, 341–2;
IT 25, 33–4, 69, 139–40, 144, 149–50,
163–6, 227–9, 232, 251, 328, 340; CL
52, 78, 88, 98, 151, 164, 197, 201, 208,
213, 219, 224, 235–9, 247–9, 298, 303;
ST 61, 103–4, 260, 297–9, 315–18; SF 17,
32, 40, 47, 57, 65, 76–8, 171–2, 179–80,
195–9, 209–10, 213–16, 222, 230.

Fierce beasts: WF 116, 128–30, 133–4, 139,
145–8, 225–9; IT 33–4, 55–7, 227–9;
CL 159, 186, 203, 211–12, 219, 224;
ST 17–19, 27–8, 32, 35–6, 41–2, 57, 64–6,
79, 87–90, 93, 97–9, 105–8, 112, 120,
126, 129, 133–42, 148, 151–6, 161,
164–5, 170–2, 181–3, 186–92, 195–
208, 214, 224–5, 230–1, 239, 244, 256–
262, 280–1, 289–90, 303, 307–8, 318,
322, 329; SF 15–17, 23, 40, 65–7, 77,
171–2, 185, 216.

Horses: WF 146, 205, 209, 268, 312, 318–
319, 334; IT 5, 33, 52, 147, 211–14,
337; CL 187; ST 63–4, 91, 103–4, 297–9,
314–19; SF 40, 117, 180–3, 190, 215–16.

Birds: WF 65, 119, 133–5, 145–8, 180–2,
185, 205, 235–6, 339; IT 26, 33, 55–7,
89, 141–2, 147–9, 163–5, 187, 196–7,
228–9, 234, 330–1, 336–7, 347; CL
88, 100, 148–9, 154, 158–60, 165, 169,

174–6, 183–8, 197–201, 208–9, 250,
287, 328–9; ST xxiii, 17, 40–1, 60–4,
75–6, 84–94, 97–8, 103–4, 111, 138–42,
155–8, 161–2, 166, 211, 214, 235, 251–
252, 272–3, 277–9, 285, 293–325, 329;
SF 17, 79, 87, 175, 209.

Phoenix: WF 235; IT 228–9, 251, 349–50;
CL 183, 195, 250, 287, 334; ST 120–1,
262, 278, 311, 320–5; SF 85, 136–9,
164; WF Part II, throughout.

Fish: WF 182; IT 155, 187, 228, 234; CL
218, 235; ST 88–91, 101, 163, 214–15,
219, 236, 245, 258.

Sea monsters, dragons: WF 185, 194; CL
211–12, 229, 235; ST 32, 97–101, 132,
174, 199, 219, 236, 258, 262, 276–80,
284, 308; SF 23, 40, 59, 67, 71, 198.

Reptiles, worms: WF 116, 145, 181; IT
139, 214, 227–8, 232–3, 252, 261, 300,
329–30; CL 39, 81, 195, 211–12, 218,
235–7, 247; ST 156, 278, 307–8, 329;
SF 23, 231, 282.

Vermin: WF 181.

Insects, spiders: WF 170, 192; IT 163,
171–2, 228, 330; CL 52, 81, 111, 154–6,
187, 198–200; ST 149, 156–8, 279; SF
23, 38–9, 213, 280–1.

V. THE SUPERNATURAL

WF 153, 157–9, 205, 253, 267; IT 28, 66,
100, 128, 334–42; CL 9, 191, 196; ST
120, 280; SF 155, 214, 221, 229, 250.

Transcendent or 'mystical' vision: WF 16,
50–1, 79–80, 203–6, 229–33, 236, 241,
244–6, 256, 262, 267, 296–7; IT v–vi,
xii–xiii, 30–1, 199–200, 217, 223, 227,
248, 254–63, 289, 317–22, 325–6,
333, 342–50, 361, 367; CL 12–31, 34,
57, 67, 72–3, 117–28, 142, 159–63,
201–2, 223–6, 243–6, 250–3, 256–8,
277–8, 318, 321–2, 331–6; ST 9–13, 53,
85, 97, 117, 217, 228, 245–92, 324;
SF 42, 52, 69, 84–7, 147, 226, 237–41,
271, 292–3.

Supernormal persons, 'supermen': WF viii,
35, 38–40, 43–4, 51, 74–83, 107–11,
114–15, 201–2, 205–6, 210–12, 215–
239, 249–51, 255, 301, 308–25, 340–2;
IT 6–8, 12, 64–6, 81–3, 92–4, 186–7,
209–10, 215, 223, 246–51, 257–63,
309–13, 325, 338; CL 25–7, 54–6,

62–6, 69–70, 73, 86, 108, 115–21, 156,
159–63, 174, 200–1, 206–8, 220–3,
231–2, 242–6, 253, 257, 277, 296, 314,
333; ST xv–xvii, xxi, 134, 160–1,
167–8, 175, 207, 265–6, 280–8, 310–11,
314–19, 330; SF 47, 69–72, 77, 80, 88–
90, 120, 132–4, 138–40, 145–60, 187,
198, 205, 213, 223, 227, 240, 273–4,
277.

Cosmic, occult or spiritualistic powers:
SF 65, 100, 138–41, 144–60; MF 14.

Myth, miraculous events: WF 16, 256,
296–7; IT 12, 325; CL 9–31, 37–40, 51,
56–7, 66–76, 90–1, 106, 109–10, 115–
128, 170–1, 202–4, 215, 221, 225–57,
294, 319, 335–6; ST 57, 120, 218,
223–4, 228–31, 239–41, 247–92, 319;
SF 69, 101, 147, 155–6, 196, 237–41.

Resurrection: WF 296–7; IT 12; CL 14–15,
18–19, 25, 30–1, 56–7, 69, 76, 91, 114–
128, 170, 189, 202, 221, 231, 252, 257,
319, 335; ST xv–xviii, xxi, 93, 126, 131,
223, 228–31, 263–6; SF 69, 101–2, 149,
155, 237–40, 251.

Immortality: WF 68, 83–4, 198, 203,
290, 296; IT 91, 249, 290, 316–22,
350, 361; CL 10, 13, 22–31, 119, 126–7,
232, 250, 294, 333–4; ST 74, 117,
136, 144–5, 276–9, 320–5; SF 66,
237–9. See also VI, 'Time and eternity'.

Visions: WF 337; CL 16, 19–23, 67,
164–202, 208, 216–17, 292–5, 318–20,
327; ST xiv–xviii, 2, 239–43, 255–7,
262–3; SF 84, 155, 238–9.

Supernatural music: IT 245, 335; CL 67,
73, 122, 168, 191, 221–2, 294; ST
xviii, 136, 215–17, 228, 239, 243, 246,
254–7, 266, 290, 329–31; SF 213–14.

Religion and religious experience: WF
190–1, 205, 212, 240–8, 270, 294–7,
324; IT 10–15, 105, 128, 317, 355, 358,
364–6; CL 14, 19, 22–3, 36–8, 69, 105,
113–14, 121, 124, 127–8, 179–83,
241–2, 273–5, 282, 286–8, 292, 299–
301, 304–7, 310–20, 324, 330–6; ST ix,
97, 119–20, 174, 241, 316; SF 36–8,
55–6, 86–8, 140, 143–6, 160, 214, 220,
223, 226–7, 240, 273, 291–3.

God: WF 36, 79, 148, 190–1, 199–200,
239, 313, 317, 322, 333–5, 340–3;

IT 4, 8, 11, 302, 309; CL 23–31, 125,
162, 201–2, 217, 226, 230–1, 242,
250, 253, 276, 287–8, 314–17; ST 34–6,
268, 274–80, 284–5, 290–2; SF 20, 23,
37–9, 42–7, 66, 83–4, 149, 156, 213,
224, 252, 267, 278.

Divine justice, anger, etc.: WF 193–5,
298–9; CL 20–1, 41, 49, 92–5, 179–82,
188–92, 202, 233–4, 248, 313, 323–6;
ST 176, 196–8, 239–41, 256; SF 30–4,
42.

Orthodox religion: WF 74–6, 84, 321;
IT 117–18, 355; CL 87, 128; ST 277;
SF 73, 141, 152, 207–8, 214, 226, 250–3.

Bible: WF 8; CL 128, 237, 333–4; ST 5;
SF 172.

Old Testament: WF 191, 235; IT 300,
303–5, 309, 316; CL 30, 92, 97, 195,
248; ST 174, 275–8, 290; SF 85.

New Testament: WF 73–96, 235, 256,
280, 315–17, 324: IT 124, 149; CL 42,
55–6, 65, 76, 101, 108, 118–19, 124–5,
179, 215–16, 230–1, 242, 253, 292–3,
329, 333; ST xx, 276, 281; SF 51–2,
140, 155, 159, 187, 196, 208, 212,
216–17, 226, 229, 233, 251, 257–8.

Christ: WF 36, 80–3, 96, 235–6, 242,
307–11, 315–16; IT xii, 24, 124; CL
22, 31, 69, 86, 231, 242, 253, 275–8,
283, 313; ST 161, 330; SF 31–2, 44,
72, 82–3, 90, 146, 159, 169, 223, 226,
236, 248, 258, 278.

Crucifixion: WF 50, 75, 235, 292; IT
321; CL 12; ST 274; SF 236, 239.

Resurrection: see above.

Christianity: WF 75–6, 280, 294–6, 321;
IT 3, 350, 355; CL 10–12, 30–1, 35,
68–9, 87–97, 113, 119, 149, 181,
202, 236, 241, 254, 274–8, 281, 288–9,
292–8, 314–16, 326–36; ST xii, xv,
286, 292; SF 21, 27, 37–9, 50–3, 73,
82, 85, 90, 104, 138, 155, 159, 169–72,
178, 187, 205–8, 211, 214, 220–2, 226,
239, 250–1, 258, 266, 271–3; 278.

Heaven: WF 24, 28, 35–6, 114–15, 148,
179, 201, 312–14, 323, 333–4; IT 104–5,
117, 142, 148–50, 360; CL 38, 174–6,
200, 292–4, 333; ST 176, 182, 221,
279, 302, 320–1; SF 82–4, 136, 141,
144, 154, 237, 250, 279, 284.

Purgatory: WF 179; IT 23, 104–5, 117;
SF 237, 250. See also III, 'Purgatorial
suffering'.

Hell, damnation: WF 21, 24–8, 40–2, 74, 114–15, 150, 179, 318; IT 52, 103–5, 109–10, 113–14, 117, 148, 331, 360; CL 38; ST 176, 182, 221, 272; SF 209, 237, 249–52, 284. See also III, 'Evil', 'Guilt and sin'.

Satan, devils, fiends: WF 24, 39, 87, 114–16, 152, 172, 182–4, 188–90, 196–7, 254–6; IT 104, 113–14, 316–17; CL 85–7, 228–30, 235–6, 240–2, 288; ST xvi–xix, 249–50, 256, 310, 322; SF 144–5, 188, 213, 252.

Grace: WF 111, 148–9, 267, 312, 317; IT 15, 103, 128, 141–3, 147–9, 231, 338–41, 350; CL 234, 239–40; ST xv–xvii, xxi–xxii; SF 59, 63–5, 72, 84, 130, 145, 214.

Prayer: WF 35–6, 87, 100, 115, 148, 171, 183, 187–9, 197, 253, 259, 309, 335; IT 3–4, 72; CL 19–20, 153, 157, 176, 179–85, 200, 254, 274, 287, 293–4, 309, 312, 316–18; ST 228, 238–41; SF 63, 77, 132, 145, 149, 265.

Religious mystics, contemplatives: WF 51, 71; IT 363–6; CL 29–31, 258, 314–15; SF 31–2, 69–70, 85–8.

Clergy, nuns, friars, etc: WF 74, 77–9, 82, 91–2; IT 10–15, 117; CL 68–70, 73, 207, 326; ST 119–20; SF 51, 146, 154, 175, 214.

Saints: WF 87, 91–5, 148, 151, 211, 315; IT 13–15; SF 36, 63–4, 69, 88, 146, 156, 159–60, 196, 251, 274. See also Index C, under individual saints.

Angels: WF 87, 115, 148, 312, 333–43; IT 13, 124, 141–3, 338; CL 156, 159, 162, 187, 190, 198–200, 208, 226, 230, 233, 243, 288, 294, 317–18; ST xv–xviii, xxi–xxii, 189, 236, 279, 290, 293, 310, 318–19, 322; SF 63, 84, 187, 214.

Virgin Mary: WF 249; IT 300, 309; SF 138.

Roman Catholicism: IT 13; CL 30–1, 35, 137, 227, 315; SF 84.

Protestantism: IT 13; CL 137, 314–18; SF 84.

Puritanism: CL 242–6, 253–5, 297; SF 217–18, 224, 271.

Gods and goddesses: WF 79, 169–71, 174, 186–94, 197–200, 205–6, 334, 338–42; IT 72, 85, 170–3, 190, 194–7, 207, 210, 218, 221–3, 246–7, 257, 307, 338; CL 14, 30, 38, 42–3, 52–3, 58, 63, 66–75, 103, 106, 114–15, 125, 156, 159, 171, 179–96, 217, 221, 237, 245, 251–4; ST xv–xviii, 60, 66, 85–6, 93, 157, 207–9, 212–13, 221, 228–9, 239–41, 249–50, 263–6, 272–5, 284, 310–11, 316–19, 326–7, 332; SF 102, 111, 114, 119, 183, 193, 196, 199, 207, 238.

Jove, Jupiter: WF 190, 237–8; IT 164, 246; CL 16, 19–23, 42, 92, 103, 159, 164–6, 171, 176, 179, 183–96, 201–2, 217, 221, 233, 257; ST xv, 2, 30–1, 38, 58, 175–6, 196–7, 206–7, 212–13, 232, 239–40, 248–50, 256–7, 265–6, 308, 323, 337; SF 78, 102, 155, 238.

Apollo: WF 190; CL 85, 91–4, 97, 103, 110, 114, 125, 183–90; ST xv, 60; SF 238–40.

Diana: CL 14–16, 42, 50, 57–8, 61, 67–8, 70–3, 168, 184–6, 189–96; ST xv, 120, 224, 228, 327; SF 102, 108–12, 134–6, 141, 155–6, 160, 238.

Olympus: IT 25, 47, 64, 165.

Mythology: WF 334–5; IT 136; CL 103, 106, 110, 128–9, 150, 183–5, 209, 226–230, 246–50, 319; ST 97, 242, 272–93, 299–300, 316–22, 330–2; SF 164–5, 207–8, 251–2.

Nymphs: ST 144, 251, 262–4.

Elysium, paradise: WF 212, 239; CL 194–5, 243, 246; ST 58, 74, 84, 97–8, 141–2, 277, 280–90; SF 201, 237, 249.

Furies: WF 155; IT 249; ST 332; SF 144, 207.

Prophecy: WF 80, 136–9, 155–7, 188, 258, 261, 264–6; IT 45–6, 57, 66, 139–40, 150–3, 252, 335–6, 361–2; CL 14, 29, 89, 164–7, 185–6, 196–7, 201, 258, 270, 306, 314–19, 322–4, 328–36; ST 33, 185, 193, 240, 246, 282–8; SF 28–31, 58, 70, 74, 78–9, 85–8, 215, 239, 253, 264–7, 277, 284.

Oracles: CL 14, 85, 91–4, 114, 123–7, 164, 190, 196, 257, 290; ST 232, 238–40; SF 102, 240.

Omens and portents, magic or weird phenomena: WF 130–6, 145–6, 205, 326–31, 337; IT 6, 56–7, 66, 70, 84, 89, 93, 102–3, 334–40; CL 86, 191; ST xvi–xvii, 33, 54, 186, 215, 271; SF 74, 233–4.

Dreams, and nightmare-consciousness: WF 126, 131–2, 146–9, 152–7, 261, 267; IT 45–6, 66, 78, 130, 134, 146–8, 258–61, 313, 339; CL 34, 65, 82–3, 97, 190–2, 204, 215, 294, 321; ST xxi, 150–4, 159–61, 329; SF 21–2, 66, 213, 220, 229, 233–7, 249, 275.

Ghosts and spirits of the dead: WF 4–5, 18–24, 30–1, 39, 42–5, 127–8, 134, 140, 146–8, 155–9, 188, 253–4, 268, 286, 299, 303, 321, 326–8, 335; IT 20–3, 28, 51–2, 62, 66, 70, 79–81, 96, 99, 102–11, 116–19, 124, 127, 136–9, 264, 340; CL 35, 86, 97–8, 114, 124, 168–72, 176, 179, 182–4, 187, 191–2, 195–6, 216–17, 220, 257; ST xvi-xxi, 151–4, 160, 179, 185–7, 191, 238–9, 305, 327; SF 21–2, 48, 155, 205–7, 225, 233–5, 239, 247; MF 14.

Apparitions: WF 146–8, 155, 159; IT 131, 139–40, 149–53; CL 192–3; ST 192–3, 331; SF 61–2, 68, 233–5, 247, 256, 270, 282; CR III.

Hecate, witches, weird sisters: WF 4, 122, 132–5, 139, 145–7, 150–1, 154–7, 178, 188, 249, 258, 265, 268, 329–30; IT 57, 108, 131, 138–9, 145, 150–3, 247, 264, 316, 329–30, 334–6; CL 86–8, 96, 124, 131, 191–13, 216, 235–41, 255; ST xvi-xix, 10, 148–54, 188–93, 238, 256, 307, 326–32; SF 61, 71, 199, 207, 233.

Black and white magic: CL 119, 124–5, 204, 211, 229, 235–42, 255; ST 33–4, 326–32; SF 71–2, 154, 198.

Superstition, folklore: WF 188–91; IT 64–6; SF 184, 207–8, 229, 272.

Enchantment: ST 154, 254–7.

Eastern or Egyptian magic: CL 56, 215.

'Magic' handkerchief in Othello: WF 108–9, 119; CL 191; SF 129, 234.

Ring in All's Well that Ends Well: SF 109, 127–9, 143–4, 147, 158.

Spirits and fairies: WF 289; CL 159, 192, 200, 204, 208–11, 215, 220, 232–5, 247–9; ST 102–3, 130, 139, 142–7, 151–61, 165–8, 260, 265–6, 273, 327–332; SF 164, 184, 198.

Mermaids, sirens: ST 71, 117, 130, 163, 178, 214, 254, 263, 275.

VI. MISCELLANEOUS

Order and disorder: WF 4, 47, 50–2, 72, 122, 130–9, 145, 150, 153–6, 221, 224, 230, 258, 261, 264, 269, 296; IT viii, 4–10, 17–19, 27–9, 40, 54–63, 67, 71–3, 80, 84, 94–5, 102, 112–13, 124–8, 134–43, 148–50, 153, 178–9, 330, 342, 363–7; CL 29, 82–3, 285, 320–6, 335–6; ST throughout; SF 13–14, 33, 38–9, 48–53, 56–9, 64, 74–5, 212–13, 222–4, 229, 233, 237, 240, 245–6, 253, 269–272, 276–9. See also II, 'Music'; III, 'Chaos and disintegration; and IV, 'Tempests'.

Time and eternity, infinity: WF 28, 57, 63–72, 84, 138–9, 180, 203, 221–33, 238–9, 244–6, 251–2, 259, 263–9, 297; IT 8–19, 25, 57–9, 93–4, 105, 116–19, 150–3, 166, 193, 198–200, 220, 248–253, 261–2, 265, 272, 285–9, 296–8, 302–4, 310–24, 334–50, 358, 364–7; CL 10–13, 17, 31, 64–7, 71–3, 77, 107–8, 114, 117–28, 175, 240, 244, 248, 251–3, 282, 331–6; ST xiv-xxii, 21, 51–3, 68, 71, 190, 205–6, 213, 254, 268–92, 321; SF 31–2, 41–2, 51–2, 57, 61–6, 69, 72, 85–90, 99–100, 147, 156, 205–206, 221–2, 226–7, 236–41, 246, 249, 253–9, 267, 271, 278–9; MF III, IV.

Fortune: WF 195, 200, 304–5, 313; IT 221, 253, 338, 356; CL 37, 42–6, 52, 57, 60–3, 68, 71, 103, 183, 195, 218; ST 22, 27, 37–9, 46–51, 68, 114, 121–4, 170, 182–4, 200, 203, 208, 212–13, 219–20, 227–8, 266–8; SF 108, 114, 190.

'Will': WF 53–4, 152–3, 158, 259–60, 305–7; IT 52, 195; CL 236; SF 22, 48, 53, 60, 67–8, 269.

'Swift thought': WF 65, 338–41; IT 332–4; CL 208–10, 240; ST 90, 138, 157, 225, 277–9, 293, 308–19; SF 184; MF 45–6.

'Nothing': WF 8, 122, 149, 153, 231–3, 245, 257–8, 264, 269; IT 115, 137, 146–9, 152, 240, 284, 331, 338, 354–5, 357–8; CL 34, 69, 82–3, 110, 127, 210; ST xvi-xix, 206, 292; SF 198, 232; CR III.

Causality: WF 158, 279; IT 289.

Anthropomorphism: CL 19, 22–5, 30, 202; ST 130, 195–6.

Index C

General Index

Abbott, C. D.: ST 306
Abercrombie, Lascelles: CL 33
Abraham: WF 235
Addison, Joseph: SF 272
Aeschylus: WF 271, 324; IT xiii, 315; CL 35, 319, 331; SF 87
  Oresteia, WF viii, 315, 333; SF 207, 253
  Prometheus Bound, CL 228
Ainley, Henry: SF 265
Alder, Vera Stanley: SF 150
Alexander, Peter: WF 239, 332, 342; CL 259; SF 280
Alexander the Great: SF 73, 205, 223
Allen, Percy: ST 235
Anne, Queen: SF 270
Apu-Ollantay (Inca drama): CL 37; SF 237
Aquinas, St Thomas: WF xiv-xvi, 337-8
Aristotle: WF 3
Arnold, Matthew: WF xiv-xv
  The Scholar Gipsy, SF 159, 258
Ascham, Roger: CL 150; SF 179
Auden, W. H.: *The Sea and the Mirror*, SF 200
Augustine, St: CL 227

Bach, Johann Sebastian: CL 243
Bacon, Francis, Lord; CL 243; ST 4
  Essay on Truth, ST 275, 284
Ball, Patricia: SF 10
Balzac, Honoré de: WF 271
Barker, Sir Ernest: SF 275
Beaumont, Francis: *see* Fletcher, John
Beethoven, Ludwig von: CL 243
Benham, Sir Gurney: ST 325
Beowulf: ST 278, 284
Berdaev, Nicholas: CL 319
Bergson, Henri: WF 137, 265; IT 244, 353-5, 358, 362; CL 82; SF 245
Berry, Francis: WF vi, 324; ST 189
  The Iron Christ, SF 263

Blake, William: CL 91, 107, 243, 250, 253; SF 231, 251, 269
  The Marriage of Heaven and Hell, IT 360; SF 272
Blunden, Edmund: IT 116, 340; ST 201
Boccaccio, Giovanni: *The Decameron*, SF 95
Bolingbroke, Henry St John, Lord: IT xiii
Bradley, A. C.: WF v-vi, 2, 125, 195; IT v-viii, 188, 341; SF 212, 287, 291
Bradley, F. H.: WF xvii, xx; IT 343-4
Brandes, Georg: WF 294
Bridges, Robert: WF 270
  The Influence of the Audience on Shakespeare's Drama, WF 272-83, 288-93
  The Testament of Beauty, WF 300; ST 274
Brontë, Charlotte: *Villette*, ST 274
Brontë, Emily: *Wuthering Heights*, ST 274
Brown, Hugh: IT 2, 5, 14, 345
Browne, Sir Thomas: WF 104
  Religio Medici, ST 288
Browning, Robert: ST 274
  Rabbi Ben Ezra, ST 279
  The Ring and the Book, SF 256
  The Statue and the Bust, SF 109
Brunton, P.: CL 56
Burke, Edmund: SF 269
  Reflections on the Revolution in France, SF 270
Burton, Robert: *The Anatomy of Melancholy*, ST 274, 287
Byron, Lord: WF 300; IT xiii; CL 100; ST 274; SF 123, 223, 229, 252, 263, 269-71
  Cain, SF 252
  Childe Harold, CL 65
  Don Juan, SF 252, 267
  Journals, SF 278

Sardanapalus, WF 239; CL 163; SF 160, 252, 268
Sonnet to George IV, SF 88–9, 277

Camden, William: SF 190
Campbell, Lily B.: IT 96
Canute: ST 271
Capell, Edward: WF 172, 180
Carlyle, Thomas: ST 276, 291
Sartor Resartus, ST 281, 287–9
The Hero as Poet, ST 289
Castiglione: *Il Cortegiano*, WF 324; CL 51, 118, 242
Castlereagh, Lord: SF 267
Caxton, William: SF 179
Chamberlain, Neville: SF 267
Chapman, George: WF xiv–xv
Chaucer, Geoffrey: CL 227; SF 250, 266, 271
Sir Thopas, CL 265
Troilus and Criseyde, CL 265
Chester, Robert: *Love's Martyr*, SF 138
Chesterton, A. K.: WF v
Christ, Jesus: *see* Index C, V
Clark, Cumberland: ST xxiii
Clemen, Wolfgang: IT ix
Coghill, Nevill: SF 188
Coleridge, Samuel Taylor: WF vi, 2, 265, 342–3; IT 166; SF 90, 95
Kubla Khan, ST xv; SF 201, 256
The Ancient Mariner, ST 279
Zapolya, CL 72, 163
Columbus, Christopher: ST 282
Confucius: WF 311, 317
Congreve, William: *The Way of the World*, SF 174, 179
Conrad, Joseph: ST 276
Copernicus: ST 15, 136
Craig, Edward Gordon: SF 3, 10, 248
Curry, W. C.: WF 341

Dale, E. A.: SF 185
Dante Alighieri: WF xiii–xx, 271, 296; CL 35, 38, 79, 110, 224–7; ST 290; SF 87, 275
Divina Commedia, WF 249, 256; IT 117, 298, 309; CL 30; ST 103, 275, 282, 332
Defoe, Daniel: *Robinson Crusoe*, CL 249
Dekker, Thomas: *The Shoemaker's Holiday*, SF 208
Delilah: IT 303–5, 309
de Vere, Edward: ST 4

Dickens, Charles: *David Copperfield*, ST 274
Dickinson, G. Lowes: IT 346
Don Juan myth: SF 251–2
Donne, John: SF 211
A Valediction forbidding Mourning, CL 157; SF 237
Sermons, ST 286
Dostoievsky, Fyodor: WF 160, 300; CL 29
The Possessed, WF 35, 174, 307, 320
Dowden, Edward: CL 168
Drake, Sir Francis: ST 282; SF 44, 268
Dryden, John: WF xiii; ST 274; SF 269, 276
Duthie, G. I.: ST ix–x, xiii

Edward the Confessor: SF 63, 87
Edwards, Harry: SF 151
Einstein, Albert: WF vii, xx; CL 243
Eleusinian *Mysteries*: CL 37
Eliot, George: WF xiii; CL 155
Eliot, T. S.: WF ix; IT vi; CL 224
Introduction to WF, xiii–xx
Marina, ST 278; SF 9
Prufrock, WF 302; SF 174
The Hippopotamus, ST 279–80
Elizabeth I: WF 328–30; CL 197, 254, 316–318, 333; SF 13–14, 86–8, 205, 265, 270
Elizabeth II: SF 13
Ellis-Fermor, Una: WF 239
Epicurus: WF xvi
Erasmus: WF xiv
Essex, Earl of: WF 328–9
Etheredge, Sir George: *The Man of Mode*, SF 170
Euripides: CL 35, 185
Evans-Wentz, W. Y.: SF 150
Eve: IT 300, 309, 316

Fairchild, A. H. R.: CL 62
Fairley, Barker: WF 271, 293
Faust myth: SF 251–2
Fitton, Mary: SF 173
Flecker, J. E.: *Hassan*, WF viii; CL 234; SF 201, 219
Fletcher, John: CL 259–73, 283, 290–2, 301; ST 2
Bonduca, CL 263–7
Philaster, CL 265
The False One, CL 263–6
The Maid's Tragedy, CL 265
Flower, Sir Archibald: SF 264

Ford, John: WF xv
Forman, R. S.: SF 9
Francis of Assisi, St: WF 315; CL 227
Fripp, Edgar I.: CL 30, 259
Furnivall, F. J.: CL 176

Galsworthy, John: *Strife*, IT 180
Gary, Franklin: ST 8
George, St: SF 13, 23, 40, 44, 57–9
Gervinus: WF 294
Goethe, Johann Wolfgang von: WF 240,
    295; CL 243; SF 229, 251, 263
    Faust, WF 114, 249, 254–6; IT 117, 345–
    346; CL 29–30, 233; ST 285; SF 239,
    251–2
Gower, John: *Confessio Amantis*, CL 37
Granville-Barker, H.: WF vi; ST 61–2
Gray, I. E.: SF 168
Gray, Thomas: *Elegy in a Country
    Churchyard*, CL 64
Greene, Robert: CL 46
    James IV, SF 217
Grosart, A. B.: ST 325

Hall, Manly: SF 150
Halliday, F. E.: SF 175
Hardy, Thomas: WF 8, 180, 202; CL
    106, 155; SF 271
    The Dynasts, SF 263
Hart, H. C.: SF 282
Hazlitt, William: WF vi, 6
Henry VII: SF 86
History of Reynard the Fox, The: SF 179
Hocart, A. M.: SF 276–8
Holinshed: WF 8; ST 10; SF 207
Homer: WF 271; IT ix; CL 215, 241
Hopkins, Gerard Manley: CL 83
    The Wreck of the Deutschland, ST 272
Horace: WF xiii
Hotson, Leslie: SF 173, 185–6
Hudson, H. N.: WF 15–16; IT 258; SF 190
Hudson, W. H.: *Green Mansions*, ST
    277, 280
Huxley, Aldous: *Do What You Will*, IT
    345
    Heaven and Hell, SF 256
Hyman, Stanley: IT vii

Ibsen, Henrik: WF 303, 325; SF 251
    Brand, WF 325
    Emperor and Galilean, WF 324; SF 274
    Love's Comedy, WF 325
    Peer Gynt, WF 325

Pillars of Society, WF 299
The Pretenders, SF 252
The Wild Duck, WF 299
When We Dead Awaken, CL 123
Isaiah: ST 246; SF 85–7

James I: SF 62, 86, 173, 205
James, D. G.: CL 72
James, Henry: WF xiii-xiv
James, William: WF 23, 29, 240–7; IT
    344; CL 11, 29; SF 293
Jezebel: IT 309
Joan, St: IT 301, 309; SF 14, 112
Job: WF 191; CL 30; ST 275, 278
John of the Cross, St: CL 250
Johnson, Samuel: SF 269–71
Jonson, Ben: WF xv, 303, 315; CL 100,
    132, 227; SF 200, 209, 213, 218
    Bartholomew Fair, SF 208
    Every Man in his Humour, SF 118, 213
    The Alchemist, SF 170, 217
Judas: WF 256; SF 31, 226
Julius Caesar: WF 328, 331; SF 73, 205, 223

Keats, George and Thomas: IT 351; SF
    268
Keats, John: WF viii; CL 29, 107
    'Bright star! would I were steadfast . . .'
    IT 59, 241, 347–8; CL 109; ST 233;
    SF 240
    Hyperion, SF 90
    La Belle Dame sans Merci, CL 38
    Letters, WF 311; IT 351–5, 361–2; CL
    233; SF 268
    Ode on a Grecian Urn, CL 121–3
    Ode on Melancholy, IT 289
    Ode to a Nightingale, IT 347; CL 102;
    ST 278, 304, 323
    Otho the Great, CL 163
    Sleep and Poetry, WF 309–11; CL 160;
    SF 268
    'Why did I laugh tonight?', IT 347
Keyserling, Count: IT 344–5, 353–5, 362
Kipling, Rudyard: *If*, WF 313
Knight, G. Wilson: Articles, lectures,
    etc., WF v; IT vii, x; CL vii-viii,
    149; ST 320; SF 7–9, 159, 205, 219,
    256–8, 263–5, 275–6; in *The Adelphi*,
    IT 16; SF 8, 280; in *The Shake-
    speare Review*, WF v; SF 8, 287; in
    The Times Literary Supplement, WF
    332; IT x-xi, 244, 250, 326, 332;

CL viii, 187; ST xiii, xxiv, 306;
SF 8, 263, 266
Atlantic Crossing, SF 12, 263, 273-4
Chariot of Wrath, SF 263
Christ and Nietzsche, WF 159, 239, 299,
310; IT xiii; CL 243; SF 88, 95,
140, 158
Hiroshima, SF 263-6
Laureate of Peace, WF ix; SF 258-9
Lord Byron: Christian Virtues, SF 89
Principles of Shakespearian Production,
WF vi, 119, 239, 323; CL 179, 191,
251, 320; SF 7, 233, 263
The Burning Oracle, WF 310; CL 100;
SF 8, 204, 263
The Christian Renaissance, CL 126, 230,
250; ST viii, xx; SF 138
The Dynasty of Stowe, SF 263
The Mutual Flame, SF 7, 18, 95, 120,
126, 129-32, 135, 138-40, 157,
257
The Starlit Dome, CL vii, 56, 163, 233;
SF 256
This Sceptred Isle, SF 7, 263-5, 273
Unpublished papers, SF 7-10, 264, *and
see under* Shakespeare Memorial
Library.
Main Shakespearian volumes not in-
dexed.
Knight, W. F. Jackson: WF ix, 343; CL
215; ST 278; SF 10, 177
Knollys, Sir William: SF 173
Knox, R. S.: ST 305
Kolbë, Mgr: IT vii-viii, 9, 96, 128, 139,
253, 316; ST xxiii, 146
Kyd, Thomas: *The Spanish Tragedy*, SF
205

Lamb, Charles: ST 330
Lawrence, D. H.: SF 215
The White Peacock, ST 291
Lawrence-Archer, J. H.: SF 9
Layamon: *Brut*, CL 166
Leavis, F. R.: IT vi
Lee, Sir Sidney: WF 240-2
Lewis, C. S.: WF 338; CL 79; SF 215
Love's Martyr, SF 138
Lowes, J. Livingston: WF 343
Lucan: WF 328
Lucretius: WF xiii
Lucy, Sir Thomas: SF 188
Lyly, John: CL 70, 79, 149, 242, 246; SF
101, 200, 205, 208, 214, 220, 227, 238

Campaspe, SF 47, 205
Endimion, CL 164-6, 197, 220; SF
78, 205, 219
Euphues, SF 208

Machiavelli: WF xiv; CL 146-9, 242, 254;
SF 59, 78, 179
Malcolm II: SF 10
Malherbe, Françoise de: WF xiii
Malone, Edmund: IT x; CL 47, 63, 68
Markham, Sir Clements: SF 237
Marlowe, Christopher: WF xv; CL 46, 149,
227, 242; SF 14, 32, 164-5, 208-9,
216-18, 227-9, 248-51, 267-8
Doctor Faustus, CL 124, 241-2; SF 134,
206, 209, 213, 217, 252
Edward II, SF 32, 209, 213, 217, 248
Hero and Leander, SF 215-17, 231
Tamburlaine the Great, WF 342; CL 218;
SF 34, 37, 41, 163, 177, 206, 209,
213, 223, 254
The Jew of Malta, SF 179
Marquard, N. J.: SF 249
Marvell, Andrew: WF 104
Bermudas, CL 247
Masefield, John: WF ix, 248; IT viii, 30-1,
61; ST 276; SF 9, 286-7
King Cole, SF 89
Massey, Gerald: WF 327
Massinger, Philip: CL 259
Melville, Herman: WF 300; CL 223
Clarel, ST 105, 279, 307
Moby-Dick, WF 285; CL 223; ST 276,
279-81
Pierre, CL 223; ST 276-7
Typee, CL 223
White-Jacket, CL 223; ST 285
Middleton, Thomas: WF xv; ST 332
The Spanish Gipsy, SF 172
Milford, Sir Humphrey: CL viii
Milton, John: WF 104, 338-9; CL 117,
202, 241; SF 164-5, 211, 229, 232,
251, 263, 267-9, 276
Comus, CL 245; SF 107, 251
De Doctrina Christiana, SF 257
History of Britain, CL 166
Il Penseroso, ST 271; SF 163
Lycidas, ST 274
Paradise Lost, WF 7; IT 297; CL 85-7,
297, 306; ST ix, 275, 281-2; SF 164,
225, 251
Paradise Regained, CL 91
Samson Agonistes, ST 275, 282

Mirandola, Pico della: WF 342
Moffatt, James: CL 119; ST 275
Molière: WF 303
    Don Juan, or Le Festin de Pierre, SF 251-2
    Le Misanthrope, WF 299
Montaigne, Michel de: WF xiv
Muir, Kenneth: WF 328; SF 10, 190, 207
Murry, J. Middleton: IT v–vi, 4, 106, 341, 352; SF 44, 226, 287, 292-3
Musgrove, S.: SF 189-90

Nero: ST 271
Newton, Sir Isaac: CL 222, 243; ST 282
Nicoll, Allardyce: IT x
Nietzsche, Friedrich: WF 239, 300-1, 308–316, 322-5; CL 250, 253, 297; SF 156, 251, 263
    The Birth of Tragedy, WF 46, 239, 300; CL 82; ST xx; SF 233, 246, 254-7
    Thus Spake Zarathustra, WF 299, 309; IT xiii, 199; CL 163, 203, 243-6
Nosworthy, J. M.: SF 197

O'Casey, Sean: SF 160
O'Neill, Eugene: WF 324; SF 160
    Mourning becomes Electra, SF 207
Orsino, Don Virginio: SF 185
Ovid: WF 8, 328
    Metamorphoses, SF 184

Partridge, Jane: ST 306
Paul, St: WF 315; CL 65, 119; SF 21, 140, 211
Paynter, William: *The Palace of Pleasure,* SF 95
Peter, St: WF 256, 299
Petrarch: CL 79
Piccarda: WF xx
Pilate, Pontius: SF 31
Planck, Max: WF xx
Plato: WF 338; CL 242, 254
    Phaedrus, CL 228
Plautus: ST 6
Pliny: SF 177
Plutarch: WF 8, 128, 327-8; ST 8-12; SF 173, 193-5, 219, 288-90
Pooler, C. Knox: CL 263
Pope, Alexander: WF xv; SF 160, 192, 269
    Essay on Criticism, WF 310-12; SF 269-70
    Essay on Man, WF 315-16; IT xiii; CL 32; ST viii; SF 140
    The Rape of the Lock, SF 174
    Windsor Forest, SF 267

Potter, W.E.: SF 168
Powys, John Cowper: *Dostoievsky,* SF 138
    Jobber Skald, SF 138
    Maiden Castle, SF 138
    Mortal Strife, CL 254
    The Brazen Head, SF 138
Price, Nancy: SF 263
Prometheus myth: SF 251
Ptolemy: CL 110; ST 15, 136

Queenborough, Lord: SF 264

Racine, Jean: *Athalie,* CL 335
    Esther, CL 335
    Phèdre, CL 335
Rampa, T. Lobsang: SF 150
'Ranjee': *see* Shahani, R. G.
Reinhardt, Max: SF 184
Richard I, 'Cœur-de-Lion': SF 25
Richards, I. A.: WF xvii; IT vi; ST 8
Ross, Elizabeth M.: ST 306
Royds, Rev. T. F.: ST 246
'Rule Britannia': ST 274
Rylands, George: SF 211

Sackville, Thomas: *Gorboduc,* SF 58
Saintsbury, George: CL 27
Sakuntala: CL 37
Samson: IT 303-5
Scott, Sir Walter: *Old Mortality,* IT 85
Seafarer, The: CL 222, 254; ST 276
Sencourt, Robert: CL 250
Seneca: WF xiv; ST 6
Shahani, Ranjee G.: IT 349-50; ST 320–323
Shakespeare Memorial Library, The: SF 7-10, 246, 264
Shaw, Bernard: WF 300, 303; SF 95, 160
    Arms and the Man, SF 174
    Major Barbara, WF 299
    Man and Superman, SF 252
    Saint Joan, SF 154
    The Apple Cart, SF 278
Shelley, P. B.: WF 342; CL 232-3, 253; ST 283, 304, 330; SF 229
    A Defence of Poetry, CL 223, 227; SF 90, 138-40, 275
    A Fragment to Music, ST 283
    Epipsychidion, ST 283
    Hellas, ST 287
    Lines Written Among the Euganean Hills, ST 283
    Ode to the West Wind, ST 274

Prometheus Unbound, WF 316; CL 160,
228, 233, 247–9; ST 282–3; SF 252
The Witch of Atlas, CL 56, 125, 233
Sheridan, Richard Brinsley: *The Critic*,
SF 170
The Rivals, SF 170
Sherriff, R. C.: *Journey's End*, WF viii,
4, 300
Shirley, James: WF xv
Sidney, Sir Philip: CL 242; SF 47
Siegel, Paul N.: SF 124
Sinsheimer, H.: SF 175
Sitwell, Sir Osbert: ST 325
Somers, Sir George: WF 49; ST 10–11
Sommers, C. A.: SF 75, 177
Sophocles: CL 35, 331
Antigone, CL 128
Oedipus Coloneus, SF 184
Oedipus Rex, CL 128
Spanish Armada, The: CL 135, 254; SF
44, 265
Spenser, Edmund: CL 79, 149, 246; ST
274; SF 227
Epithalamion, CL 149
Heavenly Hymns, SF 214
Prothalamion, CL 149
The Fairie Queene, CL 166; ST 281;
SF 47, 215, 218
The Shepherd's Calendar, SF 205
Spurgeon, Caroline: IT vii–ix, 27, 130,
146, 176, 208, 244, 331–2; CL 224,
251; ST xxiii, 87, 91; SF 212
Stawell, F. Melian: IT 346
Sterne, Laurence: *A Sentimental Journey*,
SF 174
Still, Colin: WF xx, 16, 144; IT vi–vii,
136; CL 216, 226, 230, 249; ST
xxiii, 258
Streeter, Canon: CL 22
Strindberg, August: *Lady Julia*, WF ix
Swift, Jonathan: WF 303, 315; CL 81,
232; SF 53
Gulliver's Travels, WF 58; CL 249
The Battle of the Books, CL 224
Swinburne, A. C.: WF 274; CL 263–5; SF
287

Tannenbaum, S. A.: IT 267, 291; ST
306
Taylor, F. Sherwood: WF 311
Taylor, John: SF 268
Tchehov, Anton: WF 160
The Cherry Orchard, WF 4

Tennyson, Alfred, Lord: SF 160, 263–4,
269–70
Becket, SF 84
Crossing the Bar, ST 284
Harold, SF 84
In Memoriam, SF 59
Locksley Hall, ST 283
Morte d'Arthur, ST 284
Queen Mary, SF 84
Thermopylae, battle of: SF 44
Tillyard, E. M. W.: IT xi; SF 197
Times Literary Supplement, The: see
Knight, G. Wilson, 'articles'
Titanic, The: ST 286
Tolstoy, Leo: WF v, 240–8, 270; CL 29
Resurrection, WF 248
Shakespeare and the Drama, WF 272–97
SF 144
The Kreutzer Sonata, WF 248
War and Peace, SF 137
What is Art?, WF 276
Tourneur, Cyril: *The Revenger's Tragedy*,
WF xv; SF 175–6
Treneer, Anne: ST xxiii
Tucker, T. G.: SF 126

Ur-Hamlet, The: IT 106, 123; SF 207
Ustinov, Peter: *Romanoff and Juliet*, SF
14

Van Doren, Mark: CL 236
Vergil: WF 8, 343; IT ix; CL 30, 35; SF
87, 275
Aeneid, IT 286, 297, 309; CL 214–15,
306; SF 18
Georgics, WF 328–30
Messianic Eclogue, CL 331; ST 246;
SF 85
Victoria, Queen: SF 270
Voltaire: WF 303

Waley, Arthur (translator): *Monkey*, CL
228–30
Walker, Roy: WF 298, 302, 313; IT ix;
ST x–xiii
Wanderer, The: CL 222, 254, 294; ST 276
Webster, John: WF 315; CL 227; SF 208–9,
227, 250
The Duchess of Malfi, WF 169; CL 44;
SF 206–9, 213, 217, 227–31, 235
The White Devil, SF 229
Wellington, Duke of: SF 267
White, Helen: SF 10

Whyte, Lance L.: WF vi–ix
Wilson, J. Dover: WF 326–9, 332–9, 342–3; CL 112, 324; SF 52
Wordsworth, William: CL 92, 127, 230, 243, 249–51; ST 304; SF 210, 269–71
   Ode on Intimations of Immortality, CL 72, 108, 333; ST 74, 277; SF 8
   The Excursion, CL 163

The Prelude, CL 222; ST 282
The Recluse, CL 243
Tintern Abbey, IT 352, 355
To a Skylark, SF 87

Yeats, W. B.: *Byzantium* poems, CL 64, 123; SF 201
   Resurrection, CL 123